CAMBRIDGE ... ...ENT
FOR SCHOOL ...D COLLEGES

THE EPISTLE TO THE

HEBREWS

THE EPISTLE TO THE

HEBREWS

Edited by

A. NAIRNE, D.D.

WITH INTRODUCTION AND NOTES

Cambridge
at the University Press

1957

CAMBRIDGE
UNIVERSITY PRESS

University Printing House, Cambridge CB2 8BS, United Kingdom

Published in the United States of America by Cambridge University Press, New York

Cambridge University Press is part of the University of Cambridge.

It furthers the University's mission by disseminating knowledge in the pursuit of
education, learning and research at the highest international levels of excellence.

www.cambridge.org
Information on this title: www.cambridge.org/9781107652330

© Cambridge University Press 1921

First edition 1917
First published 1921
Reprinted 1922, 1957
First paperback edition 2014

A catalogue record for this publication is available from the British Library

ISBN 978-1-107-65233-0 Paperback

PREFACE
BY THE GENERAL EDITOR.

THE General Editor does not hold himself respon- sible, except in the most general sense, for the statements, opinions, and interpretations contained in the several volumes of this Series. He believes that the value of the Introduction and the Commentary in each case is largely dependent on the Editor being free as to his treatment of the questions which arise, provided that that treatment is in harmony with the character and scope of the Series. He has therefore contented himself with offering criticisms, urging the consideration of alternative interpretations, and the like; and as a rule he has left the adoption of these suggestions to the discretion of the Editor.

The Greek Text adopted in this Series is that of Dr Westcott and Dr Hort with the omission of the marginal readings. For permission to use this Text the thanks of the Syndics of the Cambridge University Press and of the General Editor are due to Messrs Macmillan & Co.

TRINITY COLLEGE, CAMBRIDGE,
July, 1917.

PREFACE.

I THANK the Delegates of the Clarendon Press for kind permission to use and quote from Dr Souter's edition of the Revisers' Text of the Greek Testament, and Dr Souter himself for concurring in this permission and for other generous aid: Messrs T. and T. Clark, publishers of *The Epistle of Priesthood*, for allowing me with their wonted courtesy to extract the "Rhetorical Paraphrase" which had been already printed in that book: the Master of Selwyn College and the Editor of the *Church Quarterly Review* for free use of an article in that Review: the Fathers of the Society of S. John the Evangelist for placing certain numbers of the *Cowley Evangelist* at my disposal: Mr G. M. Edwards for criticism and advice especially in questions of Greek scholarship: and Dr St John Parry, the Editor of the series in which this commentary appears, to whose patience judgement and learning I am deeply indebted. Nor is it impertinent, I hope, to express gratitude to all who have been concerned with the printing of this book: under the difficult conditions of a troubled time they have persisted in the endeavour to shape it according to their scholarly tradition.

A. N.

July, 1917.

CONTENTS

INTRODUCTION

I

PLAN AND ANALYSIS OF THE EPISTLE

THE aim of this division of the Introduction is to set forth as plainly as possible the argument and intention of the epistle. For this purpose three summaries are given : (1) an outline sketch of the plan, (2) an enlargement of this in detailed analysis, (3) a very brief rhetorical paraphrase. All three are coloured by the view adopted in this commentary of the circumstances out of which the epistle arose. Their proper place would be at the end of the critical and theological enquiries which recommend that view. But it may make for clearness if the results are shortly stated first.

PRELUDE

The epistle is a λόγος παρακλήσεως (xiii. 22): to what does it exhort ? To right conduct in an approaching crisis in which the readers must choose whether or no they will be faithful to their Lord. Such faithfulness must rest on a right conception of the Person and work of Christ. Hence Doctrine is *interwoven* with Exhortation. But i.—x. 18 is mainly doctrinal, x. 19—xiii. mainly practical ; though xi. is intermediate, since *faith* partakes of both doctrine and practice, and is the affection which makes argument convincing. The author would hardly claim to have absolutely proved his doctrine by logical process, but he knows that the proof will be completed for his friends *if they will trust their Lord and follow Him where He is leading them now.*

The crisis will include persecution, abandonment of ancient forms of ritual, of ties of friendship, even of what seem to be the claims of honour, and if the right choice is made will result in actual entrance upon the complete Christian state, i.e. entrance into the very presence of God.

Hence it must be shewn that Christ has passed through suffering and death, and, according to the analogy of the ancient ritual, has opened the way to the presence of God, i.e. that He is the one true Priest who through death has offered the eternal sacrifice of life ; and withal His Person must be displayed in such a light as to win affection and be a proper object of devoted faith.

All this is summed up in the concluding Collect, xiii. 20, 21.

[If we may suppose the epistle written from a Jewish Christian in Italy to his friends (a family rather than a church) in Palestine, just before the breaking out of the Jewish war with Rome, its significance would seem to be particularly clear. But even though this must be considered unproven, still it will be necessary to recognise as its background an approaching crisis of a *very severe character* in which the readers will be obliged to make a brave and painful choice.]

Analysis is rendered difficult by the compression of the writer's thought—the style is severe rather than rhetorical ; by our want of familiarity with the pre-supposed habits of his readers' minds, which compels a certain amount of *filling in* ; and by his method of interweaving the divisions of his subject, allowing no visible articulations.   The larger divisions are: i.—iv. Preparatory ; v.—x. 18, Priesthood, subdivided into v.—vii. the High Priest, viii.—x. 18, the Sacrifice; x. 19—xiii. Exhortation, subdivided into two parts by xi., on Faith, which clinches the preceding argument and introduces the final Exhortation.

All through the idea rules that Jesus is the Forerunner. He has entered the presence of God, the heavenly sanctuary ; the readers of the epistle have not yet followed Him thither— the crisis, their choice, must first be passed : but they are in an increasingly close relationship to Him as they follow the argument of the epistle.   This is made vivid by three illustrations : the ship, vi. 19, 20 ; the race-course, xii. 1, 2 ; the sacrifice outside the camp, xiii. 10—16.

The ancient Hebrew idea of sacrifice must be kept in mind,

i.e. that the blood sprinkled was a symbol, not of death, but of life set free by death and thus presented to God.

The quotations from the Old Testament are not made arbitrarily, but according to the principle that those who were called Christs (χριστός, *anointed*) in the Old Testament, whether kings, prophets, priests, or even the people of Israel as a whole, were really Christs, or *in* THE CHRIST ; they represented God to man and man to God. The eternal Son, whom the faithful call THE CHRIST or CHRIST (as a proper name), took as His inheritance and fulfilled all that was adumbrated in them.

SKETCH

I—IV.—**Preparatory to the main theme.**

> i.—ii. 4.   The Son's inheritance as declared in Old Testament references to Israel's king and people and to the world's Creator,
>
> ii. 5—18.   and as displayed in the glorified humiliation of the earthly life of Jesus.
>
> iii.—iv.   The unity of man with God through the Christ, whose office Jesus the Son of God has inherited, fulfilling its inherent high-priestly efficacy by His ascension after suffering.

V—X 18.—**Doctrinal theme: the Eternal High Priest.**

V—VII, *The Priest* : VIII—X 18, *His Sacrifice.*

> v. 1—10.   The Christ-priest satisfies the conditions of priesthood by His sympathy in suffering and by His appointment according to the order of Melchizedek.
>
> v. 11—vi. 20.   Argument broken by warning and encouragement, but brought in again by reference in vi. 20 to this order of Melchizedek,
>
> vii.   which signifies the Priesthood of eternal life.
>
> viii.   Its sacrifice belongs to the promised New Covenant :
>
> ix.   is offered once for all in the heavenly sanctuary, and by a true outpouring of blood has been effectual for remission of sins :

x. 1—18.   effectual indeed for absolute perfecting of worshippers, since it is the personal offering of
that free will which is the meeting-point of
spiritual beings.

**X 19—XIII.—Exhortation to use the Entrance, thus
inaugurated by the High Priest,** in the one way—
like His own—which is at this very time appointed.

x. 19—39.   Therefore enter the sanctuary after Jesus, not
shrinking from His own painful way. You
will not, for yours is the life of faith :

xi.   the reality of which is proved by history.

xii.   Endure therefore, even though heaven as well
as earth is to be shaken:

xiii. 1—17.   actually overtaking the Forerunner in what
seems on earth to be His ignominious position outside the camp.

18—25.   That you may do just this, the writer (who
has done it) prays.

ANALYSIS

I—IV.

i. 1—4.   God has spoken in one who is a Son, heir of
all : who being eternal and divine has
become man, offered sacrifice for sins, and
ascended to the right hand of God, taking
His inheritance :

5—14.   which is Manhood joined to Godhead ; not
the state of the angels, for He has inherited
all that was said in the Old Testament of
anointed men and of God in manifestation.

ii. 1—4.   Parenthetic exhortation, in which the author
shews that he speaks of Him whom the
faithful call The Lord.

5—9.   The Manhood—its glory in humiliation—is
displayed by comparison of the promise of
glory for man and the actual life of Jesus
on earth.

10—18.   This was the fitting way for their Brother (Old Testament name inherited) to set men free from fear of death, and so by triumph over death and by sympathy to become their High Priest.

iii. 1—5.   This manhood, however, is not merely that of one man among many, as even Moses was, but corresponds to and fulfils the manhood of the anointed representatives of the ancient people (who were called sons by God) ; as Christ He is head of the whole house and one with its Founder :

6.   which house consists of the faithful.

iii. 7—iv. 14.   Exhortation to such faithfulness, which exhortation leads through the quotation from Ps. xcv. to the explanation of three principles in understanding the Old Testament :

(a) iii. 7—iv. 2.   much is there said which has never been satisfied till these later days ;

(β) iv. 3—10.   the description of heavenly things such as the Rest of God gives the reality which earthly things suggest ;

(γ) iv. 11—13.   sincerity of conscience is necessary for the right reading of God's Word.

iv. 14—16.   Into this Rest of God Jesus of the Old Testament did not lead the people, but Jesus the Son of God has passed into it, and stands therefore confessed the true High Priest : since the function of the high priest is to provide access to God for the people whom he represents, and Jesus has already been shewn to be the true representative of man. The section ends with exhortation : *" Let us draw near."*

V—X 18.

V—VII

> v. 1—4.   As every high priest must be sympathetic and duly appointed :
>
> 5—6.   so the Christ : for the Christ of the Old Testament, the King of Israel, was divinely addressed not only as Son, but also as Priest for ever after the order of Melchizedek :
>
> 7—10.   and the Son of God, who inherited these Old Testament appellations, sufficiently manifested His sympathy by the process of His suffering.
>
> v. 11—vi. 3.   Rebuke ; vi. 4—8, Warning ; 9—12, Encouragement, followed by
>
> vi. 13—20.   declaration of the assurance afforded by God's promise, and of the earnest of its fulfilment in Jesus' entrance within the veil.
>
> [Illustration : ship outside harbour ; anchor touching ground ; Captain already ashore.]
>
> vii. 1—3.   Melchizedek a representation (as sketched in the Old Testament) of the eternal High Priest, the Son of God :
>
> 4—10.   a greater priest than Aaron : such as our Lord has exactly shewn Himself to be,
>
> 11—14.   inasmuch as, being sprung from another tribe than Aaron's, namely the royal tribe of Judah,
>
> 15—19.   having filled up the ancient sketch by the power of an indissoluble life,
>
> 20—22.   and having been appointed by the oath of God,
>
> 23—25.   He ever liveth to make priestly intercession.
>
> 26—28.   This conclusion is confirmed by our sense of fitness : just such a High Priest were we needing.

VIII—X 18.

viii. 1—13. After repeating the chief point of the preceding argument—that we have a High Priest who has entered heaven itself and God's actual presence (1, 2), the author goes on to consider that He must offer a true heavenly sacrifice (3—6), and points out that a new and real Covenant had been promised, the Covenant in fact of which the true High Priest is Mediator (7—12), and that this implies the disappearance of the Old in the New (13).

ix. 1—5. Description of the old ritual, which

6—10. provided no real access to God's presence, and was to last only till a time of reformation.

11—14. Description of the new ritual of the true Sanctuary, Victim, and Priest, in which eternal redemption and cleansing of conscience has been provided.

15—17. And as the old ritual, according to the ancient idea of a Covenant,

18—22. involved death by representation :

23—28. so does the new ritual involve suffering, but through suffering the manifestation of abiding life.

x. 1—4. The old rule of ritual has a shadow of hope, and repeats a memorial of sins :

5—10. but Jesus Christ, the sacrificing Priest who has passed through earthly life to heavenly, has made a real offering, in which we have been really consecrated, for it is the offering of Himself made of His own free will,

11—14. and needing no repetition, for it is complete ;

15—18. and hence the prophetic promise has been fulfilled ; remission of sins has taken place ; the only barrier is removed.

X 19—XIII.

x. 19—25. *Enter* then by the way, fresh-slain yet living, the painful way of the flesh of Jesus Christ, into the true sanctuary, not forsaking the appointed methods of worship; the consolations of worship and fellowship are real to those who recognise the unseen power which is carrying on the succession of events to the appointed *Day*.

26—31. For so it is indeed; we know the truth of things, and there is no other religion to take the place of ours; we dare not despise it.

32—34. Nor will you: your former constancy must be renewed.

35—39. The Day is at hand : *He* comes, as the ancient warning says; surely the ancient *Faith* is ours.

xi. 1—2. And that there is such a power as Faith is proved

3. by our own intelligent observation of the course of history,

4—39. and by the witness borne to our forefathers, who ever looked into the unseen and chose the braver course,

40. and now wait for us to realise with them the promise they trusted.

xii. 1—3. And they, witnesses themselves to faith's reality and power, are watching us as we strip for our contest.

[Illustration : a race-course ; the readers of the epistle are stripping to run ; at the end of the course they can see Jesus who has run the race before them, and whom, as they run, they will approach.]

4—13. Endure chastisement as being yourselves sons : shrink not even from extreme suffering.

14—17. Live at peace with all if you can ; but do not, for the sake of peace, impair your consecration, as Esau, for the sake of ease, sold his birthright.

RHETORICAL PARAPHRASE

Son of God, Christ : who is He whom we thus name and who has inherited such great titles from Israel's heroes ?

One who seems far lowlier than they. But His glory was revealed in humiliation, and His humiliation was the means of His high-priestly sympathy with men.

For He shared their trials that, priest-like, He might bring them to God.

Think of Him as High Priest and you will never give Him up. Hold fast to Him in your approaching trial and you will know what His priestly salvation really is.

As High Priest: but not in the mechanical line of Aaron. That shadowy ordinance is fading ineffectually away before our eyes. Rather as High Priest in that eternal line of world-wide ancestry and living growth which the Psalmist symbolically named "after the order of Melchizedek."

Jesus, our Lord, standing on the Godward side of all men, and sacrificing His life for love of men, is the evident fulfiller of all that line of loving priestly life which has been throughout all history the visible sacrament of Godhead on earth.

Believe then that He as High Priest has opened the way for you to the presence of God.

The visible shame of Calvary was the sacrament of His entrance into the sanctuary of God's presence on our behalf. It remains for us to make the sacrament our own and to follow Him.

Remember your courage in former trials. Imitate the courageous faith of your forefathers. Follow Jesus your acknowledged Lord in the course He has run before you— do that hard duty which is now specially set before you.

Break old ties. Go forth to Him outside the camp. Enter the city of God.

Following Jesus you shall be united with the Christ.

II

HISTORY OF THE RECEPTION, CRITICISM AND INTERPRETATION OF THE EPISTLE

§ 1. *At Alexandria a tradition of Pauline authorship was criticised by scholars in the second century, but by the fourth century it prevailed and spread over the East : Clement, Origen, Athanasius.*

Eusebius in the sixth book of his Ecclesiastical History describes the attitude of the early Church in Alexandria towards the epistle to the Hebrews. It seems to have been accepted as S. Paul's ; but the acceptance was criticised. Eusebius quotes from the Hypotyposeis of Clement of Alexandria (c. 200) as follows : ἤδη δέ, ὡς ὁ μακάριος ἔλεγε πρεσβύτερος, ἐπεὶ ὁ κύριος ἀπόστολος ὢν τοῦ παντοκράτορος ἀπεστάλη πρὸς Ἑβραίους, διὰ μετριότητα ὁ Παῦλος ὡς ἂν εἰς τὰ ἔθνη ἀπεσταλμένος, οὐκ ἐγγράφει ἑαυτὸν Ἑβραίων ἀπόστολον διά τε τὴν πρὸς τὸν κύριον τιμήν, διά τε τὸ ἐκ περιουσίας καὶ τοῖς Ἑβραίοις ἐπιστέλλειν, ἐθνῶν κήρυκα ὄντα καὶ ἀπόστολον—" Paul, as the blessed presbyter used to say, did not put his name, as apostle, to this letter, since the Lord, the apostle of Almighty God, had been sent as apostle to the Hebrews. It was a matter of reverence, and because this letter lay outside his commission as apostle to the Gentiles " (*H. E.* VI. 14). From *H. E.* v. 11, VI. 13, it is reasonable to suppose that " the blessed presbyter " was Pantaenus, Clement's predecessor in the Catechetical School of Alexandria. He used to explain in this way the difficulty presented by the abrupt opening of the epistle, and the absence of the author's name and title throughout. The explanation was repeated by later writers in cruder language. Pantaenus put it in a careful, scholarly fashion, combining and interpreting iii. 1 (κατανοήσατε τὸν ἀπόστολον καὶ ἀρχιερέα τῆς ὁμολογίας ἡμῶν Ἰησοῦν) with ii. 3 f. and (which is important) those many other allusions in the epistle to the same idea. As Pantaenus put it, in harmony with his interpretation of the whole letter, the explanation was by no means trivial; it deepened the significance of many passages.

But there were other difficulties to be faced; and one, the peculiar style, was felt by Clement. Eusebius in the same chapter and still referring to the Hypotyposeis writes: καὶ τὴν πρὸς Ἑβραίους δὲ ἐπιστολὴν Παύλου μὲν εἶναι φησί, γεγράφθαι δὲ Ἑβραίοις Ἑβραϊκῇ φωνῇ, Λουκᾶν δὲ φιλοτίμως αὐτὴν μεθερμηνεύσαντα ἐκδοῦναι τοῖς Ἕλλησιν. ὅθεν τὸν αὐτὸν χρῶτα εὑρίσκεσθαι κατὰ τὴν ἑρμηνείαν ταύτης τε τῆς ἐπιστολῆς καὶ τῶν πράξεων. μὴ προγεγράφθαι δὲ τὸ Παῦλος ἀπόστολος, εἰκότως· Ἑβραίοις γάρ φησιν ἐπιστέλλων πρόληψιν εἰληφόσι κατ᾽ αὐτοῦ καὶ ὑποπτεύουσιν αὐτόν, συνετῶς πάνυ οὐκ ἐν ἀρχῇ ἀπέστρεψεν αὐτοὺς τὸ ὄνομα θείς. We cannot be sure whether Eusebius' φησί, "he says," means that these are Clement's very words or only the general sense of them. Nor is it clear whether Clement is giving his own private judgement or the common opinion of his school. There is not much significance in his habit of quoting from the Greek epistle as Paul's; that would be convenient, and if he held that it was so closely related to Paul he need have had no scruple about doing so. It should be noticed how daringly Pantaenus' explanation of the suppressed name and title is altered. After saying that Paul wrote in Hebrew and Luke translated, whence comes the likeness in style to Acts, Clement goes on to explain that Paul kept back his name because the Hebrews were prejudiced against him, and so "very cleverly he did not repel them at first start by putting his name." The ἐν ἀρχῇ, "at first start," makes us think of a converse piece of modern criticism in Wrede's *Das literarisch Rätsel des Hebräerbriefs*, who, denying Pauline authorship, thinks the conclusion a later addition by some one who wished to pass the epistle off as a letter of Paul's. Did Clement mean that the readers would perceive who was writing to them when they reached those intimate and affectionate messages? Probably not. Clement does not appear to have gone beneath the surface in his criticism and perhaps never felt how near he came to impugning the good faith of S. Paul.

Pantaenus criticised simply, yet profoundly; Clement slightly. His successor Origen has the sure touch, far sight, and caution of a real scholar, but is characteristically himself in the way he uses his scholarship; like Pantaenus, he is carried by his reverence near to the heart of the problem. Eusebius has

preserved two fragments from his Homilies on the Epistle (*H. E.*
VI. 25): περὶ τῆς πρὸς Ἑβραίους ἐπιστολῆς ἐν ταῖς εἰς αὐτὴν
ὁμιλίαις ταῦτα διαλαμβάνει· ὅτι ὁ χαρακτὴρ τῆς λέξεως τῆς πρὸς
Ἑβραίους ἐπιγεγραμμένης ἐπιστολῆς οὐκ ἔχει τὸ ἐν λόγῳ ἰδιωτικὸν
τοῦ ἀποστόλου, ὁμολογήσαντος ἑαυτὸν ἰδιώτην εἶναι τῷ λόγῳ,
τουτέστι τῇ φράσει, ἀλλὰ ἐστὶν ἡ ἐπιστολὴ συνθέσει τῆς λέξεως
Ἑλληνικωτέρα, πᾶς ὁ ἐπιστάμενος κρίνειν φράσεων διαφορὰς ὁμολο-
γήσαι ἄν. πάλιν τε αὖ ὅτι τὰ νοήματα τῆς ἐπιστολῆς θαυμάσιά
ἐστι, καὶ οὐ δεύτερα τῶν ἀποστολικῶν ὁμολογουμένων γραμμάτων,
καὶ τοῦτο ἂν συμφήσαι εἶναι ἀληθὲς πᾶς ὁ προσέχων τῇ ἀναγνώσει
τῇ ἀποστολικῇ. τούτοις μεθ᾽ ἕτερα ἐπιφέρει λέγων· ἐγὼ δὲ
ἀποφαινόμενος εἴποιμ᾽ ἂν ὅτι τὰ μὲν νοήματα τοῦ ἀποστόλου ἐστίν,
ἡ δὲ φράσις καὶ ἡ σύνθεσις ἀπομνημονεύσαντός τινος τὰ ἀποστο-
λικά, καὶ ὡσπερεὶ σχολιογραφήσαντος τὰ εἰρημένα ὑπὸ τοῦ διδασκάλου. εἴ τις οὖν ἐκκλησία ἔχει ταύτην τὴν ἐπιστολὴν ὡς
Παύλου, αὐτὴ εὐδοκιμείτω καὶ ἐπὶ τούτῳ· οὐ γὰρ εἰκῇ οἱ ἀρχαῖοι
ἄνδρες ὡς Παύλου αὐτὴν παραδεδώκασι. τίς δὲ ὁ γράψας τὴν
ἐπιστολήν, τὸ μὲν ἀληθὲς θεὸς οἶδεν· ἡ δὲ εἰς ἡμᾶς φθάσασα
ἱστορία ὑπό τινων μὲν λεγόντων ὅτι Κλήμης ὁ γενόμενος ἐπίσκοπος
Ῥωμαίων ἔγραψε τὴν ἐπιστολήν, ὑπό τινων δὲ ὅτι Λουκᾶς ὁ
γράψας τὸ εὐαγγέλιον καὶ τὰς πράξεις. The precise meaning of
some phrases here is disputed, but the general sense may be
shewn in a paraphrasing translation. " In his sermons on the
epistle to the Hebrews Origen thus discusses its authorship and
authority. He says that every one capable of distinguishing styles
would acknowledge Hebrews to be quite different from the style
of S. Paul. S. Paul was as he told the Corinthians (2 Cor. xi. 6)
'rude in speech,' and Hebrews is what may be called good
Greek. On the other hand, anyone who read S. Paul's epistles
diligently would agree that the theology of this truly wonderful
epistle is on the same high canonical level as S. Paul's." He
adds that "if I were to declare my own opinion I should say
that the theology is S. Paul's, but the actual composition of
the letter has been entrusted to some one who took notes, like a
pupil at his master's lectures, of S. Paul's ideas and then wrote
them out in his own way. So then if a church like ours at
Alexandria holds the epistle to be S. Paul's, let it not be blamed,
even though it connects the document more closely with the
apostle than I do : for it really was (as I have just shewn)

with reason that an elder generation has handed down the letter as simply 'Paul's.' But to speak accurately, S. Paul did not write the letter himself: who did, God only knows, though critical enquiry, so far as it has gone as yet, has suggested Clement, the friend of S. Paul who afterwards became bishop of Rome, or Luke the writer of the Gospel and the Acts, as in some sense the writer of Hebrews."

Origen repeats ὁ γράψας, ἔγραψεν, ὁ γράψας, in different senses because he is not sure that his predecessors did not mean more than he did by the word. He witnesses to a tradition of Pauline authorship in the Alexandrian Church without denying or affirming that it may be found in some other churches. He recognises a moderate antiquity for this tradition. He is sure himself that the letter was not composed by S. Paul, but he is also sure that it is worthy to be ranked with S. Paul's writings as a primary source of Christian theology. That being so he is not much interested in the question of authorship; a church may harmlessly quote the letter as Paul's, and he himself used to do so, as we learn from his other writings. In all this he is near to modern criticism. The difference is that he seems to recognise a closer connexion with S. Paul than most modern critics would allow. Yet even this is not absolutely clear. The word νοήματα is vague; the illustration, ὡσπερεὶ σχολιογραφήσαντος...ὑπὸ τοῦ διδασκάλου, seems to be drawn from the lecture room rather than from the letter-writing clerk; and if so it is at least possible to understand a general dependence on the apostle's theology, rather than a close following of his directions for this particular letter. It is a sad loss that we cannot read his sermons on the epistle in full; but, from their influence, which we dimly trace in Catenae and later commentators, we may imagine that he resembled his successors in this respect also, viz. that he thought more of the broad doctrine of the epistle than of special circumstances which called it forth and gave it a special character of its own.

Alexandria then witnesses to a firm conviction of the canonicity of Hebrews and of its great value; and to a vague tradition of its Pauline authorship, which we only hear of because the competent judges at Alexandria criticised it. On the other hand, Alexandria accounted for the later general acceptance of the Pauline authorship; Origen's acquiescence in the habit of quoting the epistle loosely as S. Paul's encouraged its continuance, and it spread abroad. And yet perhaps that encouragement was hardly needed. It was the Alexandrian recognition of canonicity that influenced the future. Origen was great enough to distinguish inspiration from reverence for an apostle's name. Others were less bold. And when the epistle stood firmly established in the Canon of the Eastern Church Pauline authorship became a necessary inference.

§ 2.   *There is no primitive evidence for such a tradition in the East generally: Irenaeus, Eusebius, Versions.*

But this came later. Even in the Eastern Church there is no evidence, outside Alexandria, for any early belief that the epistle was written by S. Paul. Irenaeus was bishop of Lyons in Gaul, but he was by birth a Greek of Asia Minor, and may be considered a witness to the Eastern tradition of the second century. If indeed the fragment published by Pfaff[1] were genuine, we might suspect that Irenaeus did bring a tradition of Pauline authorship with him from Asia Minor, though he afterwards gave this up in deference to the authority of the West. He is represented in this fragment as quoting Heb. xiii. 15, "let us offer up a sacrifice of praise, that is the fruit of the lips," together with Rom. xii. 1, as being both exhortations of S. Paul. It is generally supposed that the fragment is not genuine. But if it were the inference would be uncertain. The Greek runs as follows : καὶ ὁ Παῦλος παρακαλεῖ ἡμᾶς παραστῆσαι τὰ σώματα ἡμῶν θυσίαν ζῶσαν, ἁγίαν, εὐάρεστον τῷ θεῷ, τὴν λογικὴν λατρείαν ἡμῶν. καὶ πάλιν · ἀναφέρωμεν θυσίαν αἰνέσεως τουτέστι καρπὸν χειλέων (see Bleek, § 28). The καὶ πάλιν, "and again," a loose conjunctive phrase tacking on a condensed quotation illustrative of the quotation from Romans, need not imply that the ὁ Παῦλος παρακαλεῖ governs both clauses. Far

[1] *Irenaei fragmenta anecdota,* ed. Ch. M. Pfaff: Hag. Comit. 1715.

less is it a distinct assertion that S. Paul wrote the epistle to
the Hebrews ; that kind of popular quotation is allowed to
themselves by many of the ancient church writers, who speak
differently when they are to give a careful critical opinion.
If Irenaeus wrote the words and was understood to refer them
definitely to S. Paul, that would contradict what Photius cites
from Stephen Gobar, "a tritheist of the sixth century," ὅτι
Ἱππόλυτος καὶ Εἰρηναῖος τὴν πρὸς Ἑβραίους ἐπιστολὴν Παύλου
οὐκ ἐκείνου εἶναί φασιν, unless indeed we fall back on the explanation that Irenaeus had learned this denial, so displeasing
to Gobar as well as to Photius, in Gaul or Rome ; an unlikely
explanation, since Photius tells us in another place that Hippolytus learned this from Irenaeus.   But we shall return to
Hippolytus presently when we come to the witness of Rome.

Eusebius (*H. E.* v. 26) uses language of Irenaeus which
points in the same direction.   He speaks of a book of his
"in which he mentions the epistle to the Hebrews and the
so-called Wisdom of Solomon, making quotations from them."
This is not very conclusive by itself, but it fits in with the rest
of the evidence which seems to prove with sufficient clearness
that neither in the East nor in the West did Irenaeus hold
the epistle to be S. Paul's.   Eusebius himself seems to accept
the new custom of reckoning it with the Pauline epistles.   He
does so in the chapter in which he expressly declares what the
Canon of Scripture is, *H. E.* III. 25 ; for he enters therein, after
the Gospels and Acts, "the epistles of Paul," without considering it necessary to say how many there are, and he does
not name Hebrews, or any other epistle attributed to S. Paul,
among the disputed books which he presently catalogues.   But
in *H. E.* VI. 13 he does use this very term "disputed," ἀντιλε-
γομένων, of Hebrews together with the Wisdom of Solomon,
Sirach, Barnabas, Clement, and Jude, and he was of course
aware of the ancient objections.   Moreover in *H. E.* III. 37,
when he is writing about the epistle of Clement and his mind
is thereby brought to consider frankly the problem of authorship, he adopts as his own the Alexandrian mediating explanation : Clement's use of the epistle shews that it was not a new
work in his day ; hence it has been decided that it should be
included in the Pauline list ; no doubt Paul communicated

with the Hebrews in his native language, Luke or Clement (whose epistle resembles Hebrews in style) interpreted his writing.

Such was the reputable opinion of an ecclesiastical scholar just before the Council of Nicaea. At that Council Hebrews was quoted as written by S. Paul, but no discussion of the Canon of Scripture was held (Westcott, *Canon*, p. 430). It is however from this period that Hebrews does definitely take its place among the Pauline epistles. Athanasius, in his *Festal Letter* for the year 367, may be held to have declared the settled opinion of the Eastern Church. In this letter he gives a list of the canonical Scriptures, in which, after Acts and the seven Catholic epistles, he enumerates the fourteen epistles of S. Paul, placing Hebrews between the two to the Thessalonians and the Pastorals ; these are followed by Philemon, which concludes the list. Possibly the form of expression "that"—not "one"—"to the Hebrews" was intended to stand as a memorial of superseded doubt.

The order is interesting. It is familiar to us to day because Westcott and Hort have adopted it in their Greek Testament from the great uncials ℵ B and also A. The last, Codex Alexandrinus, was probably written in Alexandria. The home of ℵ and B is still disputed. Hort thought they came from Rome ; Kenyon inclines to Egypt, but admits "fair evidence of a connexion with the textual school of Caesarea, which does not exclude an actual origin in Egypt, from which the school of Caesarea took its rise[1]." Kirsopp Lake[2] says, "It is hard to realize at first that there seems to be no evidence for this order, with which we are so familiar, before the fourth century. Probably it was part of the textual and critical revision which the New Testament underwent, chiefly, but not exclusively, at the hand of Alexandrian scholars, in the fourth century." He is writing of the arrangement of the Pauline epistles, properly so called. What we, with our eyes fixed upon Hebrews, notice is, that this epistle is thus removed from the position which it elsewhere held among the early epistles[3], and is placed after

[1] *Textual Criticism of N.T.*, p. 84 f.
[2] *The earlier Epistles of St Paul*, p. 358.
[3] See Moffatt, *Historical N.T.*, p. 110.

all those addressed to churches. Here caution appears. If popular Alexandrian usage was the source of the tradition of Pauline authorship, Alexandria was also the place where that tradition was restrained by scholarship. From Alexandria a modified judgement about authorship, and a modified position in the Pauline list, were promulgated to the Eastern Church. The order of our English version, Hebrews last of all, comes to us from the Vulgate. It is found in DEKL, and perhaps in the mass of Greek cursives, but it is really Western, and reflects the never quite forgotten objection to Pauline authorship in the Latin Church.

The Syriac versions may be appealed to for the liturgical practice of the Eastern Church of the Euphrates valley, of which the metropolis was Edessa. But it is not easy to decide with certainty whether this church read Hebrews in its earliest worship. The Peshitta includes Hebrews among the Pauline epistles. But for the gospels we know that the Peshitta is not the primitive form of the version. For the rest of the New Testament we have now no "Old Syriac" to check the Peshitta. Since the Armenian version was made from the "Old Syriac," but revised from the Greek in the fifth century[1], it too fails to supply clear evidence about the early use of Hebrews in Armenia. This however may be considered. The Armenian version does include Hebrews now. If Hebrews preserves vestiges of an Old Syriac base as the rest of the Pauline epistles do in this version, we do get thereby satisfactory proof that the "Old Syriac" contained this epistle.

What it certainly did not contain, any more than the Egyptian versions did, was the Apocalypse. S. Jerome wrote to Dardanus that whereas the use of the Latins (in his day) was to exclude Hebrews, while the churches of the Greeks excluded the Apocalypse, he followed the authority of the ancient writers and accepted both as canonical. We will consider presently what this testimony precisely signifies. Meanwhile it is enough to note that he somewhat misunderstood the authority of the ancient writers. Speaking roughly we might say that the earlier

[1] Burkitt, quoting J. A. Robinson, *Enc. Bibl.*, Text and Versions, § 36.

evidence shows Hebrews received in the East and not in the
West, Apocalypse in the West not in the East ; that is, each
was suspected in that region where it was probably composed.
But for Hebrews, at any rate, even this partial acceptance must
be qualified. Only at Alexandria in quite early times does
anything like a tradition of Pauline authorship appear, and at
Alexandria we only know it because it was criticised. Nor does
criticism cease in the East even when the "use" becomes fixed.
Euthalius (c. 460) still has to defend his "use" against the old
obstinate questionings, and it is interesting to find that one of
the arguments in his defence is drawn from the false reading in
x. 34, τοῖς δεσμοῖς μου, "my bonds." Satisfaction with the Pauline
claim grows up side by side with the textual and exegetical
blurring of the individual character of the epistle.

§ 3. *In Africa Tertullian quotes the epistle as Barnabas', and
       approves it as excluding second repentance.*

In the West meanwhile there is no hint of any one reading
Hebrews as S. Paul's. Tertullian at the beginning of the third
century writes in the tract *de Pudicitia*, c. 20 : "Disciplina
igitur apostolorum proprie quidem instruit ac determinat prin-
cipaliter sanctitatis omnis erga templum dei antistitem, et
ubique de ecclesia eradicantem omne sacrilegium pudicitiae,
sine ulla restitutionis mentione. Volo autem ex redundantia
alicuius etiam comitis apostolorum testimonium superinducere,
idoneum confirmandi de proximo iure disciplinam magistrorum.
Extat enim et Barnabae titulus ad Hebraeos, adeo satis auctori-
tatis viri, ut quem Paulus iuxta se constituerit in abstinentiae
tenore : 'aut ego solus et Barnabas non habemus hoc operandi
potestatem ?' Et utique receptior apud ecclesias epistola Barnabae
illo apocrypho Pastore moechorum. Monens itaque discipulos,
omissis omnibus initiis, ad perfectionem magis tendere, nec
rursus fundamenta poenitentiae iacere ab operibus mortuorum :
'impossibile est enim,' inquit, 'eos, qui semel illuminati sunt
et donum caeleste gustaverunt et participarunt spiritum sanctum
et verbum dei dulce gustaverunt, ·occidente iam aevo, cum
exciderint, rursus revocari in poenitentiam, refigentes cruci in
semet ipsos filium dei et dedecorantes ; terra enim, quae bibit

saepius devenientem in se humorem, et peperit herbam aptam
his propter quos et colitur, benedictionem dei consequitur ;
proferens autem spinas reproba et maledictionis proxima cuius
finis in exustionem.' Hoc qui ab apostolis didicit et cum apostolis docuit, numquam moecho et fornicatori secundam poenitentiam promissam ab apostolis norat."

Here Tertullian names Barnabas as author. He seems to
have no doubt about this, but it is not therefore certain that he
witnesses to the African tradition. Zahn[1] supposes him to have
found the epistle so described in a MS. that came from some
Greek Church, and this is the more likely in that the rendering
he gives is very different from any form of the Old Latin known
to us, and appears to be his own. There is just one piece of
evidence for a real tradition behind Tertullian's assertion: in
the list of New Testament writings preserved in Codex Claromontanus "Barnabae epist." seems to have meant Hebrews.
This would be more significant if, as Tischendorf thought, that
MS. had an African origin, but Souter now gives reasons for
tracing it to Sardinia[2]. On the whole it seems probable that
there is no more value in the reference preserved by Tertullian
to Barnabas than in those of Alexandria to Clement or Luke.
Those were the guesses of a literary Church where style was
considered ; this was the guess of a simpler society which only
noticed the subject-matter and argued that the Levite of the
New Testament was likely to be the author of the epistle which
dealt with priesthood.

What Tertullian does prove is that he had no idea of the
epistle being S. Paul's, and that he rather wishes than asserts
its canonical authority. He valued it highly, but only because
it is faithful to what he believed to have been the primitive
apostolic discipline of penitence. He read it and the rest of the
New Testament in what till lately would have been thought his
own masterful way : but, as will presently appear, one of the
latest editors of Hebrews agrees with him that "no second
repentance" is the actual doctrine of the epistle. The newest
rule of interpretation is the same as that of the African master
in the second century.

[1] *Einleitung in das N.T.* VIII. 45.

[2] *Journal of Theological Studies*, Jan. 1905.

§ 4. *At Rome Clement quotes Hebrews in first century, but says nothing about authorship. Close connexion of his epistle with Hebrews throughout, and possible dependence of both on Roman liturgical use. Clement generalises doctrine of Hebrews.*

But not the same as that of the earliest reader known to us, Clement of Rome, the first "doctor" of the Church, whose motto was ἐκτενὴς ἐπιείκεια, "intense moderation." He puts no straiter limits to repentance than our Lord does in the Gospels, nor does it seem to occur to him that such limits are prescribed in this epistle or in any other part of the New Testament.

For the present however our first business is with Clement as witness to Rome's early knowledge of the epistle, and in particular Rome's knowledge that S. Paul was not the author of it.

The letter sent from the Roman Church to the Corinthian Church, where quarrels had arisen concerning the ministry, bears no writer's name. Early tradition tells us that it was written by Clement, the third bishop of Rome after the apostles, the successor, that is, of Linus and Cletus or Anencletus, and that it was written at the end of the reign of Domitian, about 95 A.D. This fits well with the indications of date afforded by the document itself, which refers to an earlier persecution (i.e. Nero's) and to one which was raging or had but just ceased when it was written. This date corresponds with Clement's position in the episcopal succession, and we may safely accept both name and date, in spite of the critics—some of them acute—who have placed the document either earlier (in the reign of Nero) or later (in the reign of Trajan or of Hadrian).

Clement, then, writing to Corinth about 95 A.D., shews, among other things in his "very adequate letter," much familiarity with the Septuagint ; names S. Paul as having written to the Corinthians ; "while expressions scattered up and down his own letter recall the language of several of S. Paul's epistles belonging to different epochs and representing different types in his literary career....The influence of S. Peter's First Epistle may be traced in more than one passage....Again the writer shews himself conversant with the type of doctrine and modes of expression characteristic of the Epistle of S. James. Just as he co-ordinates the authority of S. Peter and S. Paul, as leaders of the Church, so in like manner he combines the teaching of S. Paul and S. James on the great doctrines of salvation." But also, "It is so largely interspersed with thoughts and expressions from the Epistle to the Hebrews, that many ancient writers attributed this Canonical epistle to Clement[1]."

In ch. 36 something more than interspersion of thoughts and expressions is found. The whole passage must be quoted :

Αὕτη ἡ ὁδός, ἀγαπητοί, ἐν ᾗ εὕρομεν τὸ σωτήριον ἡμῶν Ἰησοῦν Χριστὸν τὸν ἀρχιερέα τῶν προσφορῶν ἡμῶν, τὸν προστάτην καὶ βοηθὸν τῆς ἀσθενείας ἡμῶν. διὰ τούτου ἀτενίσωμεν εἰς τὰ ὕψη τῶν οὐρανῶν· διὰ τούτου ἐνοπτριζόμεθα τὴν ἄμωμον καὶ ὑπερτάτην ὄψιν αὐτοῦ· διὰ τούτου ἠνεῴχθησαν ἡμῶν οἱ ὀφθαλμοὶ τῆς καρδίας· διὰ τούτου ἡ ἀσύνετος καὶ ἐσκοτωμένη διάνοια ἡμῶν ἀναθάλλει εἰς τὸ θαυμαστὸν αὐτοῦ φῶς· διὰ τούτου ἠθέλησεν ὁ δεσπότης τῆς ἀθανάτου γνώσεως ἡμᾶς γεύσασθαι· ὃς ὢν ἀπαύγασμα τῆς μεγαλωσύνης αὐτοῦ τοσούτῳ μείζων ἐστὶν ἀγγέλων ὅσῳ διαφορώτερον ὄνομα κεκληρονόμηκεν. γέγραπται γὰρ οὕτως· Ὁ ποιῶν τοὺς ἀγγέλους αὐτοῦ πνεύματα καὶ τοὺς λειτουργοὺς αὐτοῦ πυρὸς φλόγα. Ἐπὶ δὲ τῷ υἱῷ αὐτοῦ οὕτως εἶπεν ὁ δεσπότης· Υἱός μου εἶ σύ, ἐγὼ σήμερον γεγέννηκά σε· αἴτησαι παρ᾽ ἐμοῦ, καὶ δώσω σοι ἔθνη τὴν κληρονομίαν σου, καὶ τὴν κατάσχεσίν σου τὰ πέρατα τῆς γῆς. καὶ πάλιν λέγει πρὸς αὐτόν· Κάθου ἐκ δεξιῶν μου, ἕως ἂν θῶ τοὺς ἐχθρούς σου ὑποπόδιον τῶν ποδῶν σου. Τίνες οὖν οἱ ἐχθροί; οἱ φαῦλοι καὶ ἀντιτασσόμενοι τῷ θελήματι αὐτοῦ.

Here we seem to recognise definite quotations from Heb. i., as the uncial type shews. The latter part of these quotations, being ultimately from LXX, is introduced as scripture with γέγραπται, and Ps. ii. 7 is continued with the next verse. But the verse from Ps. civ. ends, as in Hebrews, with πυρὸς φλόγα instead of πῦρ φλέγον. Lightfoot notices that LXXA has πυρος

---

[1] Lightfoot, *The Apostolic Fathers*, Part i., *S. Clement of Rome*, vol. i. p. 95 f.

φλεγᾶ, "which shows the reading in a transition state," and
if the verse stood by itself in Clement it might be possible that
he merely used the same LXX text as the author of our epistle.
In the context that can hardly be, and the compression of ὃς ὢν
κ.τ.λ., with the variation in order, ὄνομα κεκληρονόμηκεν, makes
any explanation of the coincidence except actual quotation most
unlikely.

But there is more to be noticed than definite quotation.
The quotations are introduced by reminiscences. With αὕτη
ἡ ὁδός, cf. Heb. x. 20 ἣν ἐκαίνισεν ἡμῖν ὁδόν κ.τ.λ. Ἀγαπητοί
agrees with Heb. vi. 9. Ἀρχιερέα is the key word in Hebrews,
and προσφορῶν is explained by Heb. v. 1, while Heb. v. 2
taken with Heb. iv. 15 f. explains τὸν προστάτην καὶ βοηθὸν·
τῆς ἀσθενείας ἡμῶν. From Heb. iv. 14 we get the idea of τὰ
ὕψη τῶν οὐρανῶν, and from Heb. xii. 2 (ἀφορῶντες εἰς...ἐν δεξιᾷ
τε τοῦ θρόνου τοῦ θεοῦ κεκάθικεν) we get this again combined
with the idea of ἀτενίσωμεν. With ἄμωμον cf. Heb. ix. 14, and
with the idea of ἄμωμον καὶ ὑπερτάτην cf. Heb. vii. 26 (ὅσιος,
ἄκακος...ὑψηλότερος τῶν οὐρανῶν γενόμενος). Εἰς τὸ θαυμαστὸν
αὐτοῦ φῶς corresponds with 1 Pet. ii. 9, but when we find this
immediately followed by τῆς ἀθανάτου γνώσεως ἡμᾶς γεύσασθαι,
we cannot but recall Heb. vi. 4 f., τοὺς ἅπαξ φωτισθέντας γευσαμένους τε τῆς δωρεᾶς τῆς ἐπουρανίου καὶ μετόχους γενηθέντας
πνεύματος ἁγίου καὶ καλὸν γευσαμένους θεοῦ ῥῆμα δυνάμεις τε
μέλλοντος αἰῶνος.

This kind of reminiscence or coincidence pervades Clement's
epistle. Here are some examples : Moses flying from Egypt,
iv.=Heb. xi. 27 ; we are in the same arena (σκάμματι),
vii.=Heb. xii. 1 ; and this is followed by "wherefore let us
forsake idle and vain thoughts," "let us fix our eyes on the
blood of Christ," which is a generalising paraphrase of Heb. xii.
2 ; Moses called "faithful in all [God's] house," xvii.=Heb. iii. 2,
and θεράπων xliii., liii.=Heb. iii. 5 ; ἀνέμων σταθμοὶ κατὰ τὸν
ἴδιον καιρὸν τὴν λειτουργίαν αὐτῶν ἀπροσκόπως ἐπιτελοῦσιν, xx.,
is perhaps independently natural in its context, but cf. Heb. i.
7, 14 ; εὐεργετῶν...ἡμᾶς τοὺς προσπεφευγότας τοῖς οἰκτιρμοῖς αὐτοῦ
διὰ τοῦ κυρίου ἡμῶν Ἰησοῦ Χριστοῦ, xx., cf. Heb. vi. 18 ff. ; the
ἀπόστολον of Heb. iii. 1, is, as it were, commented upon in xlii.,
οἱ ἀπόστολοι ἡμῖν εὐηγγελίσθησαν ἀπὸ τοῦ κυρίου Ἰησοῦ Χριστοῦ,

'Ιησοῦς ὁ Χριστὸς ἀπὸ τοῦ θεοῦ ἐξεπέμφθη, cf. also Heb. ii. 3 f.;
the sacrifice of Isaac is dwelt upon in x., and many of the heroes
of faith enrolled in Heb. xi. are also celebrated by Clement. In
xvii., again, he speaks of those οἵτινες ἐν δέρμασιν αἰγείοις καὶ
μηλωταῖς περιεπάτησαν κηρύσσοντες τὴν ἔλευσιν τοῦ χριστοῦ·
λέγομεν δὲ 'Ηλίαν καὶ 'Ελισαιὲ ἔτι δὲ καὶ 'Ιεζεκιήλ, τοὺς προφήτας·
πρὸς τούτοις καὶ τοὺς μεμαρτυρημένους. ἐμαρτυρήθη μεγάλως
'Αβραὰμ καὶ φίλος προσηγορεύθη τοῦ θεοῦ κ.τ.λ., a passage which
has unmistakable points of contact with Heb. xi.; in xliii. we
find the rod of Aaron that budded = Heb. ix. 4; in lvi. is a
compound quotation from Psalter and Proverbs which coincides
with Heb. xii. 6 in the words ὃν γὰρ ἀγαπᾷ...παραδέχεται.

More fleeting recollections may perhaps be recognised in the
juxtaposition of πρόδηλον, ἑτεροκλινεῖς and the φιλοξενίαν καὶ
εὐσέβειαν of Lot (xi.), cf. Heb. vii. 14, x. 23, xiii. 2.   The phrase
σύγκρασίς τίς ἐστιν ἐν πᾶσιν, in xxxvii., which seems to be
borrowed from Euripides, may have some connexion with μὴ
συνκεκερασμένος, Heb. iv. 2; in each place the thought is of
union in one body, and it is worth noticing that in Hebrews οὐκ
ὠφέλησεν precedes, in Clement καὶ ἐν τούτοις χρῆσις immediately
follows.   Is the interesting paradox in xx., οἱ οὐρανοὶ...σαλευό-
μενοι ἐν εἰρήνῃ, at all connected with the application of Haggai's
prophecy in Heb. xii. 26?   The language of Hebrews is certainly
in favour of the reading Lightfoot adopts in ii., εἰς τὸ σώζεσθαι
μετὰ δέους καὶ συνειδήσεως τὸν ἀριθμὸν τῶν ἐκλεκτῶν αὐτοῦ·
cf. Heb. xii. 28, μετὰ εὐλαβείας καὶ δέους (though δέους, which
occurs nowhere else in N.T., has disappeared in the later text),
and for συνειδήσεως cf. Heb. ix. 9, 14, x. 2, 22, xiii. 18.

But in this last example, if there is verbal resemblance, there
is also difference.   In Hebrews συνείδησις is not used in quite
this absolute manner.   In like manner μαρτυροῦμαι is common
to Hebrews and to Clement as almost a favourite word; but
while Clement approaches the idea of Hebrews, "canonised in
Scripture," he has nothing of the development towards the idea
of "martyrdom" which we observe in Hebrews.   So again he
uses ἀρχηγός, but does not restrain it to Christ as in Hebrews:
he also uses ἡγούμενοι, βασιλεία, but extends these terms to
secular powers.   More important is his reference to the "elect"
in the passage just quoted, a Pauline thought common in

Clement, but almost if not quite absent from Hebrews. Still more remarkable is his not infrequent reference, and in contexts where there is reminiscence of Hebrews, to the Blood of Christ. The sacrificial thought of Hebrews is not Clement's ; he thinks of the "precious blood," the "price"; see vii., already referred to, "Let us fix our eyes on the blood of Christ and understand how precious it is unto His Father, because being shed for our salvation it won for the whole world the grace of repentance." Already in this very earliest, almost contemporary use of Hebrews, we find the process beginning which so quickly and thoroughly developed : the particular presentation of doctrine through the figures of priesthood and sacrifice was blurred, and Hebrews was interpreted in general terms of N.T. theology ; its peculiar language was treated as mere language, a metaphorical way of repeating S. Paul. It is obvious that this would make the acceptance of Pauline authorship more and more facile. Not that this process is carried far by Clement. It was no part of his design to interpret Hebrews ; he simply avails himself of its phrases and adapts its thoughts as he finds it convenient so to do. Thus his own theme—the ecclesiastical ministry at Corinth—leads him to touch, as Hebrews does, on the Levitical ministry. In Hebrews that ministry affords an analogy, a starting point, from which the author rises to the conception of the true priesthood which is consummated in Christ ; the Levitical order he sets aside as a shadow. In later times the Church's ministry was compared with and, so to say, justified by the Levitical priesthood as its type. Clement attaches himself neither to the one view nor the other. Like Hebrews he refers to the Levitical orders ; speaks, like Hebrews, of them as pictured in the Scriptures, rather than as actually operating in Jerusalem ; and so, he too, though their functions had certainly been interrupted when he wrote, speaks of them in the present tense (xxxii., xl.). But all he is really concerned with is the Levitical ministration as an example, among others, of good order kept.

The other point, the "sacrificial" Blood, is more important, and must here be returned to. Clement says nothing about this great subject. But he does refer more than once to the priests, i.e. bishops and presbyters, of the Church and to our Lord the High Priest, as offering sacrifice. But this sacrifice, or these sacrifices, are the same as in Heb. xiii. 15 ff. ; they are not the same as the one sacrifice mysteriously adumbrated in Heb. xiii. 10—13, and distinctly named in Heb. x. 14 ; perhaps the δῶρά τε καὶ θυσίας of Heb. v. 1 may be taken as a middle term, borrowed from the Old Testament, which connects the two. A like connexion may be perceived in the ancient, especially the Greek, liturgies. For there too special mention is made of the gifts and offerings of the people, which seem to include their alms as well as the bread and wine (originally contributed in large quantity for the social feast, the Agapé) ; but, on the other hand, these gifts and offerings are hallowed by association with the supreme offering of Christ—Himself the offerer and the offering— of which the whole liturgy is a dramatic re-presentation.

Of this idea there is in Clement no clear sign of consciousness. It seems as though Clement's language was partly moulded on the very simple liturgy in which he was accustomed to worship, while the profounder worship of later times was influenced by that great thought of the epistle to the Hebrews which Clement, in spite of his appreciation of the epistle, missed.

That Clement does owe much to the liturgical thought and language of Rome must be considered certain. "When the closing chapters, which had disappeared with the loss of a leaf in the Alexandrian manuscript, were again brought to light by the discovery of fresh documents, we could not fail to be struck by the *liturgical* character of this newly recovered portion. The whole epistle may be said to lead up to the long prayer or litany, if we may so call it, which forms a fit close to its lessons of forbearance and love." So Lightfoot writes, *Clem. Rom.* I. p. 382. And he thus explains the fact : "There was at this time no authoritative written liturgy in use in the Church of Rome, but the prayers were modified at the discretion of the officiating minister. Under the dictation of habit and experience however these prayers were gradually assuming a fixed form. A more or less definite order in the petitions, a greater or less constancy in the individual expressions, are already perceptible. As the chief pastor of the Roman Church would be the main instrument in thus moulding the liturgy, the prayers, without actually being written down, would assume in his mind a fixity as time went on. When therefore at the close of his epistle he asks his readers to

fall down on their knees and lay down their jealousies and
disputes at the footstool of peace, his language naturally runs
into those antithetical forms and measured cadences which his
ministrations in the Church had rendered habitual with him
when dealing with such a subject."

But Lightfoot continues that it is not only in the concluding
prayer that the liturgical character of Clement's language asserts
itself. This had been noticed even before the discovery of the
lost ending ; and Lightfoot himself fills five pages with parallels
between Clement's language and thought on the one hand, and
on the other such phrases and ideas in the Greek liturgies
known to us as are so deeply interfused into their characteristic
structure that those phrases and ideas may fairly be considered
primitive[1].

It is remarkable that a large proportion of those examples
can be more or less closely paralleled from Hebrews. With
προσέλθωμεν οὖν αὐτῷ ἐν ὁσιότητι ψυχῆς, ἁγνὰς καὶ ἀμιάντους
χεῖρας αἴροντες πρὸς αὐτόν (xxix.) cf. προσερχώμεθα μετὰ ἀληθινῆς
καρδίας ἐν πληροφορίᾳ τῆς πίστεως, ῥεραντισμένοι τὰς καρδίας ἀπὸ
συνειδήσεως πονηρᾶς καὶ λελουσμένοι τὸ σῶμα ὕδατι καθαρῷ,
Heb. x. 22 : with Ἁγίου οὖν μερὶς ὑπάρχοντες ποιήσωμεν τὰ τοῦ
ἁγιασμοῦ (xxx.) cf. διώκετε...τὸν ἁγιασμόν, οὗ χωρὶς οὐδεὶς ὄψεται
τὸν κύριον, Heb. xii. 14, and for the thought of μερὶς cf. ii. 11,
iii. 1, 14 : with κολληθῶμεν τῇ εὐλογίᾳ αὐτοῦ (xxxi.) cf. μὴ
συνκεκερασμένους τῇ πίστει τοῖς ἀκούσασιν, Heb. iv. 2 : with
κατανοήσωμεν τὸ πᾶν πλῆθος τῶν ἀγγέλων αὐτοῦ (xxxiv.) cf.
προσεληλύθατε...μυριάσιν ἀγγέλων πανηγύρει, Heb. xii. 22, where
the context in each case, besides affording other points of verbal
contact, has very decided liturgical affinities. On this passage
Lightfoot continues thus : "He follows up this eucharistic
reference by a direct practical precept bearing on congregational
worship : 'Let us then'—not less than the angels—'gathered
together (συναχθέντες) in concord with a lively conscience (ἐν
συνειδήσει) cry unto Him fervently (ἐκτενῶς) as with one mouth,
that we may be found partakers of His great and glorious
promises,' where almost every individual expression recalls the
liturgical forms—the σύναξις as the recognised designation of the

[1] See *Clem. Rom.* i. pp. 386—391.

congregation gathered together for this purpose, the συνείδησις which plays so prominent a part in the attitude of the worshipper, the ἐκτενῶς which describes the intensity of the prayers offered." With συναχθέντες cf. μὴ ἐγκαταλείποντες τὴν ἐπισυναγωγὴν ἑαυτῶν, Heb. x. 25 ; and note the five times repeated συνείδησις in Heb. ix. 9, 14, x. 2, 22, xiii. 18. In each of these five places συνείδησις is distinctly connected with ritual or prayer, and this perhaps may tend to explain the subtle difference which readers cannot but feel between the meaning of the word in this epistle and in S. Paul. With ἐκτενῶς there is indeed no verbal parallel in Hebrews, but it is of a piece with the greater depth continually shown by its author as compared with Clement that we do find the idea of ἐκτενῶς emphatically expressed in the description of the prayer of the Christ, Heb. v. 7—10.

We will not dwell on θυσία αἰνέσεως (xxxv.) and its parallel in Heb. xiii. 15, nor on Clement's equivalents to the εὐποιίας καὶ κοινωνίας in the same context ; nor on the light which αὐτὴ ἡ ὁδός (xxxvi.), with Lightfoot's comment, may be found to throw on ἣν ἐνεκαίνισεν ἡμῖν ὁδόν...διὰ τοῦ καταπετάσματος κτλ, Heb. x. 20—a passage which has been influential in the Greek liturgies. We will rather return to the consideration of the fuller depth which the author of Hebrews reaches in his quasi-liturgical ideas. In one sentence indeed Clement rather surprises us by an unusually philosophical phrase : Σὺ τὴν ἀέναον τοῦ κόσμου σύστασιν διὰ τῶν ἐνεργουμένων ἐφανεροποίησας. This is in his concluding prayer which has so striking a likeness to the rehearsal of the act of creation in the anaphora of the Greek liturgies ; but it is noteworthy that just here he also approaches the opening thought of the memorial of the heroes of faith in Heb. xi. Perhaps it is just worth while to point to a somewhat similar coincidence in 2 Clem. xiv. as compared with Heb. xii. 23 (ἐκκλησίᾳ πρωτοτόκων)—Ὥστε, ἀδελφοί, ποιοῦντες τὸ θέλημα τοῦ πατρὸς ἡμῶν θεοῦ ἐσόμεθα ἐκ τῆς ἐκκλησίας τῆς πρώτης, τῆς πνευματικῆς, τῆς πρὸ ἡλίου καὶ σελήνης ἐκτισμένης. "If the First Epistle of Clement is the earliest foreshadowing of a Christian liturgy, the so-called Second Epistle is the first example of a Christian homily," of the early second century, delivered either at Rome (Harnack) or at Corinth (Lightfoot). In each of these passages we find the author thinking more deeply than usual ; in each the language is linked with the exercise of worship ; and in each there is coincidence with Hebrews.

However, returning to Clement's true letter, ch. xxxvi., we do find likeness and difference as compared with Hebrews upon which we must dwell a little longer. If the reader will look back to the quotation of this chapter on p. xxx, he will notice that it begins by speaking of Jesus Christ as "the High Priest who presents our offerings." The significance of this for Clement is thus summed up by Lightfoot : "Thus all human life, as truly conceived, and as interpreted by the Church of Christ, is a great eucharistic service. It is not difficult to see how this one idea pervades all Clement's thoughts. Indeed the proper under-standing of the structure of the epistle is lost, if this key be mislaid. Our true relation to God is a constant interchange— God's magnificent gifts realized by us, our reciprocal offerings, however unworthy, presented to and accepted by Him. The eucharistic service of the Church is the outward embodiment and expression of this all-pervading lesson. The eucharistic elements, the bread and wine—and, still more comprehensively, the tithes and first fruits and other offerings in kind, which in the early Church had a definite place amidst the eucharistic offerings—are only a part of the great sacramental system. All things spiritual and material, all things above and below, the kingdom of nature and the kingdom of grace, fall within its scope. Heaven and earth alike are full of God's glory ; and shall they not be full of human thanksgiving also ? This idea underlies the earliest liturgical forms ; it underlies, or rather it absorbs, Clement's conception. There is no narrow ritual and no cramping dogma here. The conception is wide and compre-hensive, as earth and sea and sky are wide and comprehensive. It inspires, explains, justifies, vivifies, the sacramental principle."

Any one who is familiar with Clement's epistle will recognise the precision of this language ; the illustrations and similes are not ornamental, they are in Clement's own vein. But any one who is familiar with the epistle to the Hebrews will feel that, beautiful as this presentation is of the sacramental principle, that in Hebrews is grander. It is concentrated and profound ; it shews Calvary as the outward and visible sign of the sacrifice offered in the real sanctuary of heaven. Διὰ τούτου ἐνοπτριζόμεθα

τὴν ἄμωμον καὶ ὑπερτάτην ὄψιν αὑτοῦ, wrote Clement. The idea
in ἐνοπτριζόμεθα fits Hebrews well ; but it means more in
Hebrews. And this idea, as Hebrews deepens it, appears in
one prayer which is common to all the liturgies. It runs thus
in the Roman Mass : "Supplices te rogamus, omnipotens Deus :
iube haec perferri per manus sancti angeli tui in sublime altare
tuum in conspectu divinae maiestatis tuae : ut quotquot ex hac
altaris participatione sacrosanctum filii tui corpus et sanguinem
sumpserimus, omni benedictione caelesti et gratia repleamur."
There is a reason for choosing the Roman form for quotation.
The words which immediately precede this part of the prayer
contain a reference to Melchizedek as high-priest : "Supra quae
propitio ac sereno vultu respicere digneris : et accepta habere,
sicuti accepta habere dignatus es munera pueri tui iusti abel,
et sacrificium patriarchae nostri abrahae : et quod tibi obtulit
summus sacerdos tuus melchisedech, sanctum sacrificium, im-
maculatam hostiam." The liturgy of the Coptic Church refers
to the sacrifice of Melchizedek in connexion with the "offering"
of the incense after the lection from S. Paul, but the mention of
Melchizedek at this point and with this application seems to
belong to Rome alone, or to Rome and liturgies connected with
Rome[1].

A writer in the *Nineteenth Century*, Jan. 1913 (M. A. R. Tuker),
elaborating Harnack's suggestion that Prisca or Priscilla wrote
Hebrews, draws this conclusion : "The Roman origin of the
epistle indeed is enshrined in the Roman liturgy. In that
liturgy, and in no other, the priesthood of Melchizedek is in-
voked, and the words are those of the Epistle to the Hebrews—
summus sacerdos Melchisedech. Moreover, they are recorded in
the oldest reference to the Roman Canon, and must take their
place by the side of the 'Amen' of Justin as root-words of the
Liturgy." Their antiquity is confirmed by their agreement with
the old Latin ; for *summus sacerdos* is not found in the Vulgate
of Hebrews, but it does occur at v. 10 in *d*.

But what if the phrase of the Canon should go back to a
use which, however oral and unfixed, is older than the epistle ?

---

[1] For Mozarabic or Gothic parallels, cf. *Church Quarterly Review*,
Jan. 1907, also Ap. 1906 for Melchizedek's sacrifice in mosaics at
Ravenna.

What if the author of Hebrews as well as Clement has been influenced by the liturgical service at Rome in which they had both worshipped? One almost wonders that, among the various conjectures about the authorship, nothing has ever been said for Clement's predecessors Linus or Cletus. That of course would be as fanciful as to find with Mr Field a close and continuous relationship between the epistle and the later form of the Greek liturgies[1]. Nothing indeed rises above the merest conjecture in these observations. However, there is a certain liturgical flavour in Hebrews which perhaps ought not to be wholly explained as due to the influence of the Levitical analogy, and which makes itself more distinctly felt when the liturgical character of Clement's theology is brought to bear in comparison. If but little more than a fancy, it is perhaps worth considering whether further examination might not raise the fancy at least to a possibility ; that both these authors wrote from Rome; both draw consciously or unconsciously some thoughts from the eucharistic service they knew ; and their coincidences and differences tend to remind us how one aspect of a mystery is visible to one mind, another to another—so perhaps with the Christ of S. John and the Synoptists.

However the fancy is not to be pressed; especially with regard to Clement's witness to Hebrews. Even if some of his resemblances in word or thought might be due to a common liturgical influence, enough would still remain to satisfy us that he had read the epistle. Is it then clear that he knew it was not S. Paul's? Taking Clement by himself we cannot say so. It is not his way to name the authors he uses. He introduces quotations from the Old Testament with "It is written," or, more often (in the style of Hebrews), "God saith," "the scripture saith," "He saith somewhere": no writer of the New Testament is canonical for him in the same degree as the Old. He once refers to "the" letter of the blessed Paul the apostle (xlvii.), but that means the epistle Paul wrote to the Corinthians whom Clement himself is addressing ; there was a special reason for naming him in that one place. And in ch. v. Paul is named, and

---

[1] *The Apostolic Liturgy and the Epistle to the Hebrews*, by John Edward Field, Rivingtons, 1882.

from what immediately follows we might infer that Clement knew 2 Corinthians and possibly 2 Timothy, as his. But his silence about the author of the passages he quotes from Hebrews can prove but little more than his silence about S. Peter or S. James when he makes use of the teaching which comes to us under their names.

§ 5. *Clement's witness is continued by the Western denial of Pauline authorship. Till fourth century Rome and the West do not waver: Hippolytus, Muratorian Canon, Old Latin Version. Then Jerome, Augustine, Hilary begin to adopt Eastern acceptance of Paul as author; yet still witness to contrary tradition of West, which was never wholly forgotten even in the Middle Ages: Dante; Erasmus, Estius.*

But there is another consideration, in the light of which that silence does appear more significant. Clement's witness cannot be separated from the general witness of the Church in the West, which flows on from him as the starting point. That witness is against the Pauline authorship; so obstinately against it that we can hardly escape the conclusion that Rome knew S. Paul had not written the epistle. Till the fourth century Tertullian and Gregory of Elvira alone in the West make any reference to it, and both of them attribute it to Barnabas. See Souter, *Text and Canon of the N.T.*, p. 177, where the allusion is to the *pseudo-Origen Tractatus*, once attributed to Novatian. Prof. Souter would now read " Gregory of Elvira " in place of " Novatian." Indeed the silence of Novatian is eloquent. If in the middle of the third century, when he was pressing the sterner discipline at Rome, there had been any idea of the Pauline authorship in the Roman Church, he would surely have appealed to Heb. vi. 4—6. But there is no reference to Hebrews in either of Novatian's extant books, nor is he anywhere said to have made such reference.

And, going back to the end of the second century, we find the Pauline authorship distinctly denied at Rome. Eusebius, *H.E.* vi. 20, writes:

ἦλθε δὲ εἰς ἡμᾶς καὶ Γαΐου λογιωτάτου ἀνδρὸς διάλογος ἐπὶ Ῥώμης κατὰ Ζεφυρῖνον πρὸς Πρόκλον τῆς κατὰ Φρύγας αἱρέσεως

ὑπερμαχοῦντα κεκινημένος, ἐν ᾧ τῶν δι' ἐναντίας τὴν περὶ τὸ συντάτ-
τειν καινὰς γραφὰς προπέτειάν τε καὶ τόλμαν ἐπιστομίζων τῶν τοῦ
ἱεροῦ ἀποστόλου δεκατριῶν μόνων ἐπιστολῶν μνημονεύει, τὴν πρὸς
Ἑβραίους μὴ συναριθμήσας ταῖς λοιπαῖς· ἐπεὶ καὶ εἰς δεῦρο παρὰ
Ῥωμαίων τισὶν οὐ νομίζεται τοῦ ἀποστόλου τυγχάνειν.

Here we have a learned Roman, writing against the Mon-
tanists in the time of Zephyrinus, and denying that the epistle
to the Hebrews is one of S. Paul's epistles. He is checking the
licence of opponents in adducing new Scriptures, and seems to
illustrate his argument from this parallel novelty of attributing
Hebrews to the apostle. And Eusebius adds that this was
natural since even down to his own time there are some in the
Roman Church who do not allow this epistle to be Paul's; that is,
Eusebius recognises that this "very learned man" was supported
by the tradition of his church in his plain denial.

But who is this "very learned man"? Eusebius calls him
Gaius, and it is possible that there was a Gaius who was a
Roman presbyter at that time; but it is certain no Gaius wrote
the dialogue of which Eusebius here speaks. He has however
mentioned immediately before Hippolytus "bishop of some see."
Hippolytus did write that very dialogue and named the orthodox
interlocutor Gaius. It was Hippolytus the "presbyter" or
"venerable" bishop of the foreigners at the port of Rome who
denied Hebrews to S. Paul, as Stephen Gobar and Photius
distinctly say in later centuries.

The story of this remarkable person may be read in the
second volume of Lightfoot's *S. Clement of Rome*, set off with
all the riches of scholarship and all the charm of romance. Two
points only need be touched here. "He linked together the
learning and traditions of the East, the original home of
Christianity, with the marvellous practical energy of the West,
the scene of his own life's labours": and he was probably the
author of the Muratorian Canon.

As to the first point. Hippolytus does not appear to have
ever been in the East himself, but Photius tells us he was a
pupil of Irenaeus, and his own frequent references to Irenaeus
prove that true. "Not only was he by far the most learned
man in the Western Church, but his spiritual and intellectual
ancestry was quite exceptional. Though he lived till within a

d 2

few years of the middle of the third century [c. 155—236 A.D.],
he could trace his pedigree back by only three steps, literary
as well as ministerial, to the life and teaching of the Saviour
Himself. Irenaeus, Polycarp, S. John—this was his direct
ancestry. No wonder if these facts secured to him exceptional
honour in his own generation." And still, for our present
purpose, these facts are weighty. His testimony against the
Pauline authorship of Hebrews is more than ordinary. In the
face of the impression left upon us by Clement's style of
quotation and the continuous evidence for a real tradition at
Rome, it would be perversely sceptical to conjecture that Hippolytus first started that tradition, receiving it from Irenaeus.
But his learning and his connexion with Irenaeus do imply that
he had good reason for confirming the Roman tradition, and that
the earliest tradition of the East was in agreement with it.
Hippolytus is further connected with the Eastern Church in
another direction. Origen was a hearer of his at Rome. That
was not needed to start Origen on his criticism of the Alexandrian
tradition, for Clement of Alexandria had already led the way.
But it may well be that Origen did learn something from
Hippolytus which might corroborate his own inferences from
the style. He might add "external" to "internal" evidence;
and whatever he might once have meant by that ambiguous
phrase, τίς δὲ ὁ γράψας τὴν ἐπιστολήν, τὸ μὲν ἀληθὲς θεὸς οἶδεν,
it would be possible to give it the absolute significance which
would satisfy Hippolytus and Rome.

The Muratorian Canon is a document which contains a
mutilated list of the books of the New Testament. It was
"discovered and published by Muratori in 1740 from a MS. in
the Ambrosian Library at Milan...Muratori himself attributed
it to Gaius, the contemporary of Hippolytus, who flourished
under Zephyrinus....It is generally allowed that this catalogue
emanated from Rome, as indeed the mention of 'the city' implies...The general opinion also is that the document was written
in Greek and that we possess only a not very skilful, though
literal, translation." The whole of Lightfoot's § 6, pp. 405—413,
should be read to appreciate his proof that Hippolytus wrote the
Canon in Greek iambics, and that it is in fact the work included
in the list of the saint's writings which is engraved on the chair

of his third century statue, and is there called ῷδαι εἰς πάσας τὰς γραφάς. The Latin of the Canon may be found in its full and very corrupt form in Westcott's *Canon of the New Testament,* App. C.[1] The part that bears upon our enquiry shall however be quoted here from the emended text which Westcott adds:

Epistulae autem Pauli, quae, a quo loco, vel qua ex causa directae sint, uolentibus intellegere ipsae declarant. Primum omnium Corinthiis schisma haeresis interdicens, deinceps Galatis circumcisionem, Romanis autem ordine scripturarum, sed et principium earum esse Christum intimans, prolixius scripsit, de quibus singulis necesse est a nobis disputari ; cum ipse beatus apostolus Paulus, sequens predecessoris sui Iohannis ordinem, non nisi nominatim septem ecclesiis scribat ordine tali : ad Corinthios prima, ad Ephesios secunda, ad Philippenses tertia, ad Colossenses quarta, ad Galatas quinta, ad Thessalonicenses sexta, ad Romanos septima. Uerum Corinthiis et Thessalonicensibus licet pro correptione iteretur, una tamen per omnem orbem terrae ecclesia diffusa esse dinoscitur ; et Iohannes enim in Apocalypsi, licet septem ecclesiis scribat, tamen omnibus dicit. Uerum ad Philemonem unam et ad Titum unam, et ad Timotheum duas pro affectu et dilectione ; in honore tamen ecclesiae catholicae in ordinatione ecclesiasticae disciplinae sanctificatae sunt. Fertur etiam ad Laodicenses, alia ad Alexandrinos, Pauli nomine finctae ad haeresim Marcionis, et alia plura quae in catholicam ecclesiam recipi non potest : fel enim cum melle misceri non congruit.

As must necessarily be the case if Hippolytus is the writer, the testimony is clear to thirteen and only thirteen epistles of Paul. Hebrews does not appear by name, and as the title "to Hebrews" was known to Tertullian, and as Jerome says of Hippolytus "quartam decimam, quae fertur ad Hebraeos, dicit non eius esse," *de Vir. Ill.* 59, in which statement he seems to be following what Eusebius had applied to Gaius, it is difficult to suppose that "alia ad Alexandrinos" could mean Hebrews ; there is besides the possibility that Hebrews was mentioned by its usual title in the lost conclusion of the MS. Yet the language

[1] And Souter, *Text and Canon,* pp. 208—211, gives it in a corrected form with textual notes.

of Eusebius and Jerome is not decisive; to them this epistle had long been simply "to Hebrews." In the list of books interpolated between Philemon and Hebrews in Codex Claromontanus it seems to be this epistle which is entitled "Barnabas" without note of destination. And "ad Alexandrinos" does fit curiously the Alexandrine style and thought of the epistle. Nor does "ad haeresim Marcionis" = πρὸς τὴν αἵρεσιν, *bearing upon* etc., seem an impossible description of a letter which appeals so much to Old Testament testimonies and treats so deeply the real manhood of the Lord. If the identification could be upheld it would witness to a most remarkable attempt in early times to appreciate the individual and original character of the epistle. The readers who thus appreciated it would perhaps hardly be the same as those who thought it "Pauli nomine fincta."

However that may be, the mention of Marcion's name serves to remind us here that the earliest list we have of S. Paul's epistles comes from Marcion, and Hebrews is not included therein. As Marcion also omits the Pastorals, it may be best to refer to this merely in passing. At the same time it must be remarked that both omissions may be evidence of great importance. It is becoming more and more clear that some of Marcion's "readings" are not, as those who wrote against him supposed, wilful alterations of the text, but valuable evidence for at least an early text. His list of the Pauline epistles is conclusive evidence for the substantial truth of the Church's tradition of S. Paul's work and writings. And his omission of Hebrews and the Pastorals may indicate that in 150 A.D. these two elements of the final New Testament Canon were still—though it may be for very different reasons, and in different degrees—excluded.

The document called the Mommsen Canon agrees with the Muratorian in omitting Hebrews and limiting the Pauline epistles to thirteen. This document was found by Theodor Mommsen in the Phillipps Library at Cheltenham in 1885, and another copy has been found since then at S. Gall. The Canon is considered to be African, of date about 360 A.D. The Latin of the New Testament part may be read in Souter, p. 212. It adds, with a faint hint of doubt, 2 and 3 John and 2 Peter to the New Testament of Cyprian the third century bishop of

Carthage; otherwise it agrees with him. This makes it almost certain that in the earliest state of the Old Latin version Hebrews was not included; for that version arose in Africa where "Latin was the official language and the language of civilisation" while at Rome "society from top to bottom was bilingual" and from Paul to Hippolytus (56—230 A.D.) Christian literature was in Greek.

Yet we possess an Old Latin translation of Hebrews. That is true, but there is reason to suppose that it is either a late made one, or at least one that was "picked up" at a comparatively late period and added to the other books. Westcott says (*Canon*, p. 266) "The Claromontane text of the Epistle to the Hebrews represents I believe more completely than any other manuscript the simplest form of the *Vetus Latina*; but from the very fact that the text of this Epistle exhibits more marked peculiarities than are found in any of the Pauline Epistles, it follows that it occupies a peculiar position." And this becomes even more evident when we find interpolated in the MS. between the other Pauline epistles and Hebrews a list of New Testament books with the number of lines filled by each—a "stichometry"— in which the epistles of S. Paul are enumerated without Hebrews. At the end of the list Hermas, Acts of Paul, Apocalypse of Peter are added; and between the Catholic epistles and the Apocalypse (of John) comes "Barnabas," which seems to mean what we call "Hebrews," the correspondence in stichometry pointing to that identification. It seems clear that Codex Claromontanus was mainly copied from an earlier MS. which did not include Hebrews, but when this copy was made it was desired that Hebrews should be included. Dr Souter thinks that it was written in Sardinia after the island had become part of the Byzantine empire in the sixth century[1]. If so, it might seem that even so late the Latin Canon in Sardinia was enlarged in deference to Eastern custom. The peculiar character of the Vulgate translation may be mainly due to its being a revision of the Old Latin which already differed so much from the Old Latin of the other epistles.

In the fourth century we do indeed find Western doctors, such as Hilary and Ambrose, quoting the epistle freely as S. Paul's.

[1] *JTS.* Jan. 1905.

Alford accounts for this very reasonably: "About the middle of the fourth century, we find the practice beginning in the Latin Church, of quoting the Epistle as St Paul's: but at first only here and there, and not as if the opinion were the prevailing one. Bleek traces the adoption of this view by the Latins to their closer intercourse with the Greeks about this time owing to the Arian controversy, which occasioned several of the Western theologians to spend some time in the East, where the Epistle was cited, at first by both parties, and always by the Catholics, as undoubtedly St Paul's. Add to this the study of the Greek exegetical writers, and especially of Origen, and we shall have adduced enough reasons to account for the gradual spread of the idea of the Pauline authorship over the West." Perhaps the process was even simpler. There is a considerable amount of evidence for the epistle being widely known, whatever was thought about its authorship, from the earliest times[1]. Good-hearted students would come of their own accord to Origen's opinion that the theology of Hebrews was wonderful and by no means inferior to the received canonical writings; then, as with Origen himself, the step to quoting it as "the apostle's" would be easy.

But that being so the noteworthy point is the reluctance of the Latin Church to go further. This may be illustrated at two stages: first in what the two great scholars, Jerome and Augustine, write when they deliberately consider the question; secondly in the scruples against breaking with the tradition against Pauline authorship which persist to a late period.

Full and fair quotation for the mind of Jerome and Augustine may be found in that treasury of learning which all subsequent commentators have drawn upon, Bleek's edition[2], or in the excellent adaptation of Bleek's prolegomena which Alford has made in the fourth volume of his Greek Testament. S. Jerome's "usual practice is, to cite the words of the epistle, and ascribe them to St Paul." His residence in the East made this the

---

[1] See *The New Testament in the Apostolic Fathers, by a Committee of the Oxford Society of Historical Theology*, Clarendon Press, 1905, and consider Cyprian's language about the High-priesthood of Christ.

[2] *Der Brief an die Hebräer erläutert durch Einleitung, Uebersetzung und fortlaufenden Commentar.* Berlin, 1828—1840.

more natural. But it would not mean much in any one, and in him it certainly did not mean that he would assert the Pauline authorship when he gave a critical decision, such as the following: "illud nostris dicendum est, hanc epistolam quae inscribitur ad Hebraeos, non solum ab ecclesiis Orientis, sed ab omnibus retro ecclesiasticis Graeci sermonis scriptoribus quasi Pauli apostoli suscipi, licet plerique eam vel Barnabae vel Clementis arbitrentur: et nihil interesse cuius sit, cum ecclesiastici viri sit, et quotidie ecclesiarum lectione celebretur" (*ad Dardanum*, § 3). By "plerique" Jerome probably meant "many" not "most." But in any case the general sense is clear; he had learned to connect the epistle with S. Paul just so far as Origen had done. When however he goes on to contrast "nos," i.e. himself and those like-minded, with "Latinorum consuetudo," he confesses that all this is the "new learning." The liturgical use of the Latin Church was against him. The practice of the Greek churches was in accord with ancient writers whom he (and other well-read persons) considered more important than contemporary popular custom. The use of the Latins, he says, receives not Hebrews, and the churches of the Greeks reject the Apocalypse; each indulging unwarrantable licence, "eadem libertate." So that what Jerome really witnesses to is an indomitable Church tradition in the West against the Pauline authorship and even the canonical authority of Hebrews: and what he asserts is that this tradition is of late growth; the voice of antiquity is for the canonical authority, and scholars know that this, as well as the usurping tradition, can be explained by recognising that the epistle is derived, but not directly, from S. Paul. In other words he has a fairly large critical apparatus; reads its evidence with a partial misunderstanding; and leaves to later generations an unmistakable proof that even in his day the unsophisticated Western churchmen held fast to the tradition of their fathers that this epistle did not come from S. Paul.

S. Augustine's feeling may be illustrated by one short quotation from *De civitate Dei*, XVI. 22: "De quo in epistola, quae inscribitur ad Hebraeos, quam plures apostoli Pauli esse dicunt, quidam vero negant, multa et magna conscripta sunt." He was less particular as a scholar than Jerome, more philosophical as a churchman, and the mere question of authorship troubled him slightly. Moreover there is evidence that in Africa in his time such scruples were falling, perhaps more entirely than elsewhere, into the background. Whereas in the third council of Carthage, A.D. 398, Hebrews was distinguished from or among the Pauline epistles—"Pauli epistolae tredecim; eiusdem ad Hebraeos una," in the fifth council of Carthage, A.D. 419, this carefulness had ceased—"epistolarum Pauli apostoli numero quatuordecim[1]." And from this period onward in West as in East the fourteen epistles of S. Paul are regularly recognised.

The distinction between the question of authorship and canonical authority is important; it may well account for the considerable number of Western writers who cite Hebrews as Paul's from the middle of the fourth century onwards. Canonical authority admitted, only scholars when directly dealing with the question of authorship would separate this from the "corpus" of Pauline epistles: many would use Paul's name without scruple. Others, like Hilary of Poitiers (✠ 366), would cite the epistle, but would take care not to name Paul in connexion with it. That is the way most theologians treat it to day; but Souter thinks "Hilary's attitude is that of compromise. He was deeply imbued with Eastern learning, and to him Hebrews was a canonical book, but he knew the attitude of his Western countrymen with regard to it."

And that attitude altered very gradually. The ancient Roman tradition was too deeply rooted to die out. Even Dante in the *De Monarchia* (II. 8) distinguishes "Paul" or "the apostle" from the author of this epistle, introducing his one citation from it anonymously—"Scriptum est enim ad Hebraeos: Impossibile est sine fide placere Deo." And when in the sixteenth century the new learning gave fresh substance to the old doubts, we find writers within the Roman Church frankly reconsidering opinions which by that time had almost the prescription of authority. Thus Estius writes in the opening section of his Commentary that in former times catholic writers, especially among the Latins, did not recognise this epistle as canonical; that Eusebius classes it among those scriptures

[1] For S. Augustine's own progress in this respect, see Souter, *Text and Canon*, p. 191.

which were controverted by many ; and "finally in our own day Caietan at the beginning of his commentary throws doubt upon its authority, and says that a point of faith cannot be determined from it alone. Then Luther simply rejects it, because, he says, it annuls repentance. That is pretty nearly the judgement of the Lutherans and the other sectaries of our time, with the exception of Calvin and his followers, who are pleased to receive it into the number of the Holy Scriptures, not so much on the authority of the Church, as because they consider that out of the doctrine of the epistle concerning the one sacrifice of Christ, they can overthrow the sacrifice of the Mass which the Catholic Church observes throughout the world." Estius himself holds, with others, who are indeed the old Alexandrians, that the subject and its treatment were supplied by S. Paul, but the composition was entrusted to another, Clement of Rome perhaps, more likely the apostle's companion Luke. He refuses to allow that it is heresy to doubt that S. Paul was the author. The decision of the Council of Trent, by which the Epistle to the Hebrews is numbered among the fourteen epistles of S. Paul, seems only to have settled the question of its canonicity for him. Erasmus seems to promise more absolute deference to authority : Si ecclesia certo definit esse Pauli, captivo libens intellectum meum in obsequium fidei : quod ad sensum meum attinet, non videtur illius esse ob causas quas hic reticuisse praestiterit. Et si certo scirem non esse Pauli, res indigna est digladiatione." That was before the council had spoken, and the fairest way of interpreting both Erasmus and Estius is to suppose that on such a question the decision of a council was never intended to be an absolute bar to the exercise of criticism, however it might restrain promiscuous publication of results or tentative results.

§ 6.   *And was revived at the Renascence; when also the special doctrine of Hebrews, so long generalised, began to be recovered: Limborch and sacrifice, the Arminians.*

With Erasmus a new era began in the study of the New Testament. As these lines are being written it is just four hundred years since Erasmus, publishing his Greek Testament, opened the Gospels and the apostolic records in their original language to the world. That gave impulse to a movement already begun. The joy of the secular renascence had already been to recover the actual life and thought of Rome and Hellas. A *desiderium* for the real meaning of antiquity was in men's hearts, and it was in the hearts of Churchmen as well as other scholars. *Ad antiquitatem immo ad ultimam antiquitatem* was Lancelot Andrewes' appeal in the seventeenth century. And we recognise in the commentators of that time quite a novel effort to discover what was the immediate and particular sense of each of the apostolic writers.

Little of this had been attempted before. There is just a trace of it in the New Testament. At the end of 2 Peter some characteristics of the Pauline epistles are noticed. This is worth mentioning here because it has been sometimes thought that Hebrews is particularly alluded to, which seems a strange fancy. But from apostolic times till the renascence there was hardly any recognition of the individual character of epistles. Ménégoz has a chapter[1] on the theological influence of the epistle in the history of dogma. He confines his attention to the main doctrine of the sacrifice of Christ, and shows that though the peculiar language of the epistle was repeated, its peculiar idea was never grasped.

In the period of the Fathers the epistle of Barnabas comes nearest to it : the Jewish sacrifices are treated as types of the sacrifice of Christ ; Christ Himself is not represented as the High Priest ; yet there are striking affinities with the doctrine of Hebrews. Clement, in spite of his frequent quotation, and though he gives Christ the name of High Priest in the sense of head of the Church, never compares His death with the Levitical sacrifices, but considers it rather as an expiation by substitution. The same idea is admirably expressed in the Epistle to Diognetus. S. Ignatius once, in Eph. i., speaks of Christ offering Himself to God as an oblation and sacrifice for us : "but he does not develop that thought, his preoccupations were elsewhere." For during the whole of this period theological interest was in the Person of Christ. The Incarnation included

---

[1] *La théologie de l'épitre aux Hébreux* (Paris, 1894), ch. VII.

the whole of Christ's work of salvation. And so far as His death was considered separately as the means by which man was rescued, it was thought of as a ransom—an idea natural to those days of brigandage ; generally as a ransom paid to the devil, sometimes as paid to God. And though the Fathers ("apostolic" and later) adopt the term "sacrifice" from Hebrews, they use it merely as a metaphor for "ransom" : "c'est le triomphe de l'image au détriment de l'idée."

Anselm disengaged the notion of Redemption from Incarnation ; with him "soteriology" began. This, Ménégoz considers, was a return to biblical thought. But though Anselm's doctrine of "redemption by death" was biblical, his explanation was not. He drew it from Teutonic law, medieval chivalry, and the catholic system of penitence. "Satisfaction" instead of "ransom" became the idea round which thought moved. And this was continued by Aquinas, who however put Roman law, with "satisfaction by punishment"—hence the emphasis on "substitution"—in place of Teutonic law, with its "satisfaction by payment." And still, as before, the terms of "sacrifice" were adopted from Hebrews, and still they were used as metaphors ; only now, throughout the middle ages, as metaphors for "satisfaction."

The reformers accepted this doctrine from the middle ages, laying still more stress on "substitution," but still applying the sacrificial language of Hebrews in a merely metaphorical way. Calvin however took up what Eusebius, Cyril of Jerusalem, Augustine, and Aquinas had said about the threefold office of Christ as Prophet, Priest and King, and for two centuries the *munus triplex Christi* figured as an essential heading in protestant theology.

Ménégoz notices the unusual position taken by Abelard in the middle ages. He taught, and the doctrine is scriptural, that man was to be reconciled to God rather than God to man. And he developed this in his own way by declaring that the reconcilement is effected by the love that was revealed in the Saviour's death upon the cross ; there is the moving power. Perhaps, though Ménégoz does not, we may connect the line of thought thus opened with what he says of the Arminians :

"However the theology of the epistle was to find in pro-

testantism a little corner where it might fructify. The
Arminians, repelled alike by the orthodox theory of expiation
and by the superficial rationalism of the Socinians, sought an
interpretation of the death of Christ which might better respond to their religious feeling....Curcellaeus laid stress upon
the intercession of Christ in the presence of the Father, and
scarcely considered His death but as a condition of His resurrection and ascension. The Socinians too had already brought
that side of the redemptive activity of the Christ into prominence, thus approaching the views of the Epistle to the
Hebrews. But it is Limborch, the great dogmatist of the
Arminians, who entered most resolutely into this order of ideas.
...In Limborch the notion of sacrifice obliges Christ to have
died for us, but not to have suffered our punishment. His
death is thus not a substitutive expiation but a sacrificial
offering, graciously accepted by God. And as Christ has not
only been the victim but is also the high priest for all eternity,
He continues to intercede in God's presence for the sinners who
have recourse to His ministry. His sacrifice has thus a permanent value."

Once or twice Limborch drops into the more conventional
mode as when he writes "poenam peccatis nostris commeritam
quasi in se transtulit." But Ménégoz (who notices that sentence)
has given a fair description of a commentary which deserves
rather special attention[1]. Limborch seriously attempts to
realise the individual character of the epistle, as indeed (what
Ménégoz hardly appreciates enough) commentators were all
doing now both in the Roman and the reformed churches;
hence the curiosity about authorship, Luther's conjecture that
Apollos was the author and so on. Limborch thought it was
written by one of the companions of S. Paul, who knew S. Paul's
mind (*et quidem conscio Pauli*) and drew upon his doctrine.
The author wrote in order to fortify Hebrew Christians in the
faith towards which, through fear of persecution, they were
growing disaffected. He meets the excuses they might ground
on the venerable prestige of the ancient Law. And he ends
his Prolegomena with this insistence on the distinctive value

[1] *Philippi a Limborch Commentarius in Acta Apostolorum et in
Epistolas ad Romanos et ad Hebraeos*, Roterodami, 1711.

of Hebrews : "Adeo ut merito nobis summo in pretio habenda sit, sine qua multa quae ad distinctam sacerdotii Christi cognitionem spectant, ignoraremus." It is always the contrast rather than the likeness between the sacrifice of Christ and the Levitical sacrifices that he draws out, thus avoiding a style of interpretation which even in much later times has hindered the right use of the epistle. And he approaches the idea of the living power of the Blood of Christ which was not to be clearly presented till Westcott wrote.

His preface is significant, in which he lays down with no little force the principles of historical interpretation as the indispensable basis of all study, and in particular of the application of prophecy. The same kind of thing may be found in Calvin and in nearly all writers since Erasmus. In Calvin it is expressed with the beautiful lucidity of a Frenchman who is thoroughly master of a good Latin style. But in practice Calvin too often allows his scholarly principles to be wrested by party feeling. In Limborch we enjoy another atmosphere, not so brilliant but larger, more free. And this is perhaps what is chiefly to be remarked in the Arminian commentators generally. The title "Arminian" seems to be applied to a variety of theologians whose pedigree cannot always be traced very obviously from Arminius. Grotius, Bull, Jeremy Taylor, Hales, Chillingworth, Cudworth, Whichcote, and the rest of the Cambridge Platonists, are classed with Arminians by Hallam, and the bond of connexion can hardly be the original principles of Arminius. Three characteristics however belong to them all. They are remonstrants against a particular form of Augustinian doctrine: F. D. Maurice might have said that they appealed from Augustine against the Donatists to Augustine against the Manichaeans. They stood for ante-Nicene Greek theology. They were at home in learned churches where the Humanities were cared for. In all these respects they have a natural kinship with the epistle to the Hebrews, and especially in the last. The Alexandrine Platonism of the epistle, its good Greek style, its tender sympathy with the very shadows of the old Law which it shews to be vanishing away ; all this is in the broad sense of the term "Arminian."

§ 7. *The real manhood of Christ: already recognised by Nestorius as characteristic of Hebrews.*

So again is its interest in the whole of our Lord's earthly life, the frankness with which it recognises the limitations of His manhood during "the days of His flesh." And here we must go back to the fifth century, and notice a writer of that period who did remarkably appreciate this characteristic of Hebrews. He was Nestorius. Dr Bethune Baker[1] shews reason for believing that Nestorius was no "Nestorian"; the doctrine for which he was condemned was not his real doctrine. That conclusion needs to be checked by the criticism of Dr Loofs[2]. But the orthodoxy of the sermon on the Epistle to the Hebrews, of which Dr Bethune Baker gives a summary, will hardly be disputed since, until 1905, it was attributed to S. Chrysostom. Nestorius here interprets Hebrews in accordance with the tradition of the school of Antioch; Antioch "which early in the second century had had as its bishop the Ignatius who had insisted with such passionate earnestness on the reality of the human nature and experiences of Jesus, who had made his appeal above all else to the actual facts of the Gospel history—at Antioch the historical tradition had never been allowed to fade....The theologians of Antioch started from the manhood...laid stress on all the passages in Scripture which seemed to emphasize the human consciousness of the Lord...insisted on the recognition in His Person of a genuine human element in virtue of which a genuine human experience was possible. They did not for a moment call in question, or fail to recognize, the equally genuine Divine element, in virtue of which Divine experience and power was His. They did not doubt that the historical Jesus Christ was both God and man. They took their stand on history, on the primitive record, on apostolic testimony and interpretation" (Bethune Baker, pp. 3 f.).

[1] *Nestorius and his teaching.* Cambridge, 1908.
[2] *Nestorius and his place in the history of Christian Doctrine.* Cambridge, 1914.

§ 8. *Hellenistic philosophical colour: Carpzov's illustrations from Philo.*

Thus did Nestorius in the fifth century reassert one of the characteristics of this epistle, its insistence on the true manhood of our Lord. And thus, at the revival of learning, did the Arminians attempt to recover its particular doctrine of sacrifice. A third peculiarity, its affinity with the philosophical Judaism of Philo, was brought out in the eighteenth century by J. B. Carpzov, who collected parallels from Philo for almost every verse of the epistle[1]. Much has been done since his day for the text of Philo, the better understanding of Philo's philosophy, and the true relationship of Hebrews to it, but Carpzov's book is still a storehouse of material. And it marks an epoch in the exegesis of Hebrews. No one had treated the subject with anything like this elaboration before. Henceforth it was impossible to ignore the Hellenistic idiosyncrasy of author and readers. They might be " Hebrews," but they were not "Hebrews" in the narrower sense of Hebrew-speaking Jews. They belonged at least to the liberal Judaism of S. Stephen, probably to the philosophic Judaism of Apollos.

§ 9. *Interest in special character of Hebrews provokes search for suitable author: Luther's conjecture of Apollos, etc. Tradition only supports Barnabas (besides Paul) and the search is vain.*

That no doubt had already struck Luther when he conjectured Apollos as the author. Possibly Luther, and the moderns who have accepted his conjecture, read more into the few lines in which Apollos is described (Acts xviii. 24 f.) than is really to be found there. The conjecture is not supported by tradition. Harnack's idea that Priscilla was the authoress is a development from Luther's inference. Blass in the short preface to his rythmical text[2] pays no attention to the philosophical colouring,

---

[1] *Sacrae exercitationes in S. Paulli epistolam ad Hebraeos ex Philone Alexandrino.* Helmstadii, 1750.

[2] *Brief an die Hebräer, Text mit Angabe der Rhythmen.* Halle, 1903.

and accepts the Barnabas tradition, because Barnabas as a Levite would have been familiar with the cadences of the Greek Psalter. Barnabas is the only name which can be connected with anything like a real tradition. Scholarship is more respectful to tradition of late. It is felt that there are few fresh starts in thought; tradition generally lies behind, and what seems to be tradition is at least to be respectfully examined. That is the spirit of a book which has not yet been so carefully criticised as it deserves[1]. Mr Edmundson thinks Hebrews was written to Judaeo-Christians in Rome by Barnabas in 66 A.D. S. Paul was still living; had been released from his captivity; and at the close of the same year was himself in Rome, again in prison and soon to die. 1 Peter had been already written and is quoted in Hebrews. The Apocalypse was written three years later, at the beginning of A.D. 70. Early in the same year, A.D. 70, Clement, a younger brother of M. Arrecinus Clemens and the same Clement as is named in Phil. iv., gave literary expression to the message from the Church in Rome to the Church in Corinth; he was not yet the official head of the Roman Church. That is a consistent view of our epistle and the other epistles that are related to it. Without necessarily adopting the whole of it, we may at least welcome the support Mr Edmundson gives to the early date of Hebrews. That judgement is hardly fashionable at present, but, as will presently be shown, it does fit many important characteristics of the epistle.

As for the author's name, that search may as well be given up. The Barnabas tradition only emerges for a moment or two and is lost in darkness on either side. The other names proposed, Luke, Clement, Apollos, Silas, Philip the deacon, Aristion—one writer has even suggested S. Peter—are mere conjectures; some of which are surely impossible. That there should be one letter in the New Testament which was not written by any person who happens to be mentioned in the other books, is quite in accordance with the analogies of literary history. It may be added, though not as an argument, that

---

[1] *The Church in Rome in the first Century*, by George Edmundson. Longmans, 1914.

our interest in the apostolic Church and our reverence for
its rich inspiration would be increased hereby. The character,
education and to a large extent the circumstances of the author
may be gathered from the letter itself. The mere precision of a
name would not illuminate the background very much.

§ 10. *Destination more important, but precision difficult; not*
      Jerusalem. Rome proposed, and (improbably) Gentile
      readers.

It is otherwise with the question of the destination. If we
could suppose that the epistle was addressed to the Church at
Jerusalem some time between the outbreak of the war with
Rome and the fall of Jerusalem in A.D. 70, our interpretation of
the whole argument and of many difficult passages would be
confined to something like certainty. But it would be a con-
fining. Other passages would take on new difficulties. Much
is said about the tabernacle in Hebrews : there is not a line
which implies that either writer or recipients had ever seen
the temple. There may well have been Hellenistic Jews at
Jerusalem who read Greek and were accustomed to Alexandrine
terms of philosophy. But it is not at Jerusalem that we should
readily look for these, and it is certain that the epistle would
have been quite unsuited to the Church of Jerusalem as a whole.
J. J. Wetstein, in the edition of the Greek Testament which he
published at Amsterdam, 1751-2, was the first to argue for
Rome as the destination. Others, e.g. von Soden[1], have combined this view of the destination with the assertion that there
is nothing in the epistle to confirm the accuracy of the ancient
title Πρὸς Ἑβραίους, and that there is much to prove it addressed
to Gentile Christians. This is, paradoxical though the statement may sound, more agreeable to a superficial reading than
to a patient study of the epistle. The Judaic roots are there,
but they are not to be discovered in the mere obvious allusions
to Jewish ritual.

[1] *Hand-Commentar.* Freiburg, 1899.

§ 11. *Modern criticism would supersede these enquiries by re-*
garding Hebrews as a late treatise or sermon. So Moffatt,
whose view of doctrinal development may however be modified
by recognition of the "apocalyptic" origin of the Gospel:
Schweitzer;

However all such disputes may seem to have been superseded
of late. Neither author nor destination matters much. Nor do
the Jewish or Gentile antecedents of the readers. The epistle
was written at a time when the Pauline controversy about the
Law was forgotten. There is no sharply cut background. It
is a doctrinal treatise, sermon-like; very interesting as a witness
to the comparatively early development of Christian dogma, but
scarcely in touch with the vigorous life of those primitive com-
munities who had lately been making Christian history. This
is how Moffatt describes it [1]:

"The author is to us a voice and no more. He left great
prose to some little clan of early Christians, but who he was,
and who they were, it is not possible with such materials as are
at our disposal to determine. No conjecture rises above the
level of plausibility. We cannot say that if the *autor ad*
Hebraeos had never lived or written, the course of early
Christianity would have been materially altered. He was not
a personality of Paul's commanding genius. He did not make
history or mark any epoch. He did not even, like the anonymous
authors of Matthew's Gospel and the Fourth Gospel, succeed in
stamping his writing on the mind of the early church at large.
But the later church was right in claiming a canonical position
for this unique specimen of Alexandrine thought playing upon
the primitive gospel, although the reasons upon which the claim
was based were generally erroneous."

This might be almost styled great prose. It is, what
Dr Moffatt would rather care for, great scholarship; a deliberate
judgement based upon long thought and wide learning. Yet we
would set against it two passages from his earlier book [2]. The
first is a quotation from James Smetham's *Letters*:

"Is there a Christ? Is He the Heir of all things? Was
He made flesh? Did He offer the all-perfect sacrifice? Did

[1] *Introduction to the Literature of the New Testament.* T. & T.
Clark, 1911.

[2] *The Historical New Testament.* T. & T. Clark, 2nd ed. 1901.

He supersede the old order of priests? Is He the Mediator of a new and better Covenant? What are the terms of that Covenant? There are no questions like these....I am astonished at the imperative tone of this Epistle, and the element of holy scorn against those who refuse to go into these great questions carefully."

That points to one supreme characteristic of this epistle, its intensity. Here are some lines from Dr Moffatt's own pen which reveal a certain bias determining the final direction of other arguments; and it is possibly doubtful whether that bias ought to be allowed so much weight as used to be generally supposed :

" The alternative date [to A.D. 80 or later] is between 60 and 70 A.D. This largely supported view takes the epistle as implying the contemporary existence of the Jewish temple and ritual, and as written in view of the religious dissolution which (8^{13}) culminated in A.D. 70. The arguments in favour of this date have been in part already met by implication, and in part they depend upon a view of the development of early Christianity, which would require many pages to exhibit."

It is true that there is nothing in the epistle which necessarily implies the contemporary existence of temple and ritual. If the author contemplates the fall of Jerusalem as imminent, this does not mean that he mainly connects the dissolution of the Jewish religion with that catastrophe. His interest in the war is of another kind, and the signs of his interest in that, or possibly some other crisis of trial, run all through his letter. But the point to be noticed is this. The view of the development of early Christianity, in which Hebrews might bear an early date, has been re-adjusted by that "apocalyptic" reading of the primitive Gospel which was revived by Albert Schweitzer[1].

So far as affects the question before us here, the matter may be summed up as follows. The idea of what may be called liberal theologians had long been that from an early Galilean faith in

[1] In his *Von Reimarus zu Wrede*, Tübingen, 1906. An English translation with the title *The Quest of the Historical Jesus* was published in 1910, and the best introduction to the subject is Dr Burkitt's little book, *The earliest sources for the life of Jesus*, Constable, 1910.

Jesus as the Master, a Pauline, Johannine, and finally "catholic"
faith was gradually developed in the eternal and divine Son.
In such development Hebrews would come comparatively late.
There is nothing unworthy in such a view.   Development of
the faith is the counterpart to revelation through the Holy
Spirit.   But the difficulty was to find a link between Galilee and
S. Paul.   To the apocalyptic view the link is plain.   The background of the synoptic gospels is formed by those late Jewish
apocalypses of which Daniel and the Enoch literature are the
type.   Our Lord entered upon His ministry in Galilee when a
world of thoughts about the coming Kingdom of God was everywhere astir.   These thoughts were vague; spiritual hopes were
mingled with political; yet a great exalted spirit breathed everywhere.   The kingdom would not be of this world; the Christ-
king might be in some sense divine.   Our Lord accepted the
popular expectations.   How far He acquiesced in their outward
form; in what way He corrected and purified the idea; how He
came to the determination that by His own death the kingdom
must be brought in—these are the problems of the critical
historian.   But criticism tends to this broad result.   The
synoptic gospels, especially S. Mark, are good historical documents as they stand; simple souls may rightly account for the
whole course of our Lord's action by His implicit faith in the
Father's guidance; the disciples believed that He was the destined Christ who would one day come in divine glory with the
kingdom; that belief was interrupted by the crucifixion, but
was confirmed and deepened by the resurrection; and S. Paul's
faith in Christ Jesus, the exalted Son of God, hidden for a while
in heaven, His original and eternal home, whence in the great
day He would come to gather quick and dead, was simply his
ancient Jewish faith completed by his conviction that Jesus was
the Christ.

Nor was this profound theology revealed only to S. Paul.
It was the faith of the Church he entered after his conversion.
He directed it, perhaps restrained it within the lines of reasonable truth.   The tremendous spiritual impulse, which was the
main source of his inspiration, enabled him to bring what was
weak or uncertain to new and deeper expression.   But though a
high Christology may develop its expression, it will always be

a return to primitive faith, and will never involve of necessity long distance from memories of the past. There is development of that kind in Hebrews. The first readers of this epistle evidently had what we call an imperfect conception of the Person of Christ. Their friend appeals to the primitive belief in Christ as truly divine. He uses for his task of persuasion all that has been thought, said or done before his days, by the household at Jerusalem immediately after the crucifixion, by S. Paul, by Hellenists like S. Stephen and Apollos. And now he turns the ancient symbol of the Kingdom into new language for his Alexandrine friends, just as Dr DuBose in his exposition of this epistle, *High Priesthood and Sacrifice*, tries to turn its phraseology "into current coin." And he had two important aids. The crisis of the times—perhaps it really was the storm gathering over Jerusalem—was a sign that then was to be the promised Day ; in that shaking the Kingdom and the Christ were coming. And the education of author and readers in philosophy provided a set of terms in which this translation of the primitive symbol might be shaped with peculiar fitness; for the pressing difficulty lay in " the scandal of the cross," the humiliation which characterised the Christian course, and which could be shewn to run out into eternal glory by the philosophical principle of sacramental significance in the realities of life.

§ 12. *and by the now more generally recognised earliness of "catholic" thought and practice: Baur, Lake, Bousset ; Graeco-Roman influence on development.*

Schweitzer's two books—for he presently wrote another in which he showed S. Paul to be thoroughly imbued with apocalyptic Judaism—have, it seems, influenced English thought far more than German. In Germany the old "liberal" theology held on its way. The details of Baur's criticism have long been discredited. It is right that much of his principle should still be recognised as true. His *Church History*[1] is a stimulating book that should still be read by all who really care to meditate on the origins of creed and church. Very briefly his doctrine is

[1] *The Church History of the first three Centuries*, Tübingen, 1853, English Translation, Williams and Norgate, 1878.

that "the fightings without and fears within" which S. Paul, and doubtless many another of the early leaders, met patiently and faithfully, vanished in a gradual reconciliation of half views. Then, as the fit time came, the more complete idea of Christ's Person, of the Church, the Ministry, the Sacraments, descended, explained all, and took possession. "Descended" is the right word. The process came, as we should say, from God. The suspicion with which Baur is regarded, arises from his refusal to say just that. However, there is no need to speculate here as to what Baur's own opinions were about the Christian dogmas. So far as it goes the doctrine here sketched can only encourage us to more thoughtful reverence. But it begins in these days to be clear that a simpler thread of popular faith was drawn out continuously from the first, and that this popular faith was in essentials far more like the fully-developed faith of the Church's worship than used to be supposed. On this point much instruction may be gained from Professor Kirsopp Lake's book, *The earlier Epistles of St Paul*. And again and again as we pursue the enquiry we find that, while there is much truth in Baur's idea of Hebrews and other epistles belonging to a period of "reconciliation," there is no good reason for reserving that period to a late date.

The most important of what we may venture to call the successors of Baur is Dr Wilhelm Bousset, who argues[1] that it was in worship that development of faith most largely took place. This influence of ritual and of the emotion of common worship was mainly due to the Church's assimilation of Asiatic Greek ideas. In Hebrews an almost extreme example of this ritual spirit is displayed. To reach such a pitch of interest time was needed, and Hebrews is therefore separated by a considerable interval from S. Paul. Again it is evident, even from this passing reference, how much Bousset stimulates thought. Worship is still deepening—not of course without some risk of perverting—faith. This recognition of the influence of worship implies a strong united Church feeling, resting on continuous tradition, as the living soil in which new

---

[1] *Kyrios Christos : Geschichte des Christusglaubens von den Anfängen des Christenthums bis Irenaeus.* Göttingen, 1913.

thoughts and enthusiasms grow into flower. The old crude idea of a Paul or an *auctor ad Hebraeos* starting a fresh line of faith is unnatural. But, with Bousset again, sober reflection on all we know about these early days puts things in a different proportion. There is more anxiety in our author's mind about his friends' loyalty to Christ in some terrible crisis, than interest in ritual. And the reasons for placing the epistle at a late date are far weaker than those for recognising in it a new stage in the expression of ancient truth.

§ 13. *Transformation of this early "catholicism" in Windisch's representation of the ultra-dogmatic character of Hebrews.*

But, distinct from these descendants of Baur, another school of theologians has lately arisen in Germany. They might be called —with perhaps an unfair touch of caricature—the Literalists. Some of them have come to sacred literature from a previous training in classical languages. They are abundantly, if not broadly, erudite. They care little for the delicacies of language, but press the plain meaning of passages. To this class belongs Dr Windisch, author of a short book[1] full of matter, with freshly-gathered quotations from Philo and from the literature of the Graeco-Roman world. In fact, this handbook by itself supplies pretty well all the material a reader might desire for inference and discussion. The author of the epistle is left unnamed. He was a Hellenistic Jew, with the same Greek background of education as Philo, but less Greek in character, more apocalyptic. He still expects the future manifestation, therein resembling with a difference S. John. The readers were a community, mainly non-Jewish, which might be anywhere except Jerusalem. The date 80 A.D. or rather later. The author had nothing to do with the temple, but mediated Old Testament ritual for Christians. He was nearer S. Paul than any other New Testament writer, yet with many notable divergences. He has something in common with the Synoptists, whom Windisch (like Bousset) considers to represent, not quite the historical Jesus of Nazareth, but the theological belief of

[1] *Der Hebräerbrief erklärt von Lic. Dr Hans Windisch, Privat-dozent an der Universität Leipzig.* Tübingen, 1913.

the early Christian family concerning Him. Only this writer is more infected with Hellenistic ideas, more influenced by the Septuagint, than the Synoptists were. The main value of his epistolary sermon is in its doctrine of the exalted Christ, and especially in the particular aid which the author's figurative language about His high-priesthood produced (1) for the further expression of the Church's doctrine of redemption, (2) for the Church's adoption of the sacred, and especially the legal, books of the Old Testament.

But Windisch would hardly approve of the word "figurative." Though to us the language is figurative, he would take it as far more literally meant by the author himself. Windisch's exegesis is terse, crisp and full-learned. But it is as "hard" as a piece of modern carving. He writes in that most recent style of modern criticism which Reitzenstein and Norden use; to which Kirsopp Lake is somewhat inclined; and which Bousset has enriched with spiritual sympathy. This school is (against Schweitzer) zealous for Graeco-Roman influence. But beside that, it represents primitive Christianity as being from the first what the Germans call "catholic," i.e. advanced in cult and in the doctrine of the Person of Christ, but advanced in a crude and somewhat superstitious way.

A history of New Testament interpretation might be arranged on a scheme adapted from Mr Reginald Blomfield's words, "The Renaissance—one of the recurring outbreaks of humanity against the tyranny of another world[1]." Here we find this "tyranny" again coming in. So was it at the beginning with Docetism, soon met by the Church's protest. Then, according to Bousset, the "Kyrios cult," and the reaction witnessed to by Clement of Rome. So again in the eighteenth century began the "outbreak of humanity" in which critics recovered the ancient doctrine of the real manhood of Christ, but at the same time read their modern notions into that manhood. In England this culminated in the large Johannine theology of F. D. Maurice. Then Schweitzer and the eschatological school drew this out farther in their insistence on the actually Jewish, Galilean manhood. And so the "humanity" itself led on to another inrush of "the other world" with the

---

[1] *Short History of Renaissance Architecture*, p. 18.

strange and stormy figure of the apocalyptic Christ. And now, from another point of view, Windisch and this school find a crude, ultra-scrupulous reverence in apostolic days. To Windisch Hebrews has hardly any real sense of the days of the Lord's flesh, but centres on "The Heavenly Being, mythically conceived." This literalism appears in an extravagant form in a note to v. 7—the flesh was laid aside in the ascension ; our Lord took with Him only the blood. And again, on x. 28 "the Christian eschatology still knows the pitiless God of the Old Testament and of Judaism." The strong, learned excursus will be dealt with later (II. § 20) in which he almost compels assent to his thesis that "no second repentance" was the primitive, essential dogma, weakened in later days.

In the proper sense of the terms, of course, both tempers of the faith, "humanitas" and "other-worldliness," belong to Christianity. But the terms may be transferred to tempers which are not genuinely Christian. The severely historical critic will probably find that the mass of devout but unlearned Christians in every age have tended, at least in language, to insist on the "tyranny of the other world." But he will also find that the Church as a whole and in the long run, i.e. the Church guided by the Spirit, has refused to be thus enslaved. And is it not the mistake of commentators like Windisch that they interpret the apostolic writers by the ruder language of the people ? The Church, in her true catholicity, has really had the canonical writers on her side, and behind them our Lord Himself.

Yet Windisch's is a valuable commentary. If only for the illustrative material, so skilfully selected from sources hardly touched by earlier commentators, but recognised to day as highly important for the elucidation of at least a large part of the New Testament, it will be for years to come all but indispensable. And the terse, business-like expression is admirable. What Bengel's *Gnomon* is for unction, Dr Windisch is in his dry compression. His book has always been on the table at which these pages were written.

§ 14. *Some earlier German books: Bengel and text, Riehm and doctrine, Biesenthal and affinities with rabbinic type of Judaism.*

All students of the New Testament delight in Bengel's holy epigrams[1]. Here is one example from Heb. xi. 40 : " προβλεψαμένον, providente) Exquisitum verbum. Quae *nondum videt* fides, DEVS *providet*, Gen. 22, 8, 14, Joh. 6, 6. Ex hac *provisione* fluxit tota oeconomia temporum, et testimonium DEI ad veteres." But the *Gnomon* has a further interest in that it is founded upon a comparatively pure text. Bengel had already made an epoch in textual criticism by his edition of the Greek Testament. He was the first to attempt classification of authorities.

Bleek's great commentary has already been mentioned. From Riehm's *Lehrbegriff*[2] later generations have drawn. They have improved upon its conclusions. But it remains the most complete and systematic exposition of the epistle in its relation to Biblical theology.

And yet one other German book must be named[3]. It is incredible that S. Paul should really be the author of Hebrews, and Dr Biesenthal's "retranslation" into Hebrew is not retranslation but a clever exercise of his own scholarship. Nevertheless his book is worth attention. He shews how much in the epistle has parallels in Judaism on the rabbinic side. Thus he warns us against too ready trust in inferences drawn from the Graeco-Roman or Graeco-Asiatic literature which is so much relied upon of late for the interpretation of the New Testament. Even Hellenistic Judaism was Judaic, and a merely Gentile origin for this epistle is all but impossible.

[1] *D. Joh. Alberti Bengelii Gnomon Novi Testamenti, in quo ex nativa verborum vi simplicitas, profunditas, concinnitas, salubritas sensuum coelestium indicatur.* It was first published in 1742.

[2] *Der Lehrbegriff des Hebräerbriefs, dargestellt und mit verwandten Lehrbegriffen verglichen, von Lic. Eduard Karl Aug. Riehm, Privatdocent in Heidelberg.* Ludwigsburg, 1858-9.

[3] *Das Trostschreiben des Apostels Paulus an die Hebräer, kritisch wiederhergestellt und sprächlich archäologisch und biblisch-theologisch erläutert, von Joh. H. R. Biesenthal, Dr Philos. et Theol.*, Leipzig, 1878.

§ 15. *Modern English commentators. Their fine scholarship: Rendall. Their broad, practical elucidation of the theology of the epistle: Davidson and Maurice distinguish type from shadow; Bruce discovers the imperfection of the readers' faith, and the author's conception of "glory in humiliation"; that sacramental idea elaborated by DuBose, who also shows how Christ re-enacts His sacrifice in men. Westcott's explanation of the Blood as indicating life enriched through death.*

Of late however more help for the understanding of this epistle has come from England and from America. English theologians have generally been strong in that broad advantage of a classical education which combines "humanity" with grammar. For such a book as Hebrews that is a specially desirable qualification in a commentator. Hence we have a series of editions which are recommended by fine scholarship—C. J. Vaughan, Macmillan 1891; Farrar, the very interesting predecessor of this present book in the Cambridge Greek Testament series; Wickham in Methuen's Westminster commentaries 1910, a work of finished beauty; and, philologically perhaps the best of all, F. Rendall, Macmillan 1883.

Dr A. B. Davidson contributed a small edition of Hebrews to Messrs T. and T. Clark's *Handbooks for Bible Classes*, which like all, even his most unpretending work, is firm, simple and philosophical. His treatment of the theme "Priesthood after the order of Melchizedek" is particularly valuable. He, perhaps for the first time, puts the Aaronic priesthood and the Levitical sacrifices into their true proportionate place, as merely "shadow"; the author is not concerned with the comparative worth of the old ritual, but with the absolute difference in kind of the eternal priesthood which our Lord fulfilled. F. D. Maurice in his Warburton Lectures for 1845-6, had wrestled with this problem, recognising that Israelites had certainly enjoyed a real communion with God; that nevertheless their institutions, so far forth as these were institutions, lacked reality; and that though in Christ who is "a Son" reality has come, there must still be some kind of institutions in the Christian Church if this reality is not to fade away again into a vague cloudland. He solves the problem in the last lecture by distinguishing the "figurative" from the "sacramental." But he does not present his solution quite clearly. As in so much of his published work, the deep significance of these lectures comes home most effectually to those who have also learned to understand him from his letters and conversations. Two sayings of his throw much light on certain seeming inconsistencies in the epistle itself: "To me it is the pleasantest thing possible to have intercourse with men. But for shadows I have no respect at all," and "My paradox about form being more spiritual than spirit," *Life*, II. p. 299, I. p. 311.

In 1891 Dr William Milligan gave in his Baird Lecture[1] an eloquent defence and exposition of the truth, so insisted upon in Hebrews, that the doctrine of the living and exalted Christ is the indispensable complement of faith in His atoning death. A good companion to this book, as a real aid to a hearty appreciation of the epistle, would be the lately published *Letters of Richard Meux Benson* (Mowbray), which are indeed this Epistle of the Ascension translated into modern life. Dr William Milligan's son, Dr George Milligan, published in 1899 *The Theology of the Epistle to the Hebrews, with a critical introduction* (T. and T. Clark), a very useful book. Dr Moffatt's chapter on Hebrews in *The Literature of the New Testament* has been already mentioned. The commentary which he is to contribute to Messrs T. and T. Clark's *International Critical Commentaries* is eagerly expected. Meanwhile the small edition by Professor A. S. Peake in *The Century Bible* holds a distinguished place among recent commentaries. His brief introduction is commendably sober in conjecture as to author, date and destination. Yet he leans towards an early date, and is convinced that "in the argument as a whole we find decisive proof that the readers were Jewish Christians in peril of falling back into Judaism."

In a notable book[2] Dr Bruce brings the point out clearly, that the readers of the epistle had not attained to more than

---

[1] *The Ascension and Heavenly Priesthood of our Lord.* Macmillan.

[2] *The Epistle to the Hebrews, the first apology for Christianity; an exegetical study.* T. & T. Clark, 1899.

an imperfect apprehension of the faith of the Church, and that this "first apology for Christianity" was designed to set the full and generally accepted faith before them. More important still is his insistence on the teaching of the epistle about our Lord's true manhood with all its limitations, especially in what he says in his fourth chapter about our Lord's glory being in, rather than after, His humiliation ; the exaltation was latent in the humiliation. This opens the way to recognition of that sacramental principle which, sketched in Hebrews, was afterwards elaborated in the Fourth Gospel, and which perhaps alone conserves the reality, without confusion, of both the Godhead and the Manhood of the Redeemer.

What is meant by the sacramental principle of the Manhood is even more clearly brought out by Dr William Porcher DuBose in *High Priesthood and Sacrifice; an exposition of the Epistle to the Hebrews*[1]. This is the third part of the tetralogy in which he interprets the four main varieties of New Testament teaching; the others are *The Gospel in the Gospels, The Gospel according to Saint Paul,* and *The Reason of Life* (S. John). Few books prove more conclusively than these that loyalty to the complete catholic faith is no hindrance to frank originality but the most wholesome stimulus. A few quotations will best shew the line of argument :

"According to the Epistle to the Hebrews the place and part of Jesus Christ in the world is an eternal and universal one.... He is at once God in creation and creation in God ; equally God in man and man in God....That with which Christianity identifies Jesus Christ eternally and essentially and inseparably is not only God but creation and ourselves."

"It is, however, only one part of this universal process that is traced for us by this Epistle....The cosmical bearing or significance of the Incarnation is dropped, and attention is concentrated upon the act or process by which God and man become one in Jesus Christ....Not how our Lord *was* Son as God, but how He *became* Son as man, is the subject of this whole Epistle to the Hebrews."

"There is nothing said or implied of an act performed or of a becoming accomplished, apart from or instead of us. He is the expression to us of what we have to accomplish and become, and of the divine power and way of our accomplishing it....He

[1] Longmans, 1908.

does not save from having to do it all; He helps and enables to do it all. It was bound to be so, it could not be otherwise, because in the divine intention and meaning and nature of the thing, the accomplishing holiness and achieving or attaining life is just that which makes and constitutes us personal spirits, or spiritual persons."

This is theological rather than historical treatment. Dr DuBose is not concerned with the environment of the author and his first readers, or with the influence of Philonic philosophy on the author's mode of expression, and so on. He deals with the great truths themselves which mattered to the author and to the other writers of the New Testament and still matter to all readers of the New Testament at all times. It may be that he misses in consequence some of the peculiar characteristics of Hebrews. If so the deficiency may be made good from other books. The compensating advantage of the treatment he has chosen is this. He, perhaps better than any other commentator, has reached through the figures of the author's language to the realities which the figures are too apt to conceal from modern eyes. The following passage may suffice to indicate a principle which governs the whole exposition:

"And let us remember that our Author's method, while it is both, is yet more a definition of all past expressions of high priesthood by its antitype and fulfilment in Christ, than a definition of this latter by the inadequate types of it that had preceded. The method, in a word, is based upon the principle that beginnings are better explained by ends than ends by beginnings. The divine truth of Jesus Christ and His work in humanity too far transcends any or all visible human pre-intimations or prophecies of itself to be expressed within the finite limits of their meaning. But the precedent high priesthood, seen now in the light of its divine fulfilment, is seen to go along with it in accord so far as it can."

But the greatest of modern commentaries is Westcott's[1]. The Greek text itself is the best that has ever been printed of this epistle separately. The select *apparatus criticus* is easy to use, and the Introduction contains an admirable section on MSS. and versions. Then the skilfully chosen quotations from the

[1] *The Epistle to the Hebrews, the Greek text with notes and essays.* Macmillan, 1st ed. 1889.

Fathers are most instructive. Each tells, coming in appropriately. And the continuity of exegetical tradition is thus displayed, a tradition which justifies the belief that the author's meaning is always likely to be deeper than our own quick judgement would suppose. At the end of the Preface there are valuable remarks on the chief patristic commentaries, with terse indications of their several characteristics. Here, as often in this pregnant work, the student is pointed to a line of enquiry which may attract his diligence or ambition, as in this note on Origen: "Of his xviii Homilies and Books (τόμοι) on the Epistle only meagre fragments remain ; but it is not unlikely that many of his thoughts have been incorporated by other writers. An investigation into the sources of the Latin Commentaries is greatly to be desired." Of Westcott's own interpretations this may perhaps be said without impertinence. The longer they are dwelt upon the more right they are apt to prove themselves. What may seem at first too subtle turns out to be sympathetic with the author's habit of thought, and when the reader disagrees with some passage he is likely to find on further meditation that his own idea has been included and transcended in Westcott's more complete perception. The eminent service however which Dr Westcott has rendered to the study of Hebrews is this. He has carried out what (as we saw above) the Arminians attempted, viz. the true explanation of the sacrificial language ; sacrifice is offering, not loss, and "blood" in the phraseology of sacrifice means life not death, though in supreme sacrifice it does mean life enriched by death.

III

THE THEOLOGY OF THE EPISTLE

§ 1. *Hebrews was addressed to a little group of Hellenistic-Jewish friends: is a real letter; calling upon them to do a hard duty in a dangerous time, viz. to be loyal to Jesus Christ whom they worship, but as yet imperfectly, and to break with Judaism.*

The particular form which theology takes in any treatise is determined by the purpose of the writer. That purpose depends

upon the occasion of writing. Hence it is necessary to make up
our minds, as far as possible, about the date, circumstances and
destination of Hebrews, before attempting to study the characteristics of its theology. We have seen how the tendency of the
latest criticism is to give up the search for the author's name,
and the name of the place to which he sent his epistle. There
has also been a reaction against the ancient tradition that the
readers had come from Judaism to Christianity. But that
reaction has passed into another phase ; the question, Were the
readers Jewish or Gentile ? is no longer considered important,
since the epistle belongs to so late a time that this distinction
had already become almost obsolete in the Church. For Hebrews
is generally considered a late treatise, more like a sermon than
a letter. Some trouble of the day had indeed in part called it
forth. But that impulse is a secondary matter ; the dogmatic
interest is the main thing. Yet on the whole Rome is preferred
as destination. And in this connexion it is worth while perhaps
to mention an inscription which has been discovered there.
A certain Salome is described on her tombstone as the daughter
of Gadia who was πατὴρ συναγωγῆς Αἰβρέων. Zahn who draws
attention to this[1] shews that it has little real bearing on the
criticism of Hebrews, but he does press the significance of
ἐπισυναγωγὴ (Heb. x. 25), and decides from that and various
other indications that the letter was addressed to a household
community, a part of the larger church in Rome. Whether in
Rome or not may be doubtful. But this idea of the small community is winning acceptance and is probably right. Moffatt's
vaguer phrase "a little clan" is best. It is hardly likely that a
letter so polished, so full of technical philosophic language, and
so coloured with actual philosophic thought, should have been
written to any mixed assembly, however small. We had better
conclude that the author wrote to a group of friends who, like
himself, had received an Alexandrine education.

And if so, it must surely have been a Jewish-Alexandrine
education. The title "To Hebrews" may have been but an
early inference from the contents. That inference may have
been drawn from the same misunderstanding as has long

[1] *Einleitung in das Neue Testament*, I. p. 48, cf. II. pp. 113, 119 f.,
154, 1st ed.

prevailed, and of late has prejudiced the enquiry in a contrary direction. For, strictly taken, "Hebrews" means Hebrew-speaking Jews, and that—we can all see now—is just what the readers of this epistle were not. But they may have been Hellenists, may have never seen the temple, and yet the case may be strong for considering them to have been by birth and training Hellenistic Jews. And the case is strong. The argument of the epistle as a whole would have much meaning for Christians who had been Jews, little for others. Much of its difficulty for us Westerns to day arises from its taking for granted Jewish principles of sacrifice which Gentiles even then would not be familiar with. And there is a personal note. The Jewish ritual and priesthood are indeed spoken of as a mere shadow; they are not to the author the "types" which Christ "fulfilled." But Jewish "Christship" is such a real type. And even the ritual is given up with a pang; and if the ancient priesthood was but a shadow, the good priests whom author and friends had known were very far from shadowy. Start from ch. v. and see if this be not true; then read through the whole letter and see whether the impression be not confirmed.

For surely it is a letter, not a sermon. Though like 1 John it begins without a salutation, there is no need to suppose that no definite address was prefixed. Indeed, when once the view here proposed is accepted, it becomes tempting to fancy that πρὸς Ἑβραίους was originally at the head of the roll, a playful subtlety, like v. 12, xiii. 22, meaning "To you whom after all I will call Hebrews indeed." And it is a letter called forth by some very urgent occasion. The exhortations and warnings with which it is punctuated have echoes in almost every verse. The writer is throughout urging his friends to face some particular and hard duty, and in his final blessing, xiii. 20, 21, he prays that they may be enabled to make the right choice and do the duty. The ancient text with its antithesis of "you" and "us" makes this clear. The later text, conventionalised for church reading, obscures this; one of several instances which explain the tendency, so often recurring, to allow the remarkable interest of the epistle's intellectual theology to obscure the practical appeal to the will which was the supreme interest of the author.

For his theology is developed as reinforcement to his appeal. Once Jews of the broader Hellenistic party, his friends had become Christians but Christians of a most imperfect kind. They had joined the Christian Church because it offered that "reformation" of Judaism for which they had been looking, but they had not apprehended the deepest significance of this reformation. Jesus of Nazareth was indeed to them the Christ, but they had not understood all that the Church believed to be involved in that recognition. They had not properly appreciated the mystery of His Person, or of the salvation which had been wrought through His death, or of His "indissoluble life" and His exalted state and continued authority and power to aid. And now some great trial was at hand which would test their allegiance. And in face of this they were in doubt. Was it, they were asking, worth while to hold to this reformed religion when there was very strong reason for returning to the simpler faith of their fathers? See especially v. 11—vi. 8.

The strong reason was above all bound up with honour. Holding fast to Jesus as Christ might very likely bring loss of property, imprisonment, even death; see x. 32—39, xii. 4. But that was not the great difficulty. The "sin" which their friend fears they may commit is a specious one; there is an ἀπάτη about it, something that may confuse the real issue; as yet they have not done the wrong, but it is already an influence working all about them subtle in associations, clinging to them like a garment; one strong effort of will is needed to break free, and if that effort is not made the catastrophe will be irreparable. See ii. 13, vi. 4—6, x. 10, 23, 26—31, xii. 1. But these references are inadequate by themselves. There is hardly a paragraph in the letter but illustrates the situation we are imagining, and it is the letter as a whole, read with this idea in mind, which justifies our imagination. So read, it culminates at last in the appeal of xiii. 13 to go forth to Jesus outside the ancient "camp" of Israel, bearing His shame. The meaning must surely be that the hour has come when the followers of Jesus the true Christ must break with traditional Judaism. The earliest apostolic community had not done so. The apostles had frequented the temple, observing the Jewish hours of prayer (Acts iii. 1), and S. Paul's marked reverence for the mother Church at

Jerusalem had been of a piece with his claim that in standing for Jesus the living Christ he was faithful to the hope of the fathers (Acts xxvi. 5—7). But now that old alliance must be interrupted.

§ 2. *The occasion may be the outbreak of the war with Rome:*

To take that bold step, and to take it just at a time when it would be shameful, as it seemed, to take it, was the hard duty to which this letter urges the little band of thoughtful Jewish Christians, its readers. What then was the occasion? Why was this to be done, and what made the doing so particularly difficult? All becomes plain if the letter was written about A.D. 65 or 66 when the zeal of a party had become a national spirit of self-sacrifice, and the enthusiasm of the zealots had involved a whole people in war against Rome. "It was Florus," writes Josephus, "who compelled us to undertake war with Rome, seeing as we did that it would be better to perish as a nation than by partial and repeated persecution. The beginning of the war was in the second year of the procuratorship of Florus, the twelfth of Nero's reign," i.e. A.D. 66 (*Antiq.* xx. 11).

How moving the appeal would be to all Jews, in Palestine especially, but in all places too whence it was possible for Jews to travel to Palestine, and rally round the national standard, and fight for hearth and home, laying aside all party differences and uniting in the ancient, hallowed battle-cry, "The LORD our God, the LORD, one!" (cf. Deut. vi. 4, Heb. xiii. 8). And to none would it come with more force than to these "philosophic liberals," who had toyed with speculative hopes of a reformed creed, and were now summoned to play the man, and throw themselves into the stream of life in its intensity and simplicity. They were fairly well to do (vi. 10, x. 34, xiii. 5), and wherever situated, could make the journey to Palestine. They seem to have never been quite at home in the community of Christians they had joined (x. 25, xiii. 17); no doubt early apocalyptic Christianity was a rude environment for these intellectual people. They are inclined to weary themselves no more with niceties of creed ; they will return to the simplicity of the faith of their childhood, which is at least enough for men of honour. See v. 11—14, and notice the emphasis throughout the epistle on such words as καλόν, κρεῖττον.

§ 3. *when the patriotic appeal, so attractive to these imperfect disciples, was contrary to the faith of Christ.*

They were however making a double mistake. The Jewish rising was not the pure patriotism they imagined, and the Christian faith was more than a reformed Judaism.

The Jewish rising was not pure patriotism. These Christian Jews were confronted with the very choice which had been offered to our Lord when He called for the tribute money and gave His decision, "Render unto Caesar." That was no clever shelving of the question; it was a decision which cost Him life. It was a practical summing up of all He taught about the kingdom of God. That kingdom was not to be the political triumph of Judaism, but the universal victory of that true religion which had been especially entrusted to the Jews; "Blessed are the meek, for they shall inherit the earth." The quotation in Heb. x. 30, "Vengeance is mine," may have been suggested by Rom. xii. 19, but it has a more concentrated purpose in Hebrews. When this epistle was written, the problem was set for the first time which has so often been forced upon the Church again, how to apply the peaceful doctrine of the Sermon on the Mount to national politics. The solution was perhaps more simple then than it has been on some later occasions, but it was not absolutely simple. The case for the patriots must have seemed very strong. Looking back now, we can see that the author was right every way. Josephus' history of the war shews the evil passions that tainted the spirit of the heroically fighting Jews. The issue of the struggle might appear but one more of the frequent examples of might triumphing and yet not being right; but the subsequent development of Rabbinism goes near to prove that the fight was not for the truth, but for a narrow sectarian religion. And yet even now we may confuse cause and effect, and then these things were hidden from the passionate actors in the tragedy.

The author of the epistle saw the right way clearly. This—for those who accept the view here proposed of its occasion—is one proof of his inspiration. But true inspiration bears analysis, and we may further explain his insight by adding that he saw the way because he had a real apprehension of the life, work and Person of the Lord. He understood the supreme and final worth of the salvation wrought through Him, and knew that even the purest claims of patriotism could not outweigh devotion to the new faith; no such conflicting duty could be real duty; to merge the perfect work of Christ in Judaism could not be right, and on no other terms might Jewish patriotism be satisfied. To his friends he could put this in an elementary manner: You have given allegiance to the Lord Jesus as the Christ; no other plea of honour can set you free from that allegiance. That plain preliminary appeal runs through the epistle.

§ 4. *Therefore the author would deepen their faith by using the analogy of priesthood to explain the Person and the work of Christ.*

He also knew that, if he could lift the faith of these friends of his to the level of his own, they would find in the Lord Jesus Christ such strength as would enable them to make the hard choice. Hence his letter consists of an intellectual argument mingling with an emotional appeal. And the argument takes this form: Think of Him as a priest and I can make you understand. If it be asked why he threw his reasoning into that form, no certain answer can be given. No doubt the letter, like most letters, is the continuation of earlier conversations; the subject had been discussed before and this illustration had been used. Philo had used it in his theologising about the Word of God. It may be that Philo himself had not been read by these people. But, if not Philo, the masters of Philo had been theirs, and the divine High-priest was a conception that might very naturally have arisen from their Alexandrine education. But it may be there is no need to search so curiously. Christ the High-priest is an idea so frequent in the earliest Christian literature that it can hardly have been derived from this, long disputed, epistle. The germs of the idea are already to be found

in two books of the New Testament which in other respects
have affinities with Hebrews, viz. 1 Peter and the Apocalypse,
but which, again, can hardly have drawn upon Hebrews. The
instinct, inference, or possibly tradition of the Church may well
be right, not in making the Levitical Law the main interest of
the epistle, but at least in recognising in that Law a natural
analogy for the instruction of Christians who had been brought
up under it. That the analogy is not evidently used in any
other book of the New Testament, and that the two books, just
mentioned, which do approach such use are specially connected
with Jewish Christianity (cf. 1 Pet. i. 1), shows that it is not
quite reasonable to say that all Christians, Jewish and Gentile
alike, knew the Old Testament well, and might as easily have
welcomed the same analogy.

§ 5. *He does this on the lines of* atonement, mediation, approach
  to God. The Jewish ritual affords a starting point for the
  discovery of a truer type.

But this need not be laboured. Let us pass on to consider
how the analogy of priesthood is applied. The whole work of
priesthood may be summed up in four phrases from the epistle,
ἱλάσκεσθαι, ἐξ ἀνθρώπων, τὰ πρὸς τὸν θεόν, ὁδός. The priest
"makes atonement" for sins. He does this because he is a
mediator, a man "taken from among men," yet standing "on
the Godward side" of men. Thus he opens a "way" by which
men cleansed from sin may enter the presence of God. See
ii. 17 f., v. 1 f., x. 19—22. This is all part of a series of pictorial
terms derived from the Levitical ritual, which forms the starting
point for the analogy. But, before we go further, it is necessary
to state plainly that nothing more than this is derived from the
Levitical ritual. After all the Levitical priest actually effected
none of these things. Nor could they ever be effected by the
institutional means he used however far developed. If the work
of Christ is conceived as a development or fulfilling of something thus begun, the argument of the epistle becomes un-
satisfactory. It could never convince any one who had not
already accepted the reality of the salvation brought by Him ;
and even to such believers it would only be an illustration,

helping them to formulate their belief in a special manner. But the epistle reiterates the author's repudiation of that purpose. He says these ancient rites were merely "shadow," and the contrast drawn between the "shadow" and "the actual type or symbol," αὐτὴν τὴν εἰκόνα, x. 1, shews that in choosing the term "shadow" he did not mean to lay stress on its close connexion with the "reality" that cast its shadow before itself, but on the quite unsubstantial fleeting nature of these mechanical (πεποιημένων, xii. 27), temporary phases of ritual. The Levitical Law, like the Philonic philosophy, gave the author a vocabulary, and started him with an analogy. But he soon passes from analogy to a much more serious kind of reasoning. When he uses an image from the old ritual he never elaborates it fully, nor cares to get the correspondence exact. Forgetting this, we soon meet with difficulties ; first with slight ones, as when the author is thought to be detected in some antiquarian inaccuracy ; then with great ones, when we force our Lord's spiritual state into a material mould, and dispute as to when His priesthood began, or the precise relation of His intercession to His sacrifice, or enquire what the altar (xiii. 10) or the sanctuary stands for.

§ 6. *But first he shews our Lord to be the heir of Christship and Sonship:*

The epistle opens with a poet's vision of all which is afterwards to be discovered to the readers. The author stands as it were by the throne of God, and sees the light streaming from His invisible glory ; impressing itself as with a seal on certain eminences in Israel's history ; then taking definite human form in One who inherits the name of Christ and Son from those Christ-kings ; then this divine Person makes purification of sins, and returns with His achieved inheritance to the exalted throne from which He proceeded, and which He now shares as King and Priest. The readers will have little doubt from the first who is meant. In ii. 3 a passing reference to "the Lord" would remove any doubt they might have felt. The rest of chapter ii. gives another view of the work of salvation, this time from earth, as it was wrought by Jesus in His humiliation ;

and in iii. 1—6 the two lines are brought together, and Jesus is declared to be the Christ who as Christ is Son of God, and as the fulfiller of all the imperfect Christship of the past, is Son of God in the supreme sense.

So far, more has been said about our Lord's Christship than His priesthood, and this idea is never dropped throughout the epistle. But already the priesthood has been implied in καθαρισμὸν ποιησάμενος, i. 3, and expressly mentioned in ii. 17. Herein we perceive the novelty and the conservatism of the writer's design. He would interpret the old tradition, of "Jesus is the Christ," in new terms, "Jesus is our High-priest." The tradition was quite primitive. It was first expressed as the Christian creed by S. Peter when he said, in the region of Caesarea, "Thou art the Christ." It was re-affirmed, after the shock of the crucifixion, by S. Paul with the development which that trial to the faith rendered necessary. Thus in Rom. i. 2 ff. he wrote: "The gospel of God, which he promised afore by his prophets in the holy scriptures, concerning his Son, who was born of the seed of David according to the flesh, who was declared"—or "defined"—"to be the Son of God with power according to the spirit of holiness, by the resurrection of the dead."

§ 7. yet inheriting through the humiliation of real manhood.

This great confession or profession—ὁμολογία—as our author would call it, is fully adopted by him. But he retouches it, deepening some lines, the witness of the Old Testament, and (as S. Paul himself did in Colossians) the pre-existence of the divine Son; and modifying one line, since he thinks of the Lord's "raising" rather as "ascension" than "resurrection." But in particular he develops the "born of the seed of David according to the flesh." That is an assertion of the hereditary honour of our Lord's manhood. It is asserted in Hebrews also, once in plain terms, vii. 14, and throughout the epistle wherever the Christship is treated of. But for the most part our author lays the stress on another aspect of our Lord's manhood, that which S. Paul spoke about to the Philippians, ii. 5—11, His humiliation. We can see the reason for this.

The readers of the epistle, with their imperfect apprehension of the Lord's Godhead, were especially interested in His earthly ministry, "the days of his flesh," v. 7. If S. Paul's epistles were the first fruits of the Church's literature, the synoptic Gospels followed them, and we may infer that at about the time when Hebrews was written the thoughts of the brethren were being widely turned to the memories of Jesus of Nazareth. With us too a like revival of interest in the gospel story has taken place, and we know what one of the results has been; the limitations of the Lord's manhood have for a while almost daunted faith. This is a recurring illustration of what S. Paul says the Jews especially felt in his day, "the scandal of the cross," 1 Cor. i. 23. And it is evident that the friends of this author felt it painfully.

And herein is one of the causes of his choosing the analogy of priesthood. In his first mention of the priesthood he insists on real manhood being an indispensable qualification : "Wherefore it behoved him in all things to be made like unto his brethren, that he might be a merciful and faithful high priest in things pertaining to God, to make propitiation for the sins of the people. For in that he himself hath suffered being tempted, he is able to succour them that are tempted," ii. 17 f. He goes on to meet the difficulty full and square. He insists with all his power that our Lord is really "a man"—not merely the representative of man. When speaking of His earthly ministry, he reiterates the human name "Jesus." In speaking of His exalted state, he adds "Christ," or in some other way marks the difference. But he allows no infringement even thus on the very manhood. Even on earth the Lord was Christ, v. 5 ff., and in (or beyond) the heavens He is still " Jesus," iv. 14, xii. 23; "Jesus Christ, the same yesterday, to day, yea, and for ever!" is his cry, xiii. 8. And he insists on the limitations of His manhood in uncompromising language. " Though he was a Son, yet learned he obedience by the things which he suffered "; He was "made perfect" only at the last, and only after He was made perfect did He "become the author of eternal salvation," v. 8 f. He was indeed "without sin," but as His making perfect was quite parallel to the making perfect of other "just men," xii. 23, so His liability to sin was in all reality like theirs ; "For we have not a high priest that cannot be touched with the feeling of our infirmities ; but one that hath been in all points tempted like as we are, yet without sin," iv. 15. And in vii. 27 the natural meaning is that our Lord did once for all and effectually just that which the Levitical priests did often and ineffectually, i.e. offered sacrifice "first for his own sins, and then for the sins of the people." This would indeed be what S. Paul also meant in 2 Cor. v. 21, "Him who knew no sin God made to be sin on our behalf ; that we might become the righteousness of God in him." But the phrasing in Hebrews is very bold ; if it is rather careless than studied, such careless-ness is none the less significant.

In no way will the author suffer the real manhood, and therefore the real humiliation, of the Lord to be explained away. From chapter ii. it might appear that the Arian tendency had already shown itself. Some were inclined to look upon our Lord as neither quite God nor quite man, but an angelic Being. He rejects that by shewing that such Beings are on an entirely different line. According to a quotation he makes from Ps. civ. (Heb. i. 7) the angels are not persons in the sense that God and man are persons. They are what we should call "elemental forces." This was an idea which found favour in later Judaism, and has been adopted by Origen and by later theologians of undoubted orthodoxy. Something like it appears in the Apocalypse, and it is evident from Heb. xii. 22 that it is not irreverent. The irreverence lies in a mean estimate of nature. Seen from the throne of God the lightning and the wind would be, as the Old Testament habitually describes them, angels.

But the epistle merely glances at all that speculation. The author is only concerned with the truth pertinent to his purpose, that the problem of our Lord's Person cannot be solved, or shelved, by fancying Him a mingled creature, neither God nor man. He is both ; and only in frank recognition of His manhood will His Godhead be apprehended. Accordingly at ii. 5, after a final dismissal of the angelic theory, the argu-ment proceeds to a vivid picture of the man Jesus fulfilling the destiny of manhood, as it was described in the eighth Psalm. The general sense of that psalm is that man for all his feebleness

has been exalted by God to high dominion, and the author of
Hebrews says that though as yet this exaltation has not been
seen in the case of other men, we do see Jesus thus glorified.
But he chooses for the picture of this "crowning with honour
and glory" so unexpected a moment that many commentators
prefer to do violence to his Greek rather than admit what
nevertheless he plainly states, viz. that the supreme moment
of humiliation before the Lord died was the supreme moment
of His glory on earth. If as is possible he had the passage in
Philippians, ii. 5—11, in mind, he has deliberately substituted
"glory in humiliation" for S. Paul's "glory after humiliation."
In like manner the "joy set before him," xii. 2, is parallel to
"the contest set before us" in the preceding verse, and means
the joy that the Lord experienced in His endurance of shameful
death. Glory in humiliation, Godhead discovered in manhood,
death on the cross the entry as High-priest into the very
presence of God with eternal salvation found for men ; this
is the series of inward and outward, eternal and visible, perfection through limitation, that runs through the epistle : see
especially x. 19 f., where the flesh of the Lord Jesus is the way
He inaugurated into the sanctuary, and xiii. 12, where the
crucifixion which to outward appearance was like the off-
scouring of a sacrifice—the execution as it seemed of a criminal
—was the priestly entrance of the Saviour of men into the
presence of the Father.

§ 8. *In this reality of the Lord's manhood the sacramental*
principle appears which governs the whole epistle. The wide
meaning of Sacrament in early theology : a sign partaking
of the reality symbolised. So in Christ true Godhead is
involved in true manhood ; a doctrine opportune for these
Alexandrine readers.

This is the sacramental principle. The word Sacrament has
been used in a very sacred but somewhat narrowed sense of late.
In the early Church it was applied to all visible symbols of the
eternal which were not mere signs, but partook of the reality
which they symbolised. If it be objected that this is a perverse
usage of the word in modern times, appeal may be made to the
fine essay on "Sacraments" in *Lux Mundi* by Francis Paget,

late Bishop of Oxford, who shews how the two ritual sacraments of Baptism and Holy Communion, ordained by our Lord, were fitted for His purpose because they were not to be arbitrary observances, but a particular application of that unity and interfusion of the visible and the eternal with which God has ennobled the whole of His creation. The author of this epistle would agree with that. There can be little doubt that in his day the two sacraments were closely bound up with the whole church life. In vi. 4, x. 32 (φωτισθέντες), and not improbably in x. 22, he refers to Baptism, and it may be that the epistle is coloured throughout by the phraseology and thought of the eucharistic service. Yet he gives no direct teaching on these rites, whereas the larger sacramental idea pervades his letter. Thus he accepts and transfigures the scandal of the cross. Thus he restates the mystery of Christ's Person, shewing how the limitations of His environment, and—a favourite phrase—His "suffering" were the most fitting means for the interpenetration of His Godhead into earthly life. And thus, as we shall see, the doctrine of His High-priesthood becomes, in the really close reasoning of the epistle, far more than an analogy; it is an application of the sacramental principle of the unity of all life.

But before we consider that three remarks must be made.

First, sacraments are not fancies which merely stimulate thought, as when we say, "This clear sky makes me think of heaven." They are moral realities, as when an officer's courage evokes a like courage in his men; for there the appeal is from a visible act to the eternal divine quality of self-sacrifice which has been implanted in manhood. And it is more than an appeal; it is the setting free of an invisible spiritual power—we call it by an appropriate metaphor, "influence"—which overleaps the boundaries of matter, and joins the very souls of men in one; and moreover lifts them into a higher sphere of energy where physical death is made of no account. So in his doctrine of Christ's Person and saving work, our author concentrates attention on His perfect goodness—His earthly life was a manifestation in this quality above all of eternal life; and on His offering being of His own blood, His very self, consciously and willingly offered, while in chapter x. (the heart of the epistle) he all but lays aside the sacrificial figures and founds the whole in "will."

Secondly, this may be thought to prove too much. For if all this be true, where is the difference between our Lord and other men? The whole creation is sacramental; all men's lives may be effective symbols of the eternal ; how then is He unique? It may be answered that "unique" is not a happily chosen term to describe our Lord's position. Not only in this epistle, but throughout the New Testament the Godhead of Christ is represented as uniting Him with men and so carrying men with Him into God. In the end, says S. Paul, God shall be all in all, 1 Cor. xv. 28. In 2 Pet. i. 4 the promise is that men may become partakers of the divine nature. "As he is so are we also in this world," says S. John, and, "We know that, if he shall be manifested, we shall be like him ; for we shall see him even as he is," 1 John iv. 17, iii. 2. And in Heb. i. 2 the whole significance of the phrase would be spoilt if the article were added to ἐν υἱῷ : all men are sons of God, not Christ alone.

And yet that ἐν υἱῷ, "one who is a Son," does not put Him on a level with other sons. In Him, and in Him alone, the divine Sonship was always apparent. There is a Christian ideal which we keep in view but never consistently attain. Because His disciples perceived that He did always live at the level of that ideal, they recognised in Him the light and source of all life that is life indeed. Hence the primitive confession of His Christhood, and the later definition of His Godhead. And yet again that later definition was the discovery, or recovery, of some still deeper truth which again and again has proved itself a necessary truth for those who recognise the wonder and mystery of life—of all mortal life running up into eternities. There are these mysteries about and within us, and, as churchmen think, nothing can give them sense and consistency except the centering them in that supreme mystery of Christ's Person which is expressed in the sublime language of the Creed, "Light of light, very God of very God...who for us men and for our salvation came down from heaven"—all this manifested to us in One who lived as a man among men on earth. This does not separate Him from us. It brings Him closer than ever, for though there is something here which passes our understanding, it is nevertheless the indispensable presupposition to all our understanding of ourselves and our surroundings. And accordingly the author of Hebrews begins his epistle by setting forth this truth more expressly than any writer had done before. He sets it forth ; then leaves it. The rest of the epistle treats of the Lord Jesus in the days of His flesh, and of the exalted state which followed. The mode of treatment makes it seem at times that Jesus wins through suffering to Godhead. But that is the view as seen from earth ; that is the sacramental figure. The actual truth of this "perfection" is more recondite, more universally of moment. And the declaration of the Church's tradition in the introductory verses guards and gives reason to the whole complexity of the freely handled idea.

And thirdly, this sacramental principle was one which the readers could readily accept. For it is a principle which the Alexandrine philosophy had learned from Plato. S. Paul, always quick to take up words and thoughts which he could put to effective use in his teaching, every now and then adopts the sacramental phraseology, but it was not congenial to him. Philologically considered, "sacramental" and "mystical" are the same word, and in our English Prayer Book "mystical" does mean just "sacramental." But "mystical" has of late taken a more particular signification which is almost antithetical to that of "sacramental," implying the inward union of the mind with eternity, a union not mediated by outward things. And in that sense S. Paul is mystical by nature, not sacramental. It is a remarkable coincidence—but see John xiv. 26, xvi. 13—that this Alexandrine thinker, with his vivid style of picture-language, should be writing to Alexandrine Platonists, who needed instruction concerning the Person of Christ, at a time when the interest in our Lord's earthly life was being newly roused. The coincidence produced this first sketch of the application of the sacramental principle to the elucidation of the gospel story. Later, the evangelist of the fourth Gospel would use the same principle with childlike simplicity and still more profound thoughtfulness in that narrative of the life of Jesus Christ which displays, more splendidly yet quietly than any other writing, Godhead interpenetrating manhood in His Person, and from Him as from a source transfiguring the life of men everywhere.

§ 9. *Christ the High-priest is* mediator *"on the Godward side,"
consummating the eternal priesthood which runs through
nature and history.*

Now we come to the main thought of the epistle, the High-
priesthood of Christ. The idea itself, and the language in which
it is elaborated, is derived from the high-priesthood of Aaron
as described in the books of the Law. The Book, not the
contemporary usage at Jerusalem, is the source ; the Tabernacle,
not the Temple, is the illustration. And the ritual of the Day
of Atonement is especially employed. That was a service in
which the high priest took the great part, not the other priests.
When the epistle was written the distinction in Greek between
ἀρχιερεύς and ἱερεύς was not carefully observed, and we must not
too hastily read subtle significances into the author's application
of this title to our Lord ; His " priesthood " in the wide sense is
the great point, and in Ps. cx., from which the phrase "priest
after the order of Melchizedek" is taken, the word is simply
ἱερεύς. Nevertheless the author's habit is to make the most of
what is peculiar and striking in words, and it is reasonable to
suppose that when he styled our Lord " High Priest," he did
mean to emphasize His eminence in a priesthood which all men
shared. It is a title which expresses, symbolically, what we
have just now been considering, viz. that our Lord, though He
lived on earth as a man among other men, was the first to attain
" perfection " of manhood, and so became the representative of
all men in the presence of God.

For that, according to the epistle, is the essence of priesthood.
It is τὰ πρὸς τὸν θεόν, ii. 17, v. 1. In Ex. iv. 16 the Lord
promises Moses that Aaron shall be his spokesman ; σὺ δὲ αὐτῷ
ἔσῃ τὰ πρὸς τὸν θεόν, "and thou shalt be to him on the Godward
side." That is the excellent translation which has been proposed
for these words in Hebrews. " On the Godward side": George
Herbert wrote " Man is the world's High priest," and again

> " To this life things of sense
> Make their pretence :
> In the other Angels have a right by birth :
> Man ties them both alone,
> And makes them one,
> With the one hand touching heaven, with the other earth."

The whole of that poem, "Man's medley," might be quoted in illustration of some of the deepest thoughts of this epistle. This verse has obvious affinities with chapter ii. The idea recurs in other applications. Thus the Messianic quotations in chapter i. point to the Christ-kings of Israel standing on the Godward side of the nation, and the nation on the Godward side of the world. The heirship of the Son to all that has been created through Him, i. 2, and the phrase δι' ὃν τὰ πάντα καὶ δι' οὗ τὰ πάντα, ii. 10, indicate that growth of nature up to God which we term evolution, and in the quotation from Ps. cii., in i. 10—12, there is a hint of the same Godward-drawing vitality in changing and perishing things which persists throughout their mutability. So again in xi. 3 the ideal is of the successive ages of history being linked together by an influence, not material, which ever works on the Godward side, and in spite of much appearance to the contrary, still leads mankind upward and onward in steady course. The heroes of faith, who are celebrated one after the other in the rest of that chapter, stand in just this Godward relation to their several generations. The divine movement of history goes on, till at last (verses 39 f.) the priestly, Godward-drawing responsibility is found to rest upon the readers of the epistle, whose duty done or failed in will affect the perfecting of all their predecessors. We can of course see the same thing going on still, a father standing on the Godward side of his family, one who sacrifices life for a cause standing on the Godward side of his contemporaries, a parish priest standing on the Godward side of his parish, and so indeed each person who does his duty in that state to which it pleases God to call him. We might term all this "natural priesthood." The writer of Hebrews would prefer "eternal priesthood," for it is in work like this that "the other world," ἡ οἰκουμένη ἡ μέλλουσα (ii. 5), breaks in; in this the sacramental quality of life is perceptible.

§ 10. *The author names the eternal and really typical priesthood after Melchizedek, as the artificial shadowy priesthood had been named after Aaron.*

He does however distinguish this priesthood by another term, which no doubt seemed appropriate enough to his Alexandrine friends, but which obscures his meaning to us. He calls it priesthood "after the order of Melchizedek." We see from Philo how the Jewish philosophers of Alexandria had used the mysterious story of Melchizedek to illustrate their doctrine of the Word of God, a doctrine which is often near akin to the idea sketched in the last paragraph. We who have not been brought up in the Alexandrine schools have to make an effort in taking their point of view. And our author has not made that effort easier by his too scholastic treatment of the subject in chapter vii. This is the most Philonic in form of all his writing. And yet the dry, half logical, half fanciful, argument is punctuated by a few great phrases which outweigh much tediousness, and upon which if we fix our attention, we shall not miss his real meaning. What he says is in effect this. The Levitical priesthood is but a ritual institution. All such wear out and pass away. There is no seed in them which grows to perfection. And to day we see this institution proving ineffectual (ἀσθενὲς καὶ ἀνωφελές, vii. 18). Is it to make way for another ordinance of like kind?

No, a better hope (vii. 19) has arisen. In the life and death and victory over death, in the self-sacrifice of Jesus Christ, we hope that the Godward-drawing influence which the Levitical institution represented by ecclesiastical symbolism (κατὰ νόμον ἐντολῆς σαρκίνης), but which has always been a real working power in the whole world, has reached its destined perfection. This influence has been due to a divine life, always in the world, indissoluble amid all changes and chances ; and in Jesus Christ, who died for men and yet lives, we believe that we recognise the source and the complete manifestation of that life (κατὰ δύναμιν ζωῆς ἀκαταλύτου, vii. 16). He has fulfilled the typical priesthood, and His priesthood, by which we really come to God (δι' ἧς ἐγγίζομεν τῷ θεῷ, vii. 19), shall never pass away as institutional ordinances do (ἀπαράβατον ἔχει τὴν ἱερωσύνην, vii. 24). "He is

able to save to the uttermost them that draw near unto God
through him, seeing he ever liveth to make intercession for
them," vii. 25.

The institutional priesthood, which merely stimulated thought
and emotion (cf. x. 3), is named after a person in the sacred record
of Israel's history. The high priest of this artificial order is
Aaron. The High Priest of the other, real and living order is
Jesus Christ. But cannot a name be found in the same sacred
story which may stand as a type of Him, representing all the
imperfect efforts of true priesthood which He inspired and has
now carried out to their inherent perfection (ἀφωμοιωμένος τῷ
υἱῷ τοῦ θεοῦ, vii. 3) ? Will not "Melchizedek" serve this purpose ?
That personage in the dawn of history appears exercising a
priest-king's function, outside the limits of the chosen people,
dominating our great ancestor Abraham, and described in
mysterious language which suggests eternity of life, vii. 2 f.
Here surely is the world-wide, unending priesthood we are
seeking. The choice of this name might seem unimportant, but
it gains importance when we find a psalmist taking up the name
and the idea long afterwards in a psalm which not only testifies
to the inextinguishable aspiration of God's people towards the
consummation of this effectual priesthood, but also pictures so
remarkably the glory of our ascended Lord. "Thou art a priest
for ever after the order of Melchizedek," he says ; and "Sit thou
on my right hand until I make thine enemies thy footstool,"
vii. 15, 21, viii. 1, cf. i. 13, v. 6, xii. 2.

§ 11. *But another element in true priesthood is* atonement, *which
in Hebrews is oftener represented as cleansing.*

In some such terms as these our author might translate his
Alexandrine reasoning were he confronted with his modern
readers. But he would have to confess that his phrase "after
the order of Melchizedek" does not cover all he has to say about
the priesthood that was consummated by Jesus Christ. There
is nothing about "propitiation," "atonement," in the story of
Melchizedek. How did our High Priest win that forgiveness of
sins which was needed by sinful men if they were really to enter
the holy presence of God ? This question is answered in the

three following chapters, viii.—x. In these we have the ex
position of that other key-word, ἱλάσκεσθαι, ii. 17.
That verb is found elsewhere in the New Testament only
once, and there in the sincere, but as yet imperfect prayer of
a beginner in the faith, Luke xviii. 13. The reason for this
infrequency is not hard to guess. In pagan religion, and in
popular misunderstandings of Judaism and Christianity before
and since, men have conceived of "propitiation" as the changing
of God's mind from hostility to favour. No such idea is
admitted in the New Testament. Man is reconciled to God,
Rom. v. 10, 2 Cor. v. 18 ff.; only in a sense which requires
explanation can we say in the language of the second "Article
of Religion" that Christ died "to reconcile His Father to us"[1];
even of the Old Testament the consistent teaching is, "I have
loved thee with an everlasting love," Jer. xxxi. 3, "I will heal
their backsliding, I will love them freely," Hos. xiv. 4. The
"wrath" of God, in either Testament, is not contrary to His
love, but His love itself burning its way against opposition.
The same feeling about ἱλάσκεσθαι appears in S. Paul in the one
place where he uses the kindred term ἱλαστήριον, Rom. iii. 25.
He guards the true idea by adding διὰ τῆς πίστεως. Another
kindred word is ἱλασμός, twice used by S. John, 1 John ii. 2,
iv. 10, and not elsewhere in the New Testament. And this is
noticeable. For it is one of the connecting links between
Hebrews and the Johannine writings, which stand in the same
line as Ezekiel and the priestly writings of the Old Testament.
In all these books healing is provided for those who feel the
stain rather than the chain of sin. So Ezekiel, for all his
insistence upon sacrifices, shows what he recognised as the
permanent underlying significance of sacrifices, in such a passage
as xxxvi. 25 f.: "And I will sprinkle clean water upon you, and
ye shall be clean: from all your filthiness, and from all your
idols, will I cleanse you. A new heart also will I give you, and
a new spirit will I put within you: and I will take away the
stony heart out of your flesh, and I will give you a heart of
flesh." Compare with that Heb. ix. 13 f., "For if the blood of

[1] See note on "The idea of Reconciliation or Atonement" in
Sanday and Headlam's *Romans*, pp. 129 f.

goats and bulls, and the ashes of a heifer sprinkling them that have been defiled, sanctify unto the cleanness of the flesh : how much more shall the blood of Christ, who through the eternal Spirit offered himself without blemish unto God, cleanse your conscience from dead works to serve the living God ?" And here we meet with that other word, καθαρίζειν, which the author prefers to ἱλάσκεσθαι. His habit is to translate "propitiation" in terms of "cleansing."

§ 12. *This cleansing is through the Blood, which is life given by God to re-create life. Leviticus: the suffering Servant of the Lord.*

Both terms however are priestly. And this is especially evident when we observe how the cleansing is effected. It is by "blood." Here is a form of speech which would seem very strange to us if we were not so accustomed to read of the Blood of our Lord Jesus Christ in the New Testament that we have become somewhat dulled in our apprehension of the startling figure—νωθροὶ γεγόναμεν ταῖς ἀκοαῖς (Heb. v. 11). Indeed we hardly recognise anything of the nature of figure here. Our Lord's death involved bloodshed ; that violent bloodshedding was the price of our salvation. But that idea, though glanced at elsewhere in the New Testament, never enters this epistle. The bloodshedding in Hebrews, αἱματεκχυσία, ix. 22, is the blood-sprinkling of a sacrifice, and to understand—what to a Christian educated in Judaism would have been as familiar as the doctrine of sacraments is to those brought up in the church Catechism— we must turn to Lev. xvii. 10 f. :

"And whatsoever man there be of the house of Israel, or of the strangers that sojourn among them, that eateth any manner of blood ; I will set my face against that soul that eateth blood, and will cut him off from among his people. For the life of the flesh is in the blood : and I have given it to you upon the altar to make atonement for your lives : for it is the blood that maketh atonement by reason of the life."

In the Hebrew, as R.V. margin shews, one and the same word stands throughout for "soul" or "life." The sense is obscured by varying the translation. The main point is that life atones for life. Indeed we might say "life cleanses life." For the Hebrew ritual term, although in other connexions it means "cover," is very likely akin in this connexion to a similar word in Babylonian ritual which does mean "cleanse[1]." And in any case the essential idea is deeper than any ritual metaphor. It is that in sacrifice a life offered to God renews man's spoiled and broken life, re-unites it with the life of God, carries it to its destined perfection in God.

This is true even of the Levitical theology. For the theology of this passage is a conscious, an inspired transformation of an older, crude religion. The older base is a mere taboo against eating blood. That taboo is taken into the Mosaic law to stay there for a while till it passes away with the rest of the "shadow." But it is also developed into a truth about God which is to last as long as time. "Atonement" is God's grace; cf. ii. 9: He himself, so far from having to "be propitiated," provides means for reconciling His alienated children to himself. And He finds these means in the mystery of life, and through life brings new life to the dead. Life is appointed by Him to re-create life. Contrast this "life-blood...given upon the altar" for renewal of life with what Aeschylus says of life-blood spilt upon the ground: ἀνδρὸς δ᾽ ἐπειδὰν αἷμ᾽ ἀνασπάσῃ κόνις ἅπαξ θανόντος οὔτις ἔστ᾽ ἀνάστασις, *Eum.* 647 f.; cf. 1 Sam. xiv. 33 f., 2 Sam. xiv. 14.

How far, even in the Levitical conception, is this mere figure? So far as it was expressed by the use of the blood of victims it was of course mere figure. The life of bulls and goats could never be anything but external to the offerer. Unless atonement or salvation could be wrought for men entirely by an act outside themselves, these sacrifices were merely fictions. And such they were; the Levitical ritual was a shadow. But whenever the principle was transferred from the ritual sacrifices to deeds in which men willingly offered themselves to God's will—to be used by Him in life or death just as He called them to be used—then it did become possible for one man's life to re-create the life of others. And even in Old Testament history we find this happening. Very imperfectly some of the kings of Judah did

[1] See *Encyclopaedia Biblica*, art. "Ritual," § 8.

this. More perfectly the great prophets did it, especially Jeremiah. Above all that person, celebrated in Is. liii. as the Servant of the Lord, by whose suffering and death the peoples were converted and saved, did this. He may have been a historical personage, or he may have been a lyric type, the expression of an inspired prophetic poet's imagination. At any rate his ζωή ἀκατάλυτος was a supreme illustration of the Levitical theology "life re-creating life," and from apostolic times onward he stands as the forerunner of our Lord, the real "type" which could be really fulfilled in Him. We in the twentieth century can hardly avoid the presumptuous fancy that the epistle to the Hebrews would be easier for us to understand if the author had called our Lord's High-priesthood "priesthood after the order of the suffering Servant" instead of "after the order of Melchizedek."

§ 13. *The Blood of Christ is His life enriched by death, through which He appeared before God on our behalf.*

For as we read on and enter upon the profounder chapters viii.—x., it becomes clear that our Lord's "priesthood" reaches its essence in His "sacrifice," and His sacrifice is through His death. It is not His death, simply. The sacrifice is what He offered, and that was His life. But He could only offer it by dying. Yet again it was not through death, simply. The series of words concerning "suffering" are as frequent as those which concern death. The phrase in the Litany, "By thy cross and passion," is in strict accord with the theology of Hebrews. A sacrifice, an offering, is, from the very nature of such words, made at one definite time, once for all. But this is a matter that overpasses the lexicographical precision of single words. This most real offering was a moral action, a personal action with influence from persons to persons, Christ, God, men. And therefore it was bound up with the development of character— "Christ learned obedience by the things which he suffered ; and having been made perfect, he became etc.," v. 8. There was a moment when the sacrifice was offered, and there was a moment when Christ was hailed as High Priest, v. 10. But to press this very far is to make our interpretation servile to the figurative letter. The "becoming," first of Christ then of "those that

obey" Him, is as important in the argument of the epistle as is
that other point—which nevertheless is exceedingly important—
that in Christ's action, as in man's, and especially as it was
in that of the first readers, there came one supreme moment,
up to which all the past led, and upon which all the future
turned.

And that was the moment of His death. If, instructed by
the Levitical theology, we were to substitute "life" for "blood"
in all those passages of the epistle where the blood of Christ is
named, much vivid truth would be recovered for ears blunted by
convention. But something too would be lost. In Levitical
ritual the death of the victim was not the sacrifice, but the
indispensable preliminary; for except by the victim's death, its
blood (which was its life) could not be set free for sacrificial
"pouring" or "sprinkling." And, taught here by the ritual as
before by the Levitical theology, we amend our substitution, and
by the "blood of Christ" understand His "life set free and
enriched by death." We should probably come near the practical
sense of the epistle if we said this life enriched by death was
what Christ offered. But the epistle does not quite say that.
Following the analogy of the Levitical ritual, the author speaks
of His entering the true sanctuary "through his own blood,"
διὰ τοῦ ἰδίου αἵματος, ix. 12, and sanctifying the people "through
his own blood," xiii. 12, and of God bringing Him from the dead
"in the blood of the eternal covenant," ἐν αἵματι διαθήκης αἰωνίου,
xiii. 20, and of our entering the true sanctuary "in the blood of
Jesus," ἐν τῷ αἵματι Ἰησοῦ, x. 19. As Aaron entered the sanctuary
ἐν αἵματι ἀλλοτρίῳ, the sacrificial blood being but the instrument
by which, or the sphere in which, the offering—itself a mystery
not defined—was made, so also Christ. But His offering is
defined. The simplest word possible is employed. He offered
ἑαυτόν, "himself," ix. 14. Comparison with x. 34, xii. 3, shews
how high a value the author set on this colourless word. It is
as though he checked his picturesque style when he tried to
touch the very heart of things. So in the same clause, ix. 14,
he abandons even the sacred imagery of the blood, and substitutes
the sublime phrase διὰ πνεύματος αἰωνίου, which might be feebly
paraphrased "through the spiritual virtue of the divine holiness
of life." And in ix. 24 Christ enters the true sanctuary simply

to "appear before the presence of God on our behalf": even the offering of "himself" is left unmentioned: in profoundest, naked, truth there is no gift of any kind which God requires.

§ 14. *The significance of death for Christ and for all men: it is the perfecting of life.*

But all this is but an example of the translation of symbolic into "real" language which, from the very constitution of all language, it is impossible to carry out successfully; yet which must be attempted by those who would grapple closely with the mind of this most symbolising writer, and which from time to time he essays himself. Omitting further details of this kind, let us pass on to consider why he should assign so effective a value to the suffering of death. Alexander Ewing, Bishop of Argyll and the Isles, wrote to Erskine of Linlathen, "The outward sufferings of Christ were, so to speak, the accidents of His mission....But I do not know that the *dying* of Christ affects me more than the fact does, that 'He' was acquainted with grief; for in this fact, Christ being what He is, we have expressed to us the Divine sympathy with our sorrows in a way which leaves nothing to be wished for[1]." There is much harmony with the epistle in this, but not complete harmony. The author would hardly agree that the sufferings were but accidents of Christ's mission; he would say that we have to deal with sin as well as with sorrow; and he would insist that Christ's actual death was all important. And in that insistence he would be in agreement with S. Paul and S. Peter and with our Lord himself; for though it is by no means plain that our Lord started upon His ministry with a plan of salvation which included sufferings and death— in that sense these might be described as "accidents of His mission"—it is plain that when S. Peter confessed Him to be the Christ, He did receive or had received, by what we may perhaps call the inspiration of His incarnation, assurance of the Father's will that by His death He should bring the promised kingdom of Heaven. Is there here some mystery, hidden in that complete and universal nature of things which none but

---

[1] *Memoir*, p. 371. Isbister, 1887.

God can gather into view? It may be that such confession of our limits is the necessary prelude to all discussion of this matter. "We drop our plummet into the depth, but the line attached to it is too short, and it does not touch the bottom. The awful processes of the Divine Mind we cannot fathom[1]." Yet we can go some way towards gaining light from the nature of things even as we behold them. In what follows here Dr DuBose's chapter on "Human Destiny through Death" in his *High Priesthood and Sacrifice* has given much help.

Death may be considered as an evil, but also as a good. S. Paul generally speaks of physical death as an evil of the same kind as disease seems to be considered in the Gospels. In 1 Cor. xv. 24—27 he says death is "the last enemy that shall be abolished." But in Heb. ii. 14 f., a passage which looks as though it were in a manner based upon the passage in Corinthians, it is not death but "the fear of death," and the "bondage" due to that fear, which is represented as the evil. If it be objected that the devil is here said to be the lord of death, answer may be made in a fine sentence from Dr DuBose, which lovers of the Old Testament will be quick to understand; "The devil himself is the supreme evil only as he overcomes us; overcome by us, he is the supreme means of grace." What the author of Hebrews here lays stress upon is our Lord's use of death as the means of His victory. And that fits well with the heroic view in ii. 9 of Jesus crowned with glory and honour for the suffering of death. The general idea of death in this epistle is not as an evil disease of mortal men, but as the great means of fulfilling their destiny.

And that is what our Lord thought. "Whosoever would save his life shall lose it; and whosoever shall lose his life for my sake and the gospel's shall save it," Mark viii. 35 and parallels. No doubt He meant to include in this losing of life that "death to sin," or to the old self, of which S. Paul so often speaks. But when we remember what He said about the travail pangs of the Kingdom, Mat. xxiv. 8, Mar. xiii. 8, it is certain that He was also thinking of the death of the body. And indeed it is hardly possible that there can be any thorough dying to the old self

---

[1] Sanday and Headlam, *Romans*, p. 94, Note on "The Death of Christ considered as a Sacrifice."

unless it includes willingness to face physical death if God so call
a man. That was indeed S. Paul's mind too, and for himself
he did not always think of death as an evil, whatever he may
have said in some turns of his theological arguments; see
Phil. i. 21—26, and cf. Acts xx. 24.

The paradox, if it be a paradox, is indeed dissolved in the
light of ordinary life. In quiet times death may appear as the
unfortunate cutting short of pleasure or usefulness, the disease
of mortal nature, the penalty of man's sinful condition. But
at other times death for a man's country, for a cause, for "Christ's
sake and the gospel?' can well be looked upon as divinely destined
completion, τελείωσις, of a man's life, soul, self, his περιποίησις
ψυχῆς. It was in a time of severe trial that it was said of the
righteous man: "Being made perfect in a little while he fulfilled
long years" Wisdom iv. 13. "Trial," "temptation," πειρασμός,
generally bears this intense signification in the New Testament.
Probably it does in the Lord's Prayer, and "Lead us not into
temptation" ought to be interpreted by the standard of the
cross "where,"—so sang Dr Watts in the same spirit as the
Book of Wisdom—"where the young Prince of Glory died." If
we are not quite wrong in the setting we have decided upon for
Hebrews, πειρασμός bears the intense meaning there, and readers
who might soon be "resisting unto blood" themselves would be
the more apt to appreciate the pregnant issues of a heroic death.

Now transpose the key. Still remembering how great and
hopeful a crown of life is a heroic death, think not of heroism
but of the perfecting of all the "goodness" of our Lord Jesus
in His death. Then these words of Dr DuBose will seem
grounded in reverent reason: "The death of Jesus Christ was
no mere incident or accident of His human career. It was the
essential thing in it, as what it means for us all is the essential
thing in human life and destiny," for "the mystery of man is
the mystery of death, and the mystery of death is the mystery
of man; each is interpretative and explanatory of the other."

§ 15. *Third element in Christ's priesthood,* approach to God. *By the* way *He went and is men too must go : He re-enacts achievement in them.*

"What it means for us all" is the forgiveness of sin, that is the cleansing and cleansing away of sin, and in consequence our unimpeded access to the presence of God. "Having therefore, brethren, boldness to enter into the holy place by the blood of Jesus, by the way which he dedicated for us, a new and living way through the veil, that is to say, the way of his flesh ; and having a great priest over the house of God ; let us draw near with a true heart in fulness of faith, having our hearts sprinkled from an evil conscience, and our body washed with pure water," x. 19—22. Here is our fourth key-word, ὁδός. And, according to the translation here adopted and justified in the note on the passage, this way is the way of our Lord's flesh, i.e. we men must in our own lives re-enact, or have re-enacted in us, that "perfecting" which our Lord went through in His earthly life.

Now it may be that again in this connexion we ought to bear in mind the limits of our faculty for reasoning things out. It may be that there are phrases in the epistle which hint at depths beyond the reach of our plummet. And of course all the thoughts of the epistle are, as Origen recognised, "wonderful," outrunning our thought. Still it is evident that on the whole the author does mean us to believe that our sin is forgiven and the entrance is opened for us by an act of God in Christ which He enables us to make our own. The salvation is not worked upon us from outside as by a ritual ordinance. It is worked by inward moral connexion, as by a person influencing persons. The divine "way" is not a higher thing than influence. If it were it would be indeed beyond our understanding, but it would be also, as far as we can in any manner conceive, incapable of producing any effect upon us worthy of a personal, or, as the epistle puts it, of the living God. Christ enables men to be "perfected" when they pass along the way He made His own in His flesh. Only the perfection, the Godhead which, from the point of view taken in the epistle after the opening verses have removed the possibility of misconstruction, He attained, has raised His "influence" to such a pitch that this way may be represented not as "His own" but as "Himself": "for we are become partakers of the Christ, if we hold fast the beginning of our confidence firm unto the end," iii. 14. And with regard to that preliminary of perfection, the forgiveness of sin, a like process may be recognised. Sin is forgiven in being cleansed away. "Cleansed away" is part of the ritual imagery, and the author applies that imagery very boldly in vii. 27 ; see p. lxxxii above. Changing the metaphor—all language is but more or less metaphorical—and ignoring the details of ritual correspondence, we may suppose him to mean, not merely that our Lord bore our sins, but that He, as much as we, had to "overcome" sin, being as He was "tempted in all points like as we are." The result of that overcoming and its effect for His "brethren" has been set forth so well by Dr DuBose that it would only be darkening counsel to seek for other words :

"I do not know how better to express the truth of the matter than to say, in what seems to me to be the explicit teaching of our Epistle, and of the New Testament generally, that our Lord's whole relation to sin in our behalf was identical with our own up to the point of His unique and exceptional personal action with reference to it. Left to our nature and ourselves it overcomes and slays all us ; through God in Him He overcame and slew it. He did it not by His own will and power as man, but as man through an absolute dependence upon God. And He made both the omnipotent grace of God upon which He depended, and His own absolute dependence upon it, His perfect faith, available for us in our salvation. He re-enacts in us the victory over sin and death which was first enacted in Himself."

That is what the epistle would seem to mean by the phrase in ix. 12, αἰωνίαν λύτρωσιν εὑράμενος, "Christ through his own blood, entered in once for all into the holy place, having obtained eternal redemption."

§ 16. *This interaction of men with God is illustrated by the doctrine of the Covenant which the author developes from Jeremiah. His affinity with Jeremiah in respect of forgiveness, national crisis, freedom from religious bondage.*

That this interaction of man with God through Christ in the work of salvation is according to the mind of the epistle appears in its treatment of the Covenant in chapter viii., and of the Will in chapter x. The Covenant forms the transition from "priesthood" to the "priestly sacrifice" (ix.), and the passage about God's Will sums up the whole of the previous argument, and leads on to the appeal (x. 19 ff.) with which the final, practical section of the epistle begins.

The word by which the LXX translates the Hebrew *Berîth*, διαθήκη, means in Greek generally, though not always, a testamentary disposition rather than a covenant ; and it is possible that this meaning has to some extent shaped the author's phraseology in ix. 15—17. It is not however necessary to resort to that explanation of the passage, since the sacrifices with which God's covenants with His people were inaugurated, from Sinai to the Last Supper, sufficiently account for all that is there said. Some are of opinion that the choice of διαθήκη instead of συνθήκη in the LXX was meant to vindicate the peculiar character of the divine covenant, as originating from God and not as a merely mutual agreement between equals. That character of course it has, in accordance with the principle which underlies not this epistle only, but the whole New Testament and Old Testament also ; the principle so forcibly enunciated by S. Paul in Rom. viii. 12, "So then, brethren, we are debtors," but quite as plainly in Ex. xx. 2 f., "I am the LORD thy God, which brought thee out of the land of Egypt, out of the house of bondage. Thou shalt have none other gods before me." Nevertheless though not "merely" mutual, the divine covenant is a covenant, and mutual relations are its essence. In the quotation made by our author from Jer. xxxi. 31—34 this mutuality is emphasised by his use of the Greek instead of the Hebrew Bible. Where the Hebrew said "Which **my covenant they brake, although I was an**

husband to them, saith the LORD," his quotation from the
LXX has "For they continued not in my covenant, and I regarded them not." No one who interprets the details of Holy
Scripture by the whole will suppose this to mean that God
changed from love to indifference, but it does illustrate the
principle we have been examining, viz. that salvation is an act
of God on man as well as for him, and that the very nature of
God and man makes it impossible for God's forgiveness, though
God unceasingly forgives, to operate except when men answer
personally to His personal influence.

And it is clear that our author meant to bring the "Covenant" to bear on his doctrine of forgiveness especially. That
was one reason why he chose to quote from Jeremiah rather
than from any other part of the Old Testament. For Jeremiah's
oracle ends emphatically with forgiveness (Heb. viii. 12), and it
is just those words in the quotation which are repeated in x. 17,
at the end of the paragraph on "the Will." But there were
other reasons also for the choice. One was, we may suppose,
that the occasion of Jeremiah's utterance was so like the
occasion of this letter. Jeremiah spoke when Jerusalem was
about to fall before Nebuchadnezzar ; this letter was probably
written when the war with Rome was breaking out which was
to end in the calamity of A.D. 70. Then again Jeremiah spoke
of a "new" covenant, and it was the renewal of the ancient
covenant which our Lord inaugurated in His Blood at the Last
Supper ; see especially Luke xxii. 20. One chief reason against
laying stress on the coincidences of Heb. ix. 15—17 with the
language of testamentary law is that the governing thought
which underlies the whole is not Roman law, but Christ's
fulfilling of Israel's covenant hope on the night in which He
was betrayed and the day on which He died.

But above all, because it is the idea which pervades and
vivifies all the rest, Jeremiah's words are chosen as expressing
that ascent from shadow to reality which is the doctrinal theme
of this epistle, as it was the special revelation committed to
Jeremiah. Both authors wrote at a crisis when the institutional form of religion was being broken up. To those whom
they addressed this might well seem the end of religion itself.
In the narrower sense of the word religion—scrupulous reverence

—it was almost an end. But with the loss of outward bonds to God, Jeremiah saw the vision of a real union of the heart between Israel and God. And to some extent his vision was realised ; as in the Psalter of the post-exilic Jewish Church. Yet on another side the increasing domination of the Law made the later Jewish Church more institutionally scrupulous than before. And when Hebrews was written not only did the war with Rome threaten an abolition of these institutional bonds, but the larger spirit of Judaism itself was fretting to be free from them. The author, being a real churchman, would assure his friends, who as yet are so imperfect churchmen, that in Jesus Christ the whole difficulty is more than overcome. Quite freed from all the hamper of artificial religion, which is worn out and passing away, they may enjoy real forgiveness and enter really into the presence of God. The New Covenant of the heart is now being realised. Only it is a covenant. There must be an answer to the movement of God. And for these friends of his the answer must be given in the courageous acceptance of a dangerous duty, a painful dissociation from venerable traditions and ancestral friendships.

That practical appeal continually breaks in. It lends an ominous undertone to many phrases which have primarily a theological purpose. Thus ix. 22, " And apart from shedding of blood there is no remission," must be interpreted not only in the light of the doctrine of sacrifice generally, or of Christ's sacrifice eminently, but also of that sacrifice which was then being demanded from the readers, and is darkly foreshadowed in xii. 4, " Ye have not yet resisted unto blood." These men could not refuse to join the revolutionary standard without incurring the murderous resentment of their compatriots. All the more honourable was their willingness to listen to so academically reasoned a persuasion as their master sends them. If in his time of trial Jeremiah lifted some Judaeans from religion to heart-religion, this letter lifts its readers from religion to theology. " ' Theology,' " wrote Forbes Robinson, " is *the* thing and ' Religion ' is not, I think, nearly such a fine word. Theology is the Learning, Knowing, Studying God[1]." Hebrews,

[1] *Letters to his Friends, by Forbes Robinson,* p. 67.

a letter to men who may soon be martyrs, testifies more than any other book of the New Testament to the moral force of good theology.

§ 17. *This thought of interaction is carried further in the doctrine of the Will:*

The mutual, personal significance of the Covenant is developed in x. 1—18 into the still intenser theology of the Will. A short passage concerning the old sacrifices introduces this. The obvious purpose is to contrast the fictional value of a brute's blood with the real value of a person's willing act. But what has just been said about "undertones" applies here too. After all there was something not altogether unreal in these fictional sacrifices. They "called to mind"; they moved the heart. By the mere "doing" of these sacrifices nothing would ever be produced like in kind to the sacrifice of Christ. Yet the offerers wanted to become like Christ; good priests led priestly lives and helped Israelites to become like Christ; they, as well as the writer of this epistle, could deduce Christlike teaching from their sacrificial system. Another quotation from Mr Forbes Robinson well expresses this quasi-typical relationship of the Jewish sacrificial law. "It dimly hints (as sacrificial law in other nations does) at the fact that the ground of the universe is self-sacrifice—that the ground of all human, whether family or national, life is a filial sacrifice."

The Psalms however touch the reality which the Law "dimly hints." And from a psalm the author takes words which he could place quite appropriately into the mouth of our Lord as He entered upon His ministry, a ministry which overpassed the artificial bounds of Judaism and was to transform the whole world (x. 5). "I come," He said, "to do thy will, O God." The ritual imagery is for a moment dropped. The argument winds inward to the soul of truth. Christ did God's will. There was His sacrifice. That sacrifice becomes real for us when we make it our own by doing God's will as He did. Yet the two efforts, His and ours, even before they coincide, are not separate. For here is the secret power of influence again. Once He had perfectly done God's will, it became more possible for us to attempt the same, at last possible for us to succeed. That secret power is deep in the constitution of the ordered universe, the "cosmos." For in the cosmos there is but one real will, namely God's. Self will, or feeble will, in men is but their refusal of absolutely free will. For absolute freedom is security in God from all the obligations of shifting slaveries (cf. ii. 15). If, leaving what we fancy to be our private wills, we enter God's will, we are borne irresistibly on therein, "consecrated" to perfect activity ; and this entry into God's will has been opened for us by the sacrifice of Christ. He having learned obedience by suffering, at last, at the moment of His final obedience, lost and found His will perfectly in God's. That uniquely perfect consecration of a man's will to God, one perfected Son's to the Father of all, has had supreme influence ; it has, so to say, righted the tottering destiny of man. From that moment the ideal of perfect consecration has been brought again within the range of men's practical aim. Yet, since that aim is practical, they must submit to the discipline of gradually working it out.

§ 18. *which in this epistle is concentrated upon the one act of will, first wrought by Christ in dying, now to be made their own in the particular duty of the readers.*

Thus perhaps we may paraphrase the carefully distinguished tenses, ἡγιασμένοι ἐσμέν (with the supplement διὰ τῆς προσφορᾶς …ἐφάπαξ, cf. vii. 27, ix. 12, 26, 28), τετελείωκεν τοὺς ἁγιαζομένους. With the idea, here suggested, of that last present participle compare ποιῶν in the final blessing, xiii. 20 f. That may be taken to imply that, whereas the writer prays for his friends that they may do their one hard duty and so enter the will of God, he himself has already made that entry, and would have God carry on his gradual sanctification. A like thought of gradual sanctification may be involved in the two participles of ii. 11, ὅ τε ἁγιάζων καὶ οἱ ἁγιαζόμενοι, and again in the present tense of εἰσερχόμεθα εἰς τὴν κατάπαυσιν of iv. 3 as contrasted with the immediately following aorist οἱ πιστεύσαντες, "we who made the initial entry into God's will when we embraced the faith of the Church are continually pressing deeper into the peace of that will." For the two chapters on the Rest of God contain a preliminary sketch of the doctrine of God's will; cf. ii., iii. with x., and (as illustrative parallel) Dante's " E la sua volontate è nostra pace" with S. Augustine's "Quia fecisti nos ad te, et inquietum est cor nostrum donec requiescat in te."

Yet it must remain doubtful whether this thought of gradual sanctification is in harmony with the mind of this epistle; whether these present tenses are not more properly interpreted, in this epistle, of the one great conversion of will, repeated in all those who from time to time are brought into the allegiance of Christ. For, true though the other thought is generally, in this epistle the stress is almost entirely on the one decisive act. The one moment of Christ's offering His sacrifice, the one sin which may prove irreparable, the one brave act of duty which the readers are called to perform : these are the eminent ideas, and the last of them explains why. This epistle was written with one special purpose, to induce certain waverers to become by one decisive act whole-hearted followers of Christ, and this purpose moulds the whole shape of its theology.

Thus S. Paul's doctrine of the faithful being "in Christ" is known to our author, but is not much dwelt upon in the epistle. It would naturally be known to him, for S. Paul, who made it so vital and profound, did not discover it, but with the whole of the primitive Church inherited· it from Judaism. "The Christ of the LORD" had been to early Israel the king who represented the nation. Sometimes it was used as a title for the nation itself. So this author uses it, of course with a widening of the original application, in his quotation from Ps. lxxxix. 50 f. in xi. 26. In the later Jewish Church "The Christ" was recognised as a person, the King of the expected kingdom of Heaven, but the idea of inclusive representation was preserved. There was no Christ apart from his people, and, as in Dan. vii., he could be considered as almost embodying in himself "the saints of the Most High" who were to "possess the kingdom for ever." This conception of the Christ including all the faithful, "the Christ that is to be," was grandly developed by S. Paul in the Epistle to the Ephesians[1]. In Hebrews it appears more nearly in its Jewish

---

[1] See the *Commentary* and the *Exposition* by the Dean of Wells.

simplicity, as in iii. 14, "For we are become partakers of the Christ, if we hold fast the beginning of our confidence firm unto the end." Here we have the "in Christ" doctrine, but it is coupled with an "if," and that "if" is just what prevents the writer from developing it further. He had to concentrate all his might on the preliminary task of urging his friends to make the doctrine their own by loyalty to Jesus Christ,—a particular act of loyalty to the definitely envisaged person of the Lord. S. Paul, even in our author's place, might have preferred to say, "Believe that you are in Christ and you will be able to do this hard duty." Our author found it better to say, "Follow Christ loyally, do this duty, and you will know what it is to share with Him the peace of God."

His way may seem a lower way than S. Paul's. But it ought not to be so understood. His trust in the all-embracing will of God, and in the already perfected sacrifice of Christ, allows him to lay this emphasis on duty. Though he urges his friends to make their effort, he is aware of all that is being divinely done for them; their effort will not be the initial impulse in the whole complex purpose of God for their salvation. And he knew his friends, and knew what arguments would best prevail with them. They were men of fine and romantic honour and the appeal to loyalty would come home to them. Their conception of the mystery of Christ's Person was imperfect, and they could not understand properly what "in Christ" implied. Their interest in His earthly life, and the imaginative form which, if the epistle was congenial to them, thought seems to have generally taken in their minds, all this was good reason for pressing the romantic, imaginative, sacramental idea of following Christ, rather than the mystical idea of union in Christ.

§ 19. *And such concentration was natural in the crisis which the author recognised as a "coming" of Christ.*

And there was yet another peculiarity in their circumstances which made them apt to be "followers" of Christ as "captain" (cf. ii. 10, xii. 2). In the troubles of these times He was "coming," and He was coming to call His soldiers after

Him. That is a picture which is repeatedly presented in the Apocalypse. If the Apocalypse and Hebrews be not both connected with the revolt against Rome, it is at least evident that they are both connected with some crisis of like character. In the eschatological discourse of our Lord which precedes the Passion in each of the synoptic Gospels, it is difficult to avoid recognising a premonition of the fall of Jerusalem mingling with the prophecy of the final "coming" of the Son of man. Nor is it unreasonable to suppose that our Lord and other observers of the signs of the times foresaw such a conclusion to the increasing zeal of the patriots. In S. Luke's version of the discourse it seems plain that a prediction of the fall of Jerusalem is followed and completed by a prediction of the great Advent. That advent filled the horizon of the early Church. Had one of its members been asked, What is the Christian hope? he would have answered without hesitation, The coming of our Lord as Christ. And that is the hope which fills this epistle. But it is no longer a hope for the quite near future; as it was when S. Paul wrote to the Thessalonians, but not when he wrote to the Ephesians. In Hebrews, as in Ephesians, a vista opens into a long future for the Church. Writer and readers are breaking with a past which is dear to them, but regret is transformed into a vigorous outlook upon a new world (cf. τὴν οἰκουμένην τὴν μέλλουσαν, ii. 5). When once the πειρασμὸς is over, youth will be renewed under the banner of Jesus Christ (cf. xii. 24, διαθήκης νέας μεσίτῃ). And to the writer, as to S. Luke, the revelation has occurred, that "the advent" is a mystery with many senses. Whatever the great final "coming" may be, Christ can come at another time and in another way; and in the then imminent crisis he believed that Christ was really coming. That seems the evident meaning of x. 25, "...exhorting one another, and so much the more, as ye see the day drawing nigh." In the atmosphere of this thought we catch undertones—such as we have already observed to be natural to our author—in i. 6, "when he again bringeth in the firstborn into the world," or even ix. 28, "so Christ also, having been once offered to bear the sins of many, shall appear a second time, apart from sin, to them that wait for him, unto salvation."

§ 20. *This crisis explains the three passages in which*
repentance seems to be limited.

A crisis was at hand. In that crisis Christ was coming;
it was, so to say, the first stage in the realisation of all that the
traditional hope of His advent meant. The crisis would bring
the readers of the epistle face to face with a definite choice
between loyalty to Him and apostasy. The choice was of
infinite importance; its effects would reach into the sphere of
eternal realities; if they made the wrong choice it was more
than uncertain whether they would ever find opportunity for
correcting it. Take no thought for doubtful morrows but do
your duty to day, is the burden of the letter. And this concentrated anxiety of the writer ·for his friends explains those
three remarkable passages, vi. 4—8, x. 26—31, xii. 16 f., in
which he might seem to be denying the possibility of repeated
repentance. If the letter were a general treatise of theology,
laying down general rules for all Christians of all times, it
would be natural to interpret his words in that manner. The
special occasion of this, not treatise but letter, makes all the
difference.

Nevertheless "no second repentance" has been understood
at different times to be his teaching (cf. Intr. II. §§ 3, 13
pp. xxvii f., lxiii ff.). Tertullian so understood him. So does
his latest commentator Dr Windisch, whose detached note on
"The denial of the second repentance" is a valuable summary of
material for forming a judgement on the question. He argues
that the rigour of Hebrews was a logical development of the
original principle of the Church. This principle was inherited
from the Old Testament. The Law had allowed no forgiveness
for any but sins "of ignorance"; see e.g. Num. xv. 28—31.
Ezekiel implies the same in his chapter, xviii., on the wicked
man turning away from his wickedness and finding life. This
inherited principle had been intensified by the eschatology from
which the gospel started; when the Kingdom, into which the
Christian was called, was immediately expected, there was no
"place for repentance" after the one absolute repentance which
constituted his entry into the Kingdom. S. Paul implicitly,

and without perhaps conscious reflexion on the problem, held the same doctrine. That is evident from 2 Cor. vii. 10, "For godly sorrow worketh repentance unto salvation not to be repented of—μετάνοιαν εἰς σωτηρίαν ἀμεταμέλητον—but the sorrow of the world worketh death." And though it cannot be said that this austere rule was universal in the primitive Church, we do find it again in 1 John v. 16 f., "If any man see his brother sinning a sin not unto death, he shall ask, and God will give him life for them that sin not unto death. There is a sin unto death : not concerning this do I say that he should make request. All unrighteousness is sin : and there is a sin not unto death." This precept is probably connected with the passages in Hebrews, and with our Lord's word about the sin against the Holy Ghost. In fact the proclamation of forgiveness for all the world through the death of Christ involved constancy as an inherent condition. A second repentance for those who fell away from the new life thus given was impossible, except by some special command from God Himself. Such special command, for a certain limited period, was declared in the Apocalypse (ii. 5, 16, 21 f., iii. 3, 15—19 ; cf. xiv. 6 f.), and ten years later in the Shepherd of Hermas. Yet even this was but a particular indulgence, a second repentance, not a repentance that might be repeated yet again. On the other hand the epistle of Clement of Rome witnesses to a milder doctrine which was accepted in a large part of the early Church, and which became presently the general rule. The Fathers explain away the rigour of Hebrews by interpreting its language as denying second baptism but not repeated repentance.

It would not be fair to decide for or against Dr Windisch from this free sketch of his argument. Yet what we have described as his hard literalism (cf. p. lxiv f.) is evident. In the notes on Heb. vi. 4 ff. reasons will be found for supposing that the question of "second repentance" is not raised by this passage at all. The readers had been wondering whether they had not better go back to the simplicity of their ancestral Jewish faith and find a good practical "repentance" in so doing. Their friend tells them that this would be in the nature of things impossible, since to do this would be to dishonour the allegiance they have already given to Jesus as Christ. Plain honour demands faithfulness to Him. No complicated doubts about other claims of honour can annul that claim. How is it conceivable then that a new and better life can be attained in a continued state of base apostasy? A quotation Dr Windisch makes from Philo—different though his application of Philo's thought is—may be used to describe the situation : ὁ γὰρ ἀμνηστίαν ἐφ' οἷς ἥμαρτεν αἰτούμενος οὐχ οὕτως ἐστὶ κακοδαίμων, ὥστ' ἐν ᾧ χρόνῳ παλαιῶν ἀδικημάτων αἰτεῖται λύσιν ἕτερα καινοτομεῖν, *de spec. leg.* I. 193, p. 240.

This explanation of Heb. vi. 4 ff. will hardly win assent from those who recognise no connexion between the epistle and the Jewish revolt. But if any other severe crisis be taken as the occasion of writing, it will be easy to understand all the three passages on repentance in a different sense from Dr Windisch. The author is not enunciating a rule of church discipline. He is impressing the extreme peril of the situation upon his own friends. Nothing, he urges, can be compared with the gravity of this choice before you. The wrong choice will be a grievous sin. It is the one sin in all the world for you, and this choice is your one great chance. The time is perilous. In the coming disturbances you may die, or you may be involved in an inextricable tangle of evil. You will certainly not have another chance of Christian nobility like this ; it may well prove that, this neglected, you may never find the opportunity again of salvation through Christ whom you now dishonour[1].

[1] As these lines are being written a parallel is offered in the Archbishop of Canterbury's sermon in Westminster Abbey, Sunday Oct. 1, 1916—the opening message of the National Mission of Repentance and Hope: "It seems to me almost certain that if this opportunity goes by unused, it can never, never come again. Wait till six months after the war is over, and the new start, possible now, will be unattainable. At present all is tense and keen ; the spirit of sacrifice, the spirit of readiness to offer ourselves and what we love, is 'in the air.'" *Times*, Oct. 2, 1916.

§ 21. *Repentance is based upon the sacrifice offered once for all, which nevertheless must be repeated in each disciple.*

In the prayer, xiii. 20 f., with which the author concludes, the sacramental correspondence is recapitulated between the trial and the one decisive victory of the Lord Jesus in His earthly life, and the trial through which the readers are going and the one decisive duty they have to do. And the sacrificial aspect of the victory is presented in the phrase ἐν αἵματι διαθήκης αἰωνίου. This preoccupation with the need of one decisive act of will on the part of his friends may have been part of the impulse which led the writer to select the analogy of priesthood for his fresh exposition of the traditional doctrine of Christ's Person and work. For a sacrifice is an offering. The essential, generous work of a priest is to offer gifts, v. 1. It is involved in the very idea of a gift, an offering, a sacrifice, that it should be given "once for all." If it could be repeated that would mean that something had been kept back in the first giving. So far then as the analogy goes there could be but one sacrifice of Christ, offered once for all. And there is more than the truth of analogy in this. There is the emotional truth that this sacrifice, being what it was, the dreadful crucifixion, cannot be thought of as repeated, ix. 26, and even the prolongation of it, as it were (ἀνασταυροῦντας, vi. 6), by men's continued or repeated unfaithfulness would be a horrible thing. And there is the satisfaction of our need for full assurance of full free pardon ; the sacrifice is "full, perfect and sufficient," x. 14, ix. 14. Hence the greatest stress is laid in the epistle on this offering once for all. There is no repetition ; nor can the sacrifice be styled "eternal," since such an epithet might, by confusion between its temporal and moral senses, lead to misunderstanding. In ix. 14 διὰ πνεύματος αἰωνίου could not be changed into εἰς τὸν αἰῶνα without ambiguity, nor into εἰς τὸ διηνεκές without inaccuracy.

Nevertheless something is implied in διὰ πνεύματος αἰωνίου which obliges us to consider rather more carefully what we mean when we assert that the sacrifice of Christ is neither repeated nor continuous. The argument from the nature of a gift or offering becomes fallacious as soon as the offering is

pictured in the mind materially and the material picture
allowed to direct our moral apprehension of the truth.   If we
think of Christ's sacrifice as it was sacramentally worked out
on earth, it culminates in the moment of His death.   If we
insist on the ritual imagery, that moment is alone the moment
of sacrifice.   But if we let the ritual imagery go and think of
what Christ did for our salvation in His earthly course, it seems
highly artificial to separate His teaching, obedience, faith and
suffering from His death, as though the ministry were merely
moral, the death alone effectual.   For what is "merely moral"?
And how does "moral" differ from "spiritual"?   And how can
a single act be cut away from the whole process of character?
In like manner we may imagine Christ's heavenly work beginning at the moment of His death, now pictured as His
entrance into the presence of God.   At that moment He
"offers," and the offering is completed.   But just as to S. Paul
He who was once crucified abides for evermore the crucified one
(ἐσταυρωμένος), so we may think of the High Priest abiding for
ever in the state of "one who has offered."   That is to say in
modern phrase, "He pleads the sacrifice"; in the words of the
epistle, "He ever liveth to make intercession for us."   But how
difficult it is to explain what we mean by the intercession or the
pleading as distinct from the offering.   We try to do so, and
fail.   The suspicion will occur to us that we are trying to do an
impossible thing, viz. to express what is spiritually real as a
whole, in the analytic language of "appearance."   So it is when
we ask, Was there a beginning of time?   Is there a boundary
to space? and (must we not add?) "When did our Lord become
High Priest?"   In ii. 17 the present tense of ἱλάσκεσθαι is
much to be noticed.   There, at any rate, though a ritual term
is employed and Christ's work is conceived as "propitiation"
rather than "salvation," it is not contemplated as an instan-
taneous process.

Of that word however Dr DuBose writes thus: "The use of
the present tense, instead of the aorist, expresses the fact that
Christ's single, and once for all completed, act of (on the part
of humanity) self-reconciliation or at-one-ment with God, is
continuously being re-enacted in and by us, as we by His en-
abling grace and aid are enduring temptation and attaining

victory, are dying His death and rising into His life." That
may appear too subtle an exegesis of the isolated word. But
the more the epistle is studied as a whole, the more reasonable,
after all, will it prove. As S. Paul, using the figure of birth,
writes to the Galatians as though Christ should be born again
in them, Gal. iv. 19, so this author, using the figure of priesthood, writes to his friends as though they were in their own
persons to offer the sacrifice of Christ again; notice especially
xiii. 12 f. The parallel is the closer because the Galatians, like
these readers, were already Christians but needed to make a
fresh definite choice of action if they were to be fully Christian.
"My little children, of whom I am again in travail until Christ
be formed in you," is exactly like "Since Jesus suffered sacri-
ficially without the gate, let us go forth unto him without the
camp, bearing his reproach." How far the author of Hebrews
was influenced in the conduct of his analogy from priesthood by
the eucharistic service of the Church is a doubtful, if it is even
a proper question. But in the eucharistic service of the Church
in England there is a striking illustration of this idea of the
repeating of the one completed sacrifice in the persons of the
worshippers. In the prayer of consecration memorial and
dramatic representation is made of the "full, perfect, and
sufficient sacrifice," as it was first prefigured by the Saviour
himself at the Last Supper; in the following prayer that
sacrifice is re-enacted in the words "And here we offer and
present unto thee, O Lord, ourselves, our souls and bodies to
be a reasonable holy and lively sacrifice unto thee." In this
prayer it is made clear, as in the epistle, that the re-enacting
depends on the preceding completion. It might be suspected
that the separation of the second prayer from the first, with
which it was originally combined, is an instance of that bondage
to the analogy and that inopportunely logical analysis which
has unnecessarily multiplied the theological problems of the
epistle.

§ 22.   *And though, after that initial re-enacting of the one sacri-*
fice, S. Paul, S. John and Hebrews uphold the ideal of
sinlessness, they acknowledge means for the renewal of the
faithful if they do sin.

The truth might be put in this way. Though, on the one
hand, the epistle represents Christ's priesthood as culminating
in the one sacrifice, and concentrates its exhortation on the one
duty of the readers, yet on the other hand, Christ's priesthood
as a whole is its theme, and it was recognised as a canonical
scripture in virtue of its universal appeal. So regarded, the
narrower view of its doctrine of repentance appears impossible.
How can that view be thought consistent with vii. 24 f. ? "But
he, because he abideth for ever, hath his priesthood unchangeable. Wherefore also he is able to save to the uttermost them
that draw near unto God through him, seeing he ever liveth to
make intercession for them." The words are as wide as those
of our Lord, "Come unto me, all ye that labour and are heavy
laden, and I will give you rest...and him that cometh to me
I will in no wise cast out," Matt. xi. 28, John vi. 37. Neither in
this epistle, nor elsewhere in the New Testament, is the rule
of ecclesiastical discipline provided. All still moves in the
region of ideals. And the difficulty is not in the stern denial
of repentance but in the unattainable (as it seems to us) hope of
perfection.

S. Paul takes for granted that Christians have really risen
to a new life in Christ and are really free from sin. His
converts did sin, and he deals with their sins as he is inspired
to deal with them severally, cf. 1 Cor. v. 4 f. with 1 Cor. vii. 6, 25.
He goes so far as to deliver an unrepentant member of the
Church "unto Satan for the destruction of the flesh that the
spirit may be saved in the day of the Lord Jesus," 1 Cor. v. 5.
And as soon as an obstinate sinner does repent he rejoices in
his restoration, 2 Cor. ii. 5 ff. In this case extreme measures
appear to have been taken which were not generally necessary.
The main point is that in S. Paul's epistles we see Christians
guilty of sins, and yet the apostle abates nothing of his ideal of
perfect holiness. He is not laying down a rule, but undauntedly

insisting on the true life with its immense hopefulness. In the
first epistle of S. John the same ideal is insisted upon. By
this time the ardour of first conversion is no longer universal in
the Church and a twofold difficulty is arising. Commonplace
sins are frequent, and since these are inconsistent with the
ideal, some are inclined to maintain that such faults are not
actual sins. S. John answers that they are, and that whenever
a man commits them he falls out of the new life into which he
has been born : yet through the blood of Jesus he may recover
the perfect holiness. And there is no need for Christians to
sin ; his letter is written that they may not sin. If they will
but be true to the power of the new birth they will not
sin: 1 John i. 7—10, ii. 1, iii. 4—6, v. 18. But, secondly,
Christians are sometimes guilty of such sin that it is plain
they intend to persist in it, so plain that there would be in-
sincerity in praying for them. To this S. John does not answer
"You must not pray for them," but very guardedly, "There is
a sin unto death : not concerning this do I say that one should
make request." He recognises the real difficulty, and insists
upon sincerity in intercession. Whether there would be any
limit to his own intercession he does not say.

Hebrews stands in a manner outside this line of development because of the very special circumstances which called it
forth. But in the important matter of the ideal the author
is entirely at one with S. Paul and S. John. There is no
faltering in his hope. Christ's redemption (ix. 12), salvation
(i. 14), kingdom (xii. 28), sacrifice, all mean that Christians like
Christ are to be perfect. If we ask in astonishment whether
it is really to be supposed possible that a man should go through
his whole earthly life without any sin, we are indeed involved in
a difficulty, for our Lord did nothing less than that. But it is
not the interesting practical question. Our Lord did indeed no
less than that, but He did so much more. His progress ending
in perfection ; His being χωρὶς ἁμαρτίας and learning obedience
till at last He was κεχωρισμένος ἀπὸ τῶν ἁμαρτωλῶν (iv. 15,
vii. 26 ; cf. ix. 28) ; this is the great pattern. There is the same
paradox ; He is one with men yet supreme among them, in this
matter of sinlessness as in the whole mystery of His Person.
Yet that does not make the union unreal. The unreality comes

in from our reasoning by negatives. It is transmuted when we act upon the bold hope. One who strove manfully for right and conquered sins one by one in himself, would obviously be nearer to the perfect goodness of Christ, than one who committed no "sin" and lived a useless ignoble life.

§ 23. *Is this re-enacting of Christ's sacrifice accomplished in the death of self-will, or is bodily death the ultimate necessity? In the apostolic age this question would not seem important.*

Or we may put it thus : our perfection is the ideal which we go through life to realise ; but the Lord Jesus, as man, achieved that ideal : ii. 8 f., x. 9 f., 14. Does the epistle promise that we may in this life realise the ideal? In 1 John iii. 2 f. the realisation seems to wait till the great Advent. "Beloved, now are we children of God, and it is not yet made manifest what we shall be. We know that if he shall be manifested, we shall be like him ; for we shall see him as he is. And every one that hath this hope set on him purifieth himself even as he is pure." S. John substitutes "manifestation," or the showing of One already present but invisible, for "advent," παρουσία, as of One coming from another place ; but no doubt he has the great final manifestation in view[1]. With this we may compare Heb. ix. 28. But in xii. 23 another thought appears. In the heavenly Jerusalem there are already "the spirits of just men made perfect." Mr F. Field wrote of this[2]: "To avoid ambiguity a slight change is necessary ; namely 'to the spirits of just men who have been made perfect.' It is the *just men*, not the *spirits*, that are made perfect, and that not in the future state, but here on earth, where alone they can be subject to those trials and conflicts, by the patient endurance of which they are prepared for a higher state of being." He quotes examples of

[1] See Dr Brooke's note on the passage in the *International Critical Commentary*, and especially p. xxi of his Introduction.

[2] *Otium Norvicense* (*Pars tertia, Notes on selected passages of N.T.*, 1881 ; second edition published by Cambridge University Press in 1899 with title *Notes on Translation of the New Testament*).

misunderstanding of the English version. One from Archbishop Sumner's *Exposition on Ephesians* will here suffice : "The inheritance of the purchased possession when 'the spirits of just men' will be 'made perfect,' no longer clouded by the pains and anxieties which attend a fallen state." Sumner is certainly wrong and Field right. Yet there was possibly something ·in the author's mind which he has missed. There is in the epistle, combined with the idea of progressive discipline and progressive salvation, that other line of thought in which stress is laid on the decisive, culminating moment. It would seem that death, as the crowning act of life, is considered to be the moment of a man's perfecting. At death, or through death, the ideal is realised. This is well put by a writer in the *Cowley Evangelist*, April 1895 (reprinted July 1914) :

"Our Lord is leading all who are following the movements of His Holy Spirit to the *true balance* of their being. Some He deals with more strenuously and rapidly by giving them early opportunities of embracing His will, when to do so means to embrace what is hard for flesh and blood ; but sooner or later, if life is here at all prolonged, there must come the occasion when the will either surrenders itself afresh to Him in some time of great trial, or sinks back upon itself, only too soon to energize in movements of rebellion against the Divine will. It is by such ways that He reveals to men that they cannot 'live by bread alone, but by every word which proceedeth out of the mouth of God.' They are led a step nearer to the perception of what it is to be nourished by God's very life in the abeyance of all else. And all are being led to this attitude who rightly are preparing for the end, for this abeyance is a marked characteristic of death, and will be, to such as are prepared to receive it, the *blessing* which accompanies death's chastening discipline."

Almost every sentence in this quotation illustrates some point in the practical or the doctrinal exhortations of the epistle. And it indicates a right answer to a question which will have already occurred to any one who reads these notes, viz. Is the sacrifice in which we re-enact the sacrifice of Christ effected by bodily death only or also by the death of our self-will ? S. Paul would surely say that it is certainly by the death of our self-will : "I have been crucified with Christ ; yet I live ;

and yet no longer I but Christ liveth in me : and that life which I now live in the flesh I live in faith, the faith which is in the Son of God, who loved me, and gave himself up for me," Gal. ii. 20. The same answer, implied by the whole of this epistle, becomes explicit in xi. 17, where the change from the aorist of LXX to the perfect προσενήνοχεν of the quotation seems designed to show the reality, and the abiding reality, of the sacrifice of Isaac. Isaac was not slain, but he was truly sacrificed, and that sacrifice has become the type of the consecrated life of the Israel of God, and of every losing and finding of man's will in the will of God which shall have been consummated since.

Indeed the question would have been less insistent to the New Testament writers than it is to us. To them the great day for each believer was "the day" of Christ's advent or manifestation, not the day of death. And to them the life that is hid with Christ in God was so absolutely the only real life, that death was quite naturally contemplated as one act, however decisive, in the unbroken life, already being lived, of eternity. Whether that decisive act came through the "chastening discipline" of physical death, or of some earlier hour of supreme renunciation, was hardly a distinction to be dwelt upon. Perhaps in quiet times it would seem the one, in times of persecution and martyrdom the other. And, if our hypothesis be accepted, Hebrews was written at a time when martyrdom threatened. Hence in Hebrews the solemn thought of—what we should call—literal death is never far from the surface. That kind of death is chiefly glorified in this epistle; it is the longed-for "perfecting." Cf. § 14, p. xcvii f.

Yet it should also be noticed that in xi. 39 f. the Old Testament saints, celebrated in the whole preceding chapter, are said either to have waited for their perfecting till the times of Christ ; or to be still waiting, in at least partial dependence on the faithfulness of the then "militant" generation, as contributing to their perfection. With the former explanation it might seem apposite to compare 1 Pet. iii. 18 ff. Yet that is an imperfect parallel, since the heroes of Hebrews are very different from the spirits, once disobedient, in prison. And the picture which immediately follows in Heb. xii. 1 ff., of the contest to be endured by Christ's followers on earth and witnessed to by these heroes in their state of waiting, lends probability to the latter. The inconsistency vanishes if, as the arrangement of clauses in xii. 22 ff. also indicates, "the spirits of just men made perfect" are the deceased members, the *pausantes* of the Christian Church.

§ 24. *In Hebrews, as in Apocalypse, special interest in the blessed dead is shewn. The general doctrine of N.T. on this subject.*

Or perhaps Christian martyrs in particular. Among other points of contact between Hebrews and the Apocalypse is their common interest in the blessed dead. Between the writing of 1 Cor. xv. and of these two books something has happened which has multiplied, or is multiplying, the number of deceased Christians. And there are four passages in the Apocalypse which throw light on the language of Hebrews:

"(1) vi. 9—12, the vision of 'the souls' under the altar, the martyred prophets of the Old Covenant, who were to wait till the complement of the martyrs of the New had come in. For as Heb. xi. 40 says, 'they apart from us' cannot 'be made perfect.' These are clothed in white raiment and are, I imagine, merged in those who keep coming out of the great tribulation, also arrayed in white robes in vii. 13 ff., to be shepherded by the Lamb.

"(2) Look next at xiv. 13. 'Blessed are the dead that die in the Lord from this time forth. Yea, saith the Spirit, may they rest from their toiling, for their works follow with them.' This rest is not inactivity. Their powers trained by their earthly activities are from henceforth to find full scope without friction.

"(3) When we pass on to xix. 14, we are given a vision of the armies that are in heaven riding on white horses, clothed in the vesture of the Bride of the Lamb, going out to fight under their Captain Christ.

"(4) Then in xx. 4 we come back once more to the Christian martyrs, who have been faithful in their witness, and who live and reign with Christ during the mystic Millennium of the chaining of Satan. This we are told is 'the first Resurrection.'"

These paragraphs are quoted from an article in the *Church Quarterly Review*, April 1916, by Dr J. O. F. Murray, on "The Empty Tomb, the Resurrection Body and the Intermediate State." From this article, with the author's permission, some further extracts shall be made[1].

"The Resurrection of Christ is the manifestation of a force in the Universe, which, because it has been seen in operation in one instance, may be trusted to work universally....But the working of the Resurrection power, which had been manifested in the raising of Christ as the first-fruits, was not to be seen in operation again until 'the Appearing,' and then only in the case of Christians....An intermediate state is implied, not only in the doctrine of the descent into Hades, but also in the dating of the Resurrection on the third day."

"The fact seems to be that 'Resurrection,' like 'Death' and 'Life,' is a term of manifold significance, and admits of many stages and degrees....The questions of practical importance for us are two...(1) Where do we stand with regard to the 'Appearing' which St. Paul expected in his own generation? And (2) to what extent are we here and now contributing to the evolution of our spiritual bodies, building up 'the habitation, the building from God, made without hands, eternal in the heavens,' which we are to inhabit hereafter?"

Here, with regard to the first point, Dr Murray calls attention to the four passages in the Apocalypse to which we referred above. He proceeds thus:

"The sequence of events implied [in those four passages] seems to me remarkably parallel in general outline to the scheme laid down by St. Paul in 1 Cor. xv. And I am prepared to take as my working hypothesis the view that we are living now in this 'Millennium': that we are or may be, in proportion to our faith, here and now citizens of the New Jerusalem, and that, again in proportion to our faith, it is true for us that 'there is no more death'; that in fact our Lord's promises are strictly true : 'Whosoever loseth his life for my sake finds it,' not after an indefinite period, but immediately [and so S. John viii. 51, xi. 26]. Such believers have part in the first Resurrection. What further fulness of life may lie before them at the second Resurrection when the whole race reaches its consummation

[1] Cf. also "The Ascension and Whitsunday," by Father R. M. Benson, reprinted from "The Life beyond the grave," in *The Cowley Evangelist*, May 1915, especially pp. 108—112.

and each member of it is uplifted by the energy of the whole who can say ?...Meanwhile they are in life not in death, and their life is not 'disembodied.' The souls are clothed, not naked. For them Christ has come again."

With regard to the second point : "What conception can we form of the nature of our spiritual bodies ? To what extent are we here and now contributing to their evolution ?," Dr Murray finds

"that, in 1 Cor. xv. 42, St. Paul must mean 'this life in corruptible flesh in the body of our humiliation is the sowing time, the harvest will come under the transformed conditions of the body of our glory.' Certainly according to the best text he calls us expressly to begin at once to wear (xv. 49) 'the image of the heavenly,' an expression that corresponds closely to his injunction to us in Col. iii. 5 'to mortify our members that are upon earth...stripping off the old man with his ways of action, and clothing ourselves with the new after the image of Him that created Him,' further defined as 'compassion, kindness, humility, meekness,' and so forth. In other words, personal character is the most practical form under which we can conceive of our spiritual body."

"And we may conceive of the condition of the rest of the dead, 'who lived not' and have no part in the first Resurrection, not as 'disembodied,' but as in various stages of imperfect, arrested or perverted, spiritual development, without as yet the organs by which they can enter into relation with the life that is life indeed. Such a view would, I think, be in harmony with such indications as the New Testament gives us. There does not seem to be anything in the New Testament to justify the view, which has no doubt coloured all our Christian thinking for centuries, that 'soul and body meet again' at the Resurrection."

Dr Murray, though referring oftenest to S. Paul, attempts here to form a view that shall be harmonious with the New Testament as a whole. And according to this view Hebrews appears consistent in itself and with the other apostolic writings. If in ix. 27 judgement seems to follow immediately upon death, that judgement is κρίσις, a distinguishing, such as Dr Murray recognises between those who have and those who have not part in the first Resurrection. The κρίματος αἰωνίου of vi. 2 might be thought to stand in contrast with this as "final judgement," and if so the juxtaposition of ἀναστάσεως νεκρῶν might seem after all to imply that, for that final judgement, "soul and body meet again." But the reference here is probably to Jewish rather than to Christian doctrine ; ἀναστάσεως is at any rate used in no more confined a sense here than in κρείττονος ἀναστάσεως, xi. 35 ; and two considerations make it improbable that the author thought of the blessed dead as obliged to wait till a "last day." for the receiving of the spiritual body. One is the phrase in xii. 23, πνεύμασι δικαίων τετελειωμένων : the other is his silence concerning our Lord's resurrection "on the third day."

§ 25. *Application of general doctrine to Hebrews: "spirits" are not "disembodied."*

As for the first of these, the phrase in xii. 23 expresses "perfection." If there is anything in the epistle which corresponds to the partaking in the first resurrection it must be recognised here. But the word πνεύμασι might seem to contradict this. Surely not ; it is our presupposition, disproved by Dr Murray's careful analysis of the evidence, that in the New Testament "intermediate" means "disembodied," which makes us fancy this. This use of "spirit" for all that is essential in man is found in the Old Testament. In Dan. iii. 86 (LXX) "spirits and souls of the righteous," Sirach xxxi. 14, and other places, it is joined with a following genitive ; but in Sirach xxxix. 28, 2 Macc. iii. 24 (according to Codex A) it stands absolutely. It is a natural development of the expression "living soul" for a creature endowed with animal life, and S. Paul has given it the utmost dignity by his antithesis in 1 Cor. xv. 45, "The first man Adam became a living soul. The last Adam became a life-giving spirit." Since ψυχή represents the unseen natural life, in distinction from its vehicle the visible body, and since again πνεῦμα represents the more inward, more essential divine life in man, as distinguished from its mortal vehicle, πνεῦμα is especially used of men in their "freedom from the burden of the flesh." So S. Paul in 1 Cor. v. 5 would deliver the guilty man unto Satan for the destruction of the flesh, that the spirit may be saved in the day of the Lord Jesus ; cf. 1 Pet. iv. 6. In 1 Thess. v. 23 he writes more precisely : "The God of peace sanctify you wholly ; and may your spirit and soul and body be preserved entire, without blame at the coming of our Lord Jesus Christ." That is more characteristic, for S. Paul is distinguished among New Testament writers by his almost scientific interest in psychological analysis. Our author is more concerned with essence than with entirety, and prefers to sum man up as a spirit, or as "truly himself," x. 34. Nor does he, like S. Paul, oppose "flesh" to "body" as base to noble ; our Lord's earthly ministry is, in this epistle, "the days of his flesh"; and, in almost the same sense, the readers are bidden remember them that are evil entreated as being themselves also "in the body."

§ 26. *The author's silence about our Lord's rising on the third day is not inconsistent with the tradition of the Church.*

In like manner we read in x. 10 of "the offering of the body of Jesus Christ" and in x. 19 of "the way of his flesh." Both phrases describe His earthly, visible passion. Neither would be natural to this author when speaking of Christ ascended. Nor is there a word in the epistle about His resurrection in the body, on the third day. All is foreshortened, so to speak. At the moment of dying on the cross the Lord enters as High Priest into the heavenly sanctuary.

He enters as being then, and not till then, "made perfect." Helped as we have been by Dr Murray to clear the mind from servility to figures of speech, we shall not suspect that the author imagined the ascended Lord as lacking any of that complete manhood which is guarded by the doctrine of the resurrection of His body. And therefore, as we said above, this peculiar presentation of the Lord's victory over death guarantees a no less complete significance for the "spirits" of just men made perfect.

Whatever may be thought about the date of the three synoptic Gospels, S. Paul shews that the resurrection on the third day was included in the earliest tradition of the Church. Our epistle is the only book of the New Testament which could be quoted to suggest that this tradition was not held by the whole Church. And it is far more natural to suppose that the

silence of our author is due to the special direction he wished
to give to his argument. His analogy of the high priesthood
leads him to lay stress on the "indissoluble life," and on our
Lord's entering the sanctuary of the presence of God at the
moment of His death. According to his sacramental view of
things, the inward and outward offering of sacrifice are necessarily simultaneous. They are in fact one ; for the sacramental
idea is not an idea of succession in two worlds, but of time and
eternity, heaven and earth, being "inveterately convolved."

And he was quite at liberty to lay the stress thus. For
there is no contradiction of the general tradition. The "ascension" was but the last of our Lord's appearances after His
death ; S. Paul, who claimed to have seen Him also, would deny
that it was the last. The resting of His body in the tomb till
the third day may imply that, for our Lord Himself, there
were, as Dr Murray puts it, "stages" of resurrection. But the
immediate "bringing again of the great shepherd from the
dead" (xiii. 20) was itself ἀνάστασις ; our substitution of "resurrection," "rising again," for ἀνάστασις, "rising up," has
produced an unconscious prejudice in our mind. And yet we
may perhaps find in this author's liberty some encouragement
to hope that those who, like him, nourish faith more readily by
meditation on the invisible indissoluble life than by appeal to
the visible historical evidences for the resurrection, are not
condemned by the apostolic discipline. Only it must also be
remembered that these perhaps more philosophic thinkers have
to a great extent been secured in their liberty by the trouble-
some controversial labour of the historians, as our author and
his friends were secured by the simpler faith of the Church
around them.

§ 27. *The communion of saints is presupposed in this epistle:
    but the readers are not yet in full enjoyment of that com-
    munion.*

One further question must be answered before leaving this
part of the subject: what does this epistle teach about the
communion of saints, the intercourse between those who are
still in their earthly pilgrimage and those who have entered

into rest? That most comfortable doctrine is established more
firmly by S. Paul with his assurance that all the faithful live
one united life "in Christ"; and by S. John in all that per-
vading faith of his in the life eternal which is summed up in
the words he records of the Lord to Martha (John xi. 23 ff.),
to whom, when she had expressed belief in resurrection "at the
last day," He answered, "I am the resurrection and the life."
In Heb. xii. 22, "Ye are come unto mount Zion, etc.," falls
a little short of that. And, as in other places, the reason is
that, until the readers make their venture of faith, they have
but come near, they have not entered by the living way, x. 19 ff.
And in xii. 1 the "encompassing cloud" is a cloud of "witnesses," not of fellow saints in full communion. Yet it is
implied in xi. 40 that these witnesses are waiting in eager
expectation of that full communion. It might be said that
the epistle takes throughout for granted that belief in and
enjoyment of the communion of saints which was already part
of the fuller faith of Judaism, cf. Isa. liii. 10, 2 Macc. xv. 14,
and that it holds out to its readers, as part of the great peace
now to be grasped by them, the perfect enjoyment of such
communion as was the acknowledged heritage of the Christian
Church.

§ 28. *Hebrews and the Old Testament: quotations are reasonably developed from the original sense.*

This thought however brings us to the last division of our
enquiry. What is the relation of this epistle to the Old
Testament in general, and to that Alexandrian complement of
the Palestinian canon in particular which touches on so many
sides the Alexandrine or Philonic philosophy?

Few characteristics of the apostolic writers are more striking
than the respect they had for the authority of the Jewish Bible.
They appeal to it continually. They quote it continually, almost
learnedly; yet not quite with the fashionable learning of their
day. They appreciate the deeper meaning of its words, its inspiration in fact. But they take a reverent view of inspiration
and abstain far more than was usual with their contemporaries
in Judaism, and their successors in the Christian Church, from

forced interpretations, and unnatural Messianic applications. No doubt this was due to our Lord's influence who appears at the beginning of S. Luke's Gospel as a studious, but still more as a thoughtful boy, and who always reached so surely to the heart of all the Old Testament passages He dealt with in His ministry. Yet there are exceptions to this sobriety in the New Testament, as in Gal. iii. 16 where S. Paul argues rabbinically from the singular number of "seed." And, as might be expected in an author of finer education, the writer to the Hebrews is distinguished by his peculiarly reasonable use of the Old Testament.

This has been denied. It was once asserted by some one that, having opened his epistle with a magnificent assertion of our Lord's divinity, the author goes on to prove it by applying a number of passages from the Old Testament to Him, none of which were meant of Him at all. But that is just what he does not do. He does not attempt to prove our Lord's divinity in this place; he leaves proof to spring by degrees from the analogy which fills the epistle. What he uses the Old Testament for here is to show that He who came forth from God inherited the name of "Son" from those who of old, in the actual history of Israel, were entitled "Christ" or the "anointed of the Lord." And a like reverence for the original significance of the ancient words in their historical environment runs through the epistle. The quotation from Ps. viii. in Heb. ii. would have no point if the original reference to "mankind" were not recognised. The "to day" in the quotation from Ps. xcv. in Heb. iii., iv. gains its force from having been a summons in "David's" time to enter into the rest of God which was a repetition of an earlier opportunity. And throughout the epistle the real history of Israel is the main type, or the vehicle of the prophetic Spirit which revealed the ever-growing manifestation of the Christ through the Christ-bearing nation[1].

[1] See Hort's note on 1 Pet. i. 11 in his Commentary, *The First Epistle of St Peter* i. 1—ii. 17, *the Greek Text with Introductory Lecture, Commentary, and Additional Notes*, Macmillan, 1898.

§ 29. *In Hebrews the Holy Spirit is chiefly thought of as
the inspirer of Scripture:*

This prophetic Spirit is noticeable. The Spirit of God, as a
mighty all but personal influence, is prominent in the Old
Testament. It becomes, as revelation proceeds, the Spirit of
Messiah. And on this line of developing faith "the Spirit of
Jesus" (Acts xvi. 7), and "the Holy Spirit" as one of a Trinity
of divine Persons (2 Cor. xiii. 13), attracted the reverence of the
early Church. In Hebrews that line is not followed out. The
Spirit as the giver of the new life is not distinctly endowed with
a personality in this epistle. In that connexion the article is
never prefixed: see ii. 4, vi. 4, and x. 29 where the exception is
merely grammatical and depends upon the following genitive
with article. This impersonal manner of expression enables the
author to fill his phrase in ix. 14, διὰ πνεύματος αἰωνίου, with a
pregnancy of thought which may perhaps be better appreciated
in this present day than at any period since the epistle was
written. But in the three places where the Holy Spirit is represented as inspiring the sacred books of Israel the article is added,
iii. 7, ix. 8, x. 15. To this book-student the most distinctly
personal manifestation of the Spirit of God was as the inspirer
of the prophetic word[1]. And here again the affinity, with no less
marked differences, of Hebrews with the Apocalypse (xix. 10),
and with that other book which falls into the same group, 1 Peter
(i. 11), may be observed.

§ 30. *with whom, as it were, the author converses.*

This manifestation is indeed "personal" in the most popular
sense of the term. In one word it might be said that this
writer reads the sacred books as though he were "conversing"
with their ultimate author, the Holy Spirit of God. That is
what he defends in the paragraph, iv. 12 f., in which he says
the word of God is living and penetrates the conscience. The
"word of God" here is doubtless wider than the written word.

---

[1] See on this subject Swete, *The Holy Spirit in the New Testament.* **Macmillan.**

But it is wider because even the written word is wider than itself. There is for him no such thing as a merely written word. The word has been written. It was written at various times, by several men, whose circumstances contributed to the producing of their particular expressions of the mind of God. He is too good a Platonist, or sacramentalist, to slight these limitations which are the means of access to the inner life. But the inner life, the living One who speaks by these means, is the object of his affection; and since He still speaks in the new events of history and later movement of men's hearts and intellects, all these must be included in "the word" which still interprets itself to the believer in its ever-deepening and penetrating life. Hence the author's bold selection, as of Ps. civ. 4 to show the angels are wind and fire, though in other places they are otherwise figured in the Old Testament; or correction, as in xi. 27, where he denies that Moses "feared," in harmony with Moses' character as described by the whole story, but in contradiction to the particular verse referred to. Hence above all, that deepening and refining of "the lesson of the beginning of the Christ" (vi. 1) which does discover wonderful germs of the Gospel consummation in the Messianic origins of the oracles of God (v. 12), notably in the Old Testament treatment of the mystery of Melchizedek.

§ 31. *This treatment of O. T. has likeness to Philo, but is really different from his "allegories."*

But in this last instance it may be said we have overshot the mark. If S. Paul was rabbinic in some of his old-fashioned arguments, this author is Philonic in his subtleties about Melchizedek. This objection has been noticed above in § 10, and need not be more closely examined here. It may however be remarked that nothing would better serve to illustrate the likeness and unlikeness of our author to Philo than a perusal of the whole passage about Melchizedek in Philo, *Legum Allegoriarum* iii. 79 ff, pp. 102 ff. The likeness is not altogether superficial, for Philo had a beautiful mind, and to the author of Hebrews the Philonic philosophy was a real preparation for the Gospel. But Philo is diffuse and fanciful. The very title

of his commentary on the Law—"Allegories"—indicates the
gulf between him and the epistle. Philo wanders far and
wide in allegory; he employs facts as arbitrary symbols to
illustrate his own ideas. The author of this epistle is led
sacramentally through the historical facts of Israel's past and
the earthly life of Jesus Christ to firm eternal truths which can
be tested by faith (Heb. xi. 1)[1].

Philo was born about B.C. 20, studied and taught at Alexandria, was versed in Greek literature, and spent a great part of
his life in harmonising Greek philosophy, as he understood it,
with the Jewish faith. The fruits of this effort are preserved in
his chief work, the long allegorising commentary on the Law of
Moses. The date of his death is not known.

Following Dr Caird, we may briefly say that the three main
points in Philo's philosophy are these :

(1) God is absolute being and as such cannot be known
or reached; He can only be described by negatives. Philo
"carries back the finite to the infinite, but cannot think of the
infinite as manifested in the finite."

(2) Yet in some way God must reach man and man God.
Hence there must be mediation. Philo finds mediation in the
Word of God; which in the Old Testament meant God's
uttered command, His direct action, but had already been taken
by the Stoics to express "the rational principle immanent in
man and in the universe." And to describe this mediating Word
Philo employs a wealth of analogies and figures. His Word seems

---

[1] For Philo's life and works the reader may be referred to the
article "Philo" in Hastings' *Dictionary of the Bible, Extra Volume*,
by James Drummond, to Dr Bigg's Bampton Lectures, *The Christian
Platonists of Alexandria*, new edition, Clarendon Press, 1915, to the
two lectures on "The transition from Stoicism to Neo-platonism "
and "The philosophy and theology of Philo," in Dr E. Caird's
Gifford Lectures, *The Evolution of Theology in the Greek Philosophers*, Maclehose, 1904, and to Bréhier, *Les idées philosophiques et
religieuses de Philon d'Alexandrie*, Paris, 1908. The first critical
edition of Philo's works was by Thomas Mangey, Canon of Durham,
London, 1742. Later editions preserve his pagination in the margin,
and references to these page-numbers are generally given in quotation. The best modern text is Cohn's (Ed. minor, Berlin 1886—   ).

at times to be almost a person. It is really the principle of
all the activities that are involved in the connexion of man
with God.

(3) Man is a soul defiled by a body. He is indeed dwelt
in by the Word and can return to God. But to do so he must
escape from all that is himself. He must escape by losing his
will in the divine will; not realise true manhood by losing and
finding his will in the divine will.

It is evident that there is a certain amount of correspondence in these ideas with the thoughts of our epistle, though the
epistle would seem to correct Philo at least as much as it takes
from him. In language there is the same kind of cautious or
doubtful correspondence. From many pages of Philo a few
characteristic words used in Hebrews may be gleaned, and these
mount up to a considerable sum as the process is continued.
It is in Philo's abundant imagery of the Word that coincidences,
culled and brought together, are most striking. The Logos,
writes Dr Bigg, is the Impress of the mind of God, His Son, the
Archetypal Seal, the Great Pattern according to which all is
made. He is the Divider, in so far as he differentiates, and
makes each thing what it is. He is the Heavenly Man, the
Prophet of the Most High. "For his atoning function Philo
found a fitting symbol ready to hand in the High Priest....
The true High Priest is sinless; if he needs to make an
offering and utter prayer for himself, it is only because he
participates in the guilt of the people whom he represents....He
is Melchisedech, priest of the Most High God, King of Salem,
that is of peace, who met Abraham returning from his victory
over the four kings, and refreshed him with the mystic Bread
and Wine."

Again however we notice that the coincidences are not
always agreements. The main point in the representation of
Melchizedek is not the same in Hebrews as in Philo. The following words which Philo puts into the mouth of the Logos
would be utterly repudiated by the author of the epistle, as
false if applied to our Lord, and meaningless in any other
connexion: "I stand between the Lord and you, I who am
neither uncreated like God nor created like you, but a mean
between the two extremes, a hostage to either side." And

Dr Bigg rightly observes that in much of his discourse Philo is but translating the hymn of the praise of wisdom, in the Alexandrine Book of Wisdom, into scientific terminology—of that wisdom which is "the brightness of the everlasting light, the unspotted mirror of the Power of God, the image of His Goodness"; see Wisd. vii. 22 ff.

§ 32. *Hebrews is broadly Alexandrine rather than Philonic, sacramental rather than philosophic.*

Here there is a really close parallel with Heb. i. 3, and while it is doubtful whether our author had read Philo, we may be pretty certain he had read the Book of Wisdom.   It was part of that larger Greek Bible which was used by the Alexandrian Jews, and which included most of what we call the Apocrypha. The "Canon" was still somewhat vague even in Palestine.   In Alexandria it was no doubt vaguer, and we need not curiously enquire what degree of authority was recognised in these additional books.   It suffices to remember that this author knew them and that one of them was a favourite of his.   That one was 2 Maccabees, largely drawn upon in Heb. xi. and continually suggesting turns of language in the epistle.

But 2 Maccabees is not a book of philosophy.   There is a tinge of Alexandrine philosophy in it.   So there is indeed in very many parts of the LXX version; see for instance Gen. i. 2 ἡ δὲ γῆ ἦν ἀόρατος καὶ ἀκατασκεύαστος, and notice the influence of this phrase in Heb. xi. 1 ff., and frequently in Philo.   A thoughtful man who had received an Alexandrine education would not necessarily be a philosopher, but he would have looked through the window of philosophy and have become aware of that view of things which is ignored by the so-called "plain" man, or the man of "common sense," or the "materialist."   He would also have acquired a number of more or less philosophical terms with which to express his deeper thoughts more readily.

That was the kind of scholarship possessed by the author of Hebrews.   He was indeed more of an artist than a philosopher. So far from aiming strenuously at "pure thought" he frankly delighted himself with the expression of thought in visual images.   That is part of what we have termed his "sacramental" temperament. And the sacramental temper is in many respects the antithesis of the philosophical. Yet in one important point it coincides with right philosophy. It abhors "dualism." It would extend the scientific fact that all physical life is one, into the reasonable assurance of faith that all life is one, that the natural is also divine. Professor Burnet[1] speaks of "the fateful doctrine of two worlds," and shews that Plato never made that separation.

But it was that "fateful doctrine" which gave Philo so much trouble. He tried to overcome it by his mediatory Powers. He was hampered by his heritage of language. Much of what he writes about the "intelligible world" etc. is too conventional. He employs terms which the ancient Greeks had invented for their search after "reality," in his different search after the answer to the question, How can God act as a person? But the writer to the Hebrews troubles little about either of those problems. He takes for granted that God does act as a person, and asks (in his picturesque manner), How can we enter into the presence of God? And he accepts the answer of the whole Christian Church: We can do so through our Lord Jesus Christ, who, obedient to God's love for men, died to effect this. But he wrote his epistle because some friends needed further explanation of this answer. The Church in its earliest days had been content with the very simple explanation that our Lord would shortly come as Christ with the Kingdom of God, and then His people would go to God with Him. S. Paul said, Yes, and even here and now our life is hid with Him in God through the Spirit. Our author says, Christ is coming now in the crisis of these troubled times. That was a practical not a speculative assurance. He, with the rest of the Church, still expects the "final" coming. But that was for a "morrow" of which there was no need to "take thought" then, "while the summons was going forth, To day." What mattered then was the faithful following of the "Captain" who was being "brought again into the world."

Nevertheless, as a thoughtful man writing to thoughtful men, he attempts to discover a general principle which will

[1] *Greek Philosophy, Thales to Plato*, pp. 90, 345. Macmillan, 1914.

bring harmony into such ideas of extended, successive "comings" and their results. Our Lord, S. Luke records, had already said "The kingdom of God is within you," or "in your midst" (xvii. 21). And, according to the record of S. John, He had taught much about His continual presence with His disciples. This author says, The kingdom, or the new world, or the coming age, or the promised good things of God, or the inner sanctuary of His presence—call the mystery what you will—has been brought within reach of all when Christ died. These realities are here and now. They, invisible and eternal, are not separated from the visible things of this practical and responsible life of ours on earth. It is through these practical trials, duties, and affections that we deepen and intensify life till it is recognised as what it really is, the life that is life indeed. Thus we go to heaven when we pray, iv. 16. And you now, my friends, will find Jesus, and enter the sabbath rest of God, and know the vital significance of the Church's dogma concerning the Person of Christ and His strength being yours, if you will recognise "the way of His flesh" in the trial before you, and do your hard duty, and pass onward and inward with Him to God.

It is a "new world" not "another world" that Platonists seek, and Christians believe is their own to use. Only--at least so our author would put it—we have it but as we use it, and while the various persons who make up the Church linger, hesitate, or press on, a seeming inconsistency remains. We see Jesus crowned with glory and honour for the suffering of death, but we do not yet see all His disciples so ready to die (ii. 8 f.). We know Him to be exalted and apart from sin (vii. 26, ix. 28), but only one by one, as each makes the one sacrifice in his own sphere of love, do we attain to His security and propagate it in the visible world.

§ 33. *Thus "faith" in this epistle is trust intensified by hope and love. The author expresses the idea with some Platonic sympathy, but mainly rests upon the Church's doctrine of Christ.*

To take that bold step man needs an impulse. That impulse is, according to our author, faith. Lightfoot has given in his commentary on *Galatians*[1] a complete analysis of the meaning of "faith" in the Old Testament, the various New Testament writers, the Alexandrine and rabbinic schools : see his notes on "The words denoting 'Faith'" and "The faith of Abraham." On that aspect of the subject it must here suffice to say: that in the Old Testament faith is mainly trust in God ; that this primary notion persists in all the New Testament writers, but is rendered deeper and more complex by being involved with the leading passion of their particular theology ; thus S. Paul's faith is bound up with the "love" of Christ which sprang from his conversion ; S. John's with that "knowledge" of God and of His Son, which is reinforced by intellectual meditation, but is mainly (as in Hosea) personal and intuitional.

In Hebrews faith is coloured by an atmosphere of "hope," and appears as a spiritual force impelling men to endure and persevere and strive towards a holiness, a peace and a knowledge not yet realised. Whether it is innate in all men, it did not form part of the author's plan to discuss. He certainly regards it as having been implanted by God in all the men with whom his epistle directly deals, viz. the children of Israel and the Christian Church. He might, if he had chosen to adopt Platonic language, have said that faith was a form of the indwelling Word. But he prefers to put it in the opposite way, as though faith were an embracing potency in the sphere of which men live (x. 39). So faith is a bond of union between the ancient Church of Israel and Israel's heir the Christian community (iv. 2). Thus, from the beginning, faith was connected with hope ; for the Church of Israel lived on "promises," iv. 1, vi. 12, 15, 17, vii. 6, viii. 6, ix. 15, x. 36, xi. 9, 13, 17, 33, 39.

[1] Macmillan, original edition, 1865.

And so, when the great chapter xi. on faith is reached, the author introduces it by one of his terse proverbial sayings, in which he indicates the relation of faith to hope. It is the substance of things hoped for, the test of things not seen. This certainly implies that the things which may rightly be hoped for are already in being, but the stress is on "time" rather than "reality"; faith presses onwards, to the "not yet." Cf. Rom. viii. 24 (a passage which may have helped to shape this verse), τῇ γὰρ ἐλπίδι ἐσώθημεν· ἐλπὶς δὲ βλεπομένη οὐκ ἔστιν ἐλπίς, ὃ γὰρ βλέπει τίς ἐλπίζει;

A practical application of the verse will perhaps help to the understanding of our author's mind. Suppose a nation at war. If all points more and more certainly to victory the period of hope is drawing to a close. Hope has to do with things not yet seen, and flourishes in dark days. But it will flourish in dark days, if faith is there to give it substance, to "uphold" it. Such faith must obviously be faith in God who alone upholds things worthy to be hoped for. And so faith is a test of these as yet unseen but hoped for things. What then may this nation rightly hope for? Victory? No, that is on the knees of God, who designs that which is truly best for each party in the strife. Peace? Yes, but not necessarily outward peace, only the peace of God which makes for His righteousness among men. Apply the test of faith and one by one all temporal greed and private judgements about what is best for the world are stripped away. The patriotic will is not annihilated, but it is transformed into perfect union with the will of God. The test is severe, but the gold from which it purges away the dross is an inalienable possession. A nation which rejoiced in such a purified hope would conquer the world with God, though it lost what seemed its all. And it would enjoy peace in the midst of violence, and fight indomitably while convinced God bade it fight, for it would be free from all fear and all anxiety; "qui fortis est idem est fidens," Cicero, *Tusc.* iii. 14 (quoted by Lightfoot).

There is plainly a good deal of the Pauline "love" in this author's faith also. It was lack of loving loyalty which caused Israel's tragic failure of faith, iii. 16 ff. And the personal note is distinctly heard throughout chapter xi.; Moses endured as seeing "Him," not "it," which was invisible, xi. 27. It is this personal note which forbids our exaggerating the debt of this epistle to the Alexandrine philosophy. That philosophy enlarged the vocabulary of the author. It also served the intellectual interest which was strong in him, and which enabled him to intervene very weightily in the perplexed trial his friends had to face. But that trial was too real to allow him in any intellectual trifling. Alexandria had been refurbishing old-fashioned instruments of speculation. Philo followed the fashion. His earnestness made him break away again and again from the method he had imposed upon himself. But the method hampered him. There is much tediousness, much confusion in his writings. His main achievement was that "he first gave utterance to both of the two great requirements of the religious consciousness, the need for rising from the finite and relative to the Absolute, and the need of seeing the Absolute as manifested in the finite and relative ; although he could find no other reconciliation of these two needs except externally to subordinate the latter to the former" (Caird). The writer to the Hebrews knew something of this "great problem of his time," and of the manner in which educated men were approaching it. This gives his letter a peculiar sympathy which may well have won its first readers and is still appreciated by its more academic readers in these days. But his main interest was in the sufficing truth which he had found enshrined in the Christian Church, and in the life of the Lord Jesus Christ, loyalty to whom was the tradition of the Church. That made him simple, independent, original. So far as he did touch philosophy he went back, unconsciously, from Alexandrine Platonism to Plato himself. But he only touched that kind of philosophy so far as it suited his more concentrated purpose. He was convinced that in Jesus Christ the riddle of the universe was solved as far as needs be. Much more was he convinced that in Him the difficulty of living a noble and beautiful life was overcome. And out of that conviction he sent this "treatise of encouragement" to some much-loved and sorely-tried friends.

IV

THE TEXT OF THE EPISTLE

§ 1. The number of MSS. available for textual criticism has
increased so much of late that the notation in Gregory's eighth
edition of Tischendorf's Greek Testament is no longer satisfactory. Two new classifications have been proposed; an
ingenious but difficult system by von Soden, and a simple
modification of Gregory's lists. Gregory's new notation is used
in Dr Souter's Greek Testament (*Novum Testamentum Graece.
Textui a Retractatoribus Anglis adhibito brevem adnotationem
criticam subiecit Alexander Souter.* Clarendon Press, 1910), and
will be adopted in this commentary.

Dr Souter's edition, small in bulk and in cost, is invaluable.
Nowhere else is the lately discovered material so conveniently
brought together and digested. The critical notes give but a
selection of various readings and of authorities. Such a selection,
wisely made, is just what is wanted by ordinary students. The
following lists, and the critical notes, in this commentary are
founded upon Dr Souter's work. Only those MSS., Versions and
Fathers that are quoted in the notes are included, but three
early fragments of the epistle may be here mentioned as interesting.

$\mathfrak{p}^{12}$ is a single verse, Heb. i. 1, written in the margin of a
letter from a Roman Christian. It was published by Grenfell
and Hunt, *Amherst papyri*, part I (1900) no. 3 b. (c. iii. or iv.).

$\mathfrak{p}^{18}$ Heb. ix. 12—19 is part of a leaf from a papyrus book
(c. iv.); published by Hunt, *Oxyrhynchus papyri*, part VIII (1911)
no. 1078.

A fragmentary MS. of the Pauline epistles was brought to
America in 1907 by Mr Charles L. Freer. It is an uncial of
the sixth century, and has, like ℵ and B, Hebrews following
2 Thessalonians : see H. A. Saunders in *The American Journal
of Archaeology*, March 1908, and *The Biblical World* (Chicago),
Febr. 1908, and E. J. Goodspeed, Introduction to *The Epistle to
the Hebrews* (*The Bible for Home and School*), New York, 1908.
The text of this MS. is not yet published.

The New Testament used to be divided into four parts ; *Evangelium, Actus* (with Catholic epistles), *Paulus, Revelatio.* The initials e a p r shew how many of these parts are included in a papyrus, vellum or paper codex, or version.

PAPYRUS

𝔓¹³ (cent. iv.) Heb. ii. 14—v. 5 ; x. 8—xi. 13, 28 —xii. 17 (London).

UNCIALS

א (c. iv.) e a p r : Sinaiticus (Petrograd, Leipzig).

    א* = the first writing, where the first or a later scribe has afterwards corrected it : so also in A B C D H etc.

    אᵃ אᵇ etc. = correctors of the codex.

A (c. v.) e a p r (wanting in parts) : Alexandrinus (London).

    A** A² Aᶜᵒʳʳ = correctors.

B (c. iv.) e a p (Heb. ix. 14—xiii. 25, 1, 2 Tim., Tit., Philem. wanting) : Vaticanus (Rome).

    B² B³ = correctors.

C (c. v.) e a p r (fragments) : (Paris).

    C** C² etc. = correctors.

D (c. vi.) p (some lines wanting) : Claromontanus, a Graeco-Latin MS. (Paris).

    Dᵇ Dᶜ D² Dᶜᵒʳʳ = correctors.

H (c. vi.) p (mutilated) : (Athos, Kiev, Moscow, Petrograd, Paris, Turin).

    H is a copy of the edition of epp. Paul, which Euthalius put forth : *vid. infra.*

K (c. ix.) a p (Acts and part of Paul are wanting) : (Moscow).

L (c. ix.) a p (Acts i. 1—viii. 9 are wanting) : (Rome).

M (c. ix.) p (fragments) : (London, Hamburg).

P (c. ix.) a p r (mutilated) : (Petrograd), *vid.* Euthal. *infra.*

MINUSCULES

The following minuscule MSS., dating from the ninth (33) to the fourteenth centuries, are quoted in the notes

    5, 6, 33, 104, 241, 263, 326, 424, 436, 442, 456, 1908, 1912.

ω = codices plerique.

Ancient Versions

𝕷 = consensus of 𝕷 (vt) and 𝕷 (vg).

𝕷 (vt) (c. ii. (?)—iii.—iv.).   The Old Latin (e a p r) = consensus of all or most of the codices which appear to represent this version or versions.

    𝕷 (vt^d) = the Latin of D.

    𝕷 (vt^r) = fragments (c. vi.) (Munich).

𝕷 (vg) (c. iv.) = Jerome's " vulgate," recension of the Old Latin : e a p r.

𝕾 (vg) (c. v.) = the Peshitta Syriac : e a p.

𝕾 (hl) (c. vii.) = the Harklean Syriac, a version made by Thomas of Harkel, strangely " Western " in text, and having additional readings of like character entered in margin, 𝕾 (hl^mg), 𝕾 hl^(mg gr) : e a p r.

𝕾 (pal) (c. vi.) = fragments of a Palestinian Syriac version : e a p r.

[𝕰 (sah) (c. iii.—iv.) = the Sahidic version of Upper Egypt, sometimes called Thebaic : e a p r : only fragments of this version are known for Hebrews.]

𝕰 (boh) = the Bohairic version of Lower Egypt, sometimes called Memphitic : e a p (r).   The original version was probably without the Apocalypse.   Its date is disputed.   Most critics used to assign it to c. iii.—iv., some now prefer c. vi.—vii.

𝕬 (c. v. ?) = the Armenian version : e a p r.

𝕰th (c. v.—vii.) = the Aethiopic version : e a p r.

Fathers

The following Fathers are quoted in the critical notes.   In the other notes Clem. or Clement = Clemens Romanus bishop of Rome (c. i.).

The full names of the Latin writers are printed in italics.

Amb.   = *Ambrosius* bishop of Milan (c. iv.).

Ambst.   = ' *Ambrosiaster*,' a writer once confounded with Ambrose whose name may have been Isaac (c. iv.).

Aphr.   = Aphraates, wrote in Syriac (c. iv.).

Chr.   = Johannes Chrysostomus patriarch of Constantinople
        (c. iv. —v.).
Clem.   = Clemens Alexandrinus (c. ii.—iii.).
Cosm.   = Cosmas Indicopleustes of Alexandria (c. vi.).
Cyr. Hier. = Cyrillus bishop of Jerusalem (c. iv.).
Did.   = Didymus of Alexandria (c. iv.).
Eus.   = Eusebius bishop of Caesarea in Palestine (c. iii.—iv.).
Euthal. = Euthalius (ὁ αἰνιγματώδης) editor of epp. Paul., *vid.
        supra* H (c. iv.—v. ?).
Euthal.^cod. = P (*vid. supra*) to which codex notes from Euthalius
        are added by a hand of the fourteenth century.
Fulg.   = *Fulgentius* African bishop (c. v.—vi.).
Greg.-Nyss. = Gregorius bishop of Nyssa in Cappadocia (c. iv.).
Isid.-Pel. = Isidorus of Pelusium in Egypt (c. v.).
Lucif. = *Lucifer* bishop of Calaris (Cagliari) (c. iv.).
Orig.   = Origenes of Alexandria (c. iii.).
Ps.-Serap. = a writer whose work was wrongly attributed to
        Serapion an Egyptian bishop of the fourth century.
Tert.   = *Tertullianus* of Carthage (c. ii.—iii.).

§ 2. The text used in the *Cambridge Greek Testament for
Schools* is Westcott and Hort's. No one can properly appreciate
the value of this text without reading the *Introduction* (by
Dr Hort) which followed, as a second volume, the publication of
their *New Testament in Greek* in 1881. But if not the full
Introduction, at least the simplified summary must be studied,
which is printed at the end of the Greek text both in the larger
and smaller editions. It is impossible to cut the shortened
argument still shorter, and all that will be attempted here is to
indicate the conclusions in such brief fashion as may promote
intelligent analysis of the critical notes in this commentary.

Westcott and Hort aimed at establishing a securer method
than that of private judgement or rules of thumb. To say, This
reading gives the harder, but the better sense, is an example of
private judgement. To count authorities on either side, or to
prefer the older MSS., or to choose the shorter reading, are rules
of thumb. What is wanted is to discover the genealogy of MSS.,
so that a dull person may recognise as certainly as a clever one
that such and such a combination indicates the true line of

transmission ; such and such another combination indicates one of the corrupted lines.

Genealogical discovery does start indeed from private judgement. The character of a MS. is tentatively settled by the preponderance of readings on the character of which we form an opinion from what we know of the author's mind and the habits of scribes. But this preliminary judgement is superseded by degrees, as the relations of MS. to MS. begin to emerge. At last the MSS. fall into groups which represent lines of transmission. And it is no longer private judgement when, contemplated on a wide area, these groups prove their real affinity by the well marked character of the texts they reveal.

Thus the so-called "Textus receptus," derived from Erasmus, commonly printed in England till Westcott and Hort's edition appeared, and followed in our A.V., is supported by the mass of authorities from the fourth century onwards. It is a smooth, full, commonplace text, and arose from a deliberate "recension" and amalgamation of earlier diverse texts.

Neglecting then the mass of MSS. etc. which conspire to perpetuate this comparatively late form of text, we find two other forms which were already current at least as early as the third century, but which had already diverged from the true line of descent.

One of these is called the " Western " text. It represents the bold, free manner in which people in general might quote from books of which the sacred precision of each several word is not yet recognised. The primary documents for this text in Hebrews are D 𝕃 (vt), the Old Latin Fathers, and the Greek Ante-Nicene Fathers, those of Alexandria partially excepted. With these will often be ranged 104, either ℵ or B (not both together), the Syriac, Armenian, Aethiopic versions.

The other is more attractive at first sight. But close observation shows its character to be scholarly, thoughtful correction of errors or seeming errors. This is called the " Alexandrian," and in Hebrews is found in ℵ A C P, 5, 33, 1908, ℭ (boh), Alexandrian Fathers, and sometimes 𝔄 or 𝕃 (vg).

But where is the true line of transmission ? Clearly in those readings which, being of the ancient class, are neither " Western " nor " Alexandrian " in their attestation. If any group of author-

ities habitually stand for a third set of readings, that group has
the genuine ancestry. Such a group in Hebrews is ℵ B A C P
33, 424**. With these will often be ranged 𝕮 (boh) and
𝕾 (pal).

It will be noticed that these groups overlap. It must be so,
since the genealogy of MSS. is extremely complicated. They are
not simply copied one from another. In copying from one MS.
readings are brought in from another. These may have been
already written in the margin of the MS. to be copied, or they
may lurk in the scribe's memory, and so on. This is the
complication called "mixture." It can only be met by recognition of the overlapping of groups, while yet the core of each
group remains perceptible.

And if the student will be at the pains to master Hort's
close-knit argument ; or if, shirking that, he will be content to
trust Hort, he may hold fast to a simple clue through these
perplexities, and prove its worth for himself by experience.
Hort does not say that ℵ and B, especially B, are to be always
trusted because their readings on the whole are good. But he
does show how the agreement of ℵ and B assures us of the right
genealogical line. Each of them from time to time sides with
large aberrant groups. But B, standing nearly by itself, is
always worthy of at least respectful attention.

Unfortunately it is in epp. Paul. that B oftenest gets into
bad company: in this division of the New Testament it has a
considerable "Western" admixture. And in Hebrews B fails us
at ix. 14. From the middle of the word καθαριεῖ it is mutilated
to the end of the epistle. The loss is however made up in some
degree by the fragmentary 𝔓[13]. That papyrus gives a text very
like B. Or is it rather "Alexandrian"? A definite answer to
that *quaere* will be welcome. For in one or two places 𝔓[13] offers
a reading so attractive as to rouse suspicion that it is too clever ;
see iv. 4, v. 4, xi. 2.

§ 3. The text published by Westcott and Hort is generally
accepted as the working basis for all study of the New Testament.
But its details are sometimes questioned. Our R.V. for instance
represents the ancient text as against the "Textus receptus,"
but it differs in many places from Westcott and Hort. The
serious questions are these. Have Westcott and Hort really

succeeded in superseding private judgement by proved genealogy? Is not the "Western" text more true, as it certainly is more wide-spread, and probably more ancient than they knew? And is not their "neutral" text merely a variety of the "Alexandrian"?

These are the burning questions in textual criticism, and these must be borne in mind while the student considers and reconsiders the groups in Hebrews. The peculiar delicacy of language in this epistle renders the last question specially interesting. On the other hand it must be remembered that the Old Latin version, elsewhere so important a witness for the "Western" text, is represented in Hebrews almost solely by the Latin column of D, and this differs rudely from the rest of the Latin in this codex. It agrees with the quotations of Lucifer of Cagliari yet is perhaps no real "Old Latin," as a whole, but a translation picked up at the end of the fourth century.

These problems are fairly and lucidly discussed in Kenyon's *Handbook*, an excellent guide to the whole subject, complete, scholarly, urbane. The same author's *Palaeography of Greek Papyri* (Clarendon Press, 1899) is a very delightful book. Souter's *Text and Canon of the New Testament* (Duckworth, 1913) is popular and simple, but full of rare learning which no one but its author could impart. Gregory's *Canon and Text of the New Testament* (T. and T. Clark, 1907) is the outcome of vast experience and is written in a very entertaining manner. Kirsopp Lake's *Text of the New Testament* (Rivingtons, 1911) is a small and excellent book. Burkitt's article on "Text and Versions" in *Encyclopaedia Biblica* vol. IV. is of great importance. The section on the Text in Westcott's Introduction to his commentary on Hebrews should be carefully studied. The second volume of von Soden's Greek Testament, containing the text of the whole with elaborate textual notes, was published at Göttingen in 1913. The text with short *apparatus* and a brief explanatory preface was also published, a moderate sized volume, in the same year. Kenyon discusses von Soden's principles of criticism in the last chapter of his *Handbook*. Westcott and Hort's text is impugned at length and with some violence by Mr H. C. Hoskier in *Codex B and its allies, a Study and an Indictment*, 2 vols., Quaritch, 1914. Those who would learn more about the Fathers should read Swete's *Patristic Study*,

Longmans, 1902. Familiarity with S. Jerome's Vulgate is an inestimable advantage to the student of the Greek Testament. A good text of the Vulgate has been put within reach of the slenderest purse by Dr H. J. White in his (complete) *Editio Minor* of Wordsworth and White's *Novum Testamentum Latine*, Clarendon Press, 1911. Dr White wrote the masterly article on the Vulgate in Hastings' *Dictionary of the Bible* vol. IV., an article which fills the same place for this generation as Westcott's in Smith's *Dictionary of the Bible* did for a former generation.

V

THE STYLE OF THE EPISTLE

§ 1. *Character of N. T. Greek.*

Origen said that anyone who knew Greek must see that S. Paul did not write this epistle. The difference of style and language is indeed conspicuous. S. Paul, probably bilingual from early years, used Greek fluently but roughly; it is impossible, for instance, to press the delicate distinctions of classical Greek into his prepositions. He dictated his letters and they are conversational, by no means bookish. Notice in Ephesians how he thrice begins a prayer, but twice runs off into further development of his subject before completing the prayer in iii. 14—21; and contrast Heb. xiii. 20 f. Of late, the study of inscriptions, papyri etc. has enabled us to understand more precisely what this Greek of S. Paul is. It is the "common Greek" in which, since the conquests of Alexander, men of various nations could talk or write to one another throughout the civilised world. Yet this common Greek was also adapted, with more or less art, to literary purposes, and in N.T. generally we find a particular adaptation which, with variety within itself, still stands apart from the other Greek writings of the period. It is more simple; the sentences are short; it has a pleasing air of sincerity. One reason for this marked character is the influence of the LXX.

These writers were affected by the somewhat rude but vigorous and really noble effort of the translators of the Greek Bible to express holy thoughts worthily, yet in the language of the people. They repeated the effort; having new and still greater truths to tell. Thus a fresh development in vernacular literature arose which might be compared with Bunyan's English in the *Pilgrim's Progress*—the language of everyday life broken in to the grammatical terseness of book-form by the unconscious art of men inspired with an unworldly message.

Yet this N.T. Greek shews variety. The Apocalypse comes nearest to the rude ungrammatical Greek of some papyri; it is written by a foreigner who has not really mastered the idiom. In S. John's Gospel and Epistles we perhaps recognise a foreigner again who has learned to meet his difficulties by a style of extreme simplicity. S. Matthew and S. Mark are Hellenistic Bible Christians writing as they had heard the story told, yet pruning their words. S. Luke is different; a trained writer whose natural style appears in the latter part of Acts. In the first twelve chapters and in the Gospel he passes sympathetically into the more rustic style of his authorities, and in the four opening verses of the Gospel he shews that he can match the dignity of the rhetorical schools. In 2 Peter and Jude a like attempt is made but less admirably. With S. Luke however 1 Peter and James may be classed as examples of more or less literary Greek; and, supreme in this kind, stands Hebrews.

§ 2. *The Greek of Hebrews, classical but not artificial: use of LXX.*

This is but a rough classification, nor are we concerned here with critical questions about authorship; the names quoted may be taken for symbols rather than persons if any prefer to do so. As a first test of what has been said the student may refer to the lists of words at the end of Grimm and Thayer's *Lexicon of the N.T.* But it is not enough to count the mere number of words peculiar to each writer. The kind of words is the important point. In Hebrews we are at once struck by what may be termed the distinguished character of the vocabulary. Then by its classical purity; of 157 words peculiar to this epistle,

115 are current in early Greek. On the other hand when we turn from lists to the epistle itself we see that there is no affectation about this; later words or LXX words are employed where suitable. Yet there is a certain fastidiousness, as in the substitution of ἀνασταυρόω for the incorrect σταυρόω vi. 6. So in vii. after using ἱερατίαν in a reference to O. T. the author passes to his own more secular phraseology with ἱερωσύνη; and in ix. 2 he writes ἡ πρόθεσις τῶν ἄρτων, avoiding the Hebraic οἱ ἄρτοι τῆς προθέσεως. Yet he does not despise that Hebraic genitive when it contributes to a desired emphasis, as in ix. 5 Χερουβεὶν δόξης; he even imitates it (as indeed Greek quite allows) in such a phrase as καρπὸν εἰρηνικὸν...δικαιοσύνης xii. 11. That is but one instance of a frequent exercise of skill in his use of LXX. Not only does he interweave quotations, modifying them, to bring out fuller meaning, as in x. 37 ἔτι γὰρ μικρὸν ὅσον ὅσον, ὁ ἐρχόμενος ἥξει κ.τ.λ., cf. ii. 9, iv. 7, x. 10, xii. 26; but he will adopt a rude Hebraic use of the prep. ἐν, and by careful context fill it with significance, as in i. 1 f. ἐν τ. προφήταις...ἐν υἱῷ, x. 10 ἐν ᾧ θελήματι, xiii. 20 f. where notice how ἐν αἵματι and ἐν ἡμῖν explain one another. To make the most of prepositions was a delight to him, see ix. 26 ἀπό...ἐπί...εἰς...διά, ix. 28, xii. 7 εἰς παιδείαν ὑπομένετε, and the ambiguous or rather pregnant ἐκ θανάτου v. 7. Other examples of masterly conveyance from LXX are ἐπιλαμβάνεται ii. 16, τὰ πρὸς τὸν θεὸν ii. 17, v. 1— a compendium of the sacerdotal theology of the epistle, and the allusive, associative use of the title "Christ" which is continually developed—see e.g. iii. 6, v. 5, xi. 26, xiii. 21.

§ 3. *Tenses.*

In other books of N.T. it is dangerous to press the significance of tenses; in Hebrews it is hard to do so too much. Notice the aor. inf. xiii. 20 followed by the pres. part.; the combination in ii. 18 ἐν ᾧ γὰρ πέπονθεν αὐτὸς πειρασθείς, δύναται τοῖς πειραζομένοις βοηθῆσαι, with which cf. the presents in vii. 25, and the ἡγιασμένοι...ἁγιαζομένους x. 10, 14; the pres. part. in xi. 17 πειραζόμενος = "being sorely tried all the time," and the perf. προσενήνοχεν (modification of LXX) = "he hath offered and the sacrifice still stands." Perfects abound, never without proper meaning. Thus the repeatedly quoted ἐκάθισεν becomes at xii. 2 κεκάθικεν. In xi. 28 πεποίηκεν τὸ πάσχα interrupts the series of aorists because the Passover is an institution still observed. Sometimes a perfect and often a present is due to the author's habit of referring to what stands written in books or pictured in history, ii. 9 τὸν...ἠλαττωμένον βλέπομεν Ἰησοῦν... ἐστεφανωμένον, vii. 3 ἀφωμοιωμένος τῷ υἱῷ τοῦ θεοῦ, and so probably ix. 6—10 τούτων...κατεσκευασμένων...διὰ παντὸς εἰσίασιν οἱ ἱερεῖς κ.τ.λ., where the ritual of the tabernacle rather than contemporary worship seems to be described; cf. viii. 4 f. It may be remarked that the emphatic use of perfects is another example of judicious adaptation from LXX language ; see ii. 13 for quotation of a LXX compound perf. ἔσομαι πεποιθώς, and cf. e.g. Is. lx. 15 διὰ τὸ γεγενῆσθαί σε ἐγκαταλελειμμένην καὶ μεμισημένην. For a very precise use of perf. inf. see xi. 3 εἰς τὸ μὴ...γεγονέναι.

That is also an example of the inf. with article and preposition, common in later Greek, and handled by this author with freedom, e.g. in ii. 15 διὰ παντὸς τοῦ ζῆν. His use of ἐν in such phrases, ii. 8, iii. 12 ἐν τῷ ἀποστῆναι, shews how far he is from affecting classicism : for this construction, in which the inf. seems to admit a temporal sense, is hardly true to the genius of the older language. Another laudable concession to contemporary usage is the Latinising ὃ προσενέγκῃ, viii. 3.

§ 4. *Participles.*

Participles are used with nicety, terseness, and sometimes bold freedom. Notice the interwoven series in i. 3 f., v. 7—10, vi. 4—6, the terseness of μακροθυμήσας ἐπέτυχεν vi. 15, ἅπαξ κεκαθαρισμένους x. 2, γεννηθεὶς ἐκρύβη xi. 23, and the extension of formal grammar in vi. 10 ἐνεδείξασθε...διακονήσαντες καὶ διακονοῦντες, and the practical elegance of noun-phrase varied by part. in xiii. 17 ἵνα μετὰ χαρᾶς τοῦτο ποιῶσιν καὶ μὴ στενάζοντες.

§ 5. *Article.*

The article is added or omitted so as to get the utmost from the words; i. 2 ἐν υἱῷ, ix. 14 διὰ πνεύματος αἰωνίου, vi. 7 γῆ γὰρ ἡ πιοῦσα, vi. 18 (though here the text is perhaps uncertain) ἐν οἷς ἀδύνατον ψεύσασθαι θεόν, xii. 7 ὡς υἱοῖς ὑμῖν προσφέρεται ὁ θεός· τίς γὰρ υἱὸς ὃν οὐ παιδεύει πατήρ; see also xi. 16, and the scarce translatable θεὸς ζῶν. Its omission in passages of poetical elevation is effective, and reminds us of the tragedians, xi. 33 ff., xii. 22—24. The construction with a neuter adj. or part. to represent an abstract or collective is well introduced in vi. 17 τὸ ἀμετάθετον τῆς βουλῆς αὐτοῦ, vii. 18 διὰ τὸ αὐτῆς ἀσθενὲς καὶ ἀνωφελές, xii. 13 ἵνα μὴ τὸ χωλὸν ἐκτραπῇ. The rules for omitting art. in compound phrases are observed; ὃς ὢν ἀπαύγασμα τῆς δόξης is predicative i. 3, εἰς ἀπολύτρωσιν τῶν ἐπὶ τῇ πρώτῃ διαθήκῃ παραβάσεων, ix. 15, has a preposition. We are therefore inclined to suspect some deliberate purpose in the technical irregularity of ἀπάτῃ τῆς ἁμαρτίας iii. 13; it is probably meant to throw emphasis on the particular sin which the readers were in danger of committing, cf. xii. 1 τὴν εὐπερίστατον ἁμαρτίαν.

§ 6. *Order of words.*

In ix. 1 there is a double predicate, the second expressed as usual by the position of the article, the first merely by the order εἶχε μὲν οὖν καὶ ἡ πρώτη δικαιώματα λατρείας τό τε ἅγιον κοσμικόν: so in vi. 5 καλὸν γευσαμένους θεοῦ ῥῆμα δυνάμεις τε μέλλοντος αἰῶνος, cf. ix. 17, 24, xi. 26, and the compound predicate in x. 34 γινώσκοντες ἔχειν ἑαυτοὺς κρείσσονα ὕπαρξιν καὶ μένουσαν. Again and again the sense is brought out by the order of the words, e.g. the emphatic Ἰησοῦν dividing the clauses in ii. 9, cf. vi. 20, xiii. 20. Sometimes an emphatic word is postponed to the end of the clause, as in vii. 4 ᾧ δεκάτην Ἀβραὰμ ἔδωκεν ἐκ τῶν ἀκροθινίων ὁ πατριάρχης, ix. 28 ἐκ δευτέρου χωρὶς ἁμαρτίας ὀφθήσεται τοῖς αὐτὸν ἀπεκδεχομένοις εἰς σωτηρίαν with which cf. the final τὴν ἀσφάλειαν Luke i. 4. This is especially to be noticed with genitives, as in x. 20, τοῦτ' ἔστιν τῆς σαρκὸς αὐτοῦ (where see note), ix. 15, xii. 11. In xi. 1 ἔστιν stands emphatically at the beginning of the sentence. Words connected in syntax are

elegantly separated, as in Plato, iv. 8 οὐκ ἂν περὶ ἄλλης ἐλάλει
μετὰ ταῦτα ἡμέρας, ii. 17, iv. 11, x. 2.   In ix. 11, τῶν γενομένων
ἀγαθῶν διά..., the idiomatic nicety has been misunderstood by
copyists and translators, as too has the rhetorical τίνες in iii. 16.

§ 7.   *Elaboration and simplicity: no vain rhetoric.*

Long, skilfully woven periods are not uncommon, e.g. i. 1—4,
vi. 1—6; yet compared with Philo or Josephus these are plain,
with the indifference to shew that a great subject breeds.   The
antitheses too with which the epistle abounds are of such a kind
that they illustrate a certain mystery of all good language, viz.
that the understanding seems to require precisely the same
artistic form as will satisfy the ear.   Thus in xi. 1, ἐλπιζομένων
ὑπόστασις πραγμάτων, ἔλεγχος οὐ βλεπομένων, neither of the
balanced clauses could be dispensed with.   A difference in this
respect may be observed between the parallelisms of the author
and the more formal parallelisms of the O.T. poetry which he
quotes.   The same happy coincidence of sound and sense may
be observed in many of the long, swiftly-scanned perfect forms
which fit so well into their place in the sentence; e.g. κεκληρονόμηκεν ὄνομα i. 4, περικεκαλυμμένην πάντοθεν χρυσίῳ ix. 4—notice
the metrical assonance with ὑπεράνω δὲ αὐτῆς Χερουβεὶν in the
next verse.   A like good taste restrains the use of resonant compounds, μισθαποδοσία, ἐγκαταλείποντες, χειροποίητα, ὁρκωμοσία etc.
These are characteristic of the epistle; yet they are sparingly
admitted.   Contrast the profusion in 2 Peter and Jude, or even
in so pleasing a writer as Clement of Rome.   And quite as
characteristic is the effect produced by very simple words--καὶ,
ἔχω, ὦν, ὄντων, λαλέω, μένω etc.—and quiet phrases like vi. 3, καὶ
τοῦτο ποιήσομεν ἐάνπερ ἐπιτρέπῃ ὁ θεός.

Such simplicity is particularly effective when it comes by
way of contrast, as μένειν after παραμένειν vii. 23 f.   This kind
of distinction between similar words may also be illustrated by
πρόδηλον, κατάδηλον in the same chapter (14 f.).   It is one of the
author's habits to press the philological value of words in this
way; so (rightly or wrongly) πρόσφατον x. 20, and generally
τελειόω and its cognates; so again ἔκφοβος...ἔντρομος xii. 21.
This naturally lends itself to his love of antithesis, but finer

examples of that figure are to be seen in sentences like xi. 38, ὧν οὐκ ἦν ἄξιος ὁ κόσμος ἐπὶ ἐρημίαις πλανώμενοι κ.τ.λ., or in gnomic utterances like ἔμαθεν ἀφ᾽ ὧν ἔπαθεν τὴν ὑπακοήν v. 8, or ὅ τε γὰρ ἁγιάζων καὶ οἱ ἁγιαζόμενοι ἐξ ἑνὸς πάντες ii. 11.

At vii. 4 there is a sudden touch of conversational audacity— πηλίκος. This might be recondite art, as might the *meiosis* in xiii. 17 ἀλυσιτελὲς γὰρ ὑμῖν τοῦτο, or the ironic use of τις at x. 25, καθὼς ἔθος τισίν, cf. ii. 6, iii. 4, 12 f., iv. 11, xii. 15 f., xiii. 2; and indeed this kind of thing is frequent in Philo. But Philonic mannerisms were natural to the author, and (we may suppose) to his readers, and it is more respectful to take it as easy, intimate writing. Deissmann will not allow the epistle to be a letter in the true sense of the word, and Wrede considered ch. xiii. a letter-like addition to an original treatise, intended to make people think that S. Paul was the author. But ch. xiii. must surely seem to a sympathetic reader a most natural conclusion. The author himself allows that the earlier chapters are rather like a treatise (see xiii. 22 note), yet even in them intimacy sometimes intrudes; see especially the all but playfulness of v. 11—13, the reminiscences in vi. 10, x. 32 ff., and the touching sympathy of τὴν συνείδησιν ἡμῶν ix. 14, where the v.l. ὑμῶν (though fairly attested) only shews how soon and how generally such personal notes fell on deaf ears. It may be that the irregular grammar of vii. 1, x. 1, is epistolary carelessness; so too the ambiguity of expression in i. 6, iv. 7, 13 (ὁ λόγος repeated), v. 12 (τινὰ or τίνα), vi. 2, xii. 17, xii. 22 μυριάσιν ἀγγέλων [,] πανηγύρει; though the last instance should warn us against supposing that what is ambiguous to us was therefore ambiguous to native and contemporary readers. However that may be, it is certain that careful study of this epistle corrects the first impression of artificial rhetoric. Notice the truly Greek naturalness of the return to the accusative in ἀγαγόντα ii. 10; and the wakefulness against growing tedious in chs. iv. and v., where the too argumentative page is enlightened suddenly by ἄρα ἀπολείπεται σαββατισμός κ.τ.λ. iv. 9; the vivid personal ἀνατέταλκεν ὁ κύριος ἡμῶν vii. 14, and the great arresting phrases at vii. 16, 25.

§ 8. *Particles and Conjunctions.*

He uses particles and conjunctions more freely and skilfully than any other New Testament writer. For illustration take these references : οὐ γὰρ δή που ii. 16, καὶ...μὲν...δέ iii. 5 f., x. 11 f., καὶ...δέ ix. 21, ἄχρις οὗ iii. 13, καίπερ with part. v. 8, vii. 5, xii. 17, καίτοι with part. or perhaps rather introducing new sentence iv. 3 (see note), καὶ γάρ xii. 29, xiii. 22 (see note), ἄρα iv. 9, διό vi. 1, x. 5, εἰ μὲν οὖν vii. 11, viii. 4, cf. ix. 1, εἶτα xii. 9, ὥστε introducing clause xiii. 6, τοίνυν xiii. 13. Con-nexion by relatives, ὅς, περὶ οὗ, οἵτινες, ὅθεν, ὅπου, is frequent. The parenthetic, οὕτω φοβερὸν ἦν τὸ φανταζόμενον xii. 21, is a good device for heightening the imaginative effect of the passage. Variety is gained by expressing comparisons by παρά, antithetic balance by καθ' ὅσον, τοσούτῳ...ὅσῳ, i. 4, ix. 27, x. 25. In x. 33 τοῦτο μὲν...τοῦτο δέ is used in good Greek sense ; so is ὡς ἔπος εἰπεῖν (limiting the bold statement) in vii. 9. One of the simplicities of the author's diction is his frequent introduction of sentences by a plain καί—to be dis-tinguished from the emphatic καί which qualifies the opening word of a sentence introduced by some other particle : contrast ix. 21 with ix. 22, also the remarkable xi. 17. Perhaps it would be fanciful to recognise the onward pressing hopefulness of the epistle in this habit, as a sanguine temperament is sometimes discovered by an upward tending script. Yet see how a καί of this kind *appends* xi. 39 f. to the roll of by-gone heroisms, and notice the restless *desiderium* of the three last verses as contrasted with the resting places in the history which were marked by the firm words πόλιν xi. 16, and εἰρήνης xi. 31. Sometimes attention is called by an abrupt start, without connecting particle ; thus οὔπω μέχρις αἵματος xii. 4, cf. iii. 12, viii. 13, x. 8, 23, 28 f., 31, the repeated πίστει in xi., xii. 14, and often in xiii. Sometimes the author binds together a chain of nouns and phrases with καὶ and τέ, vi. 4 f. ; but again, as though weary of such precision, he pours forth additional ones rapidly and disconnected, xi. 37 f. At xiii. 8 Ἰησοῦς ἐχθὲς καὶ σήμερον κ.τ.λ. (see note) is a battle cry, not a statement, in accordance with the purpose of the epistle, which is to " witness " for the faith, not to develop it.

The author has been wrongfully accused of mistreating ὅπως in ii. 9 (see note). Another case of doubtful Greek may be worth a few remarks. No New Testament writer keeps the classical rule about οὐ and μή with participles; their rough and ready rule is, "with participle always μή." However they do use οὐ sometimes (see Blass, § 75, 5); as this author does, evidently with intention, in xi. 35. But, besides that, he preserves something of the older feeling for μή. Notice first his idiomatic ἐπεὶ μή τότε ἰσχύει ix. 17 (where see note); then the μή with part. in iv. 2, 15, vii. 3, 6, ix. 9, xi. 8, 13, 27. In most instances there is reason for μή in the syntax of the sentence, or we can discern at least a partial appropriateness in the μή : sometimes it might be translated "though...not," or "not that." Contrast xi. 1, πραγμάτων ἔλεγχος οὐ βλεπομένων, where μή would greatly weaken the thought, with xi. 27, μὴ φοβηθεὶς τὸν θυμὸν τοῦ βασιλέως = "not that, do not say that he feared"; cf. 1 Pet. i. 8, ὃν οὐκ ἰδόντες ἀγαπᾶτε, εἰς ὃν ἄρτι μὴ ὁρῶντες πιστεύοντες δὲ ἀγαλλιᾶτε, "where," however, Blass holds, "it is artificial to wish to draw a distinction between the two negatives."

§ 9. *Picturesqueness.*

Of the author's picturesque manner of thinking something has been said in another section. These characteristics may be noted here. Personification in xii. 4 and again in 5, also in 24. Yet in each case what is characteristic is the delicacy of the figure; the phrase just falls short of personification, cf. x. 23 the "confession" wavering; it is the unconscious liveliness of an ever picturing mind. And in the two instances from ch. xii., of voices in Scripture and in the mystery symbolised by "blood," there is something akin to the idea which runs through the epistle of the Spirit of God speaking in books, history and ritual. Pictures are again and again presented to the mind's eye; see the opening verses i. 1—4, xi. 13—16 the "pilgrim fathers." Sometimes these pictures are, not indistinct, but hard to interpret. They take form, dissolve, and form themselves afresh, as we ponder on their meaning; so iv. 12 f. and xiii. 7 the release of departed "leaders" from the coil of business, or their martyrdom. Mystery of a deeper kind is suggested in

such passages as xii. 18 with its undefined participles ψηλαφωμένῳ καὶ κεκαυμένῳ πυρί ; mark the φανταζόμενον immediately
afterwards, which comes in as a curious and peculiar word
that lets you into the spirit of the whole design. The converse
of this appears in sentences where difficult thought is condensed
into luminous phrases and made "clear" by being carried into
a higher region of imagination. Instances are ii. 14 τὸν τὸ
κράτος ἔχοντα τοῦ θανάτου, vi. 5 δυνάμεις τε μέλλοντος αἰῶνος,
vii. 16 οὐ κατὰ νόμον ἐντολῆς σαρκίνης...ἀλλὰ κατὰ δύναμιν ζωῆς
ἀκαταλύτου, and vii. 25 πάντοτε ζῶν εἰς τὸ ἐντυγχάνειν ὑπὲρ αὐτῶν,
where the peculiar quality of this epistle may be discerned by
comparison with the less tangible phrase of Rom. viii. 27, κατὰ
θεὸν ἐντυγχάνει [τὸ πνεῦμα] ὑπὲρ ἁγίων. Cf. also ix. 14, xi. 1, 3,
27, xii. 27. There is something of the same nature, though here
imagination more nearly approaches metaphor, in x. 20 ; worth
special reference however on account of the τοῦτ' ἔστιν, which,
perhaps always, in this epistle introduces a more profound
second thought.

Then there is the imagination of sympathy, as in the pictures of the divine humiliation ii. 8 f., v. 7 ff. ; of the unhappy
"sinners against their own selves" xii. 3, cf. χωρὶς οἰκτιρμῶν
x. 28 ; the silly, halting "multitude" xii. 13 ; the wakeful
leaders xiii. 17 ; and the recollection in v. 1 ff. of good priests
the author and his friends have known. In xi. 21 καὶ προσεκύνησεν ἐπὶ τὸ ἄκρον τῆς ῥάβδου αὐτοῦ, which we are apt to feel
an otiose addition, is probably a pathetic detail in the description
of the aged patriarch. It is generally safe to let the picturesque
emerge from our author's language. Consider how the visual
image simplifies discussion of ὑπόστασις, τελειόω, συνείδησις, and
in their context, κατὰ πίστιν xi. 13, μεσίτη xii. 24 ; and how it
adds to the value of such rememberable phrases as the "cloud of
witnesses," "land of promise," "city that hath the foundations."

§ 10. *Artistic arrangement.*

The late Dean of Lincoln, Dr Wickham, says in his edition :
"It is, in a sense beyond any other epistle in the New Testament, an artistic whole. It is a letter, but at the same time
it is an impassioned treatise or piece of oratory, having a single

purpose, ardently felt, clearly conceived, never lost to sight. The whole argument is in view from the beginning, whether in the purely argumentative passages, or in those which are in form hortatory; we are constantly meeting phrases which are to be taken up again, and to have their full meaning given to them later on. The plan itself develops. While the figures to some extent change and take fresh colour, there is growing through all, in trait on trait, the picture which the writer designs to leave before his readers' minds." This is admirably put, and we shall also listen respectfully to von Soden[1], who finds in the arrangement an exact observance of the rules of the masters of rhetoric; i. 1—iv. 13 is the προοίμιον πρὸς εὔ- νοιαν with establishment of the πρόθεσις, iv. 14—vi. 20 διήγησις πρὸς πιθανότητα, vii. 1—x. 18 ἀπόδειξις πρὸς πειθώ, x. 19—xiii. 21 ἐπίλογος, with the practical challenge that all has been leading to.

Undoubtedly there is art, much art, in the composition. If the divisions marked by von Soden do not appear at once clear cut before us, that only shews good art concealing art. In all his transitions the author hides the juncture; notice for instance how "angels" is repeated, ii. 5, as a catch-word to link the new subject of ii. 5—18 to the former. But notice also how delicately this is done; the thought of the angels itself over-laps into the new subject, and is just touched once more near the end, ii. 16; yet it is no master thought in this section, the angels, as it were, slowly fade; except for the smooth advance of the argument they need not really have been mentioned again after i. 14. To us this artistic manner is apt to cause a kind of suspicion; it seems "artificial"; we think of the author's own depreciation of the things that are transitory because they are "made up," ὡς πεποιημένων, xii. 27. And indeed his style and manner are, as with many another earnest advocate of eternal truth, transitory. They belong, like the technical vocabulary of Alexandrine philosophy which he employs, to the time and to the little circle of himself and his friends. But that means that they were natural to him and them. He has a purpose ardently felt, nothing less than to prepare some

---

[1] *Hand-Commentar*, p. 11. Freiburg, 1899.

dear friends for possible or probable martyrdom. They, like himself, live in a world of books. That explains his choice of language, and makes his purpose the more courageous. Compare the eloquent defence of S. Stephen, another "man of words" who passed from words to martyrdom with no sense of incongruity, though probably with especial difficulty ; and see how sympathetically S. Luke, himself like-minded, describes both his educated oratory and his masculine resolution. It need hardly be added that both S. Luke and our author look beyond these things—ἀφορῶντες xii. 1—to the vision of the martyr's captain and upholder, enthroned—or standing—at the right hand of God.

§ 11. *A.V. and R.V.*

Translations into modern English, such as Weymouth's or *The Twentieth Century New Testament*, are less acceptable for Hebrews than for other parts of N.T. Moffatt's earlier translation in his *Historical New Testament* (T. and T. Clark) does preserve something of the peculiar flavour of this epistle. Yet how thin is his rendering of xi. 1 : "Now faith is to be confident of what we hope for, to be convinced of what we do not see." Hardly indeed may A.V. be surpassed in that verse : "Now faith is the substance of things hoped for, the evidence of things not seen." The half philosophical, half picturesque phraseology of the original is just caught there, and the marginal note on "substance"—"Or, *ground*, or *confidence*"—goes as far as it ought to go in concession to the weaker brethren. The R.V., it must be confessed, attenuates the sense : "Now faith is the assurance of things hoped for, the proving of things not seen," and in the margin for "the assurance" "Or, *the giving substance to*," for "proving" "Or, *test*." Other, but slight, misrenderings in R.V. are vii. 9 "so to say" for ὡς ἔπος εἰπεῖν, x. 33 "partly... partly" for τοῦτο μὲν...τοῦτο δέ, xiii. 8 where the insertion of "*is*" weakens the proclamation, which in A.V. sounds forth bravely.

In Hebrews A.V. is particularly good, not merely as a piece of English, but as an equivalent of the uncommon Greek style. The advantage of reading in R.V. is not so immediately obvious

as in S. Paul's epistles, perhaps even less so when the proper
test of reading aloud is applied. Yet to the theologian, however
simple, who does not read to delight his ear but to assure his
anxious heart, the satisfaction of R.V. is presently discovered.
There is first the inestimable advantage of the pure text. At
the outset R.V. strikes the note of hope with "at the end of
these days" instead of "in these last days"; then of breadth
with " when he had made purification of sins " instead of " when
he had by himself purged our sins." It does matter whether
Christ came as a high priest of good things to come, or, R.V.
margin, of good things that have with His death already come,
ix. 11; whether we ought to "consider him that endured such
contradiction of sinners against himself," or rather "him that
hath endured such gainsaying of sinners against themselves,"
xii. 3.

Nor is the scrupulous attention of R.V. to this perf. part.,
ὑπομεμενηκότα, pedantry. As in ii. 18 and many another place
the author encourages us here by the belief that our Saviour's
pains on earth are still in Him a ground of sympathy with us.
If all the many corrections of tenses in R.V. are not so evidently
practical in their bearing, more and more are found to be so by
the student who broods over his book. Or take the article.
Is there no theological beauty in " the city which hath the
foundations" xi. 10, "the city which is to come" xiii. 14, or in
the answer of xi. 14 to xi. 9, "a sojourner in the land of promise,
as in a land not his own....For they that say such things make
it manifest that they are seeking after a country of their own"?
In xii. 2 "endured the cross, despising shame," is perhaps
wrong; the Greek has the art. with neither noun, and A.V.
reproduces the aphorism more forcibly by adding it to both.
But in xii. 14 "Follow after peace with all men, and the sanctification without which no man shall see the Lord," R.V. has
faithfully preferred an obscurity, which at least startles the
conscience, to the smooth inaccuracy, which so easily passes
through the mind as a truism, of A.V.

In that verse "no man" is a right translation. But in iii. 3,
x. 12 A.V. speaks of our Lord as "this man" without justifi-
cation in the Greek. This confuses the important doctrine of
the real manhood which the epistle illustrates continually, but

never in such crude fashion. It dwells too on His "compassion"
or "sympathy," but μετριοπαθεῖν, v. 2, is different, in some ways
more than that, and R.V. "bear gently with" is admirable.
A.V. however has "can reasonably bear with" in its margin, and
the margin deserves attention in both versions—in R.V. it is as
valuable as the text; it is very wrong to print either without
their marginal notes. If the theology of Hebrews does add
anything to the theology of the rest of the N.T., it is more
than worth while to render its peculiar theological phraseology
with particularity. That is attempted far more thoroughly in
R.V. than in A.V. In i. 14 "ministering spirits sent forth to
minister" misses the conversion of ritual idealism into practical service which R.V. expresses by "to do service." "To make
reconciliation," ii. 17, is Pauline; "to make propitiation" = ἱλάσκεσθαι. "Consecrated," vii. 28, confuses τελειόω with ἁγιάζω ; the
margin has "Gr. *perfected*," but R.V. rightly puts this into the
text. In x. 23 "faith" for "hope" is a sheer mistake, possibly
a printer's error. In xi. 2, 39 "obtained a good report" is quite
misleading. R.V. "had witness borne to them" sounds less
plain English but indicates the connexion with the other passages where μαρτυρεῖσθαι or cognates are used with more or less
approach to the idea of "martyrdom." In xii. 2 the dominant
note of τελειόω is again echoed in τελειωτήν. A.V. "Author and
finisher" has the influence of custom upon us. But the echo is
important, and "finisher" may even suggest an untrue thought if
we connect it with the popular interpretation of 1 Cor. xiii. 13.
R.V. "Author and perfecter," with the marginal alternative
"captain" for "author," carries us far deeper into the writer's mind.
In xi. 13 A.V. has "These all died in faith, not having received
the promises, but having seen them afar off, and were persuaded
of them, and embraced them," a false reading and a wrong
translation. How beautiful is R.V. "having seen them and
greeted them from afar." This is an example of that vivid
picturesqueness which really belongs to the epistle and which,
reverently preserved, may impress the writer's earnest purpose
upon more generations of readers than the sweetest compen-
sations in another idiom. So in x. 27 "fierceness of fire" R.V. is
better than "fiery indignation." It might seem wanton to alter
"Now that which decayeth and waxeth old is ready to vanish

away," viii. 13, into "But that which is becoming old and waxeth aged is nigh unto vanishing away." But the transposition of "old" knits, as in the Greek πεπαλαίωκεν...τὸ δὲ παλαιούμενον, this verse to the preceding. The compound phrase "is becoming old" shows that this is no mere proverbial appendage (which might well be introduced by "Now"), but the observation of a particular and startling process already going on before the eyes of the writer and his friends. And the "nigh unto" is one of the solemn notes characteristic of the epistle; cf. vi. 8 ἀδόκιμος καὶ κατάρας ἐγγύς, x. 25 ἐγγίζουσαν τὴν ἡμέραν, and—an answering phrase in the harmony—ἐπεισαγωγὴ κρείττονος ἐλπίδος δι' ἧς ἐγγίζομεν τῷ θεῷ, vii. 19. If this epistle really is a challenge, sounding out of an actual crisis when some great perilous change was "nigh," all this correction was worth making. It is however a pity that those who worked so carefully here should have obscured their purpose by rendering τελευτῶν, xi. 22, into "when his end was nigh."

§ 12. *Rythm.*

It would be out of place in these notes to consider the objection commonly made against R.V., viz. that its rythm is inferior, if this consideration did not help us to a more precise appreciation of the Greek rythm of the epistle. But it does. Whereas A.V. preserves the more formal Latin tradition in its grand but slightly varied cadences, R.V. approaches more nearly the freedom of the Greek. No doubt the main care of the Revisers was for exact translation and sometimes for restoring the author's meaning by attention to the order of his words. But the result unconsciously attained is, fairly often, a nearer agreement with the principle laid down by Aristotle, *Rhet.* iii. 8, that in prose there should be rythm but no metre, and that the rythm should not be too precise.

Hebrews certainly has rythm. Blass published an edition in which he shewed a metrical correspondence of clauses throughout, the beginning or ending of one answering to another near it, and not a single one failing to come into the system. He actually makes out these correspondences, but is obliged to introduce a certain number of impossible readings for the purpose. It would appear that the careful Greek rhetoricians really did

compose in this manner. But we may suspect that the author of
Hebrews was after all not one of them. Indeed his tendency to
let words run into fragments of verse forbids our recognising him
as either a very careful or a quite first-rate master of rythm.
His variety is great. To classify his cadences is a baffling task.
Finely measured yet changeful sound pervades whole sentences.
Nevertheless his variety is infected by a certain monotony of
"the metrical," here and there.

Yet the verse-metre to which he is inclined is the iambic.
Isocrates had like inclination and Aristotle says of that metre,
that in the speech of everyday life people are apt to drop into it;
which seems to provide some excuse for both writers.

Aristotle gives another hint for our guidance when he recom-
mends the paeon as a measure to be used in prose. The paeon
is a long syllable followed by three short ones, or three short
syllables followed by a long. So in the opening verse, πολυμερῶς
καὶ πολυτρόπως; and, if we extend its use by breaking the long
into two shorts, the next phrase continues in the same measure,
πάλαι ὁ θεός, for of course αι is short before the following vowel.
But if this phrase be taken, not by itself, but in its context with
the whole sentence, the last syllable of θεός is lengthened by
"position": thus monotony is avoided, and we already have
a suggestion of the many ways in which the author will adapt
this favourite element of rythm.

But another metrical equivalent of the paeon is the cretic
(– ◡ –), and this is in Demosthenes "his favourite foot throughout
the sentence." And in the epistle cretics will be found to play
an important part. The student may count the cretics in the
four opening verses; then take less rhetorical passages and
notice how the cretics diminish in number; then observe cretics
giving the "Ciceronian" character to the close of sentences,
i.e. a cretic followed by a trochaic series; yet not with Ciceronian
regularity—the modification – ◡ ◡ – is for instance common. He
will also notice how often the offending iambic combinations may
be better read as measures governed by a cretic, e.g. xii. 18, καὶ
κεκαυμένῳ πυρὶ, is notably iambic only when isolated; in its context it breaks agreeably what would otherwise have been too long
a series of cretics, ψηλαφωμένῳ καὶ κεκαυμένῳ πυρὶ καὶ γνόφῳ καὶ
ζόφῳ καὶ θυέλλῃ.

However, in spite of Aristotle and the other ancient critics, this analysis into feet is rather misleading. Walter Headlam once wrote, "I never could understand lyric metres cut up into feet: the key to understanding them is to regard them as built up from phrases, or as you would say in music 'figures.'" That is very applicable to prose; and another point to be observed is the manner in which these "figures" are linked together. In lyric metres Headlam shewed[1] that one rhythm or "figure" does not simply succeed another, but is linked with it, the last notes of the one forming at the same time the first notes of the new tune (as it were). Something of this kind may be observed in the passage just quoted, xii. 18; and continually. There indeed is a difference. Lyrics, as Headlam read them, are subtle and flexible in metre, but they have their conventionally repeated measures; the transitions occur only at certain points. In good prose there should be no convention like rhyme or metre; the transition should be continuous, like the living curve of a bough. As time went on artificiality gained on prose, and even of Isocrates Plutarch could say that he went on fitting and compacting antithetic and parallel phrases and answering cadences, smoothing away his periods almost with chisels, till he waxed aged (ἐγήρασε)[2]. In this respect, as in its language generally, Hebrews is a return towards the earlier simplicity; the precision of the schools has in the fellowship of the Church been reinforced by the racy idiom of daily life.

But this is all rather technical. Ordinary readers will be content to dwell upon the indisputable beauty of the opening verses, or such haunting cadences as iv. 16 ἵνα λάβωμεν ἔλεος καὶ χάριν εὕρωμεν εἰς εὔκαιρον βοήθειαν, viii. 13 ἐν τῷ λέγειν καινήν πεπαλαίωκεν τὴν πρώτην, τὸ δὲ παλαιούμενον καὶ γηράσκον ἐγγὺς ἀφανισμοῦ. And notice again how sound combines with sense. This epistle often if not always illustrates Landor's aphorism: "Natural sequences and right subordination of thoughts, and that just proportion of numbers in the sentences

---

[1] *Greek Lyric Metre, Journal of Hellenic Studies*, **xxii.** pp. 209—227.

[2] *de gloria Athen.* ch. 8, quoted by A. C. Clark, *Fontes prosae numerosae*, p. 8.

which follows a strong conception, are the constituents of true harmony." The "numbers," it will be found, depend on quantity not stress of syllables.   Notice at ix. 11, after the pause ...μέχρι καιροῦ διορθώσεως ἐπικείμενα, the rush of short syllables with which the new hope is introduced—Χριστὸς δὲ παραγενόμενος ἀρχιερεὺς τῶν γενομένων ἀγαθῶν διὰ..., and, on the other hand, the stately entrance of the *finale* at xii. 1—τοιγαροῦν καὶ ἡμεῖς... where the brief trochaic opening is quite appropriate.

It is trochaic because καὶ is short before the initial vowel of ἡμεῖς. This collocation is not seldom admitted, and with good effect; cf. δι' οὗ καὶ ἐποίησεν τοὺς αἰῶνας, i. 2. Except for such effects, hiatus is avoided.

In the last quotation the final ν of ἐποίησεν may be observed. This final ν, which before consonants is in this epistle as usual as in the rest of N.T., is so managed as to contribute to good rythm ; see the variety in i. 2 ἐλάλησεν ἡμῖν...ἔθηκεν κληρονόμον... ἐποίησεν τοὺς αἰῶνας, or the additional emphasis given to the initial ἔστιν xi. 1, while the omission in πνεύμασι δικαίων τετελειωμένων xii. 23 seems in turn to satisfy the ear.

§ 13. *Aids to study of language.*

The style is so important a feature of this epistle that very much more than one section of a brief introduction would be required for anything like complete treatment of the subject. The philosophical vocabulary would allow long and careful examination.   Then it would run out into consideration of the author's obligations to many other kinds of literature, especially what we now call the Classics.   Enough has perhaps been said to start the student on enquiries of his own.   A few books may be named from which he may find help.

The literature of the papyri and other documents of vulgar Greek, so necessary for the study of other parts of N.T., is not much needed here.   Milligan[1], or Witkowski[2], or Deissmann[3] will shew however that the author's literary taste has by no

[1] *Selections from the Greek Papyri*, Camb. Univ. Press.

[2] *Epistulae Privatae Graecae*, Teubner.

[3] *Light from the Ancient East* (tr. L. R. M. Strachan), Hodder and Stoughton.

means prevented his using in due measure the ordinary language of his day. Here is a list of words and phrases from Milligan which illustrate the epistle:

ἐπιδειξάτω p. 3, cf. vi. 17; εὖ γὰρ ἴσθι p. 6, cf. xii. 17; παραγενέσθαι p. 7, cf. ix. 11; λειτουργῆσαι p. 13; κεκομισμέναι, διαλυόμενοι p. 14; δι' ὀλίων (sic) p. 14, cf. xiii. 22; εὐλάβειαν p. 15; κρατεῖν p. 18, cf. ii. 14; μιανθῶσιν p. 18; ἀπολελυμένον p. 23, cf. xiii. 23; ὑπέρ = with regard to, p. 24; κατασκευάζω p. 30; καταρτίζω p. 31; τῶν ἀπό p. 52, cf. xiii. 24; ἀποκατεστάθη p. 53; σωτῆρα p. 54; χρημάτισον p. 69, χρηματίζομαι p. 112; χειροποιήτους p. 70; τὸ παρόν p. 74, cf. xii. 11; ἐγγυᾶται, ἔγγυοι p. 87, cf. vii. 22; ἡγουμένοις ἱερέων p. 88, 108, ὁ ἡγούμενος τοῦ στρατηγοῦ p. 35, cf. xiii. 7, 17; περιαιρεθῆναι p. 89, cf. xii. 1; ὅτι με ἐπαίδευσας καλῶς p. 91, cf. xii. 5 ff.; παραμένω, ἑαυτούς p. 96; εὐσέβεια p. 99, εὐσεβής p. 116; οὐ μή p. 103; νωθρεύεται p. 106, cf. v. 11; αἰωνίων p. 110; ἐπικαλοῦ p. 111, cf. xi. 16; ἐγευσάμην with gen. p. 116; ἀγαπητῷ ἀδελφῷ ἐν Κυρίῳ p. 117; πιστεύομεν, plural of one person, p. 125, cf. xiii. 18, 21; τῶν ἁμαρτιῶν καθάρσεως p. 126; τηλικαύτην p. 129; ὁ θεὸς ὁ ἅγιος ὁ ἀληθινός p. 131; εὐχαριστῶ = pray, p. 132.

On the other hand the ordinary tools of everyday Greek scholarship, Liddell and Scott and (if within reach) Stephanus' *Thesaurus*, and Goodwin's *Moods and Tenses*, will prove more necessary than might at first seem likely. And with these should be mentioned Rutherford's little *First Greek Syntax*, Macmillan, 1891. Few books reveal so vividly—what is particularly important in studying a late, classicising, though not always Atticising, but always a natural writer—the essential genius of the language. The preface to the same great master's *Romans translated*, Macmillan, 1900, is worth reading as an introduction to the really profitable lines of enquiry into the difference between S. Paul's Greek and this epistle.

There is a new edition, or revision, of Blass' Grammar by Debrunner[1], of which Dr Moulton writes "On first sight I should say that the new editor is a better qualified guide than his master for the purpose of this book. Blass was a supremely great classical scholar who could help the student of the Κοινή

---

[1] *Grammatik des neutestamentlichen Griechisch*, Göttingen, 1913.

with all manner of valuable hints from antiquity; but he almost inevitably kept to the last something of the foreigner's air of superiority on Hellenistic soil." That delightful portrait affords excuse for the frequent reference to the old edition in this commentary; for Hebrews the idiosyncrasy of Blass, the classical scholar, is still inspiring. Moreover German books are not easily got just now, and we have the advantage of Mr Thackeray's excellent translation of the second edition of the original book[1]. A very big book in English by Dr A. T. Robertson[2] may also be mentioned.

Another book by Blass[3] is extremely interesting, and to some extent certainly true. Moulton's own *Grammar of N.T. Greek*, vol. I, T. and T. Clark, 1906,—still unfortunately a fragment—must always be used. Herwerden's *Lexicon Graecum suppletorium et dialecticum* is sometimes required for the later words. And there is a wealth of entertaining and instructive material in Jannaris[4].

The Septuagint should be read in the smaller Cambridge edition[5]. This edition represents the text of the ancient MSS. faithfully. Their varieties of reading need to be observed by any one who really wishes to understand the influence of the LXX on the epistle. And, as in Westcott and Hort, it is a great thing to enjoy the original spelling: the appendix added to each vol.—"ἵνα μή τι ἀπόληται"—will serve those well who care to pursue that line of study further. So will H. St J. Thackeray's Grammar[6]—another fragment, but rich in present gratification

---

[1] *Grammar of N.T. Greek*, Macmillan, ed. 2, 1905.

[2] *Grammar of the Greek N.T., in the light of historical research.* New York, 1914.

[3] *Brief an die Hebräer, Text mit Angabe der Rhythmen.* Halle, 1903.

[4] *Historical Greek Grammar chiefly of the Attic Dialect as written and spoken from classical antiquity down to the present time.* Macmillan, 1897.

[5] *The Old Testament in Greek according to the Septuagint*, edited for the Syndics of the University Press by Henry Barclay Swete, 3 vols.

[6] *A Grammar of the Old Testament in Greek, vol. I, Introduction, Orthography and Accidence.* Cambridge, 1909.

as well as promise. And Swete's *Introduction to the Old Testament in Greek*, Camb. 1900, of which there is a new edition now revised and enlarged by Mr Ottley, should be read again and again. No one has done more than Dr Swete to help students of N.T. to regain the point of view of the first readers of the Greek Testament. He writes (p. 435), "Mediaeval Europe knew the Old Testament almost exclusively through Jerome's Latin, as the Ancient Church had known it through the LXX. When at length the long reign of the Vulgate in Western Europe was broken by the forces of the Renaissance and the Reformation, the attention of scholars was once more drawn to that which purported to be the original text of the Old Testament"—ἥτις παραβολὴ εἰς τὸν καιρὸν τὸν ἐνεστηκότα. The *Concordance to the Septuagint and other Greek Versions of the Old Testament* by Hatch and Redpath, Oxford, is all but indispensable. If however access to this is difficult, sufficient aid for everyday study may be found in Thayer's Lexicon[1]. When Dr Sanday reviewed this Lexicon on its publication in 1886, he called it a Liddell and Scott for the New Testament, and the comparison is as apt now as it was then. Grimm and Thayer like Liddell and Scott are no longer on the top of the tide ; but, like L. and S., they are wise and practical guides to plain men who do not greatly feel, and to instructed men who know whence to supply, the deficiencies due to later discovery. It is hardly necessary to mention Bruder's Concordance. Little work of any kind can be done in N.T. without it. The new Concordance of Geden and Moulton is founded on the revised and better text of N.T., but Bruder's old-fashioned text is easily controlled, and the spacious arrangement of the page is a real advantage.

---

[1] *A Greek-English Lexicon of the New Testament, being Grimm's Wilkes' Clavis Novi Testamenti translated revised and enlarged*, by Joseph Henry Thayer, T. and T. Clark.

ΠΡΟΣ ΕΒΡΑΙΟΥΣ

1 ¹ΠΟΛΥΜΕΡΩΣ ΚΑΙ ΠΟΛΥΤΡΟΠΩΣ πάλαι ὁ θεὸς λαλήσας τοῖς πατράσιν ἐν τοῖς προφήταις ²ἐπ᾽ ἐσχάτου τῶν ἡμερῶν τούτων ἐλάλησεν ἡμῖν ἐν υἱῷ, ὃν ἔθηκεν κληρονόμον πάντων, δι᾽ οὗ καὶ ἐποίησεν τοὺς αἰῶνας· ³ὃς ὢν ἀπαύγασμα τῆς δόξης καὶ χαρακτὴρ τῆς ὑποστάσεως αὐτοῦ, φέρων τε τὰ πάντα τῷ ῥήματι τῆς δυνάμεως αὐτοῦ, καθαρισμὸν τῶν ἁμαρτιῶν ποιησάμενος ἐκάθισεν ἐν δεξιᾷ τῆς μεγαλωσύνης ἐν ὑψηλοῖς, ⁴τοσούτῳ κρείττων γενόμενος τῶν ἀγγέλων ὅσῳ διαφορώτερον παρ᾽ αὐτοὺς κεκληρονόμηκεν ὄνομα. ⁵Τίνι γὰρ εἶπέν ποτε τῶν ἀγγέλων

Υἱός μου εἶ σύ, ἐγὼ σήμερον γεγέννηκά σε,

καὶ πάλιν

Ἐγὼ ἔσομαι αὐτῷ εἰς πατέρα, καὶ αὐτὸς ἔσται μοι εἰς υἱόν;

⁶ὅταν δὲ πάλιν εἰσαγάγῃ τὸν πρωτότοκον εἰς τὴν οἰκουμένην, λέγει

Καὶ προσκυνησάτωσαν αὐτῷ πάντες ἄγγελοι θεοῦ.

⁷καὶ πρὸς μὲν τοὺς ἀγγέλους λέγει

Ὁ ποιῶν τοὺς ἀγγέλους αὐτοῦ πνεύματα,

καὶ τοὺς λειτουργοὺς αὐτοῦ πυρὸς φλόγα·

πρὸς δὲ τὸν υἱόν

Ὁ θρόνος cΟΥ ὁ θεὸc εἰc τὸν αἰῶνα [τΟῦ αἰῶνοc],
καὶ ἡ ῥάβδοc τῆς εὐθΥτΗΤΟc ῥάβδΟc τῆc Βαcιλείαc
αὐτοῦ.
⁹ΗΓά́πΗὉΟΑC ΔΙΚΑΙΟὉΥΝΗΝ ΚᾺΙ ἐμίCΗCΑC ἀνομίΑν·
Διὰ τΟῦτο ἔχριcέΝ cε ὁ θεόc, ὁ θεόc cΟΥ, ἔλαιον
ἀΓαλλιάcεωc παρὰ τΟῪc μετόχΟΥc cΟΥ·
¹⁰καί
ΣῪ κατ᾽ ἀρχάc, κΎριε, τῊΝ ΓῊΝ ἐθεμελίωcαc,
ΚᾺΙ ἔρΓα τῶν χειρῶν cΟΥ εἰcιν οἱ ΟΥ̓ρανοί·
¹¹αΥ̓τῸι ἀπολΟῦΝΤΑΙ, cῪ Δὲ ΔιαμένειC·
ΚᾺΙ πάντεc ὡc ἱμάτιον παλαιωθΉCΟΝΤΑΙ,
¹²ΚᾺΙ ὡcὲι περιΒόλαιον ἑλίξειc αΥ̓τΟΎc,
ὡς ἱμάτιον ΚᾺΙ ἀλλαΓΉΟΟΝΤΑΙ·
cῪ Δὲ ὁ αΥ̓τῸc εἶ, ΚᾺΙ τὰ ἔτΗ cΟΥ ΟΥ̓Κ ἐΚλείψΟΥΟιΝ.
¹³πρὸς τίνα δὲ τῶν ἀγγέλων εἴρηκέν ποτε
ΚάθΟΥ ἐΚ ΔεξΙῶν ΜΟΥ
ἔωc ἄν θῶ τΟῪc ἐχθρΟΎc cΟΥ ὑποπόΔΙον τῶν ποΔῶν
cΟΥ:
¹⁴οὐχὶ πάντες εἰσὶν λειτουργικὰ πνεύματα εἰς διακονίαν
ἀποστελλόμενα διὰ τοὺς μέλλοντας κληρονομεῖν σωτηρίαν; 2 ¹Διὰ τοῦτο δεῖ περισσοτέρως προσέχειν
ἡμᾶς τοῖς ἀκουσθεῖσιν, μή ποτε παραρυῶμεν. ²εἰ γὰρ
ὁ δι᾽ ἀγγέλων λαληθεὶς λόγος ἐγένετο βέβαιος, καὶ
πᾶσα παράβασις καὶ παρακοὴ ἔλαβεν ἔνδικον μισθαποδοσίαν, ³πῶς ἡμεῖς ἐκφευξόμεθα τηλικαύτης ἀμελήσαντες σωτηρίας, ἥτις, ἀρχὴν λαβοῦσα λαλεῖσθαι διὰ
τοῦ κυρίου, ὑπὸ τῶν ἀκουσάντων εἰς ἡμᾶς ἐβεβαιώθη,
⁴συνεπιμαρτυροῦντος τοῦ θεοῦ σημείοις τε καὶ τέρασιν
καὶ ποικίλαις δυνάμεσιν καὶ πνεύματος ἁγίου μερισμοῖς
κατὰ τὴν αὐτοῦ θέλησιν;
⁵Οὐ γὰρ ἀγγέλοις ὑπέταξεν τὴν οἰκουμένην τὴν

μέλλουσαν, περὶ ἧς λαλοῦμεν· ⁶διεμαρτύρατο δέ πού
τις λέγων
Τί ἐϲτιν ἄνθρωποϲ ὅτι μιμνήϲκη αὐτοῦ,
ἢ υἱὸϲ ἀνθρώπου ὅτι ἐπιϲκέπτη αὐτόν ;
⁷Ηλάττωϲαϲ αὐτὸν βραχύ τι παρ’ ἀγγέλουϲ,
δόξη καὶ τιμῇ ἐϲτεφάνωϲαϲ αὐτόν,
[καὶ κατέϲτηϲαϲ αὐτὸν ἐπὶ τὰ ἔργα τῶν χειρῶν ϲου,]
⁸πάντα ὑπέταξαϲ ὑποκάτω τῶν ποδῶν αὐτοῦ·
ἐν τῷ γὰρ ὑποτάξαι [αὐτῷ] τὰ πάντα οὐδὲν ἀφῆκεν
αὐτῷ ἀνυπότακτον. νῦν δὲ οὔπω ὁρῶμεν αὐτῷ τὰ
πάντα ὑποτεταγμένα· ⁹τὸν δὲ βραχύ τι παρ’ ἀγγέλουϲ
ἠλαττωμένον βλέπομεν Ἰησοῦν διὰ τὸ πάθημα τοῦ
θανάτου δόξη καὶ τιμῇ ἐϲτεφανωμένον, ὅπως χάριτι
θεοῦ ὑπὲρ παντὸς γεύσηται θανάτου. ¹⁰ᵛΕπρεπεν γὰρ
αὐτῷ, δι’ ὃν τὰ πάντα καὶ δι’ οὗ τὰ πάντα, πολλοὺς
υἱοὺς εἰς δόξαν ἀγαγόντα τὸν ἀρχηγὸν τῆς σωτηρίας
αὐτῶν διὰ παθημάτων τελειῶσαι. ¹¹ὅ τε γὰρ ἁγιάζων
καὶ οἱ ἁγιαζόμενοι ἐξ ἑνὸς πάντες· δι’ ἣν αἰτίαν οὐκ
ἐπαισχύνεται ἀδελφοὺϲ αὐτοὺς καλεῖν, ¹²λέγων
Ἀπαγγελῶ τὸ ὄνομά ϲου τοῖϲ ἀδελφοῖϲ μου,
ἐν μέϲῳ ἐκκληϲίαϲ ὑμνήϲω ϲε·
¹³καὶ πάλιν
Ἐγὼ ἔϲομαι πεποιθὼϲ ἐπ’ αὐτῷ·
καὶ πάλιν
Ἰδοὺ ἐγὼ καὶ τὰ παιδία ἅ μοι ἔδωκεν ὁ θεόϲ.
¹⁴ἐπεὶ οὖν τὰ παιδία κεκοινώνηκεν αἵματος καὶ σαρκός,
καὶ αὐτὸς παραπλησίως μετέσχεν τῶν αὐτῶν, ἵνα διὰ
τοῦ θανάτου καταργήσῃ τὸν τὸ κράτος ἔχοντα τοῦ
θανάτου, τοῦτ’ ἔστι τὸν διάβολον, ¹⁵καὶ ἀπαλλάξῃ
τούτους, ὅσοι φόβῳ θανάτου διὰ παντὸς τοῦ ζῆν ἔνοχοι
ἦσαν δουλείας. ¹⁶οὐ γὰρ δή που ἀγγέλων ἐπιλαμβά-

A 2

νεται, ἀλλὰ cπέρματοc Ἀβραὰμ ἐπιλαμβάνεται. ¹⁷ὅθεν
ὤφειλεν κατὰ πάντα τοῖc ἀδελφοῖc ὁμοιωθῆναι, ἵνα
ἐλεήμων γένηται καὶ πιστὸς ἀρχιερεὺς τὰ πρὸς τὸν
θεόν, εἰς τὸ ἱλάσκεσθαι τὰς ἁμαρτίας τοῦ λαοῦ· ¹⁸ἐν
ᾧ γὰρ πέπονθεν αὐτὸς πειρασθείς, δύναται τοῖς πειραζομένοις βοηθῆσαι.

3 ¹″Οθεν, ἀδελφοὶ ἅγιοι, κλήσεως ἐπουρανίου μέτοχοι, κατανοήσατε τὸν ἀπόστολον καὶ ἀρχιερέα τῆς
ὁμολογίας ἡμῶν Ἰησοῦν, ²πιστὸν ὄντα τῷ ποιήσαντι
αὐτὸν ὡς καὶ Μωϋcῆc ἐν [ὅλῳ] τῷ οἴκῳ ᾳⲧοⲩ. ³πλεί-
ονος γὰρ οὗτος δόξης παρὰ Μωυσῆν ἠξίωται καθ᾽ ὅσον
πλείονα τιμὴν ἔχει τοῦ οἴκου ὁ κατασκευάσας αὐτόν·
⁴πᾶς γὰρ οἶκος κατασκευάζεται ὑπό τινος, ὁ δὲ πάντα
κατασκευάσας θεός. ⁵καὶ Μωϋcῆc μὲν πιστὸc ἐν ὅλῳ
τῷ οἴκῳ ᾳⲧοⲩ ὡς θεράπων εἰς μαρτύριον τῶν λαληθησομένων, ⁶Χριστὸς δὲ ὡς υἱὸς ἐπὶ τὸν οἶκοⲛ ᾳⲧοⲩ· οὗ
οἶκός ἐσμεν ἡμεῖς, ἐὰν τὴν παρρησίαν καὶ τὸ καύχημα
τῆς ἐλπίδος [μέχρι τέλους βεβαίαν] κατάσχωμεν.
⁷Διό, καθὼς λέγει τὸ πνεῦμα τὸ ἅγιον

Cήⲙⲉⲣⲟⲛ ἐὰⲛ ⲧⲏc φⲱⲛⲏc ᾳⲧοⲩ ἀⲕοⲩcⲏⲧⲉ,
⁸ⲙⲏ cⲕⲗⲏⲣⲩⲛⲏⲧⲉ ⲧⲁc ⲕⲁⲣⲇⲓⲁc ⲩⲙⲱⲛ ὡc ἐⲛ ⲧῷ ⲡⲁⲣⲁ-
        ⲡⲓⲕⲣⲁⲥⲙῷ,
    ⲕⲁⲧⲁ ⲧⲏⲛ ⲏⲙⲉⲣⲁⲛ ⲧοⲩ ⲡⲉⲓⲣⲁⲥⲙοⲩ ἐⲛ ⲧⲏ ἐⲣⲏⲙῳ,
⁹οⲩ ἐⲡⲉⲓⲣⲁⲥⲁⲛ οἱ ⲡⲁⲧⲉⲣⲉc ⲩⲙⲱⲛ ἐⲛ ⲇοⲕⲓⲙⲁⲥⲓᾳ
    ⲕⲁⲓ ⲉἶⲇοⲛ ⲧⲁ ἔⲣⲅⲁ ⲙοⲩ ⲧⲉⲥⲥⲉⲣⲁⲕοⲛⲧⲁ ἔⲧⲏ·
¹⁰ⲇⲓὸ ⲡⲣοⲥⲱⲭⲑⲓⲥⲁ ⲧⲏ ⲅⲉⲛⲉᾷ ⲧⲁⲩⲧⲏ
    ⲕⲁⲓ ⲉἶⲡοⲛ Ἀⲉὶ ⲡⲗⲁⲛⲱⲛⲧⲁⲓ ⲧⲏ ⲕⲁⲣⲇⲓᾳ·
    ᾳⲧοὶ ⲇⲉ οⲩⲕ ἔⲅⲛⲱⲥⲁⲛ ⲧⲁc ὁⲇοⲩc ⲙοⲩ
¹¹ὡc ὤⲙοⲥⲁ ἐⲛ ⲧⲏ ὀⲣⲅⲏ ⲙοⲩ
    Eἰ ⲉἰⲥⲉⲗⲉⲩⲥοⲛⲧⲁⲓ ⲉἰc ⲧⲏⲛ ⲕⲁⲧⲁⲡⲁⲩⲥⲓⲛ ⲙοⲩ·
¹²βλέπετε, ἀδελφοί, μή ποτε ἔσται ἔν τινι ὑμῶν καρδία

πονηρὰ ἀπιστίας ἐν τῷ ἀποστῆναι ἀπὸ θεοῦ ζῶντος,
¹³ἀλλὰ παρακαλεῖτε ἑαυτοὺς καθ᾽ ἑκάστην ἡμέραν,
ἄχρις οὗ τό Cήμερον καλεῖται, ἵνα μὴ cκληργνθῇ τις
ἐξ ὑμῶν ἀπάτῃ τῆς ἁμαρτίας· ¹⁴μέτοχοι γὰρ τοῦ
χριστοῦ γεγόναμεν, ἐάνπερ τὴν ἀρχὴν τῆς ὑποστάσεως
μέχρι τέλους βεβαίαν κατάσχωμεν.   ¹⁵ἐν τῷ λέγεσθαι
Cήμερον ἐὰν τῆc φωνῆc αγτογ ἀκογcητε,
Μὴ cκληργνητε τὰc καρδίαc γμῶν ὡc ἐν τῷ παρα-
                                        πικραcμῷ.
¹⁶τίνες γὰρ ἀκούσαντες παρεπίκρανAν; ἀλλ᾽ οὐ πάντες
οἱ ἐξελθόντες ἐξ Αἰγύπτου διὰ Μωυσέως; ¹⁷τίσιν δὲ
προcώχθιcεν τεccεράκοντα ἔτη; οὐχὶ τοῖς ἁμαρτήσασιν,
ὧν τὰ κῶλα ἔπεcεν ἐν τῇ ἐρήμῳ; ¹⁸τίσιν δὲ ὤμοcεν μὴ
εἰcελεγcεcθαι εἰc τὴν κατάπαγcιν αγτογ εἰ μὴ τοῖς ἀπειθήσασιν; ¹⁹καὶ βλέπομεν ὅτι οὐκ ἠδυνήθησαν εἰcελθεῖν
δι᾽ ἀπιστίαν. 4 ¹φοβηθῶμεν οὖν μή ποτε κατα-
λειπομένης ἐπαγγελίας εἰcελθεῖν εἰc τὴν κατάπαγcιν
αγτογ δοκῇ τις ἐξ ὑμῶν ὑστερηκέναι· ²καὶ γάρ ἐσμεν
εὐηγγελισμένοι καθάπερ κἀκεῖνοι, ἀλλ᾽ οὐκ ὠφέλησεν
ὁ λόγος τῆς ἀκοῆς ἐκείνους, μὴ συνκεκερασμένους τῇ
πίστει τοῖς ἀκούσασιν. ³Εἰcερχόμεθα γὰρ εἰc [τὴν]
κατάπαγcιν οἱ πιστεύσαντες, καθὼς εἴρηκεν
ʽΩc ὤμοcα ἐν τῇ ὀργῇ μογ
Εἰ εἰcελεγcονται εἰc τὴν κατάπαγcιν μογ,
καίτοι τῶν ἔργων ἀπὸ καταβολῆς κόσμου γενηθέντων,
⁴εἴρηκεν γάρ που περὶ τῆς ἑβδόμης οὕτως Καὶ κατέ-
παγcεν ὁ θεὸc ἐν τῇ ἡμέρᾳ τῇ ἑβδόμῃ ἀπὸ πάντων τῶν
ἔργων αγτογ, ⁵καὶ ἐν τούτῳ πάλιν Εἰ εἰcελεγcονται εἰc
τὴν κατάπαγcίν μογ. ⁶ἐπεὶ οὖν ἀπολείπεται τινὰς εἰcελθεῖν εἰc αὐτήν, καὶ οἱ πρότερον εὐαγγελισθέντες οὐκ
εἰcῆλθον δι᾽ ἀπείθειαν, ⁷πάλιν τινὰ ὁρίζει ἡμέραν,

Σήμερον, ἐν Δαυεὶδ λέγων μετὰ τοσοῦτον χρόνον, καθὼς προείρηται,

Σήμερον ἐὰν τῆς φωνῆς αὐτοῦ ἀκούσητε, μὴ σκληρύνητε τὰς καρδίας ὑμῶν·

⁸εἰ γὰρ αὐτοὺς Ἰησοῦς κατέπαυσεν, οὐκ ἂν περὶ ἄλλης ἐλάλει μετὰ ταῦτα ἡμέρας. ⁹ἄρα ἀπολείπεται σαββατισμὸς τῷ λαῷ τοῦ θεοῦ· ¹⁰ὁ γὰρ εἰσελθὼν εἰς τὴν κατάπαυσιν αὐτοῦ καὶ αὐτὸς κατέπαυσεν ἀπὸ τῶν ἔργων αὐτοῦ ὥσπερ ἀπὸ τῶν ἰδίων ὁ θεός. ¹¹Σπουδάσωμεν οὖν εἰσελθεῖν εἰς ἐκείνην τὴν κατάπαυσιν, ἵνα μὴ ἐν τῷ αὐτῷ τις ὑποδείγματι πέσῃ τῆς ἀπειθείας. ¹²Ζῶν γὰρ ὁ λόγος τοῦ θεοῦ καὶ ἐνεργὴς καὶ τομώτερος ὑπὲρ πᾶσαν μάχαιραν δίστομον καὶ διικνούμενος ἄχρι μερισμοῦ ψυχῆς καὶ πνεύματος, ἁρμῶν τε καὶ μυελῶν, καὶ κριτικὸς ἐνθυμήσεων καὶ ἐννοιῶν καρδίας· ¹³καὶ οὐκ ἔστιν κτίσις ἀφανὴς ἐνώπιον αὐτοῦ, πάντα δὲ γυμνὰ καὶ τετραχηλισμένα τοῖς ὀφθαλμοῖς αὐτοῦ, πρὸς ὃν ἡμῖν ὁ λόγος. ¹⁴Ἔχοντες οὖν ἀρχιερέα μέγαν διεληλυθότα τοὺς οὐρανούς, Ἰησοῦν τὸν υἱὸν τοῦ θεοῦ, κρατῶμεν τῆς ὁμολογίας· ¹⁵οὐ γὰρ ἔχομεν ἀρχιερέα μὴ δυνάμενον συνπαθῆσαι ταῖς ἀσθενείαις ἡμῶν, πεπειρασμένον δὲ κατὰ πάντα καθ' ὁμοιότητα χωρὶς ἁμαρτίας. ¹⁶προσερχώμεθα οὖν μετὰ παρρησίας τῷ θρόνῳ τῆς χάριτος, ἵνα λάβωμεν ἔλεος καὶ χάριν εὕρωμεν εἰς εὔκαιρον βοήθειαν.

5 ¹Πᾶς γὰρ ἀρχιερεὺς ἐξ ἀνθρώπων λαμβανόμενος ὑπὲρ ἀνθρώπων καθίσταται τὰ πρὸς τὸν θεόν, ἵνα προσφέρῃ δῶρά [τε] καὶ θυσίας ὑπὲρ ἁμαρτιῶν, ²μετριοπαθεῖν δυνάμενος τοῖς ἀγνοοῦσι καὶ πλανωμένοις ἐπεὶ καὶ αὐτὸς περίκειται ἀσθένειαν, ³καὶ δι' αὐτὴν ὀφείλει, καθὼς περὶ τοῦ λαοῦ, οὕτως καὶ περὶ ἑαυτοῦ

προσφέρειν περὶ ἁμαρτιῶν. ⁴καὶ οὐχ ἑαυτῷ τις λαμβάνει τὴν τιμήν, ἀλλὰ καλούμενος ὑπὸ τοῦ θεοῦ, καθώσπερ καὶ Ἀαρών. ⁵Οὕτως καὶ ὁ χριστὸς οὐχ ἑαυτὸν ἐδόξασεν γενηθῆναι ἀρχιερέα, ἀλλ᾽ ὁ λαλήσας πρὸς αὐτόν

Υἱός μου εἶ cύ, ἐγὼ cήμερον γεγέννηκά cε·

⁶καθὼς καὶ ἐν ἑτέρῳ λέγει

Σὺ ἱερεὺς εἰς τὸν αἰῶνα κατὰ τὴν τάξιν Μελχιcεδέκ.

⁷ὃς ἐν ταῖς ἡμέραις τῆς σαρκὸς αὐτοῦ, δεήσεις τε καὶ ἱκετηρίας πρὸς τὸν δυνάμενον σώζειν αὐτὸν ἐκ θανάτου μετὰ κραυγῆς ἰσχυρᾶς καὶ δακρύων προσενέγκας καὶ εἰσακουσθεὶς ἀπὸ τῆς εὐλαβείας, ⁸καίπερ ὢν υἱός, ἔμαθεν ἀφ᾽ ὧν ἔπαθεν τὴν ὑπακοήν, ⁹καὶ τελειωθεὶς ἐγένετο πᾶσιν τοῖς ὑπακούουσιν αὐτῷ αἴτιος cωτηρίαc αἰωνίου, ¹⁰προσαγορευθεὶς ὑπὸ τοῦ θεοῦ ἀρχιερεὺς κατὰ τὴν τάξιν Μελχιcεδέκ.

¹¹Περὶ οὗ πολὺς ἡμῖν ὁ λόγος καὶ δυσερμήνευτος λέγειν, ἐπεὶ νωθροὶ γεγόνατε ταῖς ἀκοαῖς· ¹²καὶ γὰρ ὀφείλοντες εἶναι διδάσκαλοι διὰ τὸν χρόνον, πάλιν χρείαν ἔχετε τοῦ διδάσκειν ὑμᾶς τινὰ τὰ στοιχεῖα τῆς ἀρχῆς τῶν λογίων τοῦ θεοῦ, καὶ γεγόνατε χρείαν ἔχοντες γάλακτος, οὐ στερεᾶς τροφῆς. ¹³πᾶς γὰρ ὁ μετέχων γάλακτος ἄπειρος λόγου δικαιοσύνης, νήπιος γάρ ἐστιν· ¹⁴τελείων δέ ἐστιν ἡ στερεὰ τροφή, τῶν διὰ τὴν ἕξιν τὰ αἰσθητήρια γεγυμνασμένα ἐχόντων πρὸς διάκρισιν καλοῦ τε καὶ κακοῦ. 6 ¹Διὸ ἀφέντες τὸν τῆς ἀρχῆς τοῦ χριστοῦ λόγον ἐπὶ τὴν τελειότητα φερώμεθα, μὴ πάλιν θεμέλιον καταβαλλόμενοι μετανοίας ἀπὸ νεκρῶν ἔργων, καὶ πίστεως ἐπὶ θεόν, ²βαπτισμῶν διδαχὴν ἐπιθέσεώς τε χειρῶν, ἀναστάσεως νεκρῶν καὶ κρίματος αἰωνίου. ³καὶ τοῦτο

ποιήσομεν ἐάνπερ ἐπιτρέπῃ ὁ θεός. ⁴'Αδύνατον γὰρ
τοὺς ἅπαξ φωτισθέντας γευσαμένους τε τῆς δωρεᾶς τῆς
ἐπουρανίου καὶ μετόχους γενηθέντας πνεύματος ἁγίου
⁵καὶ καλὸν γευσαμένους θεοῦ ῥῆμα δυνάμεις τε μέλλοντος αἰῶνος, ⁶καὶ παραπεσόντας, πάλιν ἀνακαινίζειν
εἰς μετάνοιαν, ἀνασταυροῦντας ἑαυτοῖς τὸν υἱὸν τοῦ
θεοῦ καὶ παραδειγματίζοντας. ⁷ΓΗ γὰρ ἡ πιοῦσα τὸν
ἐπ' αὐτῆς ἐρχόμενον πολλάκις ὑετόν, καὶ τίκτουσα
ΒΟΤΑΝΗΝ εὔθετον ἐκείνοις δι' οὓς καὶ γεωργεῖται, μετα-
λαμβάνει εὐλογίας ἀπὸ τοῦ θεοῦ· ⁸ἐκφέρουσὰ δὲ
ἀκάνθας καὶ τριβόλους ἀδόκιμος καὶ κατάρας ἐγγύς, ἧς
τὸ τέλος εἰς καῦσιν. ⁹Πεπείσμεθα δὲ περὶ ὑμῶν,
ἀγαπητοί, τὰ κρείσσονα καὶ ἐχόμενα σωτηρίας, εἰ καὶ
οὕτως λαλοῦμεν· ¹⁰οὐ γὰρ ἄδικος ὁ θεὸς ἐπιλαθέσθαι
τοῦ ἔργου ὑμῶν καὶ τῆς ἀγάπης ἧς ἐνεδείξασθε εἰς τὸ
ὄνομα αὐτοῦ, διακονήσαντες τοῖς ἁγίοις καὶ διακονοῦντες. ¹¹ἐπιθυμοῦμεν δὲ ἕκαστον ὑμῶν τὴν αὐτὴν
ἐνδείκνυσθαι σπουδὴν πρὸς τὴν πληροφορίαν τῆς
ἐλπίδος ἄχρι τέλους, ¹²ἵνα μὴ νωθροὶ γένησθε, μιμηταὶ
δὲ τῶν διὰ πίστεως καὶ μακροθυμίας κληρονομούντων
τὰς ἐπαγγελίας. ¹³Τῷ γὰρ 'Αβραὰμ ἐπαγγειλάμενος
ὁ θεός, ἐπεὶ κατ' οὐδενὸς εἶχεν μείζονος ὀμόσαι, ὤμοσεν
ΚΑΘ' ἙΑΥΤΟΎ, ¹⁴λέγων Εἰ ΜΗΝ ΕΥΛΟΓῶΝ ΕΥΛΟΓΗΣΩ ΣΕ ΚΑὶ
ΠΛΗΘΥΝΩΝ ΠΛΗΘΥΝῶ ΣΕ· ¹⁵καὶ οὕτως μακροθυμήσας
ἐπέτυχεν τῆς ἐπαγγελίας. ¹⁶ἄνθρωποι γὰρ κατὰ τοῦ
μείζονος ὀμνύουσιν, καὶ πάσης αὐτοῖς ἀντιλογίας πέρας
εἰς βεβαίωσιν ὁ ὅρκος· ¹⁷ἐν ᾧ περισσότερον βουλό-
μενος ὁ θεὸς ἐπιδεῖξαι τοῖς κληρονόμοις τῆς ἐπαγγελίας
τὸ ἀμετάθετον τῆς βουλῆς αὐτοῦ ἐμεσίτευσεν ὅρκῳ,
¹⁸ἵνα διὰ δύο πραγμάτων ἀμεταθέτων, ἐν οἷς ἀδύνατον
ψεύσασθαι θεόν, ἰσχυρὰν παράκλησιν ἔχωμεν οἱ

καταφυγόντες κρατῆσαι τῆς προκειμένης ἐλπίδος· ¹⁹ἣν ὡς ἄγκυραν ἔχομεν τῆς ψυχῆς, ἀσφαλῆ τε καὶ βεβαίαν καὶ εἰϲερχομένην εἰϲ τὸ ἐϲώτερον τοῦ καταπετάϲματος, ²⁰ὅπου πρόδρομος ὑπὲρ ἡμῶν εἰσῆλθεν Ἰησοῦς, κατὰ τὴν τάξιν Μελχιϲεδὲκ ἀρχιερεὺς γειόμενος εἰϲ τὸν αἰῶνα.

7 ¹Οὗτος γὰρ ὁ Μελχιϲεδέκ, βαϲιλεὺϲ Ϲαλήμ, ἱερεὺϲ τοῦ θεοῦ τοῦ ὑψίϲτου, ὁ ϲυναντήϲαϲ Ἀβραὰμ ὑποστρέφοντι ἀπὸ τῆϲ κοπῆϲ τῶν βαϲιλέων καὶ εὐλογήϲαϲ αὐτόν, ²ᾧ καὶ δεκάτην ἀπὸ πάντων ἐμέρισεν Ἀβραάμ, πρῶτον μὲν ἑρμηνευόμενος Βασιλεὺς Δικαιοσύνης ἔπειτα δὲ καὶ βαϲιλεὺϲ Ϲαλήμ, ὅ ἐστιν βασιλεὺς Εἰρήνης, ³ἀπάτωρ, ἀμήτωρ, ἀγενεαλόγητος, μήτε ἀρχὴν ἡμερῶν μήτε ζωῆς τέλος ἔχων, ἀφωμοιωμένος δὲ τῷ υἱῷ τοῦ θεοῦ, μένει ἱερεὺϲ εἰς τὸ διηνεκές.   ⁴Θεωρεῖτε δὲ πηλίκος οὗτος ᾧ δεκάτην Ἀβραὰμ ἔδωκεν ἐκ τῶν ἀκροθινίων ὁ πατριάρχης.   ⁵καὶ οἱ μὲν ἐκ τῶν υἱῶν Λευεὶ τὴν ἱερατίαν λαμβάνοντες ἐντολὴν ἔχουσιν ἀποδεκατοῖν τὸν λαὸν κατὰ τὸν νόμον, τοῦτ' ἔστιν τοὺς ἀδελφοὺς αὐτῶν, καίπερ ἐξεληλυθότας ἐκ τῆς ὀσφύος Ἀβραάμ· ⁶ὁ δὲ μὴ γενεαλογούμενος ἐξ αὐτῶν δεδεκάτωκεν Ἀβραάμ, καὶ τὸν ἔχοντα τὰς ἐπαγγελίας εὐλόγηκεν. ⁷χωρὶς δὲ πάσης ἀντιλογίας τὸ ἔλαττον ὑπὸ τοῦ κρείττονος εὐλογεῖται. ⁸καὶ ὧδε μὲν δεκάτας ἀποθνήσκοντες ἄνθρωποι λαμβάνουσιν, ἐκεῖ δὲ μαρτυρούμενος ὅτι ζῇ. ⁹καὶ ὡς ἔπος εἰπεῖν, δι' Ἀβραὰμ καὶ Λευεὶς ὁ δεκάτας λαμβάιων δεδεκάτωται, ¹⁰ἔτι γὰρ ἐν τῇ ὀσφύϊ τοῦ πατρὸς ἦν ὅτε ϲυνήντηϲεν αὐτῷ Μελχιϲεδέκ.   ¹¹Εἰ μὲν οὖν τελείωσις διὰ τῆς Λευειτικῆς ἱερωσύνης ἦν, ὁ λαὸς γὰρ ἐπ' αὐτῆς νενομοθέτηται, τίς ἔτι χρεία κατὰ τὴν τάξιν Μελχιϲεδὲκ ἕτερον ἀνίστασθαι ἱερέα καὶ οὐ κατὰ τὴν τάξιν Ἀαρὼν λέγεσθαι; ¹²μετατιθεμένης γὰρ τῆς ἱερωσύνης

ἐξ ἀνάγκης καὶ νόμου μετάθεσις γίνεται. ¹³ἐφ᾽ ὃν
γὰρ λέγεται ταῦτα φυλῆς ἑτέρας μετέσχηκεν, ἀφ᾽ ἧς
οὐδεὶς προσέσχηκεν τῷ θυσιαστηρίῳ· ¹⁴πρόδηλον γὰρ
ὅτι ἐξ Ἰούδα ἀνατέταλκεν ὁ κύριος ἡμῶν, εἰς ἣν φυλὴν
περὶ ἱερέων οὐδὲν Μωυσῆς ἐλάλησεν. ¹⁵Καὶ περισσότερον ἔτι κατάδηλόν ἐστιν, εἰ κατὰ τὴν ὁμοιότητα
Μελχισεδὲκ ἀνίσταται ἱερεὺς ἕτερος, ¹⁶ὃς οὐ κατὰ νόμον
ἐντολῆς σαρκίνης γέγονεν ἀλλὰ κατὰ δύναμιν ζωῆς
ἀκαταλύτου, ¹⁷μαρτυρεῖται γὰρ ὅτι Σὺ ἱερεὺς εἰς τὸν
αἰῶνα κατὰ τὴν τάξιν Μελχισεδέκ. ¹⁸ἀθέτησις μὲν γὰρ
γίνεται προαγούσης ἐντολῆς διὰ τὸ αὐτῆς ἀσθενὲς καὶ
ἀνωφελές, ¹⁹οὐδὲν γὰρ ἐτελείωσεν ὁ νόμος, ἐπεισαγωγὴ
δὲ κρείττονος ἐλπίδος, δι᾽ ἧς ἐγγίζομεν τῷ θεῷ. ²⁰Καὶ
καθ᾽ ὅσον οὐ χωρὶς ὁρκωμοσίας, (οἱ μὲν γὰρ χωρὶς
ὁρκωμοσίας εἰσὶν ἱερεῖς γεγονότες, ²¹ὁ δὲ μετὰ ὁρκωμοσίας διὰ τοῦ λέγοντος πρὸς αὐτόν Ὤμοσεν Κύριος,
καὶ οὐ μεταμεληθήσεται, Σὺ ἱερεὺς εἰς τὸν αἰῶνα,) ²²κατὰ
τοσοῦτο καὶ κρείττονος διαθήκης γέγονεν ἔγγυος Ἰησοῦς. ²³Καὶ οἱ μὲν πλείονές εἰσιν γεγονότες ἱερεῖς διὰ
τὸ θανάτῳ κωλύεσθαι παραμένειν· ²⁴ὁ δὲ διὰ τὸ μένειν
αὐτὸν εἰς τὸν αἰῶνα ἀπαράβατον ἔχει τὴν ἱερωσύνην·
²⁵ὅθεν καὶ σώζειν εἰς τὸ παντελὲς δύναται τοὺς προσερχομένους δι᾽ αὐτοῦ τῷ θεῷ, πάντοτε ζῶν εἰς τὸ
ἐντυγχάνειν ὑπὲρ αὐτῶν. ²⁶Τοιοῦτος γὰρ ἡμῖν
[καὶ] ἔπρεπεν ἀρχιερεύς, ὅσιος, ἄκακος, ἀμίαντος, κεχωρισμένος ἀπὸ τῶν ἁμαρτωλῶν, καὶ ὑψηλότερος τῶν
οὐρανῶν γενόμενος· ²⁷ὃς οὐκ ἔχει καθ᾽ ἡμέραν ἀνάγκην,
ὥσπερ οἱ ἀρχιερεῖς, πρότερον ὑπὲρ τῶν ἰδίων ἁμαρτιῶν
θυσίας ἀναφέρειν, ἔπειτα τῶν τοῦ λαοῦ· (τοῦτο γὰρ
ἐποίησεν ἐφάπαξ ἑαυτὸν ἀνενέγκας·) ²⁸ὁ νόμος γὰρ
ἀνθρώπους καθίστησιν ἀρχιερεῖς ἔχοντας ἀσθένειαν,

ὁ λόγος δὲ τῆς ὁρκωμοσίας τῆς μετὰ τὸν νόμον ΥἱΌΝ, εἰc τὸν ΑἰῶΝΑ τετελειωμένον.

8 ¹Κεφάλαιον δὲ ἐπὶ τοῖς λεγομένοις, τοιοῦτον ἔχομεν ἀρχιερέα, ὃς ἐκάθιϲεν ἐν Δεξιᾷ τοῦ θρόνου τῆς μεγαλωσύνης ἐν τοῖς οὐρανοῖς, ²τῶν ἁγίων λειτουργὸς καὶ τῆϲ ϲκηνῆϲ τῆς ἀληθινῆς, ἣν ἔπηξεν ὁ κΎριοϲ, οὐκ ἄνθρωπος. ³πᾶς γὰρ ἀρχιερεὺς εἰς τὸ προσφέρειν δῶρά τε καὶ θυσίας καθίσταται· ὅθεν ἀναγκαῖον ἔχειν τι καὶ τοῦτον ὃ προσενέγκῃ. ⁴εἰ μὲν οὖν ἦν ἐπὶ γῆς, οὐδ᾽ ἂν ἦν ἱερεύς, ὄντων τῶν προσφερόντων κατὰ νόμον τὰ δῶρα· ⁵(οἵτινες ὑποδείγματι καὶ σκιᾷ λατρεύουσιν τῶν ἐπουρανίων, καθὼς κεχρημάτισται Μωυσῆς μέλλων ἐπιτελεῖν τὴν σκηνήν, Ὅρα γάρ, φησίν, ποιΉϲειϲ πΆΝΤΑ κΑΤὰ τὸΝ τΎπΟΝ τὸΝ ΔειχθέΝΤΑ ϲΟι ἐΝ τῷ ὄρει·) ⁶νῦν δὲ διαφορωτέρας τέτυχεν λειτουργίας, ὅσῳ καὶ κρείττονός ἐστιν διαθήκης μεσίτης, ἥτις ἐπὶ κρείττοσιν ἐπαγγελίαις νενομοθέτηται. ⁷εἰ γὰρ ἡ πρώτη ἐκείνη ἦν ἄμεμπτος, οὐκ ἂν δευτέρας ἐζητεῖτο τόπος· ⁸μεμφόμενος γὰρ αὐτοὺς λέγει

ἸδοΎ ἡμέρΑι ἔρχΟΝΤΑι, λέγει κΎριΟϲ,
    κΑὶ ϲΥΝΤελέϲω ἐπὶ τὸΝ οἶκΟΝ Ἰϲραὴλ κΑὶ ἐπὶ τὸΝ
        οἶκΟΝ ἸοὔΔΑ ΔιΑθΉκηΝ κΑιΝΉΝ,
⁹οὔ κΑΤὰ τὴΝ ΔιΑθΉκηΝ ἣΝ ἐποίηϲΑ τοῖϲ πΑΤρΆϲιΝ
                                            ΑὐτῶΝ
    ἐΝ ἡμέρᾳ ἐπιλΑΒομέΝΟΥ μΟΥ τῆϲ χειρὸϲ ΑὐτῶΝ ἐξΑ-
        ΓΑΓεῖΝ ΑὐτοΎϲ ἐκ Γῆϲ ΑἰΓΎπΤΟΥ,
ὅτι ΑὐτΟὶ οὔκ ἐΝέμειΝΑΝ ἐΝ τῇ ΔιΑθΉκῃ μΟΥ,
    κἀγὼ ἡμέληϲΑ ΑὐτῶΝ, λέγει κΎριΟϲ.
¹⁰ὅτι ΑὕΤη ἡ ΔιΑθΉκη ἣΝ ΔιΑθΉϲΟμΑι τῷ οἴκῳ Ἰϲραὴλ
    μετὰ τὰϲ ἡμέρΑϲ ἐκείΝΑϲ, λέγει κΎριΟϲ,
ΔιΔΟΎϲ ΝόμΟΥϲ μΟΥ εἰϲ τὴΝ ΔιΆΝΟιΑΝ ΑὐτῶΝ,

καὶ ἐπὶ καρδίας αὐτῶν ἐπιγράψω αὐτούς,
καὶ ἔσομαι αὐτοῖς εἰς θεόν
καὶ αὐτοὶ ἔσονταί μοι εἰς λαόν.
¹¹καὶ οὐ μὴ διδάξωσιν ἕκαστος τὸν πολίτην αὐτοῦ
καὶ ἕκαστος τὸν ἀδελφὸν αὐτοῦ, λέγων Γνῶθι τὸν
κύριον,
ὅτι πάντες εἰδήσουσίν με
ἀπο μικροῦ ἕως μεγάλου αὐτῶν.
¹²ὅτι ἵλεως ἔσομαι ταῖς ἀδικίαις αὐτῶν,
καὶ τῶν ἁμαρτιῶν αὐτῶν οὐ μὴ μνησθῶ ἔτι.
¹³ἐν τῷ λέγειν Καινήν πεπαλαίωκεν τὴν πρώτην, τὸ δὲ
παλαιούμενον καὶ γηράσκον ἐγγὺς ἀφανισμοῦ.

9 ¹Εἶχε μὲν οὖν [καὶ] ἡ πρώτη δικαιώματα λατρείας τό τε ἅγιον κοσμικόν. ²σκηνὴ γὰρ κατεσκευάσθη
ἡ πρώτη ἐν ᾗ ἥ τε λυχνία καὶ ἡ τράπεζα καὶ ἡ πρόθεσις
τῶν ἄρτων, ἥτις λέγεται Ἅγια· ³μετὰ δὲ τὸ δεύτερον
καταπέτασμα σκηνὴ ἡ λεγομένη Ἅγια Ἁγίων, ⁴χρυ-
σοῦν ἔχουσα θυμιατήριον καὶ τὴν κιβωτὸν τῆς διαθήκης
περικεκαλυμμένην πάντοθεν χρυσίῳ, ἐν ᾗ στάμνος
χρυσῆ ἔχουσα τὸ μάννα καὶ ἡ ῥάβδος Ἀαρὼν ἡ βλασ-
τήσασα καὶ αἱ πλάκες τῆς διαθήκης, ⁵ὑπεράνω δὲ αὐτῆς
Χερουβεὶν δόξης κατασκιάζοντα τὸ ἱλαστήριον· περὶ
ὧν οὐκ ἔστιν νῦν λέγειν κατὰ μέρος. ⁶Τούτων δὲ οὕτως
κατεσκευασμένων, εἰς μὲν τὴν πρώτην σκηνὴν διὰ
παντὸς εἰσίασιν οἱ ἱερεῖς τὰς λατρείας ἐπιτελοῦντες,
⁷εἰς δὲ τὴν δευτέραν ἅπαξ τοῦ ἐνιαυτοῦ μόνος ὁ ἀρχιερεύς, οὐ χωρὶς αἵματος, ὃ προσφέρει ὑπὲρ ἑαυτοῦ καὶ
τῶν τοῦ λαοῦ ἀγνοημάτων, ⁸τοῦτο δηλοῦντος τοῦ πνεύματος τοῦ ἁγίου, μήπω πεφανερῶσθαι τὴν τῶν ἁγίων
ὁδὸν ἔτι τῆς πρώτης σκηνῆς ἐχούσης στάσιν, ⁹ἥτις
παραβολὴ εἰς τὸν καιρὸν τὸν ἐνεστηκότα, καθ᾽ ἣν δῶρά τε

καὶ θυσίαι προσφέρονται μὴ δυνάμεναι κατὰ συνείδησιν
τελειῶσαι τὸν λατρεύοντα, [10]μόνον ἐπὶ βρώμασιν καὶ
πόμασιν καὶ διαφόροις βαπτισμοῖς, δικαιώματα σαρκὸς
μέχρι καιροῦ διορθώσεως ἐπικείμενα.　　[11]Χρισ-
τὸς δὲ παραγενόμενος ἀρχιερεὺς τῶν γενομένων ἀγαθῶν
διὰ τῆς μείζονος καὶ τελειοτέρας σκηνῆς οὐ χειρο-
ποιήτου, τοῦτ᾽ ἔστιν οὐ ταύτης τῆς κτίσεως, [12]οὐδὲ δι᾽
αἵματος τράγων καὶ μόσχων διὰ δὲ τοῦ ἰδίου αἵματος,
εἰσῆλθεν ἐφάπαξ εἰς τὰ ἅγια, αἰωνίαν λύτρωσιν εὑράμενος. [13]εἰ γὰρ τὸ αἷμα τράγων καὶ ταύρων καὶ σποδὸς
δαμάλεως ῥαντίζουσα τοὺς κεκοινωμένους ἁγιάζει πρὸς
τὴν τῆς σαρκὸς καθαρότητα, [14]πόσῳ μᾶλλον τὸ αἷμα
τοῦ χριστοῦ, ὃς διὰ πνεύματος αἰωνίου ἑαυτὸν προσήνεγκεν ἄμωμον τῷ θεῷ, καθαριεῖ τὴν συνείδησιν ἡμῶν
ἀπὸ νεκρῶν ἔργων εἰς τὸ λατρεύειν θεῷ ζῶντι.　[15]Καὶ
διὰ τοῦτο διαθήκης καινῆς μεσίτης ἐστίν, ὅπως θανάτου
γενομένου εἰς ἀπολύτρωσιν τῶν ἐπὶ τῇ πρώτῃ διαθήκῃ
παραβάσεων τὴν ἐπαγγελίαν λάβωσιν οἱ κεκλημένοι
τῆς αἰωνίου κληρονομίας. [16]ὅπου γὰρ διαθήκη, θάνατον
ἀνάγκη φέρεσθαι τοῦ διαθεμένου· [17]διαθήκη γὰρ ἐπὶ
νεκροῖς βεβαία, ἐπεὶ μὴ τότε ἰσχύει ὅτε ζῇ ὁ δια-
θέμενος. [18]Ὅθεν οὐδὲ ἡ πρώτη χωρὶς αἵματος ἐνκε-
καίνισται· [19]λαληθείσης γὰρ πάσης ἐντολῆς κατὰ τὸν
νόμον ὑπὸ Μωυσέως παντὶ τῷ λαῷ, λαβὼν τὸ αἷμα τῶν
μόσχων καὶ τῶν τράγων μετὰ ὕδατος καὶ ἐρίου κοκκί-
νου καὶ ὑσσώπου αὐτό τε τὸ βιβλίον καὶ πάντα τὸν
λαὸν ἐράντισεν, [20]λέγων　Τοῦτο τὸ αἷμα τῆς διαθήκης
ἧς ἐνετείλατο πρὸς ὑμᾶς ὁ θεός· [21]καὶ τὴν σκηνὴν
δὲ καὶ πάντα τὰ σκεύη τῆς λειτουργίας τῷ αἵματι
ὁμοίως ἐράντισεν. [22]καὶ σχεδὸν ἐν αἵματι πάντα
καθαρίζεται κατὰ τὸν νόμον, καὶ χωρὶς αἱματεκχυσίας

οὐ γίνεται ἄφεσις.   ²³'Ανάγκη οὖν τὰ μὲν ὑπο-
δείγματα τῶν ἐν τοῖς οὐρανοῖς τούτοις καθαρίζεσθαι,
αὐτὰ δὲ τὰ ἐπουράνια κρείττοσι θυσίαις παρὰ ταύτας.
²⁴οὐ γὰρ εἰς χειροποίητα εἰσῆλθεν ἅγια Χριστός, ἀντί-
τυπα τῶν ἀληθινῶν, ἀλλ᾽ εἰς αὐτὸν τὸν οὐρανόν, νῦν
ἐμφανισθῆναι τῷ προσώπῳ τοῦ θεοῦ ὑπὲρ ἡμῶν· ²⁵οὐδ᾽
ἵνα πολλάκις προσφέρῃ ἑαυτόν, ὥσπερ ὁ ἀρχιερεὺς
εἰσέρχεται εἰς τὰ ἅγια κατ᾽ ἐνιαυτὸν ἐν αἵματι ἀλλοτρίῳ, ²⁶ἐπεὶ ἔδει αὐτὸν πολλάκις παθεῖν ἀπὸ καταβολῆς
κόσμου· νυνὶ δὲ ἅπαξ ἐπὶ συντελείᾳ τῶν αἰώνων εἰς
ἀθέτησιν τῆς ἁμαρτίας διὰ τῆς θυσίας αὐτοῦ πεφανέρωται. ²⁷καὶ καθ᾽ ὅσον ἀπόκειται τοῖς ἀνθρώποις ἅπαξ
ἀποθανεῖν, μετὰ δὲ τοῦτο κρίσις, ²⁸οὕτως καὶ ὁ χριστός,
ἅπαξ προσενεχθεὶς εἰς τὸ πολλῶν ἀνενεγκεῖν ἁμαρτίας,
ἐκ δευτέρου χωρὶς ἁμαρτίας ὀφθήσεται τοῖς αὐτὸν
ἀπεκδεχομένοις εἰς σωτηρίαν.

10 ¹Σκιὰν γὰρ ἔχων ὁ νόμος τῶν μελλόντων
ἀγαθῶν, οὐκ αὐτὴν τὴν εἰκόνα τῶν πραγμάτων, κατ᾽
ἐνιαυτὸν ταῖς αὐταῖς θυσίαις ἃς προσφέρουσιν εἰς τὸ
διηνεκὲς οὐδέποτε δύνανται τοὺς προσερχομένους τε-
λειῶσαι· ²ἐπεὶ οὐκ ἂν ἐπαύσαντο προσφερόμεναι, διὰ
τὸ μηδεμίαν ἔχειν ἔτι συνείδησιν ἁμαρτιῶν τοὺς λα-
τρεύοντας ἅπαξ κεκαθαρισμένους; ³ἀλλ᾽ ἐν αὐταῖς
ἀνάμνησις ἁμαρτιῶν κατ᾽ ἐνιαυτόν, ⁴ἀδύνατον γὰρ
αἷμα ταύρων καὶ τράγων ἀφαιρεῖν ἁμαρτίας.   ⁵Διὸ
εἰσερχόμενος εἰς τὸν κόσμον λέγει

Θυσίαν καὶ προσφορὰν ογκ ἠθέλησας, ϲῶμα δὲ κατηρ-
                                        τίϲω μοι·
⁶ὁλοκαγτώματα καὶ περὶ ἁμαρτίαϲ ογκ εγδόκηϲαϲ.
⁷τότε εἶπον   Ἰδογ ἥκω, ἐν κεφαλίδι βιβλίογ γέ-
                                        γραπται περὶ ἐμογ,

τοῦ ποιῆϲαι, ὁ θεόϲ, τὸ θέλημά ϲου.

⁸ἀνώτερον λέγων ὅτι　　Θυϲίαϲ καὶ προϲφορὰϲ καὶ ὁλο-
καυτώματα καὶ περὶ ἁμαρτίαϲ ογκ ἠθέληϲαϲ ογδὲ εγδόκηϲαϲ,
αἵτινες κατὰ νόμον προσφέρονται, ⁹τότε εἴρηκεν　　Ἰδογ
ἥκω τοῦ ποιῆϲαι τὸ θέλημά ϲογ· ἀναιρεῖ τὸ πρῶτον
ἵνα τὸ δεύτερον στήσῃ. ¹⁰ἐν ᾧ θελήματι ἡγιασμένοι
ἐσμὲν διὰ τῆς προσφορᾶς τοῦ ϲώματοϲ Ἰησοῦ Χριστοῦ
ἐφάπαξ. ¹¹Καὶ πᾶς μὲν ἱερεὺς ἔστηκεν καθ᾽ ἡμέραν
λειτουργῶν καὶ τὰς αὐτὰς πολλάκις προσφέρων θυσίας, αἵτινες οὐδέποτε δύνανται περιελεῖν ἁμαρτίας.
¹²οὗτος δὲ μίαν ὑπὲρ ἁμαρτιῶν προσενέγκας θυσίαν εἰς
τὸ διηνεκὲς ἐκάθιϲεν ἐν Δεξιᾷ τοῦ θεοῦ, ¹³τὸ λοιπὸν ἐκδε-
χόμενος ἕως τεθῶϲιν οἱ ἐχθροὶ αγτοῦ γποπόδιον τῶν
ποδῶν αγτοῦ, ¹⁴μιᾷ γὰρ προσφορᾷ τετελείωκεν εἰς τὸ
διηνεκὲς τοὺς ἁγιαζομένους. ¹⁵Μαρτυρεῖ δὲ ἡμῖν καὶ
τὸ πνεῦμα τὸ ἅγιον, μετὰ γὰρ τὸ εἰρηκέναι

¹⁶Αγτη ἡ Διαθήκη ἣν Διαθήϲομαι πρὸς αὐτούς
μετὰ τὰϲ ἡμέραϲ ἐκείναϲ, λέγει Κύριοϲ,
Διδογϲ νόμογϲ μογ ἐπὶ καρδίαϲ αγτῶν,
καὶ ἐπὶ τὴν διάνοιαν αγτῶν ἐπιγράψω αγτογϲ,—
¹⁷Καὶ τῶν ἁμαρτιῶν αγτῶν καὶ τῶν ἀνομιῶν αγτῶν
ογ μὴ μνηϲθήϲομαι ἔτι· ¹⁸ὅπου δε ἄφεσις τούτων, οὐκέτι
προσφορὰ περὶ ἁμαρτίας.

¹⁹Ἔχοντες οὖν, ἀδελφοί, παρρησίαν εἰς τὴν εἴσοδον
τῶν ἁγίων ἐν τῷ αἵματι Ἰησοῦ, ²⁰ἣν ἐνεκαίνισεν ἡμῖν
ὁδὸν πρόσφατον καὶ ζῶσαν διὰ τοῦ καταπετάσματος,
τοῦτ᾽ ἔστιν τῆς σαρκὸς αὐτοῦ, ²¹καὶ ἱερέα μέγαν ἐπὶ τὸν
οἶκον τοῦ θεοῦ, ²²προσερχώμεθα μετὰ ἀληθινῆς καρδίαϲ
ἐν πληροφορίᾳ πίστεως, ῥεραντισμένοι τὰς καρδίας ἀπὸ
συνειδήσεως πονηρᾶς καὶ λελουσμένοι τὸ σῶμα ὕδατι
καθαρῷ· ²³κατέχωμεν τὴν ὁμολογίαν τῆς ἐλπίδος ἀκλινῆ,

πιστὸς γὰρ ὁ ἐπαγγειλάμενος· ²⁴καὶ κατανοῶμεν ἀλλή-
λους εἰς παροξυσμὸν ἀγάπης καὶ καλῶν ἔργων, ²⁵μὴ
ἐγκαταλείποντες τὴν ἐπισυναγωγὴν ἑαυτῶν, καθὼς
ἔθος τισίν, ἀλλὰ παρακαλοῦντες, καὶ τοσούτῳ μᾶλλον
ὅσῳ βλέπετε ἐγγίζουσαν τὴν ἡμέραν. ²⁶Ἑκουσίως
γὰρ ἁμαρτανόντων ἡμῶν μετὰ τὸ λαβεῖν τὴν ἐπίγνωσιν
τῆς ἀληθείας, οὐκέτι περὶ ἁμαρτιῶν ἀπολείπεται θυσία,
²⁷φοβερὰ δέ τις ἐκδοχὴ κρίσεως καὶ πγρὸϲ ζΗλοϲ ἐϲθίειν
μέλλοντος τοὺϲ ὑπεναντίογϲ. ²⁸ἀθετήσας τις νόμον
Μωυσέως χωρὶς οἰκτιρμῶν ἐπὶ Δγϲὶν Η τριϲὶν μάρτγϲιν
ἀποθνΉϲκει· ²⁹πόσῳ δοκεῖτε χείρονος ἀξιωθήσεται τιμω-
ρίας ὁ τὸν υἱὸν τοῦ θεοῦ καταπατήσας, καὶ τὸ αἷμα τῆϲ
Διαθήκηϲ κοινὸν ἡγησάμενος ἐν ᾧ ἡγιάσθη, καὶ τὸ
πνεῦμα τῆς χάριτος ἐνυβρίσας. ³⁰οἴδαμεν γὰρ τὸν
εἰπόντα Ἐμοὶ ἐκδίκηϲιϲ, ἐγὼ ἀνταποδώϲω· καὶ πάλιν
Κρινεῖ Κύριοϲ τὸν λαὸν αγτογ̂. ³¹φοβερὸν τὸ ἐμπεσεῖν
εἰς χεῖρας θεοῦ ζῶντος. ³²Ἀναμιμνήσκεσθε δὲ τὰς
πρότερον ἡμέρας, ἐν αἷς φωτισθέντες πολλὴν ἄθλησιν
ὑπεμείνατε παθημάτων, ³³τοῦτο μὲν ὀνειδισμοῖς τε καὶ
θλίψεσιν θεατριζόμενοι, τοῦτο δὲ κοινωνοὶ τῶν οὕτως
ἀναστρεφομένων γενηθέντες· ³⁴καὶ γὰρ τοῖς δεσμίοις
συνεπαθήσατε, καὶ τὴν ἁρπαγὴν τῶν ὑπαρχόντων ὑμῶν
μετὰ χαρᾶς προσεδέξασθε, γινώσκοντες ἔχειν ἑαυτοὺς
κρείσσονα ὕπαρξιν καὶ μένουσαν. ³⁵Μὴ ἀποβάλητε
οὖν τὴν παρρησίαν ὑμῶν, ἥτις ἔχει μεγάλην μισθαποδοσίαν, ³⁶ὑπομονῆς γὰρ ἔχετε χρείαν ἵνα τὸ θέλημα τοῦ
θεοῦ ποιήσαντες κομίσησθε τὴν ἐπαγγελίαν·
³⁷ἔτι γὰρ μικρὸν ὅϲον ὅϲον,
  ὁ ἐρχόμενοϲ Η̂ξει καὶ ογ̂ χρονίϲει·
³⁸ὁ Δὲ Δίκαιόϲ [μογ] ἐκ πίϲτεωϲ ζΉϲεται,
καὶ ἐὰν ὑποϲτείληται, ογ̂κ εγ̂Δοκεῖ Η ψγχΉ μογ ἐν αγ̂τῷ.

³⁹ἡμεῖς δὲ οὐκ ἐσμὲν ὑποстολῆς εἰς ἀπώλειαν, ἀλλὰ πίϲτεως εἰς περιποίησιν ψυχῆς.

11 ¹Ἔστιν δὲ πίστις ἐλπιζομένων ὑπόστασις, πραγμάτων ἔλεγχος οὐ βλεπομένων· ²ἐν ταύτῃ γὰρ ἐμαρτυρήθησαν οἱ πρεσβύτεροι. ³Πίστει νοοῦμεν κατηρτίσθαι τοὺς αἰῶνας ῥήματι θεοῦ, εἰς τὸ μὴ ἐκ φαινομένων τὸ βλεπόμενον γεγονέναι. ⁴Πίστει πλείονα θυσίαν "Αβελ παρὰ Καὶν προσήνεγκεν τῷ θεῷ, δι' ἧς ἐμαρτυρήθη εἶναι δίκαιος, μαρτυροῦντος ἐπὶ τοῖϲ Δώροιϲ ἀϒτοῦ τοῦ θεοῦ, καὶ δι' αὐτῆς ἀποθανὼν ἔτι λαλεῖ. ⁵Πίστει Ἐνὼχ μετετέθη τοῦ μὴ ἰδεῖν θάνατον, καὶ οϒχ ηϒρίϲκετο Διότι μετέθηκεν ἀϒτόν ὁ θεόϲ· πρὸ γὰρ τῆς μεταθέσεως μεμαρτύρηται εϒαρεϲτηκέναι τῷ θεῷ, ⁶χωρὶς δὲ πίστεως ἀδύνατον εϒαρεϲτῆϲαι, πιστεῦσαι γὰρ δεῖ τὸν προσερχόμενον [τῷ] θεῷ ὅτι ἔστιν καὶ τοῖς ἐκζητοῦσιν αὐτὸν μισθαποδότης γίνεται. ⁷Πίστει χρηματισθεὶς Νῶε περὶ τῶν μηδέπω βλεπομένων εὐλαβηθεὶς κατεσκεύασεν κιβωτὸν εἰς σωτηρίαν τοῦ οἴκου αὐτοῦ, δι' ἧς κατέκρινεν τὸν κόσμον, καὶ τῆς κατὰ πίστιν δικαιοσύνης ἐγένετο κληρονόμος. ⁸Πίστει καλούμενος Ἀβραὰμ ὑπήκουσεν ἐξελθεῖν εἰς τόπον ὃν ἤμελλεν λαμβάνειν εἰς κληρονομίαν, καὶ ἐξῆλθεν μὴ ἐπιστάμενος ποῦ ἔρχεται. ⁹Πίστει παρῴκηϲεν εἰς γῆν τῆς ἐπαγγελίας ὡς ἀλλοτρίαν, ἐν σκηναῖς κατοικήσας μετὰ Ἰσαὰκ καὶ Ἰακὼβ τῶν συνκληρονόμων τῆς ἐπαγγελίας τῆς αὐτῆς· ¹⁰ἐξεδέχετο γὰρ τὴν τοὺς θεμελίους ἔχουσαν πόλιν, ἧς τεχνίτης καὶ δημιουργὸς ὁ θεός. ¹¹Πίστει καὶ αὐτὴ Σάρρα δύναμιν εἰς καταβολὴν σπέρματος ἔλαβεν καὶ παρὰ καιρὸν ἡλικίας, ἐπεὶ πιστὸν ἡγήσατο τὸν ἐπαγγειλάμενον· ¹²διὸ καὶ ἀφ' ἑνὸς ἐγεννήθησαν, καὶ ταῦτα

νενεκρωμένου, καθὼς τὰ ἄстρα τοῦ οὐρανοῦ τῷ πλήθει
καὶ ὡς ἡ ἄμμος ἡ παρὰ τὸ χεῖλος τῆς θαλάσσης ἡ ἀνα-
ρίθμητος. ¹³Κατὰ πίστιν ἀπέθανον οὗτοι πάντες,
μὴ κομισάμενοι τὰς ἐπαγγελίας, ἀλλὰ πόρρωθεν αὐτὰς
ἰδόντες καὶ ἀσπασάμενοι, καὶ ὁμολογήσαντες ὅτι ξένοι
καὶ παρεπίδημοί εἰσιν ἐπὶ τῆς γῆς· ¹⁴οἱ γὰρ τοιαῦτα
λέγοντες ἐμφανίζουσιν ὅτι πατρίδα ἐπιζητοῦσιν. ¹⁵καὶ
εἰ μὲν ἐκείνης ἐμνημόνευον ἀφ᾽ ἧς ἐξέβησαν, εἶχον ἂν
καιρὸν ἀνακάμψαι· ¹⁶νῦν δὲ κρείττονος ὀρέγονται, τοῦτ᾽
ἔστιν ἐπουρανίου. διὸ οὐκ ἐπαισχύνεται αὐτοὺς ὁ
θεὸς θεὸς ἐπικαλεῖσθαι αὐτῶν, ἡτοίμασεν γὰρ αὐτοῖς
πόλιν. ¹⁷Πίστει προσενήνοχεν Ἀβραὰμ τὸν Ἰσαὰκ
πειραζόμενος, καὶ τὸν μονογενῆ προσέφερεν ὁ τὰς ἐπαγγελίας ἀναδεξάμενος, ¹⁸πρὸς ὃν ἐλαλήθη ὅτι Ἐν
Ἰσαὰκ κληθήσεταί σοι σπέρμα, ¹⁹λογισάμενος ὅτι καὶ ἐκ
νεκρῶν ἐγείρειν δυνατὸς ὁ θεός· ὅθεν αὐτὸν καὶ ἐν
παραβολῇ ἐκομίσατο. ²⁰Πίστει καὶ περὶ μελλόντων
εὐλόγησεν Ἰσαὰκ τὸν Ἰακὼβ καὶ τὸν Ἠσαῦ. ²¹Πίσ-
τει Ἰακὼβ ἀποθνήσκων ἕκαστον τῶν υἱῶν Ἰωσὴφ
εὐλόγησεν, καὶ προσεκύνησεν ἐπὶ τὸ ἄκρον τῆς ῥάβδου
αὐτοῦ. ²²Πίστει Ἰωσὴφ τελευτῶν περὶ τῆς ἐξόδου
τῶν υἱῶν Ἰσραὴλ ἐμνημόνευσεν, καὶ περὶ τῶν ὀστέων
αὐτοῦ ἐνετείλατο. ²³Πίστει Μωυσῆς γεννηθεὶς ἐκρύβη
τρίμηνον ὑπὸ τῶν πατέρων αὐτοῦ, διότι εἶδον ἀστεῖον
τὸ παιδίον καὶ οὐκ ἐφοβήθησαν τὸ διάταγμα τοῦ
βασιλέως. ²⁴Πίστει Μωϋσῆς μέγας γενόμενος ἠρνή-
σατο λέγεσθαι υἱὸς θυγατρὸς Φαραώ, ²⁵μᾶλλον ἑλόμενος
συνκακουχεῖσθαι τῷ λαῷ τοῦ θεοῦ ἢ πρόσκαιρον ἔχειν
ἁμαρτίας ἀπόλαυσιν, ²⁶μείζονα πλοῦτον ἡγησάμενος
τῶν Αἰγύπτου θησαυρῶν τὸν ὀνειδισμὸν τοῦ χριστοῦ,
ἀπέβλεπεν γὰρ εἰς τὴν μισθαποδοσίαν. ²⁷Πίστει

κατέλιπεν Αἴγυπτον, μὴ φοβηθεὶς τὸν θυμὸν τοῦ βασιλέως, τὸν γὰρ ἀόρατον ὡς ὁρῶν ἐκαρτέρησεν. ²⁸Πίστει πεποίηκεν τὸ πάσχα καὶ τὴν πρόσχυσιν τοῦ αἵματος, ἵνα μὴ ὁ ὁλοθρεύων τὰ πρωτότοκα θίγῃ αὐτῶν. ²⁹Πίστει διέβησαν τὴν Ἐρυθρὰν Θάλασσαν ὡς διὰ ξηρᾶς γῆς, ἧς πεῖραν λαβόντες οἱ Αἰγύπτιοι κατεπόθησαν. ³⁰Πίστει τὰ τείχη Ἰερειχὼ ἔπεσαν κυκλωθέντα ἐπὶ ἑπτὰ ἡμέρας. ³¹Πίστει Ῥαὰβ ἡ πόρνη οὐ συναπώλετο τοῖς ἀπειθήσασιν, δεξαμένη τοὺς κατασκόπους μετ᾽ εἰρήνης. ³²Καὶ τί ἔτι λέγω; ἐπιλείψει με γὰρ διηγούμενον ὁ χρόνος περὶ Γεδεών, Βαράκ, Σαμψών, Ἰεφθάε, Δαυείδ τε καὶ Σαμουὴλ καὶ τῶν προφητῶν, ³³οἳ διὰ πίστεως κατηγωνίσαντο βασιλείας, ἠργάσαντο δικαιοσύνην, ἐπέτυχον ἐπαγγελιῶν, ἔφραξαν στόματα λεόντων, ³⁴ἔσβεσαν δύναμιν πυρός, ἔφυγον στόματα μαχαίρης, ἐδυναμώθησαν ἀπὸ ἀσθενείας, ἐγενήθησαν ἰσχυροὶ ἐν πολέμῳ, παρεμβολὰς ἔκλιναν ἀλλοτρίων· ³⁵ἔλαβον γυναῖκες ἐξ ἀναστάσεως τοὺς νεκροὺς αὐτῶν· ἄλλοι δὲ ἐτυμπανίσθησαν, οὐ προσδεξάμενοι τὴν ἀπολύτρωσιν, ἵνα κρείττονος ἀναστάσεως τύχωσιν· ³⁶ἕτεροι δὲ ἐμπαιγμῶν καὶ μαστίγων πεῖραν ἔλαβον, ἔτι δὲ δεσμῶν καὶ φυλακῆς· ³⁷ἐλιθάσθησαν, ἐπειράσθησαν, ἐπρίσθησαν, ἐν φόνῳ μαχαίρης ἀπέθανον, περιῆλθον ἐν μηλωταῖς, ἐν αἰγίοις δέρμασιν, ὑστερούμενοι, θλιβόμενοι, κακουχούμενοι, ³⁸ὧν οὐκ ἦν ἄξιος ὁ κόσμος ἐπὶ ἐρημίαις πλανώμενοι καὶ ὄρεσι καὶ σπηλαίοις καὶ ταῖς ὀπαῖς τῆς γῆς. ³⁹Καὶ οὗτοι πάντες μαρτυρηθέντες διὰ τῆς πίστεως οὐκ ἐκομίσαντο τὴν ἐπαγγελίαν, ⁴⁰τοῦ θεοῦ περὶ ἡμῶν κρεῖττόν τι προβλεψαμένου, ἵνα μὴ χωρὶς ἡμῶν τελειωθῶσιν.

12 ¹Τοιγαροῦν καὶ ἡμεῖς, τοσοῦτον ἔχοντες περι-

κείμενον ἡμῖν νέφος μαρτύρων, ὄγκον ἀποθέμενοι πάντα
καὶ τὴν εὐπερίστατον ἁμαρτίαν, δι᾽ ὑπομονῆς τρέχωμεν
τὸν προκείμενον ἡμῖν ἀγῶνα, ²ἀφορῶντες εἰς τὸν τῆς
πίστεως ἀρχηγὸν καὶ τελειωτὴν Ἰησοῦν, ὃς ἀντὶ τῆς
προκειμένης αὐτῷ χαρᾶς ὑπέμεινεν σταυρὸν αἰσχύνης
καταφρονήσας, ἐν Δεξιᾷ τε τοῦ θρόνου τοῦ θεοῦ κεκάθικεν.
³ἀναλογίσασθε γὰρ τὸν τοιαύτην ὑπομεμενηκότα ὑπὸ
τῶν ἁμαρτωλῶν εἰς ἑαυτοὺς ἀντιλογίαν, ἵνα μὴ κάμητε
ταῖς ψυχαῖς ὑμῶν ἐκλυόμενοι. ⁴Οὔπω μέχρις αἵματος ἀντικατέστητε πρὸς τὴν ἁμαρτίαν ἀνταγωνιζόμενοι,
⁵καὶ ἐκλέλησθε τῆς παρακλήσεως, ἥτις ὑμῖν ὡς υἱοῖς
διαλέγεται,
Υἱέ μου, μὴ ὀλιγώρει παιδείας Κυρίου,
μηΔὲ ἐκλύου ὑπ᾽ αὐτοῦ ἐλεγχόμενος·
⁶ὃν γὰρ ἀγαπᾷ Κύριος παιΔεύει,
μαστιγοῖ Δὲ πάντα υἱὸν ὃν παραΔέχεται.
⁷εἰς παιδείαν ὑπομένετε· ὡς υἱοῖς ὑμῖν προσφέρεται ὁ
θεός· τίς γὰρ υἱὸς ὃν οὐ παιδεύει πατήρ; ⁸εἰ᾽ δὲ χωρίς
ἐστε παιδείας ἧς μέτοχοι γεγόνασι πάντες, ἄρα νόθοι καὶ
οὐχ υἱοί ἐστε. ⁹εἶτα τοὺς μὲν τῆς σαρκὸς ἡμῶν πατέρας
εἴχομεν παιδευτὰς καὶ ἐνετρεπόμεθα· οὐ πολὺ μᾶλλον
ὑποταγησόμεθα τῷ πατρὶ τῶν πνευμάτων καὶ ζήσομεν;
¹⁰οἱ μὲν γὰρ πρὸς ὀλίγας ἡμέρας κατὰ τὸ δοκοῦν αὐτοῖς
ἐπαίδευον, ὁ δὲ ἐπὶ τὸ συμφέρον εἰς τὸ μεταλαβεῖν τῆς
ἁγιότητος αὐτοῦ. ¹¹πᾶσα μὲν παιδεία πρὸς μὲν τὸ
παρὸν οὐ δοκεῖ χαρᾶς εἶναι ἀλλὰ λύπης, ὕστερον δὲ
καρπὸν εἰρηνικὸν τοῖς δι᾽ αὐτῆς γεγυμνασμένοις ἀπο-
δίδωσιν δικαιοσύνης. ¹²Διὸ τὰς παρειμένας χεῖρας καὶ
τὰ παραλελυμένα γόνατα ἀνορθώσατε, ¹³καὶ τροχιὰς ὀρθὰς
ποιεῖτε τοῖς ποσὶν ὑμῶν, ἵνα μὴ τὸ χωλὸν ἐκτραπῇ,
ἰαθῇ δὲ μᾶλλον. ¹⁴Εἰρήνην διώκετε μετὰ πάντων,

καὶ τὸν ἁγιασμόν, οὗ χωρὶς οὐδεὶς ὄψεται τὸν κύριον,
¹⁵ἐπισκοποῦντες μή τις ὑστερῶν ἀπὸ τῆς χάριτος τοῦ
θεοῦ, ΜΗ ΤΙΣ ῥίΖΑ ΠΙΚΡίΑϹ ἄΝω φΎΟΥϹΑ ἐνοχλῇ καὶ δι᾽
αὐτῆς μιανθῶσιν οἱ πολλοί, ¹⁶μή τις πόρνος ἢ βέβηλος
ὡς Ἠϲαῦ, ὃς ἀντὶ βρώσεως μιᾶς ἀπέδετο τὰ πρωτοτόκια
ἑαυτοῦ. ¹⁷ἴστε γὰρ ὅτι καὶ μετέπειτα θέλων κληρονο-
μῆσαι τὴν εὐλογίαν ἀπεδοκιμάσθη, μετανοίας γὰρ
τύπον οὐχ εὗρεν, καίπερ μετὰ δακρύων ἐκζητήσας
αὐτήν. ¹⁸Οὐ γὰρ προσεληλύθατε ψηλαφωμένῳ
καὶ κεκαγμένῳ πυρὶ καὶ ΓΝόφῳ καὶ Ζόφῳ καὶ θΥέλλῃ ¹⁹καὶ
ϹάλΠιΓΓΟϹ ἤχῳ καὶ φωΝῇ ῥΗΜάτων, ἧς οἱ ἀκούσαντες
παρῃτήσαντο προστεθῆναι αὐτοῖς λόγον· ²⁰οὐκ ἔφερον
γὰρ τὸ διαστελλόμενον Κἂν θΗρίον θίΓῃ τοῦ ὄρουϲ, λιθο-
Βοληθήϲεται· ²¹καί, οὕτω φοβερὸν ἦν τὸ φανταζόμενον,
Μωυσῆς εἶπεν Ἔκφοβός εἰμι καὶ ἔντρομος. ²²ἀλλὰ
προσεληλύθατε Σιὼν ὄρει καὶ πόλει θεοῦ ζῶντος, Ἱερου-
σαλὴμ ἐπουρανίῳ, καὶ μυριάσιν ἀγγέλων, ²³πανηγύρει
καὶ ἐκκλησίᾳ πρωτοτόκων ἀπογεγραμμένων ἐν οὐρανοῖς,
καὶ κριτῇ θεῷ πάντων, καὶ πνεύμασι δικαίων τετελειωμένων, ²⁴καὶ διαθήκης νέας μεσίτῃ Ἰησοῦ, καὶ αἵματι
ῥαντισμοῦ κρεῖττον λαλοῦντι παρὰ τὸν Ἄβελ. ²⁵Βλέ-
πετε μὴ παραιτήσησθε τὸν λαλοῦντα· εἰ γὰρ ἐκεῖνοι
οὐκ ἐξέφυγον ἐπὶ γῆς παραιτησάμενοι τὸν χρηματίζοντα,
πολὺ μᾶλλον ἡμεῖς οἱ τὸν ἀπ᾽ οὐρανῶν ἀποστρεφό-
μενοι· ²⁶οὗ ἡ φωνὴ τὴν γῆν ἐσάλευσεν τότε, νῦν δὲ
ἐπήγγελται λέγων Ἔτι ἅΠαΞ ἐΓὼ ϲείϲω οὐ μόνον τΗΝ
ΓῆΝ ἀλλὰ καὶ τὸΝ οὐρΑΝόΝ. ²⁷τὸ δέ Ἔτι ἅΠαΞ δηλοῖ
[τὴν] τῶν σαλευομένων μετάθεσιν ὡς πεποιημένων, ἵνα
μείνῃ τὰ μὴ σαλευόμενα. ²⁸Διὸ βασιλείαν ἀσάλευτον
παραλαμβάνοντες ἔχωμεν χάριν, δι᾽ ἧς λατρεύωμεν
εὐαρέστως τῷ θεῷ μετὰ εὐλαβείας καὶ δέους, ²⁹καὶ γὰρ
ὁ θεὸς ἡμῶν πῦρ καταναλίϲκον.

13 ¹Ἡ φιλαδελφία μενέτω. ²τῆς φιλοξενίας μὴ ἐπιλανθάνεσθε, διὰ ταύτης γὰρ ἔλαθόν τινες ξενίσαντες ἀγγέλους. ³μιμνήσκεσθε τῶν δεσμίων ὡς συνδεδεμένοι, τῶν κακουχουμένων ὡς καὶ αὐτοὶ ὄντες ἐν σώματι. ⁴Τίμιος ὁ γάμος ἐν πᾶσιν καὶ ἡ κοίτη ἀμίαντος, πόρνους γὰρ καὶ μοιχοὺς κρινεῖ ὁ θεός. ⁵Ἀφιλάργυρος ὁ τρόπος· ἀρκούμενοι τοῖς παροῦσιν· αὐτὸς γὰρ εἴρηκεν ΟΥ ΜΗ ϹΕ ΑΝΩ ΟΥΔ᾿ ΟΥ ΜΗ ϹΕ ΕΓΚΑΤΑΛΙΠΩ· ⁶ὥστε θαρροῦντας ἡμᾶς λέγειν

ΚΥΡΙΟϹ ΕΜΟΙ ΒΟΗΘΟϹ, ΟΥ ΦΟΒΗΘΗϹΟΜΑΙ·

ΤΙ ΠΟΙΗϹΕΙ ΜΟΙ ΑΝΘΡΩΠΟϹ;

⁷Μνημονεύετε τῶν ἡγουμένων ὑμῶν, οἵτινες ἐλάλησαν ὑμῖν τὸν λόγον τοῦ θεοῦ, ὧν ἀναθεωροῦντες τὴν ἔκβασιν τῆς ἀναστροφῆς μιμεῖσθε τὴν πίστιν. ⁸Ἰησοῦς Χριστὸς ἐχθὲς καὶ σήμερον ὁ αὐτός, καὶ εἰς τοὺς αἰῶνας. ⁹διδαχαῖς ποικίλαις καὶ ξέναις μὴ παραφέρεσθε· καλὸν γὰρ χάριτι βεβαιοῦσθαι τὴν καρδίαν, οὐ βρώμασιν, ἐν οἷς οὐκ ὠφελήθησαν οἱ περιπατοῦντες. ¹⁰ἔχομεν θυσιαστήριον ἐξ οὗ φαγεῖν οὐκ ἔχουσιν [ἐξουσίαν] οἱ τῇ σκηνῇ λατρεύοντες. ¹¹ὧν γὰρ εἰσφέρεται ζῴων τὸ αἷμα περὶ ἁμαρτίας εἰς τὰ ἅγια διὰ τοῦ ἀρχιερέως, τούτων τὰ σώματα κατακαίεται ἔξω τῆς παρεμβολῆς· ¹²διὸ καὶ Ἰησοῦς, ἵνα ἁγιάσῃ διὰ τοῦ ἰδίου αἵματος τὸν λαόν, ἔξω τῆς πύλης ἔπαθεν. ¹³τοίνυν ἐξερχώμεθα πρὸς αὐτὸν ἔξω τῆς παρεμβολῆς, τὸν ὀνειδισμὸν αὐτοῦ φέροντες, ¹⁴οὐ γὰρ ἔχομεν ὧδε μένουσαν πόλιν, ἀλλὰ τὴν μέλλουσαν ἐπιζητοῦμεν· ¹⁵δι᾿ αὐτοῦ ἀναφέρωμεν θυσίαν αἰνέσεως διὰ παντὸς τῷ θεῷ, τοῦτ᾿ ἔστιν καρπὸν χειλέων ὁμολογούντων τῷ ὀνόματι αὐτοῦ. ¹⁶τῆς δὲ εὐποιίας καὶ κοινωνίας μὴ ἐπιλανθάνεσθε, τοιαύταις γὰρ θυσίαις εὐαρεστεῖται ὁ θεός. ¹⁷Πείθεσθε τοῖς ἡγουμένοις ὑμῶν καὶ ὑπείκετε, αὐτοὶ γὰρ

ἀγρυπνοῦσιν ὑπὲρ τῶν ψυχῶν ὑμῶν ὡς λόγον ἀποδώσοντες, ἵνα μετὰ χαρᾶς τοῦτο ποιῶσιν καὶ μὴ στενάζοντες, ἀλυσιτελὲς γὰρ ὑμῖν τοῦτο. ¹⁸Προσεύχεσθε περὶ ἡμῶν, πειθόμεθα γὰρ ὅτι καλὴν συνείδησιν ἔχομεν, ἐν πᾶσιν καλῶς θέλοντες ἀναστρέφεσθαι. ¹⁹περισσοτέρως δὲ παρακαλῶ τοῦτο ποιῆσαι ἵνα τάχειον ἀποκατασταθῶ ὑμῖν. ²⁰Ὁ δὲ θεὸς τῆς εἰρήνης, ὁ ἀναγαγὼν ἐκ νεκρῶν τὸν ποιμένα τῶν προβάτων τὸν μέγαν ἐν αἵματι διαθήκης αἰωνίου, τὸν κύριον ἡμῶν Ἰησοῦν, ²¹καταρτίσαι ὑμᾶς ἐν παντὶ ἀγαθῷ εἰς τὸ ποιῆσαι τὸ θέλημα αὐτοῦ, ποιῶν ἐν ἡμῖν τὸ εὐάρεστον ἐνώπιον αὐτοῦ διὰ Ἰησοῦ Χριστοῦ, ᾧ ἡ δόξα εἰς τοὺς αἰῶνας τῶν αἰώνων· ἀμήν. ²²Παρακαλῶ δὲ ὑμᾶς, ἀδελφοί, ἀνέχεσθε τοῦ λόγου τῆς παρακλήσεως, καὶ γὰρ διὰ βραχέων ἐπέστειλα ὑμῖν. ²³Γινώσκετε τὸν ἀδελφὸν ἡμῶν Τιμόθεον ἀπολελυμένον, μεθ' οὗ ἐὰν τάχειον ἔρχηται ὄψομαι ὑμᾶς. ²⁴Ἀσπάσασθε πάντας τοὺς ἡγουμένους ὑμῶν καὶ πάντας τοὺς ἁγίους. Ἀσπάζονται ὑμᾶς οἱ ἀπὸ τῆς Ἰταλίας. ²⁵Ἡ χάρις μετὰ πάντων ὑμῶν.

NOTES

CHAPTER I

I. 1—4. The Son Eternal.

1 Gradually and variously, abundantly yet still imperfectly, in the ancient days God revealed His mind to our spiritual ancestors, the Hebrew Fathers of the faith. He entered into the hearts of His **2** prophets and each of them uttered the word He gave. Now at the end of this period to which we belong the same God has spoken to us in One whose eternal unity with Him we are taught to recognise in the name "Son": One whom He appointed from eternity to be the heir of the whole universe of life, through whom also He created those successive ages of time in which life goes on, ascending ever back to **3** Him through whom it first sprang forth from God: One who, like the effulgence of a hidden glory or the engraven form that perfectly expresses an artist's idea, has never ceased to shed the divine light and impress the divine seal upon creation: One too who in the passage through humiliation which He undertook as well as in the new exaltation thus achieved, bore and still bears onward all things to their destined goal, as He was authorised to do by the commandment issuing from the effectual power of God. For this eternal Son entered into the life of men, and like a priest made purification of those sins which had become the characteristic stain of humanity; and so, triumphant, He sat down on the right hand of majesty divine in sublime state. Thus in bold concrete terms borrowed from holy writ we figure His heavenly reign, while by adding abstract terms of reverence we confess how little language can describe or mind con- **4** ceive the co-equality of Godhead. Thus then He reigns, having become in the mysterious progress of that earthly career by so much greater than the angels—those spiritual beings whose glory and beauty it might be imagined He would resemble in His journey through creation—as that name of "Son," so homely sounding, which He, the heir of all, inherited by human fashion of inheritance, is more distinguished in real worth than any that belongs to them.

1. πολυμερῶς καὶ πολυτρόπως. A famous opening in the contemporary style of rhetoric. Maximus Tyrius (fl. 150 A.D.) uses the corresponding adjectives in like conjunction: πολυμερὲς is an epithet of πνεῦμα in Wisd. vii. 22, and πολύτροπος is a favourite word in 4 Macc. The spirited rendering of the Old Latin, *Multifarie multisque modis ante deus locutus patribus in prophetis*, remains, a little polished in Vg., *Multifariam et multis modis olim deus loquens*, etc. The phrase has come into prominence in another way since criticism has directed attention to the gradual development of theology in the Old Testament. "In divers portions and in divers manners" well expresses the progressive revelation given through the prophets to Israel, e.g. the judgement of God in Amos, His love in Hosea, His holiness in Isaiah, the new covenant in Jeremiah, law and sacrifice in Ezekiel.

It might be questioned whether the prep. ἐν does not point to the disproportionate stress which the Alexandrines had laid on the passive disposition of the prophet; God spoke in him as though he were merely the instrument of revelation. The author of this ep. however is apt to give the deepest meaning to his phraseology, whencesoever borrowed; and when he says God spoke in the prophets he is not likely to have intended less than the fullest inspiration of most reasonable heralds. See Intr. III. 29, 30. Indeed this appeal to prophecy at the opening of the ep. sets the key of the whole. Not mechanical law but the inspiration of men is the line along which God's purpose will be found to reach fulfilment in Christ. This is in harmony with the whole N.T. The Christian Church was at one with the more liberal Judaism of the day in its peculiar reverence for the prophetic augmentation of the original Torah. In this our Lord had set the example. Canon Box says:

"Nor must it be forgotten that our Lord's attitude towards the old religion of Israel was that of the prophet rather than the priest. The fulfilment of the Law of which He spoke was essentially prophetic in character. He breathed into it fresh life, deepened and extended its moral significance and claim. And above all He took up a position towards it of sovereign freedom. It is in the prophetic Scriptures that He finds the most adequate expression of His own Messianic consciousness, especially in Isaiah liii. The people instinctively recognised in the new teacher the voice of a prophet. And in fact the whole character of the Christian movement depicted in the New Testament is prophetic. The Day of Pentecost marked the outpouring of the prophetic spirit and gifts. 'The testimony of Jesus is the spirit of prophecy[1].'"

2. ἐπ' ἐσχάτου τῶν ἡμερῶν τούτων. This is the ancient text; "at the end of these days" not "in these last days." It is opposed to πάλαι like "modern" to "old time." At the end of the modern period to which the author belonged the Son entered upon His ministry. The addition of τούτων makes the phrase different from anything else in N.T. (cf. 1 Pet. i. 20, 2 Pet. iii. 3, Jude 18), and it indicates the peculiar attitude of the author to the Messianic ideas of the Church. Intr. iii. 19.

ἐλάλησεν. Does this refer specially to our Lord's teaching, or more generally to His whole life and work in which God spoke to men? See the last pages of Milman's *Latin Christianity* for an eloquent appeal to the words of Christ as "the primal, indefeasible truths of Christianity," which, however our understanding of them be deepened, "shall not pass away." There is little more in this ep. about His words; the theme is His act of sacrifice. But His words form here a just antithesis to the ancient prophecy, and ii. 3 agrees with that interpretation. Only, the reference there is less to continuous teaching than to the proclamation of σωτηρία. Such a proclamation is the beginning of the gospel in Mark i. 15.

ἐν υἱῷ. "His Son," A.V. and R.V., spoils the grandeur of the thought. The author sets us for the moment in the sphere of heavenly pre-existence where logical ideas of personality are out of place; these will come presently as part of the fruitful limitations of "the days of His flesh." Yet R.V. mg., "Gr. *a Son*," is hardly correct. The Greeks, with their frequent omission of the article in the large tragic style, could express just what is wanted here, but there is no equivalent in English. In many of those tragedy lines the idea of class and character is thus presented, as in the fragment from Euripides, θεῶν δὲ θνητοὺς κόσμον οὐ πρέπει φέρειν. Hence Westcott's paraphrase (which he does not offer as adequate) "One who is Son." He carries us further by his remark that we should lose as much by omitting the article before προφήταις as by inserting it here.

κληρονόμον πάντων. The noun is rich in associations from O.T., Philo, and the gospel tradition. In O.T. the "inheritance" of Abraham and his descendants in Canaan, and hence in spiritual privileges, is a common theme: Israel too is the κληρονομία of the Lord. The subject of one of Philo's treatises is Τίς ὁ τῶν θείων ἐστὶν

---

[1] "How should we teach the Old Testament?" *Guardian*, July 13, 1916.

κληρονόμος; In the gospel tradition our Lord was remembered as having described Himself as the heir of the vineyard, slain by the husbandmen, and thereby opening the vineyard to other husbandmen : Matt. xxi. 33 ff., Mark xii. 1 ff., Luke xx. 9 ff. The particular noun κληρονόμος is rare in LXX. In N.T. it is used by S. Paul, elsewhere only in Jas. ii. 5 and those three passages of the gospels, and this ep. But in this ep. the three words κληρονομέω, κληρονομία, κληρονόμος, are characteristic : see i. 4, 14, vi. 12, 17, ix. 15, xi. 7, 8, xii. 17. From Noah onwards the chosen people are represented as heirs of God's blessing in the future. The Christian people have inherited their hope and are entering, heirs in their own turn, upon its fulfilment. All this heirship springs from Christ's universal and eternal heirship. Through Him all nature was created and to Him it all reverts in holiness historically perfected by the ascending strain of life towards its Lord. The commencement of His visible act of heirship is indicated in *vv.* 5 ff. : He takes by right of inheritance the ancient names of Christ and Son.

καὶ ἐποίησεν τοὺς αἰῶνας. αἰὼν in LXX represents 'olam, "age." In late Hebrew 'olam had the meaning " world," κόσμος, but perhaps not when this ep. was written[1]. " Ages " is a fuller sense and therefore likely to be our author's. It corresponds with " these days," i.e. this period or age, just above; and a like full meaning suits best in xi. 3. The ancient text has the order of words as quoted. The later text puts τ. αἰῶνας before ἐποίησεν, a false emphasis, and perhaps inferior rythm though Blass thought otherwise. In the true order καὶ simply connects ἐποίησεν with ἔθηκεν as contemporaneous or immediately successive.

3. ἀπαύγασμα τῆς δόξης, *splendor gloriae* (latt.). Whatever may have been the original meaning of the Hebrew *chabod* the context often shows that it expressed the idea of glorious light in O.T., and so its LXX rendering δόξα ; e.g. Isa. lx. 1, φωτίζου φωτίζου, Ἱερου σαλήμ, ἥκει γάρ σου τὸ φῶς, καὶ ἡ δόξα Κυρίου ἐπὶ σε ἀνατέταλκεν. This was consonant with the Hebrew mind. " The sky had cleared after some days of south-westerly weather, and morning broke in that rare splendour which persuaded the Hebrew poets, that perfect bliss will be perfect light[2]." Ἀπαύγασμα might mean " reflection " but is more properly " effulgence," and that suits this context; the Son is the stream of light from the innermost glory.

χαρακτὴρ τῆς ὑποστάσεως, *figura* (vg.), *imago* (d), *substantiae.* So. χαρακτήρ, which might be the impression, is here used in the

1 Dalman, *The Words of Jesus*, p. 153.
2 Hogarth, *Accidents of an Antiquary's Life*, ch. v.

more primary sense of the engraved seal itself which expresses the
idea in the artist's mind : cf. Liturgy of Serapion, ὁ θεὸς....ὁ τὸν
χαρακτῆρα τὸν ζῶντα καὶ ἀληθινὸν γεννήσας, and Cic. *Or.* 8, 9, ...*sed
ipsius in mente insidebat species pulcritudinis eximia quaedam, quam
intuens in eaque defixus, ad illius similitudinem artem et manum dirige-
bat.* Cicero had just written *quasi imago exprimatur,* so that the rendering of d, Erasmus' *expressa imago,* and A.V. "express image," may
be approved. But A.V. "person " for ὑποστάσεως is an anachronism :
ὑπόστασις was not used for " person " till the fourth century. See
three articles by Dr Strong, Dean of Christ Church[1], for full treatment of this and kindred words. A.V. here follows the Geneva
version, and may be compared with Wisd. ii. 23, ὁ θεὸς ἔκτισεν τὸν
ἄνθρωπον ἐπ' ἀφθαρσίᾳ καὶ εἰκόνα τῆς ἰδίας ἰδιότητος ἐποίησεν αὐτόν.
But that is not the idea in our author's mind. He treats ὑπόστασις
throughout the ep. more as a philologist than a philosopher. It
means that which, in the deepest sense appropriate to the context,
underlies, supports, or as here originates expression, and it is always
associated with a genitive ; cf. iii. 14, xi. 1, and contrast 2 Cor. ix. 4.
Cf. also Coleridge[2], " *Quod stat subtus,* that which stands beneath,
and (as it were) supports the appearance." Milton, who conveys so
much from this ep., says in *Paradise Lost,* x. 63 ff. :

> " So spake the Father, and unfoulding bright
> Toward the right hand his Glorie, on the Son
> Blaz'd forth unclouded Deitie ; he full
> Resplendent all his Father manifest
> Express'd, and thus divinely answered milde."

ὤν...φέρων τε "being and bearing." The mode of conjunction
emphasises the difficult assertion that throughout the days of His
flesh the Son was still revealing Godhead and bearing the universe
to its goal. But this is the assertion which the author justifies by
his sacramental view of glory in humiliation; cf. Intr. ii. 15, iii. 7.
In B and ps.-Sarap. φανερῶν is read for φέρων. That suits the
immediate context but would impoverish the general theology of
the ep. It is an instance of B losing weight by association with one
other and inferior authority. For the pres. part. cf. xi. 17, and ὑπάρ-
χων in Phil. ii. 6, where however the compound " being originally "
is less absolute than the simple ὤν.

τῷ ῥήματι τῆς δυνάμεως αὐτοῦ " by the commanding word (cf. xi. 3)
of His power." *Virtutis suae,* latt. ; and so the ancient commentators

---

[1] "The history of the theological term 'Substance,'" *JTS.* Jan., Oct., 1901
Oct. 1902.
[2] *Aids to Reflection,* Intr. Aphorisms xii n.

But the second αὐτοῦ, especially in a balanced piece of rhetoric like this, would surely have the same reference as the first. And this fits the context; the Son reveals or mediates God's power as He does His glory and inmost being. This αὐτοῦ is omitted by M 424** Orig. Perhaps the ancient commentators and translators were unconsciously influenced by their general view of the passage as a declaration of the essential unity of the Son with the Father. But it is more than that. It starts from the prophets, and joins the high doctrine of the contemporary Church concerning the Godhead of the Son with the old prophetic idea of the Christ, the LORD's Anointed, representing God in His people. The theme is not so much the uniqueness of the Son's relation to the Father, as His uniting men with God. This becomes plainer as the ep. proceeds; so far it is partly obscured by the technical terms which are borrowed from Alexandrine Judaism, e.g. ἀπαύγασμα Wisd. vii. 25 f. and Philo, χαρακτήρ and φέρων (τὰ πάντα) Philo.

καθαρισμὸν τῶν ἁμαρτιῶν ποιησάμενος. So, without δι' ἑαυτοῦ or ἡμῶν in the ancient text. The middle, ποιησάμενος, is in accordance with the rule that a verb in Greek may be resolved into the corresponding noun with the middle ποιεῖσθαι.

ἐκάθισεν ἐν δεξιᾷ. First allusion to Ps. cx. which will supply the guiding thought of the ep., viz. the royal High Priest after the order of Melchizedek. Cf. Mark xiv. 62, which is reminiscent of this psalm and of Dan. vii. 13.

μεγαλωσύνης. Used in the doxologies of Jude (25) and Clem. Rom. xx. 12. In viii. 1 it is joined with ἐν τοῖς οὐρανοῖς; in this rhetorically finished passage the author substitutes ὑψηλοῖς in a peculiar sense partly for the alliterative music, partly to give distinction and variety to the style; so διαφορώτερον and παρ' αὐτοὺς in next verse.

4. κεκληρονόμηκεν. This long word with its running metre is also chosen partly for its combination with ὄνομα into a musical cadence; cf. vii. 28, xii. 2. But there are no idle graces in the author's style, and the perfect is needed here. The Son has inherited that name and still keeps it. In d the translator justifiably renders by a present tense, thus also getting a good Latin cadence of his own, *pŏssĭdēt nōmĕn*. Intr. v. 12. This verb is also a stylistic echo of κληρονόμον in v. 2; yet more than stylistic. Hitherto we have been mainly concerned with the pre-existent state of One who received in time the name of Son, also of Christ, and the dignity of Lord, King and High Priest. But the rest of the ep. is chiefly taken up with tracing His inheritance and achievement of these names and dignities

on earth. "Most of what is said of the Son in His pre-existing state
is contained in i. 2, 3, though some of the things said there are
repeated in other passages. The pre-existing state is alluded to very
little, and chiefly because it explains the present condition of exaltation, which was not possible except to a being essentially Son of
God...Beyond the assumption of the pre-existence of the Son, the
epistle seems nowhere to desert the region of history" (Davidson,
pp. 40 and 74). Davidson thinks the appointment as heir in *v.* 2
refers to the historical exaltation after the death on the cross.
Westcott, surely better, says "There is nothing to determine the
'time' of this divine appointment. It belongs to the eternal order."
It is in fact the whole of which our modern notion "evolution" is a part.
But with κεκληρονόμηκεν ὄνομα we pass to another special part or line
of this whole in history. The next section looks back upon the
Christs of Israel's history who have, in O.T., received the name of
Son, and regards this as the process of inheritance, by which One,
who will later in the ep. be styled Lord and King and High Priest
and Christ, inherited His name of Son.

I. 5—14. The Son's Inheritance. Christ-sons in History.

5   The angels I say; for angels have nothing to do with such a
name as "Son." God, who speaks in the writers and personages
of our sacred books, did not say, "My son art thou; this day have I
begotten thee," to any angel. He said that to one of those kings of
Israel who were also called the Christs of the LORD, and who, being
themselves faint reflections of the divine effulgence and copies from
the divine seal, made history prophetic of the perfect Christ. It was
again to the best and greatest of those Christ-kings that God said
through Nathan the prophet, "I will be to him a father, and he shall
6 be to me a son." And whenever God brings back again the people
whom He had called His firstborn son into the family of nations
after one of those repeated humiliations which make the paradox of
their spiritual history and are prophetic of a far more transcendent
glory through humiliation still to come, He says, "And let all the
angels of God worship him." The quotation is apt for our argument,
since this nation, itself too, bore the title "Christ": through all this
varied line of Christship our Christ, who crowns the line, inherits
His name of "Son."

7   And on the other hand while God, speaking in a psalmist about
Himself, utters words concerning angels which indicate their dignity

in the sacramental order of nature—"Who maketh His angels winds, and His ministers a flame of fire," concerning the Son God indi- 8. cates His place in a more mysterious line along which manhood and Godhead, history and its fulfilment in the eternal sphere, are inexplicably brought together—"Thy throne is God (or does He even say, O God?) for ever and ever, and the sceptre of righteousness is the sceptre of God's kingdom. Thou lovedst righteousness and didst hate 9 iniquity; therefore God, even thy God, hath anointed thee with the oil of gladness above thy fellows." And, going deeper still, bringing 10 seen and unseen, time and eternity, into still closer union, He uses the person of a psalmist to address Himself by His own ineffable name; yet utters words which certainly have reference to the Son through whom He made all things, and to whom, the abiding heir of all things, they return through all their change and perishing as His inheritance—"Thou in the beginning, Lord, didst found the earth, and works of Thy hands are the heavens. They shall perish, but Thou 11 still remainest. And they all as a garment shall grow old, and as a 12 vesture shalt Thou roll them up; as a garment shall they be utterly changed. And Thou art the same, yea Thy years shall not fail."

And finally, concerning the Son and not concerning any angel, God 13 signifies in a mysterious oracle which a psalmist was inspired to express in human words, that One (whom we well recognise to day) is to reign with Himself in co-equal majesty till the victory over evil is wholly won—"Sit thou on my right hand until I make thine enemies the footstool of thy feet." Such an awful summons was 14 never given to an angel. The angels serve, they do not reign. In the universal temple of creation they are the priestly winds, the holy spirits, ceaselessly sent forth to do God's service for the sake of those who are to inherit salvation in that divine victorious act which lay quite in the future when the doctrine of angels was first made known to man, and still we await its full completion.

5.   τῶν ἀγγέλων. This takes up κρείττων τῶν ἀ. in the last verse, and introduces a formal proof of the Son's superiority to the angels. We are reminded of Col. ii. 18 and i. 16, and wonder whether the author is correcting a tendency of his day to angel worship. But there is no further hint of this in the ep. unless the further parallel with Col. in xiii. 8 f., be thought to support the conjecture. And the positive argument of the section, that the Son has received His name by inheritance through the line of the Christ-nation and its kings, is far more essential to the ep. than the negative argument, that the inheritance has not come through the line of the angels. The main

point comes out at last in ii. 16; the Son is truly man and therefore truly mediator between man and God.

υἱός μου εἶ σύ, κ.τ.λ. From Ps. ii., which is addressed to a king of Israel. Apart from the more transcendent Messianic significance which this Psalm would probably have in the Jewish church of the later centuries B.C., it is justly quoted by the author in its context here for this reason. In O.T. kings of Israel are styled "the LORD's Messiah." In the English Bible "Messiah" is rendered "Anointed," but in the LXX, which was the Bible of the author, the rendering is ὁ χριστός. Hence he quite fairly thinks of our Lord as "inheriting" this title through the Christs of the past. He also thinks of these Christs of the past as being themselves, in their degree, revelations of the one divine Christ (cf. xi. 26). And he is confirmed in this bold idea by finding that even these Christs of the past were called "sons" of God. Intr. III. 6.

ἐγὼ ἔσομαι αὐτῷ, κ.τ.λ. This appears in a striking manner in Nathan's oracle to David, 2 Sam. vii., from which this quotation is taken. The deep solemnity of that passage was felt of old as much as by this author. That is proved by the allusion to it in Ps. lxxxix. 26 ff.

6. ὅταν δὲ πάλιν εἰσαγάγῃ, κ.τ.λ. The meaning of this appears from the quotation which follows, καὶ προσκυνησάτωσαν αὐτῷ, κ.τ.λ. This nearly corresponds to the LXX of Ps. xcvii. (xcvi.) 7, and exactly to the B text of a LXX addition to Deut. xxxii. 43. Each poem celebrates the restoration of the people of Israel, who are in Ps. lxxxix. 51 associated with David in the office of Messiah. It is, therefore, when God brings His people, after their humiliation (of exile, etc.), into the fellowship of the nations (τὴν οἰκουμένην) again, that He bids all the angels worship this people who are His firstborn son (Jer. xxxi. 9, Hos. xi. 1). In Ps. xcvii. (xcvi.) ἄγγελοι of LXX represents the Hebrew 'elohim. This indicates the answer to an objection that might be raised, viz. that angels are called "sons of God" in Job i. 6, ii. 1, xxxviii. 7. In the author's Bible, the LXX, ἄγγελοι is the rendering of bne 'elohim in each place. Nor is this a false rendering. 'Elohim is used in the O.T. in various senses, of false gods 1 Kings xix. 2, of judges etc. Ps. lxxxii. 6, of spiritual beings or angels. This last is the use in the passages of Job, and bne 'elohim is the regular Hebrew phrase for the class or company of 'elohim, as bne neb'iim is for the class or professional guild of prophets; sonship in the sense of "descent from" is not implied.

A question still remains about the force of the temporal clause ὅταν εἰσαγάγῃ. Being completed by the present λέγει in the apodosis it should mean "whenever he brings again." And this would suit

the repeated humiliations of Israel very well: "The exile of Israel
in its deepest sense has lasted from Nebuchadnezzar's burning of
Jerusalem to the present day[1]." But the imperative προσκυνησάτωσαν might be considered the real apodosis; cf. Apoc. iv. 9 f. Then
the reference would be to an event in the future, and it is very possible
that the author had also in mind that "second" advent of his Lord
(ix. 28) of which he treats in a somewhat unusual manner in this
epistle; cf. Intr. III. 19.   πάλιν might be taken as in preceding verse,
but whenever it is followed by a verb in this ep. it is construed with
the verb; iv. 7, v. 12, vi. 6.

7.   καὶ πρὸς μέν, κ.τ.λ.   Not "to" but "with regard to." No
address to angels follows, but a description of angels from Ps. civ. 4.
It matters little whether the Hebrew makes "winds" (πνεύματα) and
"fire" predicate as the Greek does, or the other way. The meaning
will be really the same. Other pictures of angels might be collected
from O.T., but this accords with the ancient and deepest idea of
the Hebrews. To them the thunderstorm was in very truth the
manifestation of the LORD their God. The thunder was His voice,
the winds and lightnings His angels. So in N.T. the law, given in
the thunder of Sinai, is spoken of as ordained by angels, and the
coming of the Son of man is expected sometimes with angels, sometimes with clouds; cf. also John xii. 29. That this implies no
derogation from the angels' glory is shewn by the author's language
in xii. 23, and the symbolic exaltation of nature and "forces of
nature" in the Apocalypse[2]. All this however is but hinted here.
The main thing is that angels are shewn to stand in another line
of life from that along which the Son lifts man to God.

8.   πρὸς δὲ τὸν υἱόν.   πρὸς must have the same meaning as
before. Yet the quotation, from Ps. xlv., is in the form of an
address. This might be explained by the consideration that it
would be more in accordance with N.T. usage to speak of the
vocative, ὁ θεός, as applicable to the Son, than to use it as a direct
address to the Son: even S. Thomas' words in John xx. 28 are
different from the absolute "O God." But, besides that, there is
some doubt whether ὁ θεός here is intended to be taken as a vocative.
In אB, that very strong combination of textual authority, τῆς βασιλείας αὐτοῦ, not σου, is read. With αὐτοῦ, the natural (though not
quite inevitable) translation of the sentence would be "Thy throne
is God...and the sceptre of righteousness is the sceptre of His

---

[1] Cheyne, *Jewish Religious Life after the Exile*, p. 159.
[2] See further Sanday, *The Life of Christ in recent research*, on "The Symbolism of the Bible," and "A Sermon on Angels."

kingdom." It is a further argument for following the strong MS.
authority that the author has made another adjustment of his
LXX text by writing καὶ ἡ ῥάβδος τῆς εὐθύτητος ῥάβδος τῆς βασιλείας
instead of ῥάβδος εὐθύτητος ἡ ῥάβδος τῆς βασιλείας, shifting the predicate as though to imply that wherever righteous rule is found it
will be God's rule.   One who could make such a thoughtful correction as that might make the other to avoid what he felt to be
somewhat crude theology.   It would be possible to construe the
original Hebrew in this way, and it would make the immediately
following "God, even thy God" easier. Most O.T. commentators
however think this unnatural, and all ancient exegesis is against it
in the quoted Greek.   The extraordinary arrangement in d perhaps
shows how remarkable that translator found the passage.   He
translates καὶ πρὸς μὲν τοὺς ἀγγέλους αὐτοῦ λέγει (so in D) by *Et angelus
ipsius dicit* and then arranges all that follows down to the end of *v.* 12
as one utterance or oracle.

That of course is merely curious.   But the solution of the problem
in *v.* 8 does depend in part upon the interpretation of *vv.* 10—12.
These are quoted from Ps. cii. 25 ff.   As generally in LXX Κύριε
represents the ineffable name.   Hort writes in his Commentary on
1 Pet. ii. 3 "It would be rash to conclude that he meant to identify
Jehovah with Christ.   No such identification can be clearly made out
in the N.T."   It would seem right therefore to say that here again,
as in the last quotation, O.T. language is applied to the Son to
describe His divine character ; He is not Himself addressed as
"God" or "Lord."   But if so, the whole series of quotations
might seem to be in an ascending scale.   First, His inheritance of
the name Son is illustrated from passages in which that name is
given to the anointed kings or to the people of Israel.   Then, after
a verse in which the "nature-glory" of angels is indicated, a second
application of O.T. language is made, assigning to the Son the
attributes of a king who is addressed as "God," and finally even
the attributes of Him who is the Lord God of Israel are associated
with Him.

On the other hand it must be noticed that not all those attributes
are presented.   These verses from Ps. cii. seem to correspond to the
"nature" character of the angels in *v.* 7 and to the Son's work
of creation in *v.* 2.   The mark of His divinity is here mainly recognised in this, viz. that while created nature changes and passes,
He as χαρακτὴρ τῆς ὑποστάσεως abides unchangeable : cf. xii. 27 f.,
xiii. 8.

See a paper printed by Hort in 1876 *On Hebrews* i. 8.   Westcott agrees with him both in reading αὐτοῦ, and in translating " God is Thy Throne.''

13. κάθου ἐκ δεξιῶν, κ.τ.λ. From Ps. cx., which dominates in the ep.; cf. i. 3, v. 6, 10, vi. 20, vii. 11, 15, 17, 21, 24, 28, viii. 1, x. 12 f., xii. 2. 'Εκ δεξιῶν is LXX; in mere allusions the author writes ἐν δεξιᾷ. In the last two quotations the name "Son" was not expressed. In this verse that thought is quite superseded by the culminating glory of exaltation to co-equality in kingly rule; cf. Mark xii. 37, 1 Cor. xv. 28. This quotation brings us to the personal history of our Lord on earth, the humiliation in which this glory was achieved; that subject will be taken up at ii. 5.

14. πνεύματα. Here we must translate "spirits" in spite of v. 7. But the Greek reader, certainly the Jewish Greek reader, would feel no difficulty in that. He had not learned, nor found in his Bible, the separation between symbol and reality which confuses us. Thus in Gen. i. 2 the wind on the dark water actually was to him the Spirit of God; cf. Ps. xxxi. 5, Eccl. xii. 7, Luke xxiii. 46, John iii. 8, xx. 22.

λειτουργικά. This adj., like λειτουργεῖν λειτουργία, is used of the Levitical service in LXX (not in Leviticus); cf. Rom. xv. 16. The angels minister in the "temple" of God, which is the universe, as often in the Psalter. See especially Ps. xxix. 9 and cf. John xiv. 2, Luke ii. 49. "Ministering angels" are spoken of in Philo and the Talmud.

ἀποστελλόμενα. Pres. part. of continual activity. A part. is similarly used in the Hebrew of the seraphim in Isa. vi. So Milton, "Thousands at his bidding speed And post o're Land and Ocean without rest "; cf. Lucr. v. 297 ff., *ardore ministro...tremere ignibus instant, Instant, nec loca lux inter quasi rupta relinquit.*

διὰ τοὺς μέλλοντας κληρονομεῖν σωτηρίαν. The periphrasis with μέλλω indicates "imminence in past time" (Blass 62, 4). S. Paul's doctrine of election does not enter into this ep., not even in iv. 3; it is the salvation that is predestined not the number of the saved. All that is read in O.T. of angels is here represented as having reference to the salvation to be fulfilled in the latter days; cf. ix. 28, xi. 40.

Hence σωτηρία is to be interpreted from O.T. usage not, as perhaps in some parts of N.T., from the contemporary Greek world[1]. Hort has fine notes on the word in his comm. on 1 Pet., pp. 38 f.,

---

[1] See Deissmann, *Bible Studies*, p. 83 f., *Light from the Ancient East*, index, s.vv. σωτήρ, σωτὴρ τοῦ κόσμου, σωτηρία.

48, 103 ; see also Sanday and Headlam on Rom. i. 16. The dominant idea is that of victorious rescue, as in Ps. xxxv. (xxxiv.) 3,
Isa. lix. 16—20, cf. Eph. vi. 17. But " salvation in the fullest sense
is but the completion of God's work upon men, the successful end of
their probation and education " (Hort) ; so in this ep. it is associated
with " progress " and " perfection," ii. 10, v. 9, vi. 9. Σωτήρ,
frequent in Pastorals and 2 Pet., cf. also Phil. iii. 20, does not occur
in this ep.

CHAPTER II

Such being the mysterious origin, office and achievement of Him **1**
to whom our allegiance has been rendered, we are bound more exceedingly to give heed to the tradition of life and doctrine on which
we (unlike the earlier disciples) mainly depend. More exceedingly : **2**
for we are in a time of trial, and we must be vigilant lest by however
unexpected a chance the tide of trouble sweep us away from our
loyalty. More exceedingly again: for we run a risk like that of
ancient Israel, but of deeper consequence. Their Law was a word
spoken through the angels of the storm at Sinai; and in due course
it was firmly established, and every refusal to walk in its path or
to listen to its meaning, though it delayed complete establishment,
received just and due payment of the wage it merited. So costly
was the establishment of the Law: and how shall we escape away **3**
if by our neglect we hinder—no mere word spoken through angels
but—salvation itself? And such a great salvation! A proclamation
of victorious mercy, which received its impulse in the speech of Him
we adore as Lord, has been handed on unimpaired so far as to us by
those who heard the very accents of His voice. So far in its course **4**
it has been firmly established: God as well as the disciples witnessing
to its truth all the way with signs and wonders as of old ; with
exquisitely varied acts of power ; with breathings of a holy Spirit
such as inspired creation and our national history, each duly appor-
tioned according to His ever active will.

1. Set. This verse (omitted in M Orig.) introduces the first of
those exhortations which are so closely interwoven with the argument
of the ep. that the author justly styles it a " word of exhortation "
in xiii. 22. So, in an ancient prologue to the Pauline epp., Hebrews
is described simply thus—*Ad Ebreos quos hortatur ad similitudinem
thesalonicensium ut in mandatis Dei persecutiones prumptissime
patiantur*[1].

---

[1] Gwynn, *Liber Ardmachanus*, p. 209.

τοῖς ἀκουσθεῖσιν. The tradition of the Church on which the whole ep. rests. Like the ancient prophets, the author disclaims innovation; cf. xiii. 8 f.

παραρυῶμεν. Cf. Isai. xliv. 4, παραρρέον ὕδωρ. The passive here (2 aor. subj.) implies being carried away by the tide of temptation ; "lest we drift," ne casu lebemur (sic) d, ne forte effluamus vg.

2. ὁ δι' ἀγγέλων λαληθεὶς λόγος. The Law at Sinai, διαταγεὶς δι' ἀγγέλων ἐν χειρὶ μεσίτου as S. Paul says, Gal. iii. 19; see note on i. 7 above.

ἐγένετο βέβαιος. From xii. 19, 25 we see how the author (so imaginatively reading his Bible) felt that a risk was run at Sinai; Israel's fear made the acceptance of God's commandments uncertain. Moses the "mediator" saved them from the peril then, but the "word" did not become really firm till the whole troubled course of the nation's political ambition was ended by the exile. This verse like i. 1 is a curious anticipation of modern O.T. criticism.

3. ἀμελήσαντες. "If we should have," not "since we have neglected." A like risk was before the author's friends, but he had good hope of them; cf. vi. 1—12.

ἀρχὴν λαβοῦσα. Cf. xi. 29, 36. The phrase has almost a personal ring, like "receiving impulse from." Thus it gives to ἐβεβαιώθη something of the idea of confirmation by "development."

λαλεῖσθαι. Probably refers to actual "speaking," i.e. to our Lord's proclamation "The kingdom of God is at hand," or to the whole of His teaching during His ministry; xi. 4, xii. 24 are not parallels. That teaching would include such pregnant sayings as Mark viii. 35, x. 45, which are the germ of the apostolic doctrine of salvation by the cross. In this ep. the high-priestly entrance into the heavenly sanctuary is contemplated timelessly or as simultaneous with the act of dying; therefore no reference to the forty days of Acts i. 3 is likely.

τοῦ κυρίου. Here first the author names his Master plainly. The readers would have recognised to whom he was pointing throughout ch. i., but there he set them, as it were, by the throne of God in heaven, and opened a vision of eternal things. That would have lost its mystery if he had introduced a defining title which rose out of the earthly limitations of "the days of" the Saviour's "flesh."

It rose out of those days, yet perhaps not immediately. The title κύριος is not often found in the synoptic gospels in the full sense which it has in the rest of N.T. In many places S. Luke's ἐπιστάτης, "Master," might be substituted for it without apparent loss. In Luke xxiv. 3 τοῦ κυρίου Ἰησοῦ is quite unusual. But all three words are omitted by authorities which have peculiar weight in these last chapters of Luke, and the closest parallel to them is in Mark xvi. 19 f., which according to the most ancient evidence are no part of the original book. Bousset in his study of early Christian doctrine, *Kyrios Christos*, shews that this title, Κύριος, was characteristic of certain religious fellowships in the Graeco-Roman world which may have influenced the Christian Church in the development of faith through worship—*lex orandi, lex credendi*. Such influence would not be alien to the followers of Him who is Himself the truth wherever found (John xiv. 6). But there are passages in the gospels (though hardly in Mark) which at least raise the question whether the impulse had not been given earlier and elsewhere; e.g. Matt. vii. 21 f., xx. 31. And the influence of the LXX with its Κύριος (see above on i. 10) must also be taken into account.

ὑπὸ τῶν ἀκουσάντων, κ.τ.λ. S. Paul, who claims immediate revelation so earnestly (see Gal. i. 1, 11 f., 16), would hardly have written this. But, taken by itself, it does not put the author and his friends farther from the "beginning" than S. Paul. They had not listened to the teaching of our Lord himself; that is all that is necessarily implied; cf. Acts i. 21 f., and Hdt. ix. 98 καὶ τάδε ἴστω καὶ ὁ μὴ ἐπακούσας ὑμέων πρὸς τοῦ ἐπακούσαντος.

4. σημείοις τε καὶ τέρασιν. So often in Acts and thrice in Paul; cf. also John iv. 48. A frequent collocation in LXX of Deuteronomy, which was rather a favourite book with our author. The idea has some resemblance to the concluding verses of Mark which may have been written by the presbyter Ariston; see Swete's Commentary, pp. ciii.—cv.; there are also other coincidences in language. Closer attention shews that the resemblance is probably superficial. In particular, Ariston makes much of the outward signs; our author passes from his almost conventionally quoted O.T. words to the deeper things of spiritual life.

πνεύματος ἁγίου. Without article, as always in this ep. unless the Spirit is connected with O.T. inspiration. The exception in x. 29 is a grammatical necessity. Intr. iii. 29.

θέλησιν. This abstract noun (only here in N.T.) suits the "movement" of the passage; contrast x. 36, xiii. 21.

II. 5—18. Jesus the man: glory in humiliation: priesthood through death.

5   The Lord speaking, God witnessing, Holy Spirit operating! Yes, for it was not to mere angels that God subjected the spiritual world of which we are speaking, our home long destined and now within our
6 reach. To whom then is it subject? Why, to man. Does not some one somewhere call God to witness to this paradox? "What is a man," he says, "that Thou art mindful of him; mortal man, that
7 Thou visitest him? Thou didst humble him indeed, but only a little below angels; with a wreath of glory and honour didst Thou deck him.
8 All things didst Thou put in subjection under his feet." Glory in humiliation! Strange but true, for there it stands written, "all things in subjection"; there is no exception at all. Well, as yet at any rate we do not see those "all things" in subjection to man.
9 But we do behold One, who stands visible to memory and faith, a little below angels, humbled—he is Jesus, the man: and but a little below angels indeed—it is for the suffering of death that He wears a wreath of veritable glory and honour, so that He may,—thus God of His free favour granted— on behalf of every one of us taste death.

10   Manhood, suffering, death! Yes, for it was befitting Him, for whose good pleasure "all things" came into being, and through whose direction "all things" hold their course, after bringing many sons "to glory" in the psalmist's dream, to carry Him who was to lead the way in realising that glorious victory of theirs, through
11 sufferings to His purposed goal. For suffering is the faculty of mortal man, and in suffering we find the pledge of real communion; not only the sanctifier but those too whom He sanctifies are seen thereby to have the same divine origin. And that is why He is not ashamed to call them brothers. Who so well as He can give full meaning to those often-repeated words of Israel's martyr and Israel's
12 prophet? "I will declare Thy name to my brothers, in the midst of
13 the church of our people I will praise Thee." And again, "It is I who will be a man of faith in Him." And again, "Behold I and the children whom God gave me." Now there we hear the accents of
14 a common piety and kindred. And since kindred as regards these "children" implies physical relationship, He too partook of that just as they do; for the sake of that great purpose already named, viz. through death to bring to nought the potentate of the realm of death,
15 the awful Adversary; and so to give quittance to all the multitude of those who by fear of death throughout the course of natural life were

liable to slavery. For I hardly fancy you will say that such physical 16
relationship, such "taking hold of," is likely with regard to angels.
No, it is Abraham's human seed He takes hold of. And therefore He
was bound in all respects to be made like to these "brothers" of His.
For this is the sum of all that purpose indicated by manhood, suffer- 17
ing, human piety and death, namely that He may become, in regular
process, pitiful and faithful as a High Priest on the Godward side,
to the end that He may continually do priestly work in taking away
the sins of the people of God. For, having gone through the tribu- 18
lation of trial, He has in Himself the lasting experience of suffering,
and in that quality is able to come to the rescue of those who, as
their turn comes round, enter into trial.

5. οὐ γὰρ ἀγγέλοις, κ.τ.λ. The LXX of Deut. xxxii. 8 says that
"when the Most High gave to the nations their inheritance he set
the bounds of the peoples according to the number of the angels of
God" (Heb. "of the children of Israel"). This might imply that
when the world became an οἰκουμένη, a society of men, it was put
under the control of the angels. Thus τὴν οἰκουμένην τὴν μέλλουσαν
might mean "the social world which lay in the future at the time of
creation." If so the author denies the inference (cf. xi. 27). But it
is more likely that he is giving a varied expression of the thought
which recurs in vi. 5, δυνάμεις μέλλοντος αἰῶνος, xii. 28 βασιλείαν
ἀσάλευτον, xiii. 14 πόλιν τὴν μέλλουσαν, cf. also iii. 5, iv. 9, viii. 13,
ix. 10, x. 1, 20, xi. 10, 16. The world or city or good things to come,
the kingdom that cannot be shaken, the opened way to God, are the
"kingdom of God," promised in O.T., proclaimed at hand by our
Lord, brought in some sense by His death, still to be consummated at
His "coming" (ix. 28). That passage, ix. 28, shews that the author
holds the ancient faith of the Galilean disciples (Acts iii. 21) concerning the final advent. But it is enlarged and deepened in his
epistle. A "coming" in the trial of his own day is recognised,
x. 25, 37, Intr. iii. 19; and the seeming confusion of past, present and
future is removed by his Platonic conception of eternity as reality not
length of time, cf. ix. 11 f. To him there was no antithesis between
this world and "the world to come," a favourite formula in Judaism,
but only in late Judaism, see Dalman, p. 147 ff. If, as the coincidence in quoting Ps. viii. suggests, he knew Eph. i. 21 f., he would
feel that he could not quite adopt the phrase used there. His
"world to come" is more akin to S. Paul's doctrine of the Spirit,
and nearer still to S. John's sacramental thought. It is "the higher
hidden life which lies at the roots of the visible life," Gardner, *The
Ephesian Gospel,* p. 194.

6. διεμαρτύρατο δέ πού τις. A favourite verb in Acts: "to call (God) to witness to the truth of what some one says[1]." Thus the Alexandrine formula πού τις is used here with precision. In the quotations of this chapter it is no longer God who speaks in the person of the O.T. writer; here it is a man concerning mankind, in 12 f. the man Jesus concerning His relation towards men. Throughout this chapter the point of view is from earthly history.

τί ἐστιν ἄνθρωπος, κ.τ.λ. From Ps. viii. The Psalmist contemplates the grandeur of creation and feels the littleness of man. But, remembering Gen. i. 26 ff., he appeals to the LORD to confirm his faith in man's high destiny. In the Hebrew he says, "thou hast made him little lower than God." That becomes in LXX "than the angels." The rendering might be justified from the ambiguity of *'elohim* (cf. note on i. 8). But it is rfot necessary to press this. The real subject of interest in this chapter is not the angels but the humiliation of Jesus as the means of His glory. The omission of καὶ κατέστησας...χειρῶν σου in the next verse (so BD^c) helps to bring out the simplicity of the argument.

υἱὸς ἀνθρώπου. So far as there is real antithesis in the original Hebrew, this second term for "man" means "ordinary man," "mankind." It may be that the lowly idea of this psalm and of Ezekiel (ii. 1 and *passim*) was combined with the grand idea in Dan. vii. 13 by our Lord when He called Himself "The Son of Man." There is no direct reference to that title in this epistle.

8. ἐν τῷ γὰρ ὑποτάξαι αὐτῷ τὰ πάντα. Is there reminiscence of 1 Cor. xv. 25—28 in the language here? That passage shews at any rate how naturally association of ideas would lead the author from Ps. cx. (i. 13) to Ps. viii. B, still simplifying, omits αὐτῷ.

The inf. with art., an interesting feature of N.T. Greek, is handled with skill in this ep. (cf. ii. 15, Intr. v. 3). Its tenses signify state not time; Goodwin, § 96. But with ἐν τῷ the use is not classical, and in this use the tense of the inf. perhaps can indicate time. Blass 71. 7.

9. τὸν δὲ βραχύ τι, κ.τ.λ. Throughout *v.* 8 αὐτῷ means "man" in general, in whom the psalmist's faith is not yet seen fulfilled. In the one man, Jesus—note the name of His manhood, here first introduced, so frequent in the rest of the epistle—we do behold it. As He passes to His death, we behold Him glorified in humiliation: see John xiii. 31.

βραχύ τι in the Ps. appears to mean "only a little," here "at least a little," or possibly "for a little while." The distinction is

---

[1] Cf. W. Wallace, *Lectures and Essays*, p. 205, Man "has claimed God for his everlasting ally, and been content with nothing less than immortality."

not important, nor is the comparison with angels. The stress is on
ἠλαττωμένον. The author keeps to the main idea of his quotation,
"glory in humiliation," but gives a deft turn to this particular phrase.
ἐστεφανωμένον under same article as ἠλαττωμένον. The picture is
of one who stands ever before our view (note pres. indic. and perf.
part.) as both humiliated and glorified. This compound phrase is
divided into two parts by the emphatic βλέπομεν Ἰησοῦν, and διὰ τὸ
πάθημα...ἐστεφανωμένον go together. The prep. has its "forward"
sense, "crowned for the purpose of," not "in recompense for" death.
Thus ὅπως...γεύσηται "that he may taste" (vivid subj. in due sequence
to pres. and perf.) follows intelligibly. There is no other way of
construing grammatically¹. Blass recognises this so clearly in his
rythmical edition that without any authority he alters γεύσηται into
ἐγεύσατο. He does that, because, with so many others, he sees a
reference to the ascension, as in Phil. ii. 5—11. But in this ep. our
Lord becomes king by enthronement not by crowning, and that is in
general accordance with ancient custom. Properly indeed στέφανος
is not a kingly crown at all but an athlete's wreath, cf. 2 Tim. ii. 5,
iv. 8. But the usage of LXX perhaps forbids our pressing that.
The title "Christ" which belongs to His exalted perfection is not
added to the name of His manhood in this place; it first appears at
iii. 6; cf. the antithesis in xiii. 20 f. Throughout this chapter the
work of the Lord on earth is in view. Only in the perf. partt. here
and in *v.* 18 are glimpses of that completed glory which will be the
theme of later chapters. Intr. II. 15, III. 7.

χάριτι θεοῦ. M 424** have χωρὶς θεοῦ and this reading was known
to Origen and other Fathers. Textual authority may be considered
decisive against it, and it might seem to have arisen from theological
reflexion, orthodox or docetic; Godhead could not taste death. Comparison with v. 7 f. makes one wonder whether it was not due to
recollection of the cry *Eloi, Eloi, lama sabachthani,* by which the
evangelists mark the supreme moment of glory in humiliation.
There is a curious allusion to this passage in conjunction with xii. 2
in *Ap. Const.* VIII. 1: συγχωρήσει θεου σταυρὸν ὑπέμεινεν αἰσχύνης
καταφρονήσας ὁ θεὸς λόγος, which in the *Constitutions of Hippolytus*
runs οἰκείᾳ συγχωρήσει καὶ βουλῇ σταυρὸν...θεὸς ὢν λόγος. Behind both
forms actual words of Hippolytus probably lie². Is it possible that

¹ Dr J. O. F. Murray however writes in a letter: "I have in times past taken
ὅπως...γεύσηται θανάτου as referring not to the Cross but to a present activity of
the ascended Lord, taking the bitterness out of the cup of death for everyone—
as He did in the case of S. Stephen, Acts vii. 55. S. Paul suggests that He is
present at every death bed (1 Th. iv. 14) lulling to sleep, κοιμηθέντας διὰ τοῦ
Ἰησοῦ. This would prepare the way for ii. 15, and xii. 4."
² See Frere, *JTS,* Ap. 1915.

Hippolytus found συγχωρήσει in Hebrews, and should this good Platonic word be added to the classical vocabulary of the author? Stephanus quotes from Chrysostom: ὅπου γὰρ χάρις συγχώρησις· ὅπου δὲ συγχώρησις οὐδεμία κόλασις.

10. ἔπρεπεν of Christ befitting us vii. 26, cf. Matt. iii. 15. Philo uses the word boldly, as here, of God the Father. Cf. ὤφειλεν, v. 17.

δι' ὅν...δι' οὗ. Cf. Rom. xi. 36, 1 Cor. viii. 6.

πολλοὺς υἱούς, not merely the Christ-sons of O.T. as in ch. i., but all men as in Ps. viii. That follows from the obvious reference in ἀγαγόντα. Rutherford, § 220, says: "The use of the aorist participle to denote an action anterior to that of the principal verb is a sense acquired by it, and cannot be explained as other than a convention sanctioned by its utility. Still there are no exceptions of any sort to this convention, such exceptions as are commonly recorded being no exceptions." Here at any rate there is no need to dispute that *dictum*; εἰς δ. ἀγ. refers back to δόξῃ κ. τ. ἐστεφάνωσας, "having brought to glory as we have just heard." The breaking of the apposition by the acc. ἀγαγόντα is according to the genius of Greek which exchanges stiff accuracy readily for the ease or emphasis of the sentence; cf. Plato, *Ion* 540 c, ἀλλ' ὁποῖα ἄρχοντι κάμνοντος πρέπει εἰπεῖν ὁ ῥαψῳδὸς γνώσεται κάλλιον ἢ ὁ ἰατρός;

ἀρχηγόν. Cf. xii. 2, Acts iii. 15; in the earlier classical Greek of a prince; in LXX and later Greek of a leader or author. Aristotle calls Thales ἀρχ. τοιαύτης φιλοσοφίας; often joined with αἴτιος, cf. v. 9. The rendering of d is *ducem* here, *principalem* xii. 2; vg. *auctorem* in both places.

τελειῶσαι. The phrase τελειοῦν τὰς χεῖρας is used of appointing a priest in Ex., Lev., Num., e.g. Lev. iv. 5, ὁ ἱερεὺς ὁ χριστὸς ὁ τετελειωμένος τὰς χεῖρας. The ritual association may have suggested its use in N.T. where it is characteristic of John as well as of Hebrews. In Hebrews τελειότης, τελείωσις and τελειώτης are also found. But the author's habit of pressing the root-significance of words best explains the varied force he gives it. In each context "bringing to the destined perfection" is the idea. So in Jas. i. 25 νόμον τέλειον is "a law that involves its own end," the converse of what this ep. says of the Levitical law. Cf. Philo, *migr. Abr.* I. 457, τελειωθεὶς ὁ νοῦς ἀποδώσει τὸ τέλος τῷ τελεσφόρῳ θεῷ.

11. ὅ τε ἁγιάζων. Another Levitical word. The refrain of the "Law of Holiness" (Lev. xvii.—xxvi.), ἅγιοι ἔσεσθε ὅτι ἅγιος ἐγὼ Κύριος ὁ θεὸς ὑμῶν—with variations, in one of which, xxi. 8, Κύριος ὁ ἁγιάζων αὐτούς, is the cadence—shews how deeply moral feeling entered into Israel's ritual. Jesus, whose forerunners speak in the next series of quotations, is ὁ ἁγιάζων: οἱ ἁγιαζόμενοι are the πολλοὺς υἱούς, i.e. mankind, cf. John i. 9. The tense of the partt. serves this large faith; contrast x. 10, xii. 14, and note the emphatic πάντες: Intr. III. 18.

ἐξ ἑνὸς completes δι' ὃν...δι' οὗ, cf. Luke iii. 38. But Bruce, borrowing the phrase though not the judgement of Davidson, suggests "of one piece, one whole." But cf. also the Greek gnome, ἐν ἀνδρῶν ἐν θεῶν γένος, Pind. *Nem.* VI. and Adam's development of the thought[1]. Add Acts xvii. 28, 2 Pet. i. 4.

οὐκ ἐπαισχύνεται, of God in xi. 16. Here the condescension, or cheerful humility, of Jesus the Son is declared by putting into His mouth three verses of O.T. in which representative personages call those whom they save by suffering (Ps. xxii. 22), or train as disciples (Isa. viii. 17 ̅), "brothers" and "children," and confess themselves to be like them dependent upon God.

13. ἔσομαι πεποιθώς. An emphatic periphrasis as in class. Gk., Goodwin § 45, Moulton, p. 226 f.

ἰδοὺ ἐγώ, κ.τ.λ. Cf. Odes of Solomon xxxi., "He lifted up His voice to the Most High, and offered to Him the sons that were with Him[2]."

14. αἵματος καὶ σαρκός. The physical constitution of man, as in Matt. xvi. 17, 1 Cor. xv. 50, Gal. i. 16, Eph. vi. 12, John i. 13. So in Philo and Sirach xiv. 18. Not however in the Hebrew Bible where "blood," as in all other places in this ep., signifies "life"; see Lev. xvii. 11 and Intr. III. 12, 13.

τὸν τὸ κράτος ἔχοντα τοῦ θανάτου. The English versions might remind us of Luke xii. 5, but the ἐξουσία there is God's; here the devil has τὸ κράτος (*imperium* d and vg.) of death. There is something vague and shadowy about the phrase. The author, who nowhere else mentions the devil or evil spirits, would be in sympathy with Dr Swete's view of "the personal or quasi-personal ' Satan,'"[3] and with Jas. iv. 7 "Resist the devil, and he will flee from you." Our Lord died, he says, to "do away with" this lord of death; death itself, says S. Paul in 1 Cor. xv. 26 (that passage seems to be still in the author's mind). He holds firm to our Lord's victory over the realm of evil, but does not define the persons of its agents. Nor does our Lord in the synoptic gospels; He condescends to the popular language of the

---

[1] "The doctrine of the divine origin of the soul from Pindar to Plato." *Cambridge Praelections.*
[2] Rendel Harris, *The Odes and Psalms of Solomon*, p. 129.
[3] *Th Holy Spirit in the New Testament*, p. 370.

time, but with a quiet correction of its grossness, which impresses
the mind of the reader more and more. In those gospels the devil
or Satan is mentioned comparatively seldom, with reticent and perhaps symbolical solemnity[1]; it is the many evil spirits that are
oftener spoken of. In the Pauline epp. of the captivity these spirits
take on a certain grandeur, so that it is not always easy to decide
whether powers of good or evil are meant; see Eph. ii. 2, iii. 10,
vi. 12; Col. i. 13, 16, ii. 10, 15. In S. John's Gospel and 1 Ep. they
almost disappear, but "the devil" is freely and frankly introduced.

In LXX διάβολος is the rendering of "satan"=adversary, and is
used of a human adversary Ps. cix. (cviii.) 6, and of that angel whose
office it is to try the servants of God, Job i. and ii.; Zech. iii. 1 ff.
Except possibly in 1 Chr. xxi. 1 this angel is not a rebel or an
evil one; and in 1 Chr. xxi. 1 the LXX translator, prefixing no
article, seems to have understood a human adversary to be meant.
Wisd. ii. 24 gives the first hint of the later explanation of the
serpent in Gen. iii. as being the devil. Rabbinical Judaism was
inclined to the ancient simplicity. "Satan and the evil impulse and
the angel of death are one," said Simon ben Laqish (c. 260 A.D.)[2].

15. ἀπαλλάξῃ only Luke xii. 58, Acts xix. 12 elsewhere in
N.T., nor there in this sense or construction. With the thought of
this clause cf. Rom. viii. 20 f. But ἀπαλλάσσω, "give quittance," is
a less noble word than ἐλευθερόω which S. Paul uses there. Neither
that word nor the Pauline καταλλάσσω, καταλλαγή, "reconcilement of
man with God," come into this epistle.

ὅσοι...δουλείας. Such a state is well illustrated by the hymn of
Hezekiah in Isa. xxxviii., and by all that pagan doctrine of *Sheol*
which long hindered true religion in Israel. But the author shows
abundantly in ch. xi. that he does not consider that to have been the
real faith of O.T. saints. True faith, though still expectant not
fulfilled, could always rise above the imperfections of its environment:
see below on v. 1 f. That holds good of the ancient pagan world as
well as of Israel, but this ep. is mainly concerned with Israel.

16. ἐπιλαμβάνεται. O.L. *adsumpsit* or *suscepit* represents the
interpretation of the Fathers "who understand the phrase of the fact
of the Incarnation"—"when He took upon Him man "; Westcott
prefers the unclassical meaning "help," understanding it "of the
purpose of the Incarnation"—"to deliver man." Isa. xli. 8 f. seems
to have been in the author's mind. But he substituted ἐπιλαμβάνεται
for the LXX ἀντελαβόμην, which does mean "helped"; cf. Luke i. 54.

---

[1] See Sanday, *The Life of Christ in recent research*, pp. 28 ff.
[2] See Box, *Ezra-Apocalypse*, p. xli.

The picturesque expression is quite in his manner; it is faithfully translated by vg. *apprehendit*; it has a broader significance than either of the other translations allow; and the ironical δή που (a literary nicety not found elsewhere in the Greek Bible) serves partly as an apology for its rather rude vigour. "The seed of Abraham" instead of "men" was suggested by the passage of Isaiah, but is in harmony with the whole ep., cf. Matt. i. 2.

17. ἐλεήμων...πιστός. Epithets separated, like the partt. in *v.* 9, to distribute the emphasis.

ἀρχιερεύς. The figurative title, derived from Ps. cx., which rules throughout the ep. Here first pronounced, it has been prepared for, more or less subtly, in i. 3, 13, 14, ii. 9—11; indeed almost every word of this chapter has been pregnant with an expectation which is now explained. The psalm has ἱερεύς. This author often, not always, prefers the full-sounding ἀρχιερεύς. In the Greek of his time the words were used indifferently.

τὰ πρὸς τὸν θεόν. This has been well translated "on the Godward side." In Ex. iv. 16 the LORD tells Moses that Aaron shall be a mouth to him: σὺ δὲ αὐτῷ ἔσῃ τὰ πρὸς τὸν θεόν. Intr. III. 5, 9.

ἱλάσκεσθαι. Elsewhere in N.T. only Luke xviii. 13 (ἱλάσθητι). It is connected with ἵλεως viii. 12, ἱλαστήριον ix. 5 (and, in another sense, Rom. iii. 25), ἱλασμός 1 John ii. 2, iv. 10. In LXX ἐξιλάσκεσθαι is more frequent, and often represents Hebrew *Kipper*, e.g. Lev. xvii. 11. Both Heb. and Gk. verb can take acc. of person in sense of conciliate, e.g. Gen. xxxii. 20 (Jacob and Esau). But in the Hebrew scriptures this construction is never applied to God; God reconciles man to himself, man does not appease or propitiate God in the true theology of Israel. Intr. III. 11.

τοῦ λαοῦ. The doctrine of priesthood in this ep. starts from the analogy of the Levitical priesthood though its reality is found in another line. This is one of the terms of the analogy; ὁ λαός is the regular word for the people of Israel, see antithesis in Luke ii. 32.

18. πειρασθείς...τοῖς πειραζομένοις. In N.T. πειρασμός has an intense meaning which springs from the great trial that shall precede the coming of the kingdom of God, cf. Ap. iii. 10. In the Lord's Prayer, "Lead us not into temptation" is tinged with that thought, cf. Luke xxii. 40, 46. The first readers of this ep. were entering upon a trial of just that nature. The Lord was "coming"; loyalty involved a hard choice, which might mean martyrdom; Intr. III. 19.

CHAPTER III

III. 1—6. JESUS IS CHRIST, THE SON.

1   That is what the humiliation of the Lord Jesus really means. Wherefore, ye brothers in a consecrated life, partakers like Him in a summons to heavenly exaltation through the trials of earth, penetrate into the heart of Him whom God sent on such a mission and made High Priest of the creed which you are destined to confess
2 courageously. We name Him Jesus, man among men, faithful with manly faithfulness to God who appointed Him His task. So, Scripture
3 says, was Moses faithful in God's family. But His faithfulness has richer consequences. For He stands before us endued with a glory more abundant than Moses had, the glory of kinship with the founder
4 of the family Himself. I mean God, and I mean a larger family than Moses knew as God's; Israel was God's family indeed, but God's true
5 family is everywhere. And further, if it was in that universal family that Moses served, still he was but the servant; when God called him faithful, that was but a guarantee that he would faithfully make
6 known to the people what God purposed to tell him; while God's Christ (even the Christ-kings of Israel's monarchy) was to be styled "Son," and the son, as founder's kin, is in authority over the family. That family, ruled by the supreme Christ, are we, if we resolve to hold fast the boldness and the boast of the hope with which such a divine pedigree invests us.

    1. ἀδελφοὶ ἅγιοι...μέτοχοι take up thoughts already thrown out in i. 9, ii. 11 f., 17. So too κατανοήσατε answers to βλέπομεν ii. 9. It is still Jesus, the man, on whom attention is fixed; not till *v.* 5 are the two lines of ch. i. (the divine Son) and ch. ii. (the fellowman) brought together in the title Christ. The reading Χρ. Ἰησοῦν here has no place in any type of ancient text.

    τὸν ἀπόστολον καὶ ἀρχιερέα: as effluence of the divine glory, as proclaimer and leader of salvation He was "sent." Cf. Gal. iv. 4, but more especially John xvii. 3. The idea is characteristic of John, Gospel and 1 Ep In 1 John iv. 10, ἀπέστειλεν τὸν υἱὸν αὐτοῦ ἱλασμόν, it is combined, as here, with the sacerdotal analogy. In Paul the word ἀπόστολος has generally a more technical ring. Here it has a larger sense as in John xiii. 16: so also in that place in the synoptic gospels where it is used for the first time, Mark iii. 14 (אB), Luke vi. 13; contrast Matt. x. 2. Cf. Clem. xlii., οἱ ἀπόστολοι ἡμῖν εὐηγγε-λίσθησαν ἀπὸ τοῦ κυρίου Ἰησοῦ Χριστοῦ, Ἰησοῦς ὁ χριστὸς ἀπὸ τοῦ θεοῦ ἐξεπέμφθη.

τῆς ὁμολογίας ἡμῶν twice again in the ep. iv. 14, x. 23; in a more general sense 2 Cor. ix. 13; in 1 Tim. vi. 12 f. of the brave confession of faith which, after the example of Christ, a churchman ready for martyrdom makes. That passage helps us to understand both ὁμο-λογίας and κλήσεως here.

2. The reference in this and the following verses is to Num. xii. where Moses is vindicated by God against the complaint of Miriam and Aaron. Moses is no mere prophet to whom God makes himself known in vision and dream; στόμα κατὰ στόμα λαλήσω αὐτῷ: the fut. λαλήσω explains λαληθησομένων below. But θεράπων gets an emphasis in LXX by repetition; Moses is intimate with God, yet still a servant. Cf. Philo, *Leg. All.* III. 128: πιστὸς δὲ μόνος ὁ θεός, καὶ εἴ τις φίλος θεῷ, καθάπερ Μωυσῆς λέγεται πιστὸς ἐν παντὶ τῷ οἴκῳ γεγενῆσθαι. In Wisd. x. 16 Moses is called θεράπων Κυρίου, and Lightfoot says (on Clem. iv.) that in ecclesiastical literature "ὁ θεράπων τοῦ θεοῦ was a recognised title of Moses, as ὁ φίλος τοῦ θεοῦ was of Abraham."

τῷ ποιήσαντι αὐτόν, i.e. "made Him apostle and high priest." This is obvious and natural; "created," absolutely, would—apart from the question of orthodoxy—bring a superfluous thought into the context.

ὅλῳ om. p¹³B 𝔉𝔱𝔥 Cyr. Amb.: a strong combination; the omission here would add force to the inclusion in *v.* 5. But does that consideration point to an "Alexandrian" touch? Intr. IV. 2, 3.

4. ὁ δὲ πάντα κατασκευάσας θεός. Cf. i. 2, God made all things through the Son. This is not a declaration of the divinity of Jesus as creator, but a step in the argument for His divinity as Son.

6. Χριστὸς δὲ ὡς υἱός. Another step in the same argument. "Christ" in N.T., but especially in this ep., links the history of Israel with the Gospel, the adoption of the people of God with the incarnation of the Son. Here as in *v.* 5 the title looks backwards and forwards; Moses was not one of those Christs who were of old called "sons," Jesus is the Christ in whom that Sonship is perfected.

οὗ (ὅς D*M 6 424**𝔏 Lucif. Amb. *al.*) οἶκός ἐσμεν ἡμεῖς. The house throughout this passage is a house of persons, a family. Cf. Abbott[1]. "These things reveal the object of Jesus as being, from

[1] *The fourfold Gospel, section* III. *The Proclamation,* pref.

the first, not the establishment of what men would commonly call a
Kingdom, but the diffusion of what we should rather call the atmosphere of a Family, a spiritual emanation spreading like a widening
circle from a source within Himself as a centre, and passing into the
hearts of all that were fitted to receive it, so as to give them something of His own power or ' authority '—a term defined in the
Prologue of the Fourth Gospel as being ' authority to become children
of God.' " This quotation helps us also to appreciate the paradox
(a favourite one in S. Paul) of Christian boasting (τὸ καύχημα τῆς
ἐλπίδος).

μέχρι τέλους βεβαίαν *om.* 𝔭¹³B 𝕮𝔩𝔥 Lucif. Amb. The phrase is
unnecessary here and (after τὸ καύχημα) grammatically awkward. In
v. 14 it is otherwise, and it would gain force there by coming freshly.
But cf. *v.* 3 *supra.*

III. 7—IV. 2. Therefore listen to the call.

7   Loyalty and hope is the tradition in God's family. Therefore,
as the Holy Spirit saith in Scripture, "To day if ye should hear
8 His voice harden not your hearts as in the Provocation after the
9 manner of the day of the Temptation in the wilderness; in which
wilderness your fathers became God-tempters in the time of His
assay, "when," saith God, "they saw my works full forty years."
10 Wherefore He continueth, "I was wroth with that generation and
said, ' Ever do they wander in heart, they are the people that know
11 not my ways. As I sware in my anger; certainly they shall not
12 enter into my rest.'" Look to it, brothers, that there be not in any
one of you an evil heart of mistrust, manifesting itself in apostasy
13 from God who lives; but encourage one another from day to day
while still the call "To day" is sounding; that no one of you be
hardened by the speciousness of that sin which fills our thought
14 at this time. There is ground for encouragement, for partakers in
the fellowship of the Christ-nation we long have been, and still shall
be, if we will but hold fast the principle of its foundation firmly to
15 the end; the while it is still said, "To day, if ye shall hear His voice
16 harden not your hearts as in the Provocation." For who were they
that heard and provoked? Why, were they not all those who came
17 out of Egypt under the leadership of Moses? And with whom was
He wroth full forty years? Was it not with those who sinned, whose
18 limbs, saith Scripture, fell in the wilderness? And to whom sware
He that they should not enter into His rest, but to those who refused
19 to trust Him? Indeed we plainly see that the reason they could not

enter was just that—mistrust.   Let us therefore fear, lest while the iv. 1
promise of entering into His rest survives though they perished, any
one of your number shall be found (a thing scarce credible) to have
deserted your post.   Your post, I say, for we too have now heard 2
that same good tidings of rest which they did, though the sense of
what they heard was no use to them—those unhappy men whom we
still remember as lost from the company of the true hearers who have
been welded into one body by faith.

7. καθὼς λέγει τὸ πνεῦμα τὸ ἅγιον.   So x. 15, cf. ix. 8; Intr.
III. 29. The quotation is from Ps. xcv. in which the psalmist's
invitation to worship passes into warning; then, at οὗ ἐπείρασαν, the
voice of God himself breaks in.   The author follows LXX, though
not agreeing exactly with any one known MS., and perhaps adapting
at his own will.   Thus διὸ is probably his own addition.   He divides
the sentence where the "first person" begins, and so lays emphasis
upon the conclusion.   This brings the "forty years" into connexion
with the "tempting" or "trying," and comparison with Deut. viii. 2 f.
suggests that δοκιμασία means the proof to which God put the Israelites
during the whole period of their wandering; for the metaphor cf.
Sir. vi. 21; 1 Pet. i. 7.

11. εἰ εἰσελεύσονται.   A strong negative, as often in LXX
(cf. Mark viii. 12).   It represents a Hebrew idiom, an aposiopesis
frequent in oaths.

12. καρδία πονηρὰ ἀπιστίας.   Moulton, p. 74, compares Soph.
O.T. 533, τόσονδε τόλμης πρόσωπον.   But in classical Greek καρδία was
not thus used except in poetry, proverbs etc.[1].   The force of ἀπιστία
here may be felt by comparing 2 Tim. ii. 13, εἰ ἀπιστοῦμεν ἐκεῖνος
πιστὸς μένει.   But πίστις, with its cognates, gradually reveals its definite
significance in this ep. as the argument develops.

ἐν τῷ ἀποστῆναι ἀπὸ θεοῦ ζῶντος.   Cf. 1 Tim. iv. 1 for the verb,
and contrast it for the noun.   The phrase θεὸς ζῶν, frequent in N.T.
and nearly always (in the true text) without article, is used with
special emphasis in this ep., cf. ix. 14, x. 31, xii. 22.   To readers
brought up in Judaism it would imply the essential energy of Godhead,
cf. Matt. xvi. 16, xxvi. 63.   To Grecized ears the epithet ἀληθινὸς
might mean more, cf. 1 Thess. i. 9, 1 John v. 20.   In ix. 14 a later
text betrays itself by adding καὶ ἀληθινῷ.

13. ἀπάτῃ τῆς ἁμαρτίας.   Cf. 2 Thess. ii. 10, ἐν πάσῃ ἀπάτῃ
ἀδικίας.   The phrase in 2 Thess. is good classical Greek, even if

---

[1] G. M. Edwards' *English-Greek Lexicon*, App. A, "Notes on Greek words
for Mind, Heart, etc."

τῆς be inserted with the later text. But here the single article is irregular since the governing substantive does not depend upon a preposition (Rutherford § 18); and since the author does not elsewhere offend in that way, it may be supposed that he intended to mark thus unusually the definite character of the sin. He means some particular sin to which his friends were immediately liable, cf. xii. 1, 4.

14. μέτοχοι τοῦ χριστοῦ. In i. 9 (= Ps. xlv.) μέτοχοι had the same meaning as in Luke v. 7. Here it is used as in iii. 1, vi. 4, xii. 8, *participes Christi*, Lat. Nor is there any difficulty in this if the O.T. idea of "the inclusive Christ" be remembered: Intr. III. 18.

τὴν ἀρχὴν τῆς ὑποστάσεως. ὑπόστασις may mean "firmness" of character or resolution. It is so used in 2 Cor. ix. 4, xi. 17, and it is a natural extension of the word into metaphor. But the author's habit is to press the literal sense, and if the idea expressed in the last note be just we may suppose him here to be referring, in quasi-philosophical phrase, to the principle of Christship founded upon which his readers had started upon their spiritual course, cf. vi. 1. The vg. with its *initium substantiae eius* (so A ὑπ. αὐτοῦ) might seem to support this explanation. Westcott quotes Primasius: "Initium substantiae dicit fidem Christi, per quam subsistimus et renati sumus, quia ipse est fundamentum omnium virtutum. Et bene substantiam eam vocat, quia sicut corpus anima subsistit et vivificatur, ita anima fide subsistit in Deo et vivit hac fide. Substantia autem Christi appellatur fides vel quia ab illo datur, vel certe quia ipse per eam habitat in cordibus fidelium." He had xi. 1 in mind, and it may be noticed that one MS. (424**) gives πίστεως here instead of ὑποστάσεως.

15. ἐν τῷ λέγεσθαι...παραπικρασμῷ. Either a complete sentence in itself with apodosis at μὴ σκλ. (A.V., W.H.); or a continuation of the last sentence (R.V.); or it might be printed with a dash after παραπικρασμῷ, the form of the warning being rhetorically altered at τίνες γάρ.

16. τίνες γάρ. A.V. "For some" (τινές) was no doubt influenced by vg. *quidam enim*. It is not impossible for the (properly) enclitic τινὲς to stand at the beginning of the sentence (cf. Luke xi. 15; John xiii. 29; Acts xvii. 18, 34, xix. 31, xxiv. 19; 1 Cor. xv. 6; Phil. i. 15; Wisd. xvi. 18 f.), but here the position would be too emphatic and the series of rhetorical questions would be broken. The idiomatic ἀλλὰ (L. and S. *sub voc.* II. 1) misled the old Latin translators from whom *quidam* of vg. is derived; see however Blass 77. 13. For the historical fact see Num. xiv. 28—35 (to which there is verbal allusion in next verse), xxvi. 64, Deut. ii. 14.

CHAPTER IV

1. ἐπαγγελίας. This word, which in Acts xxiii. 21 bears the more classical sense of "announcement," is often used by Paul of the promises made to Israel. In LXX it is used of God's promise or announcement in Ps. lv. (lvi.) 9, Amos ix. 6, which latter (half) verse might almost serve as a motto to this ep.: ὁ οἰκοδομῶν εἰς τὸν οὐρανὸν ἀνάβασιν αὐτοῦ καὶ τὴν ἐπαγγελίαν αὐτοῦ ἐπὶ τῆς γῆς θεμελιῶν.

δοκῇ...ὑστερηκέναι. A convenient form for expressing the future-perf. (cf. xi. 3), which also allows the author to mitigate the harshness of his warning (cf. vi. 9).

2. εὐηγγελισμένοι. By the time the heading to Mark was written τὸ εὐαγγέλιον had come to mean "The Gospel of Jesus Christ." But when our Lord proclaimed "the gospel of the kingdom," or spoke of "losing life for my sake and the gospel," He was, like the author of this ep., carrying on the idea of the "good tidings" already declared to Israel. The use of the verb in Isa. xl.—lxvi. especially prepared the way for N.T. See Isa. xl. 9, lii. 7 and Rom. x. 15, lx. 6, lxi. 1 and Luke iv. 18 f.

ὁ λόγος τῆς ἀκοῆς. Cf. 1 Thess. ii. 13, Rom. x. 16 f., Gal. iii. 2, 5. The phrase almost looks like an improvement upon Paul's vague "Hebraism" λόγος ἀκοῆς. It is not "the word heard" but "the sense of what was heard"; cf. Ez. xii. 23, ἠγγίκασιν αἱ ἡμέραι καὶ λόγος πάσης ὁράσεως.

2. μὴ συνκεκερασμένους...τοῖς ἀκούσασιν. So W.H., R.V., A.V. mg., von S. One minuscule has, what seems to have been a conjectural emendation of Theodore of Mopsuestia, τοῖς ἀκουσθεῖσιν: cf. 𝔏 vg. *non admixtis fidei ex his quae audierunt.* D* 104 𝔏 (vt^d) 𝕾 (hl. mg.) have τῶν ἀκουσάντων. But τοῖς ἀκούσασιν of all other MSS. may be accepted as certain, and the only variant which need be considered is συνκεκερασμένος: so W.H. mg., Tisch., Westcott Comm., and (with correction to the more classical συγκεκραμένος) Steph. followed by A.V. text. The chief authorities for this are ℵ 𝔏 (vt) 𝕾 (vg.): for συνκεκερασμένους p^13ABCD and most Greek MSS., 𝔏 vg. (though Sixtine and Clementine editions print *admistus*), 𝕾 hl. 𝕰 (boh).

𝔄 𝔈𝔱𝔥. The testimony of the Fathers is divided, and perhaps only shews, what mss. and versions have already shewn, that both readings were widely and early current. Since W.H. the accession of 𝔭¹³ to the larger group may almost turn the scale, especially if it can be demonstrated that συνκεκερασμένους best fits the context. It surely does. The author's mind is intensely set upon the peril to his readers' loyalty. He looks back for illustrative warning to Israel's history. He sees the disobedient Israelites standing as it were pictured before him; hence the perfect which well describes those persons but would ill fit the abstract λόγος ἀκοῆς (cf. ii. 9, vii. 3, xii. 2, 23). But some (spite of ἀλλ' οὐ πάντες;) did listen to that "gospel." Caleb did then (see reff. to Num. and Deut. already given), and the Lord's disciples did afterwards (cf. ii. 3). With that company of faithful listeners the "generation" whom Moses led out of Israel are not (not "were not") "very members incorporated in the mystical body." For the metaphor in συνκ. see reff. to Hdt. in L. and S. *sub voc.* 3, and cf. Aesch. *Ag.* 321 ff. There is a note on this passage in W.H. Intr. in which Westcott is inclined to accept a modern emendation ἀκούσμασιν and to combine it with συνκεκερασμέ-νους; Hort suspects "primitive error." Intr. IV. 2.

IV. 3—10. REST IS OFFERED YOU.

3　For there is a rest into which we are entering even now, we who have made the venture of faith, according to that He hath said, "As I sware in my wrath, certainly they shall not enter into my rest."...

4 And yet...after the six days' work of creation was finished, He hath said somewhere I think concerning the seventh day words like these,

5 "And God rested on the seventh day from all His works."...And then in this Psalm again, "Certainly they shall not enter into my rest."...What do these deep hints and disappointing contradictions

6 mean?　Why surely this: since the fulfilment of the promise demands that certain persons should enter, and since those who heard the good tidings in former days did not enter because of their

7 stubbornness, He now again defines a particular day, saying "To day" in the person of David after all this long time; it is with prophetic significance that the proclamation comes to us, "To day if ye shall

8 hear His voice, harden not your hearts." It comes to us; for if it had been "rest" that their Jesus gave to them when he led the second generation of the wanderers into Canaan, the Holy Spirit would not be speaking in the later period of the psalmist about

9 another fateful day.　There remaineth therefore a divine rest for the

people of God. For whoso hath entered into that rest which God 10
offers is witness to a bold analogy. Such a one needs no more to
choose and see. He has found rest from the anxieties of effort, even
as God, after what we can only imagine as the six days' effort of
creation, returned into the tranquil energy of Godhead.

3. γάρ. 𝔭¹³BDωℋ ℨ (hl) 𝔅𝔱𝔥 Chr. Cyr. Lucif. *al*: οὖν ℵACM
1908 *al pauc* 𝔅 (boh). If τ. ἀκούσασιν refers (as is supposed in the
last note) to the Christian Church, γάρ gives much the best sense.
Without 𝔭¹³ the authorities would be too strong on either side to
allow that consideration to be decisive. The accession of 𝔭¹³ to the
first group turns the scale. So again with the omission of τὴν before
κατάπαυσιν in 𝔭¹³BD*. The small but strong group assures us that
we may recognise a certain subtlety in our author's language; this
is not "the rest" of the psalm in its primary sense, but "a rest"
which new experience reads into the old words. Intr. IV 2.

οἱ πιστεύσαντες. Is this technical, "those who have become
Christians," cf. Rom. xiii. 11? or quite general, the antithesis to
δι' ἀπιστίαν, iii. 19? Or may we compare xiii. 21 and understand
that deep conversion which is peace indeed, already enjoyed by the
author, who, because he desires it for his friends, writes them this
earnest letter?

καίτοι, with part. classical: but καίπερ is more regular and is
always used elsewhere in this ep., v. 8, vii. 5, xii. 17; Blass 74. 2.
Here this construction yields a rather dim sense. W.H. print a
comma after as well as before the clause; but if, with 𝔭¹³ only, we
might omit γάρ after εἴρηκεν, all would run plainly. Thus καί τοι
(rather than καίτοι, cf. xiii. 22) would mean "and further"; as
e.g. in Hdt. v. 31, Σὺ ὦν στρατηλάτεε...καί τοι...ἐστι ἕτοιμα παρ' ἐμοὶ
χρήματα, κ.τ.λ., and possibly Acts xiv. 17. Cf. the old Latin rendering, *et cum opera ab origine mundi facta sunt dixit tamen.*

7. ἐν Δαυείδ. More like ἐν τ. προφήταις, i. 1, than Rom. ix. 25, xi. 2.
But the stress is on the Holy Spirit who speaks (iii. 7) not on the
tradition of human authorship. Σήμερον may be second accusative
after ὁρίζει. Then λέγων would introduce the repeated quotation, and
καθὼς προείρηται, *sicut supra dictum est,* vg. would refer back to iii. 7,
15. That is a legitimate rendering of προείρηται, though it is not
certain (in spite of R.V.) that the verb is so used elsewhere in N.T.
Here it may be noticed that B 𝔅 (boh) Orig. read προείρηκεν and that
the old Latin rendering of ὁρίζει is *praefinivit.* Reading and rendering
seem to point to a deeper significance in this return upon the already
repeated quotation. The psalm is now recognised as prophetic of
a further future which is pressing to fulfilment while this letter is

being written : "again He defines beforehand...saying To day...even
as He has foretold."

8. εἰ γὰρ αὐτοὺς Ἰησοῦς...οὐκ ἄν. Cf. xi. 15 f. This name
"Jesus," as sometimes "Christ" in this ep., sounds confusing to
ears accustomed to the English Bible. To readers of LXX there
would be no doubt about the reference to "Jesus the son of Naue"
who brought Israel into Canaan; to converts from Judaism that
Jesus would be the old familiar name. But the coincidence enriches
old and new with interchange of associations; the emphatic position
of αὐτοὺς helps to keep the distinction clear; presently, in *v.* 14, it
will be strikingly asserted.

9. σαββατισμός, a noun (found also in Plutarch, not in LXX)
formed from the Hebrew *sabat*, which is translated κατέπαυσεν in
LXX of Gen. ii. 2 quoted above. Wetstein quotes passages from
rabbinical writings in which the sabbath is a type of "the age to
come which is all sabbath and rest unto life eternal"; cf. Abelard's
hymn, "O quanta qualia sunt illa sabbata Quae semper celebrat
superna curia." But our author knows a sabbath rest which may
be enjoyed here and now; the aorists in *v.* 10 are neither "gnomic"
nor "post futurum"; they spring from experience, cf. xiii. 21.

IV. 11—13. BE ZEALOUS AND SINCERE.

11   Zealous therefore let us be to enter into that rest, in order that no
one of us may chance to fall, involved in that same ruin which is the
12 type of all resistance to God's purpose. For the Word of God, where-
ever heard, is His reason and is alive. Practical it is, and cuts both
ways, for comfort and for judgment, more sharply than any two-edged
sword; and penetrates to that inmost centre of our being where the
immaterial and material elements combine to form a person; and
analyses the prudent calculations and the quick intuitions of the
13 heart. No corner of our nature is obscure to Him, but all is naked
and exposed before His eyes, to whom the reasonable conscience He
Himself has planted in us must give answer.

11. ἵνα μή...ἀπειθείας. Notice the emphatic final genitive, as
in *v.* 8 *supra* and x. 20; the separation of τῷ αὐτῷ from its noun; and,
possibly, the variation ἐν...πέσῃ for ἐμπέσῃ. In such a vigorously
composed clause it would be rash to deny that the strange expression
"fall into a type or example" is possible. But it would be strange,
and πέσῃ is weightier if taken absolutely; cf. παραπεσόντας vi. 6.
Ὑπόδειγμα is "a sign suggestive of anything" (viii. 5, ix. 23),

and so may signify a crime or horror which is a world's wonder, cf. 2 Pet. ii. 6.

12. ζῶν γὰρ ὁ λόγος, κ.τ.λ. This explains the fresh interpretation which has just been put upon the written word of the psalm. But so much in the following paragraph resembles what Philo says of the "logos" in a wider sense, that it is necessary to recognise something of the larger sense here also¹. The predicate "living" makes this possible. The written word is no mere fixed letter; it is the means of conversation—a "reasonable service"—with the living and still speaking God. Intr. III. 30.

ἐνεργής. B has ἐναργής, "flashing," or perhaps "perspicuous," see Cic. *Acad.* II. 17. Cf. i. 3, where B has φανερῶν for φέρων. In Philem. 6 the Latin *evidens* seems to be a translation of the same variant.

μάχαιραν. Cf. Luke ii. 35, "Yea and a sword shall pierce through thine own soul; that thoughts out of many hearts may be revealed"; a saying which really illustrates this passage, with its keen analysis of conscience, more vividly than the more intellectual parallels in Philo: see Intr. III. 32. But in Luke "sword" is ῥομφαία a "great sword," elsewhere in N.T. only in Ap. Here μάχαιρα may have its general N.T. meaning "sword," as in xi. 34, 37, or its more proper meaning "knife," and the grim realism of the whole simile may be drawn from fighting, or from the butcher-work of sacrifice, or possibly from surgery. Cf. note on vi. 19.

13. τετραχηλισμένα. The choice between these alternatives might be decided if we could recover the primary meaning of this word, but that is not easy. Philo speaks (*de praem.* p. 413) of an athlete ἐκτραχη-λιζόμενος by superior strength, Theodoret says the metaphor is from victims in sacrifice. Hesychius, the (late) Alexandrian lexicographer, says τετραχηλισμένα· πεφανερωμένα; so the Latin and Syriac versions, *aperta*, made manifest. The general idea may be illustrated by a passage in Dr H. F. Hamilton's book, *The People of God*, vol. I.: "What causes Isaiah's apprehension is the very vividness of his consciousness, *the nakedness with which he sees his soul contrasted against another Personality.* If death is sometimes apprehended because consciousness is felt to be dying out, in this case death is apprehended because consciousness is passing the bounds of life in the opposite direction. It is becoming so acute and so intense,...

---

¹ In *The origin of the prologue to St John's Gospel* (Camb. 1917) Dr Rendel Harris compares this ep. with John i. 1—18, Col. i. 15—20, and all three with Prov. i., viii., Sir. xxiv., Wisd. vi., vii., and Cyprian's *Testimonia*, etc. Hence he concludes that the doctrine of Christ as the Word grew out of an earlier doctrine of Christ as the Wisdom of God, and that it depends on the Jewish Sapiential tradition rather than on the Philonic.

that the prophet feels that soul and body are on the point of being
torn asunder."

πρὸς ὃν ἡμῖν ὁ λόγος. Windisch translates "of whom we
speak," comparing περὶ οὗ νῦν ὁ λόγος in Philo and πρὸς ὑμᾶς οἱ λόγοι
μου in Wisd. vi. 9. Westcott, "to whom we have to give account,"
which agrees with the Syriac and the Latin of d, *ante quam nobis
ratio est.* Having no equivalent in English to this Greek word with
its complex associations we can hardly express the effect, which
nevertheless we feel, of its emphatic position at the beginning and end
of the sentence.

IV. 14—16.   THE COMPASSIONATE HIGH PRIEST.

14   Having then a High Priest who is supreme above all others, and
has passed right onward beyond all our imaginations of heaven,
Jesus, the Son of God, let us be loyal in our allegiance to One who
15 is so great yet so kind.   For we have not such a High Priest as
cannot be touched with the passionate trouble of our infirmities.
He has gone through every kind of temptation that men are subject
to; He has been as liable to fall as other men; but through all He
16 has kept innocence.   Trusting therefore in His real victory over sin,
let us draw near with boldness to the throne of God's grace, that
we may receive the royal boon of God's pity, and find His Fatherly
countenance turned graciously upon us, for rescue in each time of
need.

14.   ἔχοντες οὖν.   οὖν may mean "therefore," marking logical
consequence as in *v.* 16; or "then," indicating resumption of argument after digression as in x. 19.

ἀρχιερέα μέγαν.   Philo twice has ὁ μέγας ἀ.   In 1 Macc. xiii. 42
the phrase marks a turning-point in Jewish history: cf. x. 21, xiii. 20.
Here the argument begins to rise from mere analogy to the doctrine
of real priesthood.

διεληλυθότα τοὺς οὐρανούς.   Cf. 2 Cor. xii. 2, ἁρπαγέντα ἕως
τρίτου οὐρανοῦ.   But the compound part. is the emphatic word.   All
that we call "heaven" has been passed through and left behind.
The real presence of God is reached.   The plural certainly need not
be an allusion to the rabbinic idea of successive heavens.   The
Hebrew word is a dual form.   Yet the sing., οὐρανός, is the regular
rendering in LXX.   The plural is common in Psalms and is
found in passages which have a grand ring—poetry, prayer, etc.
In this ep. the sing. is only used in ix. 24, xi. 12, xii. 26.   The
distinction is illustrated in the Lord's Prayer.   The opening is

solemn, Πάτερ ἡμῶν ὁ ἐν τοῖς οὐρανοῖς ; the antithesis is simple, ὡς ἐν οὐρανῷ καὶ ἐπὶ γῆς.

15. συνπαθῆσαι, used of God in 4 Macc. v. 25; in N.T. only here and x. 34; συμπαθής in 1 Pet. iii. 8. Both verb and adj. possess an intensity which "compassion" and "sympathy" have lost in English; cf. Luke xxiv. 26, Acts xxvi. 23, Intr. III. 14.

πεπειρασμένον—χωρὶς ἁμαρτίας, see quotation from DuBose, Intr. III. 15. It may be asked whether our Lord was tempted or tried in all points like all men, if, as the silence of the gospels perhaps implies and ecclesiastical tradition almost asserts, He never suffered sickness; and if that be so, whether He overcame disease in and for man in the same way as He overcame sin[1]. It is certainly the will of God that the evil of sickness should be overcome as much as the evil of slavery or ignorance. And perhaps the true succession of the miracles of healing is the advance of science. It seems reasonable as well as reverent to recognise a discipline of sickness; we cannot think of a discipline of sin. This ep. would seem to promise real freedom for man from sin, not from suffering.

16. προσερχώμεθα. A sacerdotal word, Lev. xxi. 17—23, cf. Ez. xliv. 9—16; it is used in 1 Pet. ii. 4, never in Paul except, somewhat strangely, 1 Tim. vi. 3. And "the throne of grace" makes one think of the mercy seat (LXX ἱλαστήριον) where the LORD promised to commune with Moses, Ex. xxv. 20 ff. Thus the new and living way of x. 20 is here anticipated, and here as there παρρησία has a special force. Philo has τὸν ἐλέου βωμόν (cf. Statius, *Theb.* XII. 481 ff.), but the fine phrase of the ep. is probably formed on O.T. models; see especially Isa. lxvi. 1. For χάρις see Hort on 1 Pet. i. 2, "It combines the force of two Hebrew words *chen* and *chesed*... *chen*, a comprehensive word, gathering up all that may be supposed to be expressed in the smile of a heavenly King looking down upon His people (Num. vi. 25)...*chesed*, the coming down of the Most High with help to the helpless (Ps. lxxxv. 7)." Cf. Culverwell on Ps. iv. 6, "The words are plainly put up in the form of a petition to Heaven, for some smiles of love, for some propitious and favourable glances, for God's gracious presence and acceptance[2]." Both χάρις and ἔλεος are found in LXX as renderings of both *chen* and *chesed*, and their combination, as in this verse, is natural; cf. Wisd. iii. 9, iv. 15, 1 Tim. i. 2, 2 Tim. i. 2.

εἰς εὔκαιρον βοήθειαν. Ps. ix. 10, καὶ ἐγένετο Κύριος καταφυγὴ τῷ πένητι, βοηθὸς ἐν εὐκαιρίαις ἐν θλίψει, cf. Ps. ix. 22 (x. 1).

[1] See a paper by the Rev. F. M. Downton in *The Cowley Evangelist*, July, 1914; and cf. note on xii. 2.
[2] Campagnac. *Cambridge Platonists*. p. 263.

CHAPTER V

V. 1—10. THE PRIESTHOOD OF OUR HIGH PRIEST FULFILS THE UNIVERSAL RULE; CONSUMMATION THROUGH INFIRMITY.

1   Yes, infirmity is characteristic of priesthood. For every high priest of whatever religion is taken from among men, and on men's behalf is established on the Godward side in order that he may, like any ordinary worshipper, bring gifts and sacrifices before God for 2 relief from sins. He is himself one of the people, no austere saint in whom the passions of humanity are quenched, but one who is able to bear gently with the ignorant and wandering just because he, 3 like them, is compassed about with infirmity, and owes the debt of moral weakness, and while he offers for the people must himself 4 also make offering for sins. He has indeed a distinctive office. And yet that is no prize of successful effort; he is priest simply because God calls him.

5   So it was with Aaron. So also with the LORD'S Anointed whose priesthood is celebrated in the Psalm. He did not glorify himself in order to be made High Priest. God called him; God who in one 6 psalm spoke of his sonship, in another assigned him priesthood; 7 "Thou art priest," He said, "after the order of Melchizedek." And when this anointed Son manifested Himself wholly, as Jesus Christ, the same rule held. He, in the days of His earthly sojourning, made offering of prayers and supplications, with a great cry and with tears, to Him who was able to lead Him in salvation out of the valley of 8 death. In awful reverence He cried and at once was heard. Then, Son though He was, He learned by the sufferings appointed Him the 9 obedience that might be achieved no other way. At last, perfected by the death through which God conducted Him, He became to all men who, obeying Him, share His obedience, author of salvation that 10 is eternal; being hailed by God in the eternal sphere " High Priest," after the order of Melchizedek.

    1. ἵνα προσφέρῃ. προσφέρειν, προσφορά, ἀναφέρειν, and (rarely) ἀναφορά, are sacrificial words in LXX. The first three are frequent in Hebrews, and ἀναφέρειν seems to be distinguished from the more general προσφέρειν as it is in some passages of LXX where "προσφέρειν is used of the offerer bringing the victim to present before the altar, ἀναφέρειν of the Priest offering up the selected portion upon the altar, Lev. ii. 14, 16, iii. 1, 5. In the Canons of Councils προσφορά and προσφέρειν are used absolutely for 'offering the Holy Sacrifice,' and 'the offering' itself[1]." Ἀναφορά, which does not occur in N.T., became important in later liturgical language—it comes in rubrics of the Barberini S. Basil and S. Chrysostom[2]—as the title of the more solemn part of the service which begins with "Lift up your hearts." The common verbs in the liturgies themselves are προσφέρειν of the "elements" or the "sacrifice," ἀναπέμπειν of the prayers. The nouns are δῶρα, θυσία, θυσίαι, λατρεία, ἐπιθυσία, προσφορά.

ὑπὲρ ἁμαρτιῶν. περὶ ἁμαρτίας is the usual phrase in LXX. It is often used as a noun in itself, even without article, = "sin-offering." So in Ps. xl. quoted in ch. x. In LXX ὑπὲρ ἁ. is rare; in N.T. only in Hebrews, but cf. 1 Cor. xv. 3, Gal. i. 4. The collocation in ix. 7 suggests the feeling of the phrase.

2. μετριοπαθεῖν δυνάμενος, *mensurate pati potens*, Arias Montanus, "can reasonably bear with," A.V. mg. Windisch quotes from Philo (*Leg. All.* III. p. 113), ὁρᾷς πῶς ὁ τέλειος τελείαν ἀπάθειαν αἰεὶ μελετᾷ. ἀλλ' ὅ γε προκόπτων δεύτερος ὢν Ἀαρὼν μετριοπάθειαν ἀσκεῖ, ἐκτεμεῖν γὰρ ἔτι τὸ στῆθος καὶ τὸν θυμὸν ἀδυνατεῖ.

τοῖς ἀγνοοῦσι. In the Greek liturgies the priest prays that he may offer "for his own sins and the ignorances of the people": cf. ix. 7.

4. καθώσπερ καὶ Ἀαρών is omitted by 𝔭[13]. The paragraph is about high priests in general; καθώσπερ (altered to καθάπερ in the later text) is a strange word; another MS. omits οὕτως καὶ ὁ χριστός, which might hint at some early disturbance in the text. Is the reading of 𝔭[13] primitive, or a thoughtful "Alexandrian" correction? Intr. IV. 2.

5. ὁ χριστὸς: significantly printed without capital by W.H. The psalms about to be quoted referred primarily to "Christs" of O.T.; not till *v.* 7 is attention concentrated upon the consummator of their Christhood.

οὐχ ἑαυτὸν ἐδόξασεν γενηθῆναι, not "imagined that he had been made"; δοξάζω (only here in Heb.) always = "glorify" in LXX and N.T.

---

[1] Hammond, *Liturgies Eastern and Western*, pp. 376, 389.
[2] Swainson, *Greek Liturgies*, pp. 79, 89.

7. ταῖς ἡμέραις τῆς σαρκὸς αὐτοῦ. Cf. 2 Cor. v. 16, 1 Cor. xv. 50, and x. 20 below.

πρὸς τὸν δυνάμενον. Cf. Mark xiv. 35 f., εἰ δυνατόν ἐστιν...πάντα δυνατά σοι. The whole passage seems to allude to Gethsemane; hardly to the narrative as it stands in any of our gospels. The clause which is doubtfully attested in Luke xxii. 43 f. perhaps indicates considerable variety in the tradition behind those gospels. The language has many affinities with the Maccabean books, 2 Macc. xi. 6, 3 Macc. i. 11, 16, vi. 13 f.

σώζειν ἐκ θανάτου. Syr. "to quicken him from death"; vii. 16 and the whole idea of this ep. justify such a paraphrase, though the everyday meaning of the three Greek words would be "to save from dying."

εἰσακουσθεὶς ἀπὸ τῆς εὐλαβείας. John Smith, the Cambridge Platonist, said, "*He was delivered from what he feared;* for so the words being nothing else but an Hebraism are to be rendered[1]," but there are no such Hebraisms in this ep. *Pro sua reverentia* is the good translation of vg., well explained by Primasius, "Reverence sometimes stands for love, sometimes for fear; here for the supreme charity and supreme obedience of the Son of God."

8. ἔμαθεν ἀφ' ὧν ἔπαθεν, proverbial in Greek from Hdt. to Philo, but the acc. τ. ὑπακοήν gives the phrase distinction here.

In Ignatius παθεῖν has almost the same sense as in the creed, "suffered and died." That sense is approached in ix. 26, xiii. 12, Luke xxii. 15, Acts i. 3, xvii. 3. In 1 Pet. the verb is very frequent, and generally illustrative of the idea that Christ's disciples are made one with Him by suffering. The theology of 1 Pet. iv. 1 (cf. Rom. vi. 7) is near akin to that of our author, but less carefully expressed: Χριστοῦ οὖν παθόντος σαρκὶ καὶ ὑμεῖς τὴν αὐτὴν ἔννοιαν ὁπλίσασθε, ὅτι ὁ παθὼν σαρκὶ πέπαυται ἁμαρτίαις.

9. αἴτιος σωτηρίας. A phrase twice found in Philo. "While αἰτία generally means an accusation or charge, a *crimen*, it is sometimes used by Plato for a cause or source (αἰτία ἀγαθοῦ). Thus in Pindar, *Nem.* VII. 11, a μελίφρον' αἰτίαν ῥοαῖσι μουσᾶν means 'a pleasing subject (*motif*) for the flow of song': and αἴτιος, though usually 'the culprit' or 'accused,' is also the author or originator: so Plato, *Rep.* 379, τῶν μὲν ἀγαθῶν οὐδένα ἄλλον αἰτιατέον[2]."

10. προσαγορευθείς. Cf. 1 Macc. xiv. 40, and Clem. xvii., a ch. which has other coincidences with the ep. The parts. τελειωθείς

---

[1] Campagnac, p. 156.
[2] Wallace, *Lectures and Essays*, pp. 302 f.

(catching here that shade of meaning which it has in Wisd. iv. 13,
"perfected by death") and προσαγ. are grammatically synchronous,
both marking a moment just anterior to ἐγένετο. But the emphatic
epithet αἰωνίου complicates the symmetry. It might be said that
ἐγένετο depends on τελ. grammatically, philosophically on προσαγ.
For αἰώνιος in this ep. is quasi-philosophical: cf. vi. 2, ix. 12, 14 f.,
xiii. 20. It mingles in conversational freedom ideas from O.T. and
from the Alexandrine schools. In LXX αἰών = Hebrew 'olam, "age,"
and αἰώνιος represents the same noun modified by dependent words;
it means in general "everlasting." In Philo χρόνος is distinguished
from αἰών as the measurable system of days, years, etc. which is but
an image of the archetypal αἰών; for αἰών is the life of the "intelligible" world and must be sought among the immaterial things of
the pure intellect (*Quis rerum div.* p. 496, *De mut. nom.* p. 619). This is
like Plato in *Timaeus*, 37 D, E; time with its parts is an eternal image
of the eternity which has no parts or tenses. Only in calling the
image also "eternal" Plato shews the difference between his true
idealism and the vulgar fancy of "two worlds" which most of his
successors indulged in (Intr. iii. 32); moreover Plato is not speaking
here with philosophic strictness. He is dealing with the "eternal,"
not with the "intelligible," and only gives a poetic hint, in
picturesque terms, of "time untimed." Our author is nearer Plato
than Philo in this respect. He has not thought out the problem so
far as perhaps S. John did. But in his free artistic deepening of
O.T. phrases he does so use αἰώνιος that at each of its occurrences the
reader must pause, as though before the opening of a spiritual vista
which outshines the current thought. "Divine" would be no rendering, but a suggestive substitution. After all the usage of O.T., to
a sympathetic reader, will seem different in degree, not kind: see esp.
Psalms, and Eccl. iii. 11 R.V. mg.

V. 11.—VI. 8. It is impossible to sink the difference
between Judaism and Christianity: return to the
simplicity of childhood would be unmanly betrayal
of our Lord.

Of Melchizedek our discourse might be much, and it would be 11
difficult to explain in sufficient argument what we mean by putting
his priesthood in the same line as our Lord's, since of late you have
grown so lazy-eared. For just when you ought to be commencing 12

teachers, now that you have been so long in our Christian school, you say that you yourselves have need of a repetition of the old pre-Christian teaching as to what the very elements of the earliest lessons in the oracles of God may mean. You have come round again to this; you have need (such is your iterated plaint) of the milk of simple religion, not of the strong food of the controversy between the Churches. I play upon your words as you do upon our master,

13 Paul's. But I am anxious. For any who casts in his lot with that kind of simplicity, avoids the discipline which produces a reasoned

14 morality; he is in fact a babe. And full-grown men do require the strong food; the kind of men, I mean, who by reason of habitual exercise have their faculties in good training, so that they can discern in a crisis between the noble course and the base.

vi. 1 Wherefore let us leave behind the simple theme of the mere origins of Messianic doctrine, and let us be borne onward by the tide of duty to the consummation of that doctrine in thought and action. Let us not be laying over again a foundation for the conventional religious life of renouncing the works of the devil and of

2 faith towards God; the foundation which consists of teaching about ceremonial washings, and imposition of hands, about the resurrection

3 of the dead, and judgement at the eternal assize. And indeed we are to go forward, if, as I surely believe, God will presently commission us for a time of trial.

4 It is a critical hour. For as to your plan of shirking responsibility by retiring into the Church of your fathers, that is in the very nature of things impossible. Your eyes have been opened once for all to the truth; you know the taste of the gracious gift that comes from heaven: you have become members of the body which

5 the Holy Spirit vivifies; you have tasted the excellence of God's promise; you have anticipated its fulfilment in the age that is to come when our Lord comes as Christ triumphant, for you already experience the spiritual powers that issue therefrom. That is Christianity; not an academic problem, but a profound spiritual experience, a

6 gift received, a loyalty to be rendered. If you fall away from this, it is impossible to start you again fair and fresh in the recovered simplicity of childhood's mind, while by the very act of this fresh start you are crucifying the Son of God—not being "crucified with Christ," but crucifying Him for your pleasure and putting Him to open shame by the renunciation of allegiance which your new life will daily proclaim.

7 Take a parable from Genesis to enforce my warning. The ground that (in the time of man's innocency) drinks the rain which comes

often upon it and brings forth herb meet for those for whose sake
it is also, by God's ordinance, tilled, partakes of the blessing of the
whole creation. But when (after the mortal change) it produces 8
thorns and thistles, it is reprobate and nigh the fulfilment of the
curse which God pronounced, and its destiny is to be cleansed of its
weeds by fire.

11. περὶ οὖ, κ.τ.λ., *de quo grandis nobis sermo et ininterpretabilis
ad dicendum*, vg. Cf. Dion. Hal. *de Comp.* viii., περὶ ὧν καὶ πολὺς ὁ λόγος
καὶ βαθεῖα ἡ θεωρία. These four verses are more than usually tinged
with the literary flavour of the period, but beneath the surface they
are "biblical." S. Paul had written about στοιχεῖα, Gal.iv. 3 (where see
Lightfoot's note), and 9, Col. ii. 8, 20, and about "feeding babes
with milk," 1 Cor. iii. 1 f., cf. 1 Pet. ii. 2. The author gives a half
playful turn to words which he and his friends knew well (cf. xiii. 25).
Then in the next paragraph this friendly intimacy passes into the
severity of anxious love.

12. τινά, so W.H., R.V., Blass. But most ancient authority is
for τίνα. Greek ears could perhaps catch the rythm better than ours,
the bare, active inf. is untranslatable but idiomatic, τίνα τὰ στοιχεῖα
has a touch of lively irony, τινά, "some one," is a mannerism already
repeated to satiety, and on the whole it seems better to read the
interrogative with A.V., von Soden, and probably Euthalius.

CHAPTER VI

1. τὸν τῆς ἀρχῆς τοῦ χριστοῦ λόγον. Cf. iii. 14, but there is a touch of depreciation here as in v. 12.

καταβαλλόμενοι *diruentes* 𝔏 vt, but Josephus and other late writers use the word in the sense required here, 'lay foundation.'

νεκρων ἔργων. Elsewhere in N.T. νεκρὸς only of persons, except Rom. vii. 8, viii. 10, and Jas. ii. 17—26, where it is predicate to ἁμαρτία, σῶμα, πίστις. Tertullian felt the personal sense of ν. so strongly that he translated here *operibus mortuorum*. The metaphor is bold, "deeds which belong to that realm of death" spoken of in ii. 15. There is probably no thought of Paul's "works of merit."

2. διδαχήν. So B 𝔏 vt and d (though the Greek of D is διδαχῆς). The attestation though limited is important; and the acc., which makes a certain ecclesiastical system the foundation of repentance and faith, suits one interpretation of the passage very well. With the genitive, the θεμέλιον is not defined; "laying foundation" is but an ornamental phrase for starting upon repentance, faith, doctrine of washings, etc.

It will be noticed that all the elements of this foundation belong to Judaism as much as to the Christian faith. They are the στοιχεία τῆς ἀρχῆς τῶν λογίων τοῦ θεοῦ as held by a Pharisee like S. Paul or a Hellenistic Jew like S. Stephen before their conversion to Christianity. The plural βαπτισμοῖς occurs again at ix. 10 of Jewish "washings"; cf. Mark vii. 4, 8, Lev. xiv. 7 f., xvi. 4, 24, 26, 28 etc.[1] For ἐπιθέσεως χ. cf. Acts vi. 6, viii. 17, ix. 17, xiii. 3, xix. 6, xxviii. 8, 1 Tim. iv. 14, 2 Tim. i. 6, also Lev. i. 4 etc., xvi. 21, Num. xxvii. 18. For ἀναστάσεως...κρίματος αἰωνίου, Acts xxiii. 6, xxiv. 15, 25, Dan. xii. 2 f., 2 Macc. vii. and the teaching of our Lord in the gospels. Of course the last three doctrines were inherited by the Christian Church. That can hardly be said of the (plural) "washings," and this phrase seems to make it plain that "the foundation of repentance and faith" which the readers of the ep. propose to lay again would be, should they carry out their proposal, a return to the Jewish Church. This they think an abandonment of useless controversy,

---

[1] For the "baptism" of proselytes, etc., see Box and Oesterley, *The Religion and Worship of the Synagogue*, ch. xiii.

a simple and sufficient basis of noble life and true faith in God. Their friend answers that their purpose is an "impossible" (*v.* 4) one. They would be abandoning not useless theological controversy, but their Lord himself to whom (whatever they think of the doctrine of His Person) they have given allegiance. Their new start in the simple faith of their fathers would be an act of gross dishonour; it would not be a new start at all, but a base desertion. The idea is in the very nature of things impossible. Intr. III. 1—3, 20, 22.

3. ἐάνπερ ἐπιτρέπῃ, perhaps "commission" rather than "permit." The nature of the commission may be inferred from x. 25, xii. 4, xiii. 3.

4. φωτισθέντας. In eccl. writers φωτίζω, φωτισμός, mean the illumination of baptism. This passage and x. 32 perhaps lead up to that technical usage. For the tense cf. Rom. xiii. 11. The following phrases carry on the description of the manifold character of "the new life." They are tersely suggestive and lose their pregnancy by detailed explanation. A few parallels will shew how church tradition lies behind the whole passage: τ. δωρεᾶς 2 Cor. ix. 15, 2 Pet. i. 3, 4; καλὸν γ. θεοῦ ῥῆμα 1 Pet. i. 24f.; δυν. μέλλοντος αἰῶνος Luke i. 17, v. 17, 1 Cor. v. 4, Gal. iii. 5. For μετόχους πν. ἁγίου it is unnecessary to quote. It is taken for granted throughout Acts and Epistles that the Christian life is new life springing from the Holy Spirit, the life-giver. But the form of the phrase, μετόχους γενηθέντας, indicates rather strikingly one characteristic of this thought as N.T. holds it. In F. D. Maurice's words, "The Spirit dwells in the Body, and in each of its members *as such*, and not in individuals. The Spirit in an individual is a fearful contradiction," *Life,* I. p. 209. For absence of art. see Intr. III. 29, v. 5 but here the style of the context would be sufficient explanation: καλόν is only marked as predicate by position: Intr. v. 6.

5. δυνάμεις τε μέλλοντος αἰῶνος. In Tertullian's copy what might be a full line in a papyrus roll, ΑΜΕΙϹΤΕΜΕΛΛ, had dropped out, and he translated with dark grandeur *occidente iam aevo.* Intr. II. 3.

6. ἀνακαινίζειν, ἀνασταυροῦντας. Neither verb carries the meaning "again" in itself; ἀνασταυροῦν is good Greek for "crucify," "impale," whereas σταυροῦν, which is always used elsewhere in N.T., meant in the classical period "make a palisade": Intr. v. 2. What is implied here by this part. may be seen by comparing Gal. ii. 19, iv. 19; when one entered the Christian family he shared the crucifixion of his Lord and so found the Lord's life his own. If these disciples desert Christ they are enacting the crucifixion in another manner, declaring their fellowship with the crucifiers instead of with

E 2

the Crucified. For παραδειγμ. cf. iv. 11 with Gal. iii. 1, Matt.
x. 33, Mark ix. 39, Luke xii. 9, 1 Cor. xii. 3, and Matt. i. 19.

7 f. An analogy in confirmation of what has been said, drawn
from Scripture; cf. Gen. i. 11 f., iii. 17 f.

VI. 9—12. YOU ARE DILIGENT IN CHARITY ; BE ZEALOUS ALSO IN THEOLOGY.

9   But we have really no doubt about you, my very dear friends ; you
are certainly destined for those grander efforts which lay fast hold of
10 salvation, even though we do speak thus. For God is not a task-
master, too austere to care for equity. He does not forget your work
and the love of which you gave proof in the service you devoted
to the honour of His name. You ministered in former days to His
covenanted saints, in whom the ancient communion in His name is
continued and renewed. You are still ministering to them. And God
whose memory is effective love will not let you break away from our
11 loving fellowship. But we set our heart on your doing something
further. We would have each one of you continue to prove the same
zeal in another line of service ; i.e. in expanding, deepening and
assuring our common hope till at last, matured, it passes into fulfil-
12 ment. That is the impulse we desire to save you from treating with
lazy indifference, and so to make you imitators of your companions
in the faith who through loyal trust in God and a steady enduring
spirit are entering upon the inheritance of the ancient promises in all
their modern complexity.

9. ἐχόμενα σωτηρίας. Hdt. often uses this construction as periphrasis, e.g. τὰ τῶν ὀνειράτων ἐχόμενα = "dream-matter." But the
gen. σωτηρίας rather recalls such personal usage as in Eur. *Ino*,
ἐλπίδος κεδνῆς ἔχου : cf. xii. 5.

10. ἄδικος. Cf. God's δικαιοσύνη in O.T., e.g. Ps. ciii. 17.

τῆς ἀγάπης. Most mss., but hardly one of weight, prefix τοῦ
κόπου (from 1 Thess. i. 3). It mars the force of ἐνεδείξασθε.

διακονήσαντες...διακονοῦντες. The tenses are in logical relation
to the present position of the readers. Pedantic grammar might have
given ὡς διακονησάντων...διακονούντων. Intr. v. 4.

τοῖς ἁγίοις = "the Christians," but in this ep. only so here and
xiii. 24 (cf. iii. 1). This is the regular use in Paul. Lightfoot, on
Phil. i. 1, explains it as "a term transferred from the old dispensation
to the new"; Israel had been chosen by God as His λαὸς ἅγιος ; the
Israelites were called in LXX οἱ ἅγιοι ; now the Christian Church
takes over the title ; the main idea is "consecration." Perhaps it

may be added that in his two earliest epp., to the Thessalonians, Paul uses οἱ ἄγιοι in a rather different sense of the "holy ones" who shall accompany the Christ at His advent, 1 Thess. iii. 13, 2 Thess. i. 10. Is it possible that this apocalyptic colour always affects his application of the term? Cf. below, x. 25, xii. 14, and 1 Cor. vi. 1 f.

11. ἕκαστον. Cf. τις, iii. 12 f., iv. 1, 11. It is correlative to the affectionate ἀγαπητοί, frequent in Paul; the writer is very anxious for his friends and "calleth them all by their names."

πληροφορίαν. Cf. x. 22, 1 Thess. i. 5, Luke i..1, Col. ii. 2 where Lightfoot says that "full assurance" seems to be the meaning of this substantive wherever it occurs in N.T. Elsewhere only in ecclesiastical writers, e.g. Clem. xlii. μετὰ π. πνεύματος ἁγίου. In this ep. d has *confirmatio* in both places, vg. *expletio* here, *plenitudo* in x. 22.

12. κληρονομούντων, as in i. 14. Abraham "found" the promise (15); he did not "carry home the harvest" (x. 36, xi. 39). That remained for those who "in the end of these days" are entering into the various labours of their predecessors (John iv. 37). The word was suggested to the author by the quotation he is about to make (14) from Gen. xxii. 17, where the sentence continues, καὶ κληρονομήσει τὸ σπέρμα σου.

VI. 13—20. THE OATH OF GOD, AND THE ANCHOR OF HOPE.

The promises are ancient, and they are a real ground for hope. 13 For it was to Abraham that God made promise. And since He had no greater person to swear by, He sware (we read) by Himself, saying 14 "Surely, with great blessing will I bless thee, and with great abundance will I multiply thee." And that was how Abraham, 15 after spirited endurance, met with his promise. An encouragement to us as well as to him. For when mere men swear, they swear by 16 some one who is greater than themselves, and however hot their dispute, it is brought to a close and the agreement is decisively fixed by an oath. And so it was by oath that God, deliberately purposing 17 to demonstrate with excessive clearness to the future heirs of the promise made to Abraham the unalterable firmness of His plan, took the position of an umpire between himself and Abraham. He 18 bound Himself by an oath sworn by His own person, in order that, through two unalterable sanctions—the oath He sware and His own Divinity that He sware by—we may have strong encouragement. We were the final cause, we who have now fled for refuge from the

storm of this troubled world to seize the hope thus long ago held
19 forth to us. That hope we are attached to as an anchor to which we
may entrust the keeping of more than physical life; an anchor
soundly forged and firm in its hold. Such an anchor as it drops
into the mysterious deep and bites the ground is a symbol of the
high priest's entry into the presence of God behind the sanctuary
20 veil. And indeed One has entered into that presence as a forerunner of our own entry to do priestly service there for us, namely
Jesus. He entered at the moment of His death, having in that
moment become "High Priest," "after the order of Melchizedek,"
"eternally."

13. ἐπαγγειλάμενος. Cf. Rutherford quoted on ii. 10, and see
Moulton, p. 130 f. for the sense in which it is legitimate to call this
an "aorist part. of coincident action."

ὤμοσεν καθ' ἑαυτοῦ. Philo (*Legg. all.* III. p. 127) presses the
argument from κατ' ἐμαυτοῦ ὤμοσα of LXX in the same manner.

14. εἰ μὴν. The classical ἦ μὴν was often spelt εἰ μὴν in Hellenistic
Greek. Moulton (p. 46) seems to object to the spelling εἰ in W.H.,
Tisch., v. Sod. But the variant εἰ μή, both here and in LXX,
suggests that "connexion with εἰ, *if,*" was long ago, though wrongly,
supposed. This oath-formula is not unfrequent in LXX; in N.T. the
quotation here is the only instance.

εὐλογῶν εὐλογήσω. A common mode of representing an emphatic
Hebrew idiom which throws the stress on the root idea of the verb;
so A.V. and R.V. in Luke xxii. 15, where A.V. mg. is less good.
Moulton calls it "possible, but unidiomatic Greek," p. 76.

15. ἐπέτυχεν. The part. attached here, and the context in xi. 33,
shew that this word implies boldness in accepting a promise of which
the fulfilment is hidden in the future. It means properly to fall in
with on the way; cf. Thomas Aquinas' prayer, "Concede mihi
dilectum filium tuum, quem nunc velatum in via suscipere pro-
pono, revelata tandem facie perpetuo contemplari." A Christian
gem in Brit. Mus. has a fish and anchor with the legend ΕΠΙ-
ΤΤΝΧΑΝΟΤ[1].

17. ἐπιδεῖξαι. There seems to be a contrast with ἐνδείκνυσθαι
above (11), and it is tempting to fancy that the author wished thus
to imply "additional proof"; cf. vii. 14 f.

18. ἐν οἷς ἀδύνατον. Num. xxiii. 19, 1 Sam. xv. 29. ℵ*AC
have τὸν θεόν, BD θεόν, v. Sod. like W.H. allows the alternative; τὸν

---

[1] Westcott, *Religious Thought in the West*, p. 307.

θεόν corresponds to our "God" without article, an emphatic *name* at the end of the clause; cf. xiii. 16. Cf. Clem. xxvii. οὐδὲν γὰρ ἀδύνατον παρὰ τῷ θεῷ εἰ μὴ τὸ ψεύσασθαι.

19. τῆς ψυχῆς. In iv. 12 ψυχή seems to signify one of the physical elements in man's constitution, his living power as distinguished from (what is intimately connected therewith) his πνεῦμα or breath. Yet even there the physical analysis is an illustration of the keener analysis of conscience by God's Word. Here ψυχή evidently has a higher meaning in itself. The following extract from Coleridge[1] explains this meaning: "Life is the one universal soul, which, by virtue of the enlivening Breath and the informing Word, all organised bodies have in common, each after its kind. This, therefore, all animals possess, and man as an animal. But, in addition to this, God transfused into man a higher gift, and specially inbreathed :— even a living (that is, self-subsisting) soul, a soul having its life in itself. *And man became a living soul.* He did not merely possess it, he became it. It was his proper being, his truest self, the man in the man." Coleridge perhaps refines too subtly upon the Hebrew idiom of Gen. ii. 7. But he has caught the main feeling of the O.T., viz. that the natural and spiritual are one : and natural life has moral and so eternal life folded up within it. One writer of O.T. questioned the sharp division between the "soul" of man and the "life" of brutes, Eccl. iii. 21 R.V. Perhaps that writer's real thought went deeper than his cynical expression of it. And perhaps there is just a hint in our author of sympathy with his question. In x. 34, xii. 3, he seems to recognise that a man's "very self" is a deeper reality than even his "soul." Hort's notes on ψυχή in 1 Pet. i. 9, 22, ii. 11, should be read[2].

εἰσερχομένην, i.e. the anchor, to which the hope, according to a common metaphor of Greek writers of every period, is compared. To break the metaphor at this point and apply εἰσερχ. merely to the hope is tame. And the harshness is lessened when εἰσερχ...καταπετάσματος is recognised as all but a quotation from the well-known account of the day of atonement in Lev. xvi. This quotation is introduced in order to bring the argument back to Melchizedek and priesthood. The general picture is one of three noticeable ones with which the ep. is punctuated, cf. xii. 1 f., xiii. 11 f. The faithful are

---

[1] *Aids to Reflection*, Introd. Aphorisms, ix.
[2] Cf. also Wallace, *Lectures and Essays*, pp. 131 f., 204. App. A of Edwards' *English-Greek Lexicon* gives briefly the classical usage. And very instructive is Burnet's *Socrates and the Soul* (Milford for the British Academy, 1916), in which the high Platonic idea of ψυχή, as that true life which a man ought most to care for, is proved to have been originated by Socrates.

likened to the crew of the ship which has run to port from the storm. The anchor, dropped into the mysterious deep, already holds the ground. The captain has gone ashore, and the crew await orders to follow him. The imagery is only touched in with a stroke or two. But the point is that the submerged bottom which the anchor holds is continuous with the shore. So in ix. 4 the altar of incense "belongs to" the Holy of Holies, in xii. 22 the readers have "come to" the heavenly Sion; all this is ἐχόμενα σωτηρίας, vi. 9.

CHAPTER VII

VII. 1—3. MELCHIZEDEK THE TYPE.

Melchizedek; for now I am going to talk about him after all. **1**
See him, as he appears in that mysterious chapter of Genesis ; King
of Salem, Priest of God most High ; who met Abraham as he was
returning from the slaughter of the kings and blessed him ; to whom **2**
also Abraham gave as portion a full tithe of all the spoil :—he being
first by the interpretation of his name King of Righteousness, and
then also being entitled King of Salem, which is King of Peace ; one **3**
to whom no father, mother or descent is assigned ; one who has
neither beginning of days nor end of life in the history ;—we behold
in short a picture drawn after the likeness of that Son of God whom
antiquity faintly discerned, and whose true features we have learned
to day from those who saw the Lord and by our own communion
with Him :—this Melchizedek abides a priest continuously.

For the meaning of " priesthood after the order of Melchizedek "
see Intr. III. 10.

1. ὁ συναντήσας, ὅς ℵABC²DK33. This attestation is so strong
that we must suppose either that it represents a very early scribe's
error which has only been corrected in comparatively late times ; or
that it was a carelessness of the author himself, who began a relative
sentence which he never finished. Cf. x. 1, xi. 35; also Acts xix. 40,
xxiv. 5—8, but in each of these passages Luke seems to be purposely
representing the embarrassment of the speakers. It may be noticed
that there are other confusions of text in D and 𝔏 vt in *vv.* 1 and 2 ;
these perhaps indicate some interruption in the transmission which
we cannot fully trace.

κοπῆς. Cf. Aesch. *Ag.* 1276 :

βωμοῦ πατρῴου δ' ἀντ' ἐπίξηνον μένει
θερμὸν κοπέντος φοινίῳ προσφάγματι.

See W. Headlam *ad loc.*

3. ἀγενεαλόγητος. Gen. says nothing about Melchizedek's father,
mother or descent ; none could declare his " generation," cf. Isa. liii.
8 (LXX).

ἀφωμοιωμένος. Used of statues or pictures that "resemble" their original. Melchizedek is like our Lord, not our Lord like him.

εἰς τὸ διηνεκές, x. 1, 12, 14. The author uses this phrase instead of εἰς τὸν αἰῶνα when he wishes to express the simple idea of time ; so πάντοτε v. 25. Cf. note on v. 9. The phrase is frequent in Greek inscriptions.

VII. 4—10. A GREATER PRIEST THAN LEVI.

4   Look at him. What a large figure he stands there ; one to whom Abraham gave tithe of the choicest spoils, Abraham the first father 5 of our holy race. It is true that those who, being of the sons of Levi, receive the legal office of the priesthood, are authorised to tithe the people of God according to the Mosaic Law, that is their own brothers ; the family of Abraham is quite accustomed to being tithed 6 by their own kin. But here is one who does not count his ancestry from the sons of Levi, and he has exacted tithe from Abraham, and upon the holder of the divine promises himself he has pronounced 7 blessing. Now there is no dispute at all about the principle, Less 8 receives blessing from greater. And while in our nation mere men, dying one after the other in the course of nature, take tithes, in that ancient mystery it is a far greater Person who takes them, One 9 who, according to the witness of Scripture, absolutely lives. Indeed we may almost venture to reduce it all to the matter-of-fact assertion 10 that through Abraham Levi also the tithe-taker has been tithed, for as Levi had not yet been born, he was still part of Abraham his ancestor when that meeting with Melchizedek took place.

4. πηλίκος = "how large" cf. Gal. vi. 11, or "how old." There seems no parallel in Greek literature for the meaning "how great in character." And θεωρεῖτε (only here in this ep., contrast κατανοήσατε iii. 1) is probably used as in Luke and Acts of literal "seeing," not as in John. This is one of the author's bold, vivid phrases = "what a big one." The "apodeictic" οὗτος adds to the effect.

ᾧ. So BD* 𝕃 (vt, vg.codd) 𝔖 (vg.) 𝔆 (boh.) Ambst.: ᾧ καὶ אACDcω 𝕃 (vg.codd) 𝔖 (hl) 𝔄 Chr. Cyr. al.

The opposed groups in vv. 23 and 26 should be compared. In v. 23 no doubt is possible. Here and in v. 26 the authority on either side is weighty enough to make W.H. give a marginal alternative. But few who have observed the groupings throughout the ep. will hesitate to prefer their text. And in all three cases this interpretation of documentary authority supports the reading which minute study of the context approves. In this verse καί does not connect an additional relative clause as in *v.* 2. And it would throw the emphasis where emphasis is not required.

ὁ πατριάρχης. Here is the true emphasis of the sentence, cf. xi. 17. For πατριάρχης cf. Acts ii. 29, vii. 8, and 4 Macc. vii. 19, xvi. 25, an Alexandrine work which " approaches nearer than any other than the Greek Bible to the models of Hellenic philosophy and rhetoric " (Swete).

8. μαρτυρούμενος. The grandeur of this undefined part. is more easily expressed in the Latin versions (*ibi autem contestatus quia vivit*) than in English ; R.V. " one," suggests " one man " in the context, and hardly improves upon A.V.

9. ὡς ἔπος εἰπεῖν. Here again R.V. is not satisfactory. Not "as it were " but " one might almost say " is the meaning of this Greek idiom.

Λευίς. So best MSS. This nom. form is found in LXX also ; above, *v.* 5, Λευεί is the gen.[1]

VII. 11—25. The moral necessity for the Levitical priesthood to pass away.

So then Levi is demonstrated less than Melchizedek. And now let us come somewhat nearer to reality in considering why our Lord should be priest after the order of Melchizedek, not of Levi.

The real reason is the failure of the Levitical priesthood to achieve 11 what priesthood is meant to achieve. For if the Levitical priesthood had achieved that, what need would there still have been for a psalmist to prophesy that after the order of Melchizedek a quite different priest should arise, and so be reckoned *not* after the order of Aaron? We see from the book of Leviticus that the whole law 12 for Israel rests upon the institution of Aaronic priesthood. The psalmist's word is therefore a bold one. It is the sacred law of Moses that he is daring to repeal, for the law goes with the priesthood. He speaks boldly and therefore with as deep a significance as may be conceived. And so I do not scruple to believe that he 13 spoke prophetically of our Lord Jesus Christ, and contemplated an astonishing break with ancestral faith and custom in these days of ours. For He towards whom this oracle is directed is a member of a different tribe from Levi, and of His tribe no one has ever paid

[1] Thackeray, *Grammar of O.T. in Greek*, § 11. 6 (3), W.H., *Intr. to N.T. in Greek*, p. 155.

14 any attention to the service of the altar. That is plain, for every one knows that it is from Judah that our Lord is sprung, and Moses never said a word about priests with reference to the tribe of Judah.

15 And to come back from contemporary fact to scriptural inference, the setting aside of the merely instituted priesthood of Aaron is even more plainly commended, if the oracle be true, and if after a real, moral likeness to Melchizedek there is to arise a priest of so different

16 a character that he has entered upon his office, not according to law, which (for all its divine sanction) is nothing but a material system of authority, but according to the ever freshly operating power of

17 life which passes indissolubly through death. For that is what the witness of Genesis as completed by the psalmist means—"Thou art

18 a priest eternally after the order of Melchizedek." It means first indeed that an ordinance we have received from the church of our fathers is being set aside to day, because it has proved weak and

19 useless; for the Law has really accomplished nothing of that priestly mediation for which it was designed. But more important is this; a stronger kind of hope is being brought forward in its place, through the transforming power of which we are in these days of change and trial actually entering into the presence of God.

20 And there is also that matter of the oath. Whatever divine sanction there may have been for the Levitical priesthood, the sons of Aaron have become priests without an oath from God to establish

21 them, but this Priest received his priesthood with the giving of an oath by God through the psalmist who brought God's word to him— "The Lord sware, and will not repent; Thou art priest eternally."

22 This oath implies covenant, and makes a great difference. Our Priest has become surety for a covenant, and a greater covenant than even Abraham knew. And what this suretyship means we remember when we call Him Jesus, the man who suffered for us.

23 And yet another point. Those priests have been appointed one after the other in considerable numbers. They had to be, for they were always prevented by death from lasting out the office which

24 itself survived them. But our Priest "abides" "eternally"; and so the priesthood which He holds can never be passed on to another.

25 Hence He is able to *save*, and that all-completely, those who from generation to generation draw near through His priestly aid to God; seeing that at all times He is living to do in the reality of the eternal sphere all that the analogy of priesthood indicates for a priest to do after he has offered his sacrifice. This He does uninterruptedly on their behalf.

11. τελείωσις. Cf. vii. 28, ix. 12, x. 19—22, xii. 28 f., xiii. 13 f. Windisch quotes *Testament of Levi* xviii. 1 f., καὶ μετὰ τὸ γενέσθαι τὴν ἐκδίκησιν αὐτῶν παρὰ κυρίου ἐκλείψει ἡ ἱερωσύνη, καὶ τότε ἐγερεῖ κύριος ἱερέα καινόν, ᾧ πάντες οἱ λόγοι κυρίου ἀποκαλυφθήσονται, and viii. 14, βασιλεὺς ἐκ τοῦ Ἰούδα ἀναστήσεται καὶ ποιήσει ἱερατείαν νέαν. He thinks this clause (viii. 14) a Christian interpolation; Charles thinks it proves a Maccabean date. Ἱερατεία (ἱερατία *v.* 5 *supra*) is a LXX translation word, ἱερωσύνη (11, 24) is found in Sirach and the Greek books of LXX; it belongs to the more literary Greek.

οὐ, not μή, because "it is not the inf. but only the idea κατὰ τ. τάξιν Ἀ. which is negatived," Blass 75. 4.

13. προσέσχηκεν τῷ θυσιαστηρίῳ. A.V. and R.V., "give attendance at," seem to follow the Latin versions (*praesto fuit ad aram— altario*) with a kind of allusion to the common, and regular LXX, meaning of the verb "pay attention to." Note the assonances in these verses, μετ(α)- thrice, -εσχηκεν twice; cf. i. 1, *v.* 25 below.

14. ὁ κύριος ἡμῶν. Cf. ii. 3. The familiar title goes naturally with πρόδηλον, "obvious, as a historical fact"; contrast κατάδηλον in next verse.

16. ἀκαταλύτου. Cf. 4 Macc. x. 11 d. βασάνους, but the idea here is far deeper. It is part of the whole conception of death revealed by the cross as a mysterious act of one indissoluble life, which conception is characteristic of this ep. Like ψυχή, ζωή is a physical term with sacramental extension: John i. 4.

18. ἀθέτησις...προαγούσης ἐντολῆς. How bold this declaration is, may be seen from Lev. xxix. 9, καὶ ἔσται αὐτοῖς ἱερατία μοι εἰς τὸν αἰῶνα.

τὸ αὐτῆς ἀσθενὲς καὶ ἀνωφελές. See Blass 48. 8 n. who says this use of αὐτῆς without emphasis would hardly be tolerable with a substantive—τὴν αὐτῆς ἀσθένειαν.

21. κατὰ τ. τάξιν M. was added to this line from *v.* 17 at an early stage, but the authorities against it are decisive.

22. κρείττονος διαθήκης. "Covenant," διαθήκη in LXX, *berith* Hebrew, is an idea which fills O.T. What has already been said about Abraham and the Law (12) implies it, cf. Gen. xv. 18, Ex. xxiv. 7. The word itself is introduced here to prepare for fuller treatment in the next two chapters. That here, at any rate, it is used in the O.T. sense, is proved by the addition of ἔγγυος, for neither a "testament" nor an "agreement" in Greek law required a surety. Ἔγγυος is an ordinary Greek word, μεσίτης (only once in LXX, Job ix. 33, though the thought is found in Deut. v. 5) is found in Philo and late Greek as well as in N.T. In this ep. it is used only

of Christ, viii. 6, ix. 15, xii. 24; elsewhere 1 Tim. ii. 5 of Christ,
Gal. iii. 19 f. of Moses. Here it might have caused confusion,
coming so soon after vi. 17, and ἔγγυος has a more affectionate ring,
cf. Sir. xxix. 15, χάριτας ἐγγύου μὴ ἐπιλάθῃ, ἔδωκεν γὰρ τὴν ψυχὴν
αὐτοῦ ὑπέρ σου. It gives a hint of the reason for κρείττονος, which
will be shewn in full presently.

23. γεγονότες ἱερεῖς ℵBωℤ (vtʳ, vg.) 𝔖 (vg. hl. pal.) ℭ (boh.)
𝕬 ℭⁱʰ Chr. *al*: ἱερεῖς γεγονότες ACD33 ℤ (vt) Cyr.: ἱερεῖς *solum* Cosm.
The reading of ℵB is confirmed by the rest of the group. The order is
varied from that in *v.* 20 in order to mark the parallel with ἀπαράβατον ἔχει τ. ἱερωσύνην in the next verse; πλείονες is emphatic and
ἱερεῖς is not part of the predicate.

25. εἰς τὸ ἐντυγχάνειν, perhaps suggested by Rom. viii. 26f., where
however it is the Spirit who intercedes, yet cf. *v.* 34. In Romans vg.
has *postulat*, here the celebrated phrase *semper vivens ad interpellan-
dum pro eis*.

VII. 26—28. OUR HIGH PRIEST, ETERNAL, SON OF GOD.

26   A long argument, but now you have the heart of it. For such a
High Priest as my last words describe is the High Priest for whom
we were always waiting. He is God's loving saint, doing no ill,
pure from the least stain, now quite removed from the hindrance
that sinful men could cause to His perfect work, and lifted high
27 above the highest symbols that we know. He is One who hath no
need (as the high priests on earth have) to multiply sacrifices day
after day, first for His own sins and then for those of the people.
Nothing less than that effective two-fold offering did He make once
for all when He offered up Himself, visibly on the cross, eternally in
28 heaven. Once for all; for there is the difference. The law of Moses,
literal and fixed, appoints mortal men to be priests, with an inherent
weakness, that repeatedly saps their priesthood. The living reason
with which God swears His oath of appointment after the discipline
of law has failed, exalts a Son, "eternally," for the consummation of
His filial work.

26. [καὶ] ἔπρεπεν. ABD𝔖 (vg. hl.) Eus. add καί. The group
looks "Western" but the reading is attractive. Yet καί weakens the
sense. It is indeed a startling assertion that such a High Priest
"became" us, cf. ii. 10, Ps. lxiv. (lxv.) 1; but the sublime description
of this High Priest, and the paradox of His priestly offering, are what
the author would chiefly desire to be noticed.

ὅσιος, often in Psalms for *chasid*, in English versions "saint."

The *chasidim* were the little band who stood with Judas Maccabeus as martyrs for the faith. This ep. is an encouragement, xii. 4 f., xiii. 22, to just that kind of martyrdom, and a like spirit breathes through the Psalter. But the word had a tender and beautiful sense of its own before it received that associated splendour. Cheyne translates, "the man of love," God's "duteous loving ones"; for *chasid* is connected with *chesed* "lovingkindness," the special attribute of God in Hosea¹. The epithets that follow may be illustrated from Philo's allegorisings of high priesthood, but the terse language of the ep. touches the heart as Philo does not. The author is thinking of one who had really lived on earth as man. In κεχωρισμένος ἀπὸ τῶν ἁμαρτωλῶν he does indeed pass to the exalted state of this High Priest, cf. ix. 28, xii. 2, but it is still the manhood that is exalted, and carries our affection with it. Intr. III. 7.

27. ἀνενέγκας. אA 33, 436, 442, Cyr. have προσενέγκας. If the distinction noticed on v. 1 be true, this would seem to refer to the death on the Cross, wherein our Lord, before becoming High Priest, gave Himself to be the victim, whereas ἀναφέρειν, just before, refers to His function as High Priest in heaven. But textual authority is not in favour of the verbal distinction, and the idea itself cannot be analysed with so mechanical a logic. The sacrifice on the cross is sacramental: earth and heaven, now and after, are not twain and separated; they stand to one another as outward visible sign to inward spiritual reality. Intr. III. 8, 32.

More important it is to notice that τοῦτο implies all that follows ἀνάγκην. The sacrifice needs no repetition, but when the Lord offered it, He offered ὑπὲρ τῶν ἰδίων ἁμαρτιῶν as well as for the people's. In what sense that should be understood may be gathered from ix. 28, 1 Pet. ii. 21—24 (a passage which also explains ἄκακος, ἀμίαντος) Gal. iii. 13. The N.T. doctrine is deeper than "vicarious suffering." Intr. III. 15.

28. ὁ λόγος τῆς ὁρκωμοσίας, rather "the divine reason with which God sware" than "His commanding utterance" or "our argument about the oath-giving." This vigorous conclusion brings us face to face at last with the practical earnestness of the author. Philo and Leviticus, whose fashion and speech he has partly followed in the preceding paragraphs, only reach the threshold of his house of thought.

---

¹ *The Book of Psalms, or the praises of Israel,* pp. 9, 29, 141.

CHAPTER VIII

VIII. 1—13. The New Covenant.

1   Here is the climax of the argument: our High Priest's work is
real, it is not limited by the terms of the analogy. Such a High
Priest as has been described we certainly have. When He was enthroned in essential unity with the Godhead in heaven, He entered
2 on a priestly service which is no less essentially divine. It belongs
to the sanctuary and tabernacle of truth not of appearance; the
tabernacle or tent, says Scripture. which the Lord pitched, not man.
3 For Scripture hallows this picture-language of analogy, and as every
high priest is appointed for the offering of gifts and sacrifices, we say
of our High Priest too that it was necessary for Him to have a
4 "sacrifice" to "offer." Now if He had remained on earth to exercise His priesthood, He would not have been a priest at all. There
was no room among the regular priests with their traditional cere-
5 monial for His quite different action to be counted a sacrifice. (I do
not mean that those priests have nothing to do with heavenly things,
but it is only in a shadowy imitation of the spiritual realities that
they perform their unreal ritual. Imitation; that is the gist of the
oracle announced to Moses when he was to inaugurate the ceremonial
of the tabernacle. See, says the divine voice, that thou do everything
6 in imitation of the pattern shewn to thee in the mount.) But our
High Priest has succeeded to an office different in kind from theirs.
Indeed the analogy as applied to Him gets its peculiar distinction
by reason of the covenant which it implies. The covenant which
our High Priest establishes between God and man is a better one
than that which Moses mediated. It is a covenant that has, on
the basis of larger promises, become the gospel law. Scripture
7 justifies our calling it "better." For if no fault could have been
found with the Mosaic covenant, there would be no looking for
8 a second to take its place. But we see just such a searching of faith
in one who was—in a time of trial like the present—carried beyond
the external guarantees of religion. For there is a divine oracle in
the book of Jeremiah which does find fault with people, and says,

Behold days are coming, saith the Lord, when I will bring my sacred relationship towards the separated houses of Israel and Judah to completion in a new covenant. It shall go deeper than the cove- 9 nant that I made with their fathers in the day when I took them by the hand to lead them out of the land of Egypt. For, according to the divine sanction of that covenant, as they did not abide by my good purpose toward them, so I ceased to be careful on their behalf. For this is the covenant which I will grant to the house of united 10 Israel, now that those days have passed away; again establishing it with my "thus saith the Lord." I will give them an affectionate understanding of my laws, and upon their hearts will I write them. So, with mutual trust, I renew the essential bond between us: "I will be to them God, they shall be to me my people." Brothers 11 and fellow-citizens as they shall now be, they will not have to teach one another, saying, Know the Lord. For they shall all know me in their own consciences, young and old, the great men and the simple alike. For with mercy will I now meet the ingratitude of their 12 offences, and their sins will I never remember any more.

A new covenant! The first He declares outworn. That which is 13 wearing out and growing old is nigh unto vanishing away.

1. κεφάλαιον. *Capitulum* 𝔏 = the capital point; if an argument is well knit its capital point is also the "sum" of it. Here the capital point is that the High Priest of the Christian faith has entered the real presence of God; His work is a spiritual reality. The author still expresses this by visible imagery, taken from scripture, and as it were etherealised by a few touches; cf. Ps. cx. as in i. 3, Ex. xxix. 30, and Num. xxiv. 6. For ἀληθινός, the antithesis of χειροποίητος, cf. ix. 24.

2. τῆς σκηνῆς τῆς ἀληθινῆς, κ.τ.λ. There is a verbal reference here to Num. xxiv. 6, but the underlying thought is of Ex. xxiv. 18— xxv. 40. And by the epithet ἀληθινῆς the author colours the simplicity of the Hebrew story of the pattern on the mount with a philo- sophic tinge. As in ix. 24 we seem to catch a glimpse of Plato's "intelligible" world. The epithet applies also to τῶν ἀγίων. The great High Priest exercises His function in a reality which transcends our images of thought. For λειτουργός cf. i. 7, Rom. xiii. 6, xv. 16, Phil. ii. 25. The word is used both of civil and of sacred officers; to ancient thought the service of the state was all sacred and Godward. In Rom. xv. 16 Paul associates the word with priestly phraseology, in Phil. ii. 25 with civil.

3. ὁ προσηνέγκῃ: unclassical subj. cf. xii. 28. See Blass 65. 8, and for τι...ὅ 50. 1.

4. οὖν: so the good mss., though the mass of mss. have γάρ. Οὖν is used here in the "looser way to resume or continue," Blass 78. 5. Μὲν corresponds to δὲ in v. 6.

To what point of time is the reference in ἀναγκαῖον...εἰ ἦν...οὐδ᾽ ἂν ἦν? Are we to translate, "it is necessary...if He were...He would not be" (so 乱 *necesse sit, est*), or, "it was necessary...if He had been ...He would not have been"? The first might perhaps be defended by vii. 25, and the tense of ἰλάσκεσθαι ii. 17, as an allusion to continual intercession. But that would involve a strange use of προσφέρειν, and if we ask what the author meant by the "somewhat to offer," it is difficult to answer otherwise than in the words of ix. 14. The second translation must therefore be accepted, at least for ἀναγκαῖον. The conditional clause is less definite; but its point is that, but for His passing through death to the eternal sphere, the spiritual priesthood of the Lord would have been impossible. So here too the thought is carried back to the crucifixion. Thus the question whether ὄντων τῶν προσφερόντων proves the ep. to have been written before the fall of Jerusalem becomes superfluous. Westcott says indeed that "the tense of the principal verb (λατρεύουσιν) fixes the translation of the participle to the present." But is λ. the principal verb? It stands in a relative clause introduced by the generalizing οἵτινες.

5. σκιᾷ. Cf. Ps. cii. (ci.) 12, cix. (cviii.) 23, cxliv. (cxliii.) 4, Eccl. vi. 12 (vii. 1), Wisd. ii. 5, v. 9, in all of which LXX expresses the idea of a vain thing passing away. So Col. ii. 17, and in this ep. (cf. x. 1) σκιὰ indicates the arbitrary, allegorical symbol, as opposed to the "image itself," or real symbol which partakes of the reality it symbolises. Intr. III. 8.

τύπον, from LXX of Ex. xxv. 40. Philo (*vit. Mos.* II. p. 146) in his comment on the same passage makes τύπον something like the Platonic "idea." Our author glances at that fancy (see note on v. 2, *supra*), but after all lets the word rest in the simple sense of "pattern," which was all the translator intended. He changes the tense of LXX δεδειγμένον because perfects, frequent as they are in the ep., are never employed without a particular reason; cf. xi. 17, xii. 2, Intr. v. 3.

6. λειτουργίας...διαθήκης...ἐπαγγελίαις νενομοθέτηται: a striking sequence, leading swiftly to the doctrine of the new covenant which will be introduced at v. 8 by the quotation from Jeremiah. Νενομο-θέτηται is almost paradoxical like ἕτερον νόμον...τῷ νόμῳ τοῦ νοός μου, Rom. vii. 23, since in vii. 16 *supra* we have been carried beyond "law." Such paradoxes may be reduced to order by reference to Jas. i. 25.

8. αὐτούς. Textual authority is almost evenly divided between αὐτοὺς and αὐτοῖς. Both are legitimate with μεμφόμενος, but αὐτοῖς was perhaps intended to go with λέγει. This phrase of introduction is made as vague as possible. The subject is best understood from iii. 7, iv. 7, but the tense of λέγει is the noticeable point. The inauguration of the promised new covenant now, "at the end of these days," is in the author's mind ; the original occasion of the prophecy is of secondary importance to him.

Yet it is of some importance. He has chosen his quotation carefully. It is from Jer. xxxi. (xxxviii.) 31—34. Whether those critics are possibly right who think the passage does not come from Jeremiah himself, hardly matters ; inspiration, not authorship, is what the writer of Hebrews cares about. And indeed it seems more characteristic of Jeremiah than the prophecies of restoration which immediately precede it. The material symbolism of those prophecies is not what Jeremiah specially stands for in O.T.; the daring "heart-religion" of this place is. We are inclined to connect it rather with the chapter that follows it, and to think of Jeremiah imprisoned as a traitor, suspected as a free-thinker in religion, certain of the speedy ruin of Jerusalem, and the abolition of all the ancient institutions of the faith. In these straits he is lifted to such a pure conception of spiritual and therefore "indissoluble" communion with God, as might be considered the culmination of O.T. prophecy. He calls this a "new covenant." But the terms of the covenant are the same as they always have been and will be, "I will be their God, and they shall be my people." It is new because it shall now be written on the heart, instead of in law, priesthood, monarchy, temple, sacrifice. Moreover, thus inwardly and spiritually written, it shall at last be effectual ; it shall bring "knowledge of God" to "perfection," and supersede "merit" by "grace "; cf. John i. 17.

The idea of this new covenant inspired the author of the "Comfort ye" prophecy (Isa. xl. ff.). The very phrase is recorded by S. Paul and in one version of the gospel narrative as having been uttered by our Lord at the last supper, 1 Cor. xi. 25, Luke xxii. 20. In Mark (xiv. 24 f.) the two words are spoken, but the "new" has rather a different significance: "This is my blood of the covenant, which is shed for many. Verily I say unto you, I will no more drink of the fruit of the vine, until that day when I drink it new in the kingdom of God."

The author of Hebrews probably knew 1 Corinthians. He knew the tradition of the Lord's words which lies behind the gospels. He saw the covenant developing in one unbroken line from Abraham,

through Moses and Jeremiah, to the last supper. At the last
supper the new covenant, promised by Jeremiah, received a fresh
sanction in the Saviour's blood (cf. ix. 15—17) and a final promise of
fulfilment when the Lord Jesus came as Christ with the Kingdom.
In the trial of his own days he believed that, in some real sense, that
coming was to be. Hence he quotes Jeremiah here as a prophecy
for the immediate present. The new covenant was "in a very
little while" to reach perfection. Even now the obsolete ceremonial,
which Jeremiah had long ago recognised as no necessity for faith, was
dropping away. Intr. III. 16.

συντελέσω seems to be the author's own substitution for διαθή-
σομαι of LXX. Like ἐπιτελεῖν in *v.* 5, ix. 6, it has perhaps a ritual
colour, cf. ἐκτελεῖν τελετήν, ἐπιτελεῖν λειτουργίαν in Greek liturgies.

9. **κἀγὼ ἠμέλησα.** The Hebrew *ba'alti* either means "although
I was an husband to them," cf. Jer. iii. 14, or perhaps "and I was a
master to them," which would be explained by Hosea ii. 16, "thou
shalt call me Ishi, my husband, and shalt call me no more Baali,
my master." The mistranslation of LXX may itself be taken in a
sense not unlike Hosea's. In Ex. xix. 5 the covenant is made conditional on Israel's obedience, cf. Lev. xxvi. 14 ff., especially 40 f.
The new covenant, being written on the heart, needs no such condition; it will continually be renewed by forgiveness, cf. Lev. xxvi.
44 f. This is the main teaching in Deuteronomy (see especially
x. 12—xi. 1), though in some places the more rigorous doctrine of
retribution is enforced, cf. iv. 24 quoted in this ep. xii. 29. The
repeated λέγει Κύριος (*vv.* 9, 10) represents the divine sanction, first
for the old promise, with conditions, then for the new promise of
grace.

10. **διάνοιαν**, cf. John xv. 15.

11. **πολίτην.** For this there is in LXX as in ep. a v.l. πλησίον;
a scriptural commonplace instead of the idiomatic but free rendering
of the translator.

γνῶθι...εἰδήσουσιν. Thus Jeremiah anticipates a richer fulfilment of Hosea's desire, Hos. vi. 3. To both these prophets, as to
S. John, to know God is eternal life.

13. **πεπαλαίωκεν**: perf. corresponding to pres. λέγει in *v.* 8. It
also frames the picture which is carried vividly through the "imperfect" participles to the sudden close in ἀφανισμοῦ (frequent in
LXX of Jeremiah for sudden violent removal)—"A certain moment
calls the glory from the grey."

CHAPTER IX

Now the ordinances of the first covenant were ritualistic and its 1 holiness was materially conceived. A tabernacle was constructed after 2 the fashion of a double tent. In the first tent are placed the candlestick and the table and on the table the rite of setting forth the loaves before the LORD is celebrated. This tent is called "Holy Place." Then beyond the inner veil is a second tent which is called "Holy of 3 Holies," the ritual of which is mainly connected with the altar of incense and the ark of the covenant; the altar is golden and the ark 4 all covered with gold. In this tent the pot, also golden, containing the manna is kept; also the rod of Aaron which budded, and the tablets on which the "words" of the covenant at Sinai were written. Above the ark are the cherubim, the angels of the LORD's presence, 5 overshadowing the mercy-seat with their wings. Everywhere pomp and glory of which it is not possible to speak now in detail.

That is the tabernacle and its furniture as we see it in the sacred 6 books. And this is the divine service of the tabernacle. The outer tent is entered continually by the priests as they perform their various ministries. But the great ceremony takes place within the inner 7 shrine. Once and once only in the year, by himself alone, the high priest enters there. He carries blood. Blood is life, and on this great occasion no less significant a sacrificial act is admissible. He offers the blood, bringing it to the LORD at the mercy-seat where He has promised to be present; a living soul for the renewal of his own soul and for cleansing the LORD's people from those sins of popular ignorance for which their priest is so largely responsible. Yet why 8 should they be shut out? The Holy Spirit, through whom the written record of this institution comes to us, makes it particularly clear that the way to the inner mysteries has not yet been revealed to the common gaze; the outer tent still stands to hide it. But we 9 are meant to recognise in this outer tent a kind of premeditation of the change in these days of ours. The gifts and sacrifices of the old order are offered duly though they cannot bring the worshipper to

10 real communion with God. They are but part of an external system
of rules about eating and drinking and various ceremonial washings.
As ordinances of worship they are confined within the limits of
earthly ideas. But their significance springs from their transitory
claim. They have been appointed in expectation of a reformation
which inaugurates a new epoch.

1. μὲν οὖν might be taken together = "so then." But the strong
contrast Χριστὸς δὲ... in *v.* 12 requires μὲν to correspond to that long-
delayed δέ. If so, καὶ is rather superfluous: the emphasis is on the
predicative λατρείας, κοσμικόν, for which latter adj. cf. Tit. ii. 12.
Καὶ is omitted by B *al. pauc.* ℵ (vg) ℭ (boh) Orig.

ἡ πρώτη. The mass of mss. add σκηνή. But the simple ἡ πρώτη
of all the good authorities shews that "the first covenant" (as in
viii. 13) is meant.

τό τε ἅγιον. This or, less often, τὰ ἅγια = the outer tent, the
"Holy Place" in LXX. But in this ep. the plural is always used in
that sense. Is not this τὸ ἅγιον a neuter abstract = "its holiness"
(Intr. v. 5)? Cf. the confused rendering in d, *habuit autem et quidem
prior eius iustitia constitutionis cultura sanctum saecularem.*

2. Ἅγια. Not ἁγία, as the following ἡ λεγ. Ἅγια Ἁγίων shews.
B has τὰ ἅγια, and in next verse (with considerable support) τὰ ἅγια
τῶν ἁγίων. But B also inserts καὶ τὸ χρ. θυμιατήριον after ἄρτων,
omitting χρ. ἔχουσα θ. in *v.* 4. All these variations seem to arise
from a desire to harmonise ep. with LXX.

For the construction and furniture of the tabernacle, see Ex. xxv.—
xxvii., xxx. 1—10, xxxvi.—xl. But some details in the ep. are taken
from other places in O.T.; cf. especially Lev. xvi.

ἡ πρόθεσις τ. ἄρτων. Substituted, as better Greek, for the more
usual οἱ ἄ. τῆς προθέσεως.

τὸ δεύτερον καταπέτασμα. See Ex. xxvii. 16.

4. θυμιατήριον. So Aquila, Symmachus, Philo, Josephus, for
θυσιαστήριον (θυμιάματος) of LXX. This was outside the veil. But
when Aaron entered the Holy of Holies the cloud of incense penetrated to the Mercy-seat. Hence in Lev. xvi. 12 f. it is "before the
LORD," and is here said to "belong to" the Holy of Holies.

στάμνος, κ.τ.λ. Ex. xvi. 33; ἡ ῥάβδος Ἀαρὼν κ.τ.λ., Num. xvii. 10;
αἱ πλάκες κ.τ.λ., Ex. xxv. 16, Deut. xxxi. 26, 1 Kings viii. 9. The
manna and the rod are not mentioned in 1 Kings viii. Josephus,
Bell. v. 5. 5, says ἔκειτο δὲ οὐδὲν ὅλως ἐν αὐτῷ, ἄβατον δὲ καὶ ἀχραντον
καὶ ἀθέατον ἦν πᾶσιν, ἁγίου δὲ ἅγιον ἐκαλεῖτο. Cf. Tac. *H.* v. 9, *vacuam
sedem et inania arcana.* But the ep. refers to the tabernacle in the
wilderness, not to the temple and the later state of things.

5. Χερουβεὶν δόξης. A phrase formed by the author after the fashion of those Hebrew compounds in which the second noun concentrates attention upon the characteristic feature of the first, cf. Moulton, pp. 73 f. So Gen. i. 21 "bird of wing" (cf. Ps. lxviii. 13, where we should say "as a dove" in English). Here the glory is the presence of the LORD, Ex. xxv. 22, Num. vii. 89, Ez. xi. 22 f., xliii. 1—4. In tabernacle and builded temple the LORD "speaketh from between the cherubim," and " above Him stand the seraphim," Isa. vi. 2. In the temple of the universe (cf. Ps. xxix. 9), a more ancient conception, He dwells in the "thick darkness" of the storm, 1 Kings viii. 12; rides upon the cherubim, the angels of the wind; the seraphim, angels of fire and lightning, go before Him, Ps. xviii. 6—14, cf. *supr.* i. 7; the thunder is His voice, Ps. xviii. 13, Ex. xix. 19, Deut. iv. 12, cf. *infr.* xii. 19. For a beautiful refinement upon the ritual conception see Ps. xxii. 3.

περὶ ὧν...κατὰ μέρος. No doubt this simply means "I have no time or space to dwell on further details." Yet this earnest haste of the author does itself distinguish him from the allegorical school in which he had received some instruction, and with which (as he seems to acknowledge in v. 11) he had a certain sympathy. He refuses ἀκριβεύεσθαι περὶ τῆς σωτηρίας which in the allegorical Ep. Barn. (ii. 10) is considered necessary. "The writer of the Epistle... mentions the cherubim and the mercy-seat. Of these, he says, we cannot now speak particularly. Could any allegorist have resisted the temptation to speak most particularly on these subjects?" Maurice.

6 f. For the entrance of the priests, the sons of Aaron, see Ex. xxviii. 1, Num. xvi. 40, xviii. 3—7. For the yearly entrance of Aaron (the "high-priest" is hardly mentioned in the "Law") see Lev. xvi. and Ex. xxx. 10.

7. οὐ χωρὶς αἵματος. Cf. Lev. xvi. 14 ff., 18 f., with Lev. xvii. 11; Intr. III. 12, 13.

ἀγνοημάτων, cf. Ez. xlv. 20, Lev. iv. 2, 22, 27, and especially LXX of 13 ἀγνοήσῃ ἀκουσίως. Perhaps accidental uncleannesses rather than what we should call sins are primarily meant by this word. But v. 2 shows that our author has a deeper thought, and Lev. xvi. 16 justifies it.

8. Here, and in ix. 25, x. 19, xiii. 11, τὰ ἅγ. seems = "Holy of Holies." It is more likely that this reflects the usage of Lev. xvi. There after the full phrase, εἰς τὸ ἅγιον ἐσωτέρω τοῦ καταπετάσματος εἰς πρόσωπον τοῦ ἱλαστηρίου ὅ ἐστιν ἐπὶ τῆς κιβωτοῦ τοῦ μαρτυρίου, the brief τὸ ἅγιον is used inclusively of the whole tabernacle.

9. προσφέρονται like the perfect πεφανερῶσθαι is in accord

with the author's habit of beholding pictures in the sacred records,
standing as present things before his eyes: Intr. v. 3. Thus, again
(cf. viii. 4), no inference can be drawn from this passage as to the
date of the ep.

10. βαπτισμοῖς. Cf. vi. 2; σαρκὸς, cf. ii. 14, v. 7 and contrast
vi. 1 νεκρῶν ἔργων which does not refer to ritual.

δικαιώματα ℵABP 33 𝔖 (vg) ℭ (boh) 𝔄 Cyr. Euthal.ᶜᵒᵈ is the
well attested reading, not δικαίωμα nor δικαιώμασιν. Though B agrees
with the mass of Greek mss. in prefixing καί, the authorities for its
omission, ℵ*AD*P 33 𝔏 (vt) 𝔖 (vg) ℭ ℭᵗ𝔥 Orig. Cyr. Euthal.ᶜᵒᵈ, seem
sufficient. Both the insertion of καί and the alteration to δικαιώμασιν were meant to make the grammatical construction easier.
But δικαιώματα, in apposition to δῶρα, θυσίαι, gives a sense more
agreeable to the context. The author is concerned about the abolition
of the sacrifices rather than the petty rites and rules.

διορθώσεως. A medical word, used by Aristotle and later writers
in moral sense as here. Cf. Acts iii. 21. The next verse shews that
in one sense this "reformation" has already come. The primitive
and popular faith of the Church would look for it in the "day of the
Lord" (cf. x. 25, Apoc. i. 10), the great Advent still expected.
In this ep. a "critical moment[1]" is expected "to day," in which
"reformation," "new covenant," entrance into heaven (x. 19 ff.),
receiving of the kingdom (xii. 28), peace in union with the will
of God (x. 10, xiii. 21) may be realised by the readers for whose
encouragement in stress of trial their friend is writing.

IX. 11—14. The reality of life laid down to cleanse.

Such is the tabernacle of the Old Covenant and its ritual, splendid,
making no mean appeal to religious emotion, but unfit to fulfil that
new life for which conscience yearns.

11 But when, Levi fading, Christ came, as High Priest of the loving
mercies of God the only good, which found expression through the
tabernacle that has nought to do with ritual splendour or precision,
the tabernacle not made with hands, not of this ordinary earthly
12 building; then He cared no more about the figurative blood of beasts
than about the pomp of worship, but entered by the sacramental
virtue of His own blood, once for all, into the sanctuary: having
found, when all seemed lost upon the cross, such deliverance for
men as can be measured by no temporal standard, nor rendered
13 ineffectual by any limitations of material circumstance. It is a moral

---

[1] For καιρός see Trench, *New Testament Synonyms*, § LVII.

deliverance. Let it be acknowledged that the ritual observances do effect such cleansing as the use and wont of mere humanity demands. Here there is more than that; the "other world" breaks in. Our **14** Lord Jesus completes the long line of the Christs of history with all their filial yearnings towards the Father. He died willingly, lovingly, and His life thus consecrated really became what the Levitical theology defined "blood" to be, viz. life set free for the renewing of lives. As Aaron approached the mercy-seat enveloped in the cloud of incense, so the dear memory of our dying Lord is interfused with the mystery of the all-embracing Spirit who makes all life by His inspiration eternal and divine. So, an immaculate victim, He offered Himself to God. Such goodness is more intelligible than any analogy. It is our consciousness of God, who is above and through and in us all, that He died to restore, cleansing away the evil which is death to hide; so that, sharing in what He has made priestly service mean, we too may serve God who lives indeed.

11. γενομένων. This, the reading of BD* 𝔏 (vt) 𝔖 (vg. hl. pal.) Orig. Chr. (Aphr.), must be accepted, though Tisch., v. Sod., R.V. text prefer μελλόντων with אADᶜω 𝔏 (vg.) 𝔖 (hlᵐˢ) 𝕮 (boh) 𝔄 𝕮𝔱𝔥 Eus. Cyr-Hier. Chrᶜᵒᵈᵈ Cosm. ⅔ al. Doubtless the second group is strong. But the first may reasonably be interpreted as a consensus of all three ancient lines of transmission. And this is one of the few passages in which intrinsic probability is important in itself. As Rendall has pointed out, the construction is τῶν γενομένων...διὰ τῆς μείζονος κ.τ.λ. But even Westcott, who keeps γενομένων but translates "good things realised," has missed this piece of rather distinguished idiom. The correction to μελλόντων would therefore be obvious: cf. ii. 5, vi. 5, x. 1, xiii. 14. Nor did the difficulty arise entirely from the construction. Even with the right construing, the "good things" are said to have come already into being, and such sayings in N.T. have always proved hard: cf. Acts xv. 11, ἀλλὰ διὰ τῆς χάριτος τοῦ κυρίου Ἰησοῦ πιστεύομεν σωθῆναι καθ' ὅν τρόπον κἀκεῖνοι, where A.V. and R.V. "we believe that we shall be saved" is possible grammatically but improbable in the context. Here is in fact a test passage of the credibility of B joined with the great "Western" authorities and Origen.

ἀγαθῶν. Only here and x. 1 in true text of this ep., in which καλός and κρείττων are so frequent with their ideas of "nobility" and "superiority." From such passages as Mark x. 18, Luke xxiii. 50, Acts xi. 24, Rom. v. 7, 1 Pet. ii. 20, ἀγαθός would seem to imply goodness in the divine degree, which is goodness touched with affection.

κτίσεως. 𝔏 *creationis*, so R.V., but "there is no occasion to take κτίσις in any other sense than that in which κτίζειν is commonly applied to a city (3 Esdr. iv. 53) or to the tabernacle itself (Lev. xvi. 16)[1]." A.V. "building" does very well.

12. αἰωνίαν λύτρωσιν εὑράμενος. For αἰωνίαν, "in the eternal sphere," see note on v. 9. This is the only place in the ep. where λύτρωσις or any of its simple cognates occur. In ix. 15, xi. 35 we find the Pauline ἀπολύτρωσις, but hardly in Pauline sense. These words are an inheritance from O.T. through LXX, especially from the latter part of Isaiah, where they are mostly renderings of some form of the Hebrew *goel* = "avenger," and then more generally "rescuing with might." So Isa. lxiii. 4 ff.: ἡμέρα γὰρ ἀνταποδόσεως ἦλθεν αὐτοῖς, καὶ ἐνιαυτὸς λυτρώσεως πάρεστιν. καὶ ἐπέβλεψα, καὶ οὐκ ἦν βοηθός· καὶ προσενόησα, καὶ οὐθεὶς ἀντελαμβάνετο· καὶ ἐρρύσατο αὐτοὺς ὁ βραχίων μου, καὶ ὁ θυμός μου ἐπέστη. In Mark x. 45 = Matt. xx. 28 our Lord says that the Son of man came to be a servant and to give His life λύτρον ἀντὶ πολλῶν, which may shew that to Jewish ears these words implied "ransom" or "price[2]." Yet that saying too is part of the Isaianic language of deliverance: "I have given Egypt as thy ransom, Ethiopia and Seba for thee.. I have loved thee; therefore will I give men for thee, and peoples for thy life," Isa. xliii. 3 f. The mystery seems deeper when coordinated with John xv. 13, than when explained in terms of law or commerce. On the whole we may consider that the main idea in our author's mind is "deliverance" raised to sublimity by divine self-sacrifice. And this deliverance the Saviour "found." In the divine will it already was; not to be bought with a price, but an "ideal" which has now been realised in obedience, cf. v. 8. The aor. part. might be described as "of coincident action" (Moulton, p. 130 ff.), but it might also be said to represent the moment before εἰσῆλθεν just as τελειωθείς, προσαγορευθείς in v. 9 represent the moment after.

14. αἰωνίου. ἁγίου is read by ℵᶜD*P *al* 𝔏𝔖 (pal) 𝔊 (boh.) Did.½ Chr.½ *al*. The attestation of αἰωνίου is sufficient, and it suits the context. The thrice-repeated "eternal" (cf. *vv.* 12, 15) is set over against the "gold and glory" of the tabernacle. For the vast theological idea see Intr. III. 13, 29. "The Christ" offered Himself through the medium of that divine, essential life in which the whole spiritual movement issues from and returns to God—"When that which drew from out the boundless deep, Turns again home."

---

[1] Field, *Otium Norvicense*.
[2] Cf. Sanday and Headlam, *Commentary on Romans*, p. 86.

τὸ αἷμα τοῦ χριστοῦ. Intr. III. 12, 13.
καθαριεῖ. Cf. ii. 17. In the middle of this word Codex B is mutilated, and fails us for the rest of the ep.
συνείδησιν. A Pauline word; five times in this ep., cf. ix. 9, x. 2, 22, xiii. 18. Rom. ii. 15 shews conscience in its troubled, 1 Pet. ii. 19 in its cleansed and truly natural state, viz. the enjoyment of the presence of God. This state is perhaps less often remembered than the other. Hence a later reading in 1 Pet. ii. 19, σ. ἀγαθὴν for σ. θεοῦ, and R.V. as well as A.V. renders "conscience toward God," relegating "of God" to mg: the meaning rather is that because of his "consciousness of God," in communion with whom he is supported and at peace, a man can well bear injuries and injustice. The word, with its commoner equivalent in secular writers, τὸ συνειδός, has passed from this ep. into the Greek liturgies, wherein, as here, it lifts the mind to reality, and determines the true moral sense of such ritual terms as ἄμωμος. The whole passage, culminating in θεῷ ζῶντι, is artistically ordered to that end.

ἡμῶν. W. H. give ὑμῶν as mg. alternative, the attestation being strong on either side. In xiii. 21 a like variation is important; here the sense is hardly affected, but see Intr. v. 7.

νεκρῶν ἔργων. Cf. vi. 1 and Sirach xviii. 29 (cod. 248, see Hart, *Ecclesiasticus in Greek*, pp. 24, 146) κρείσσων παρρησία ἐν δεσπότῃ μόνῳ · ἤπερ νεκρᾷ καρδίᾳ νεκρῶν ἀντέχεσθαι.

IX. 15—22. TO LIFE THAT RENEWS LIFE DEATH IS
THE ONLY WAY.

And this life-renewing life can only be through death. That is 15 why in the new covenant Christ is a mediator between God who makes the covenant and men with whom God makes it. God dies not; but in Christ the mystery of life through death has been enacted. So the divine purpose is achieved. From the transgressions, by which (as we are told in Jeremiah) the first covenant was marred, deliverance has been and is still effected. So those who have heard the call of God to day may recognise in their clean conscience the fulfilment of the promise; the inheritance long waited for is theirs to take; the eternal inheritance of spiritual freedom.

The analogy of ancient custom points to the same truth. Where 16 there is a covenant, the death of him who makes it has to be represented. For the ritual of a covenant is that it must be confirmed

17 over slain victims; since the idea is that it avails not so long as he
who made the agreement lives.

18   Hence the first covenant too is recorded to have been inaugurated
19 not without blood. For when each commandment had been spoken,
in its proper place in the law which God gave at Sinai, by Moses to
the people, Moses took the blood of the calves and the goats with
water and scarlet wool and hyssop, and sprinkled both the book of
20 the covenant and all the people, saying, This is the blood of the
covenant which God ordained to establish his relationship with you.
21 And, to speak generally, it is in the touch of blood that all things
22 are cleansed according to that law, and without bloodshedding there
is no remission of legal offences.

15. διαθήκης. Cf. vii. 22, viii. 8. For the question whether
the author passes here from the meaning "covenant" to the
meaning "testament" see Intr. III. 16. The point may be left
doubtful. It is the sacrificial analogy that is affected by the alternative, not the deeper sense, viz. that our Lord laid down His life
for His friends, and that in no other way might the great salvation
be perfected.

16. τοῦ διαθεμένου. Cf. Luke xxii. 29, Acts iii. 25, Jer. xxxi.
(xxxviii.) 31, and Aristophanes, Av. 439; ἣν μὴ διάθωνταί γ᾽ οἵδε
διαθήκην ἐμοί, where the terms of the agreement follow, on oath.

17. ἐπεὶ μὴ τότε. So ℵ*D* Isid-Pelus. The other mss. have
ποτε. Blass says that in either case the sentence must be interrogative; "never" would be μηδέποτε or οὐδέποτε, 75. 3, App.
p. 332. But the μὴ might come under Goodwin's "cautious assertion" § 269 = "I am of the opinion that," or perhaps "the idea is."

19. See Ex. xxiv. 6—8, to which details are here added from
Lev. xiv. 4—7, Num. xix. 6, 17 f. So in v. 21 the sprinkling of
"all the vessels of the ministry" comes from the "law of Moses"
not from the particular narrative of the inauguration of the covenant.

The phrase ἔριον κόκκινον, which occurs nowhere in LXX, is found
in a curious compound quotation or reminiscence in Ep. Barn. vii.
about the scapegoat: καὶ ἐμπτύσατε πάντες καὶ κατακεντήσατε καὶ
περίθετε τὸ ἔριον τὸ κόκκινον περὶ τὴν κεφαλὴν αὐτοῦ καὶ οὕτως εἰς ἔρημον
βληθήτω.

22. αἱματεκχυσίας. Not found in LXX or profane authors.
It is a general word which includes the "shedding" as the necessary
and terrible preliminary to the "sprinkling"; cf. Matt. xxvi. 28,
Mark xiv. 24, Luke xxii. 20. This would suggest the thought of
the "precious blood," 1 Pet. i. 19; cf. Ps. cxv. (cxvi.) 6.

IX. 23—28. CHRIST IN HEAVEN, OUR REFUGE AND OUR HOPE.

It is therefore necessary that if the imitations of things heavenly 23 be cleansed by these means, the ultimate realities themselves should be cleansed by mightier than legal sacrifices. That necessity conducted Christ. For He entered no manufactured sanctuary, an echo 24 of the true, but penetrated that very heart of goodness which "heaven" symbolises, to be manifested now, before the face of God, in His compassionate divinity which is the refuge of us men. Nor did He purpose either to repeat that solemn act. He was not 25 going to offer Himself many times. The very idea of such repetition is paradoxical. There is no analogy here with the Aaronic high priest's entering the sanctuary year after year in the fiction of a blood-life not his own. If that were a true symbol, Christ must have 26. suffered many times in the long repetition of such rites; for ritual sacrifice is as old as the world. No; it is now and only now. At this moment which sums up and sweeps into desuetude the series of the ages, for the annulling of the sin which till now has obstinately held its ground, through the sacrifice of Himself, He has been seen of men and passed to God. And in as much as it is the spiritual 27 destiny of men once to die, and after death the discernment and separation of judgement; so also He, who as the Christ shares our 28 manhood and shall at last complete our hope, having once been taken to God that He might (like the prophetic servant of the LORD) take upon Himself the sins of many, shall in the sequel, separated from that burden of sin, be seen by those who are longingly expecting Him. And that vision shall be rescue from all ill.

23. κρείττοσι θυσίαις. For the pl. cf. xiii. 16, but the reference can hardly be the same. The pl. here is merely the antithesis, in a general statement, to τούτοις; in the particular application which immediately follows, the sacrifice by which the realities of heaven are cleansed is shown to be one and only one.

The cleansing of the heavenly realities might also be explained as a mere extension of the Levitical analogy. But from xii. 26 f. more would seem to be meant. Even the things of heaven shall be shaken. Even the saints at rest watch anxiously the issue of God's will on earth, cf. xii. 1 with xii. 23, also Ap. v. 11 f. with vii. 16 f. In heaven itself the intercession of the High Priest is still required, vii. 25, cf. ii. 18. As yet there is no place, however near to God, where His will is not working against opposition. Only within that will itself is peace **x. 10, xiii. 21.** The same idea is expressed in the Lord's Prayer, at least in the Greek form in which it has come to us; γενηθήτω τὸ θέλημά σου, ὡς ἐν οὐρανῷ καὶ ἐπὶ γῆς.

24. ἐμφανισθῆναι. In LXX of manifestation of God Ex. xxxiii. 13, 18, cf. ἐμφάνηθι Ps. lxxix. (lxxx.) 2, Zeph. ii. 11.

26. παθεῖν. See note on v. 8. Two cursives have ἀποθανεῖν here.

νυνί does not respond to ἐπεί = "now as things are," for the intensive form is not used in that sense. Both νυνί and νῦν in *v.* 24 refer to that act which to men is still visible in memory (πεφανέρωται, cf. Gal. iii. 1) as the crucifixion, while in eternity beyond the veil it was the manifestation of the consummated work of redemption (cf. *v.* 12). The νῦν, *v.* 24, is not quite logically appropriate. But "To day" rings too insistently in the author's ear for him to heed that. Moreover there is a sense in which loyal following of Christ brings the completed sacrifice "again" into present time, cf. xiii. 13, Intr. III. 21.

συντελείᾳ. Five times in Matthew (not elsewhere in N.T.) with sing. αἰῶνος: where, as in Dan. ix. 27, xii. 4, 13, it looks forward to the Messianic "end." Here it is rather different; the final age, in the successive periods of history, had been reached when the Lord died. Cf. i. 2, xi. 3.

27. μετὰ δὲ τοῦτο κρίσις. Cf. Box, *The Ezra-apocalypse*, pp. xlv f. "While the theology of S (that part of 2 Esdras which Mr Box calls the 'Salathiel-apocalypse') recognises the Day of Judgement and an intermediate state for the soul between death and Judgement, it knows of no resurrection of the body. In the description of the state of the soul after death it is made clear that the soul enters at once into a state of blessedness or the reverse....These conditions—though they will be intensified—are not to be essentially altered on the Day of Judgement itself. This practically means that judgement sets in immediately after death, and that a man's fate is virtually determined by the present life—which is the doctrine of Wisdom and of Hellenistic Judaism." Cf. xi. 40, xii. 23, but also vi. 2, xi. 35. Intr. III. 24, 25.

28. πολλῶν ἀνενεγκεῖν ἁμαρτίας. From Isa. liii. 12, cf. 1 Pet. ii. 24, also John i. 29. Elsewhere in this ep. ἀναφέρω is only used in sacrificial sense, but Rom. viii. 3, 2 Cor. v. 21, shew how the two meanings might run into one another.

ἐκ δευτέρου. Cf. Collects for I Advent, VI Epiphany "come again," "appear again." But that is not the usual N.T. conception, cf. Mark xiv. 61 f., Acts i. 11 (where a few MSS. add πάλιν); ἐκ δευτέρου ὀφθ. simply answers to ἅπαξ προσενεχθείς.

χωρὶς ἁμαρτίας. Cf. vii. 26.

τοῖς αὐτὸν ἀπεκδεχομένοις. Cf. Luke i. 21; but in Paul ἀπεκδ. is a strongly Messianic word, Rom. viii. 19, 23, 25, 1 Cor. i. 7, Gal. v. 5, Phil. iii. 20.

εἰς σωτηρίαν. Cf. ii. 3. σωτηρία is the whole of which redemption, cleansing, sacrifice, etc. are parts.

CHAPTER X

X. 1—18. THE WILL OF MAN UNITED TO THE WILL OF GOD THROUGH THE WILLING SACRIFICE OF CHRIST.

1   The Levitical Law carries with it an imaginary shadow of the good things which God purposed for man, not the consubstantial symbol which is a vehicle of the realities it symbolises. So year by year the sacrifices go on in monotonous succession. Men are ever approaching God, but are unable to reach by such merely ritual
2 means His very presence. If it were otherwise these sacrifices would have ceased, since they would have already brought about the desired result; the ritual cleansing of the worshippers would have passed once for all into spiritual cleansing, and they would no longer be let
3 and hindered by the consciousness of sins. But it is not so. There is some good in the ritual, especially of the Day of Atonement. It
4 awakes the sense of sins year after year. But it never passes into the eternal order, for bulls' and goats' blood cannot take sins away.
5   Wherefore, on His entrance into the created world, One whom we know saith: "Sacrifice and offering Thou wouldest not—a body didst
6 Thou prepare for me. In burnt-offerings and sin-offerings Thou
7 didst not take pleasure. Then said I, Lo, I am come—as in a written book my commission is recorded—to do, O God, Thy will."
8 In the first part of this quotation (which is so prophetically applicable to the Person and work of our Lord) the legal sacrifices are spoken of
9 as quite apart from the inmost mind of God. Then follows an answer to God's appeal which has abiding validity. The consent of Christ is in real correspondence with the will of God. Remove sacrifices: then God's will is established as the source and goal of salvation.
10 And God's will envelopes us with complete and permanent conse- cration, since Jesus, a man like us in the body, used these human limitations to realise His representative, inclusive Christship, and to make an offering to God through which, once for all, we are brought into God's very presence, i.e. into union with His good will.
11   This union of men's wills with God's will is the reality of which sacrifice is the figure. Priesthood in general is merely figurative.

We see priest after priest standing up in history and offering sacrifices, all of the same fictional, ineffective kind. The sacrifices are offered, and still sins bar the entrance. But this Priest of ours 12 offered one sacrifice for the continuous taking of sins out of the way. That was the real sacrifice of a will lost and found in God's will. And so it ensued that having offered it, He was enthroned in high 13 collateral glory at God's right hand; whence, as from the centre of life, He henceforth directs the process which shall at last be completed by the utter defeat of the powers of evil. That end is certain; 14 the one true sacrifice assures it, for that sacrifice has already brought perfection. And He has made those partakers of His own perfected holiness who in continual succession are called to realise their consecration in the school of life.

These reflections on the life and death of our Lord, as interpreted 15 by the experience of our hearts, are confirmed by the witness of the Holy Spirit in Scripture. For in the promise of the New Covenant 16 already quoted from Jeremiah, forgiveness of sins is the concluding assurance—"of their sins and of their iniquities I will have no more 17 remembrance at all." The peace of the Christian conscience answers to the promise of prophecy; and where such remission is effectual 18 there is no place for any further offering for sin.

1. σκιάν—εἰκόνα. Cf. viii. 5: εἰκὼν here, as in Col. i. 15, iii. 10 = Gen. i. 27, indicates a true type, symbol or sacrament, in which the visible actually partakes of the eternal reality signified. What the ep. implies throughout is here plainly said, that the Levitical rites, however they may furnish an analogy, are no "type" of the sacrifice of Christ; Intr. III. 5.

There is some uncertainty about the text of this verse, as will appear from the following conspectus of readings:

θυσίαις] *add.* αὐτῶν ℵP (𝔏 (vg.)) ἃς ℵCDωChr. *al.:* αἷς D* HL 5 263 442 456 *patres:* om. A 33 1908 ᕦ (vg. hl.) 𝔄 διηνεκὲς] *add.* αἱ Aᵃ 104 (ᕦ (hl.) 𝔄) δύνανται ℵACDᵇP 33 424** 436 442 1908 *al.* ᕦ (vg. hl.) 𝔄 Chr. *al.:* δύναται DHKL 5 326 *al. pauc.* 𝔏 (vt.ᵈʳ vg.) ℂ (boh.) Orig. Chr.

The v.l. δύναται makes a complete, but not so neat a sentence as we might desire, and textual authority points to its being an ancient attempt at emendation. We might be content to suppose that the author left the sentence unfinished with unconscious, or perhaps with deliberately rhetorical carelessness. But the other variations suggest further disorder. Hort proposed as the original text, καθ' ἣν κατ' ἐνιαυτὸν τὰς αὐτὰς θυσίας προσφέρουσιν αἱ εἰς τὸ διηνεκὲς οὐδέποτε δύνανται τοὺς προσερχομένους τελειῶσαι—, after which double relative the author will have broken off and begun a new sentence. The usage of the ep. is against connecting εἰς τὸ διηνεκὲς with a following verb, but its peculiarly emphatic position in the clause thus fashioned might meet that objection. On the other hand the accumulation, κατ' ἐνιαυ-τὸν ταῖς αὐταῖς θυσίαις...εἰς τὸ διηνεκές, is perhaps not so pointless as Hort felt; the printed text of W.H. is faithful to the actual evidence; the author may have written vigorously rather than beautifully here; and, if the ep. be regarded as a real letter, such a touch of roughness is acceptable.

τελειῶσαι. D has καθαρίσαι, the part for the whole; cf. next verse.

2. οὐκ. A few authorities omit this, as though the sentence were not interrogative, thereby bringing ἂν into an awkward position.

3. ἀνάμνησις. [Com]memoratio, Latt. But the Greek implies an awakening of mind rather than an external making of remembrance; cf. Clem. liii., ἐπίστασθε...εἰς ἀνάμνησιν οὖν ταῦτα γράφομεν. Here and elsewhere the author recognises a sympathetic influence in the old ceremonies which, as mere ceremonies, were shadows.

5. εἰσερχόμενος εἰς τὸν κόσμον. It is not of course meant that our Lord uttered these words at His birth or when He began His ministry. Nor need we suppose that our author thought the psalm was composed as a direct prediction of our Lord in the days of His flesh. But he did consider it a prophetic psalm, which expressed, by more than mere coincidence, the very mind of his Lord. He writes τὸν κόσμον, "the universe of natural law," not τὴν οἰκου-μένην, "the society of men"; there are no limitations in nature which are not transformed to instruments of the true freedom when a will in harmony with God's will operates.

λέγει. The unexpressed subject harmonises with the idea of the eternal, variously manifested Christ which pervades the ep. There is more in the quotation than a dramatic application of ancient words to the Lord's earthly circumstances ; cf. 1 Pet. i. 11.

The quotation is from Ps. xl. (xxxix.). It follows LXX, with εὐδόκησας for ἤτησας and τὸ θ. σου after instead of before ὁ θεός. That transposition gives the key, and removes the suspicion of unfaithful-ness which might be aroused by the adoption of the LXX "body" for the Hebrew . "ears." Ṣ (hl^mg) gives "ears," like Aquila and Symmachus. But though the author alludes to the word σῶμα in v. 10, the doctrine of that allusion permeates the ep., and does not depend on this quotation. And this particular word has nothing to do with the purpose for which he quotes the psalm. That purpose is to introduce the main subject of this section, Christ's union with the will of God and our union through Him in that same will.

6. περὶ ἁμαρτίας. A compound noun representing the Hebrew word for " sin-offering": cf. v. 1.

7. κεφαλίδι. Properly the *umbilicus* or horn of the rod round which the writing was rolled. But here and elsewhere in the LXX it is used for the roll itself. So we might say, " between the covers of a book." It is possible that the psalmist had no definite book in view, but meant simply, "my duty is as plain as if it were written down," cf. perhaps Ps. cxlix. 9. But Cheyne says, " To the psalmist, there was a Bible within the Bible, and the books of Deuteronomy and Jeremiah formed principal elements in its composition. 'The law within my heart' reminds us at once of Deut. vi. 6 and Jer. xv. 16, xxxi. 33."

9. τότε εἴρηκεν. τότε is part of the quotation: the perf. εἴρηκεν sums up the argument emphatically, as in i. 13. What the psalmist has said of old stands confirmed by the obedience of Christ: union in the will of God is consecration and perfection.

10. ἡγιασμένοι : the perfect corresponds to ἐφάπαξ. Whatever their subsequent failures, those who have entered upon the Christian allegiance are sanctified ; nothing but renunciation of their ἁγιασμός (cf. xii. 14) cancels that. In those early perilous times, entrance upon such allegiance could seldom be anything but a sincere act of will. But the thought here is deeper than that. The security is guaranteed by the greater will of God : cf. 1 John iii. 20.

11. ἱερεύς. This is to be read with 𝔭¹³ אD, not ἀρχιερεύς with AC. That, after ix. 7, might seem inconsistent with καθ᾽ ἡμέραν. Indeed, the view here may extend beyond the bounds of Judaism to all the ritual priesthood of the wide world: cf. v. 5. The history of religion —the satisfying of man's heart-restlessness for God—is here presented as a consistent whole. The cross is the focus. Thither all past yearning tends ; thence all new confidence proceeds. There a devotion of will is apparent which goes beyond all that even the analogy of sacrifice can picture. Yet the analogy is necessary, else language would be cold and loveless. Moreover sacrificial language brings the mystery home to the only men who will recognise the cogency of the argument of these verses, in which, considered as logic, too much is taken for granted. For in no other language can the relief of forgiveness be so movingly expressed.

περιελεῖν : cf. περίκειται, v. 2, and εὐπερίστατον, xii. 1. The word is precisely appropriate to the context so charged with yearning for freedom. Yet the author's instinct for rythm must have helped him to find it. Contrast ἀφαιρεῖν, v. 4, in both tense and prefix.

13. As in ch. i. the whole circle of the Incarnation and Redemption is contemplated in this paragraph about the Will. And, as there, all closes on the oracle from Ps. cx., which tells of exaltation to the throne in heaven, and then looks on to the great Advent; cf. 1 Cor. xv. 25.

14. τετελείωκεν...ἀγιαζομένους. As in Acts ii. 47 (τοὺς σωζο-μένους), the thought of progress in the Christian life is not excluded. But the argument of the ep. as a whole would lead us to recognise the succession of those who one after another in perpetuity (εἰς τὸ διηνεκές) are called: Introd. III. 18, 21. As there is one divine will and all wills freed in it, so there is one achieved perfection and each successive perfecting of men is by partaking in that one.

X. 19—25. THE VENTURE OF FAITH.

19 So then, brothers, argument ended, let us clinch it by action. We are emboldened to venture upon the way into the sanctuary, 20 spiritually united and vivified in the life-blood of Jesus. It is the way which He inaugurated for us, a way fresh-slain yet living, the way that leads through the veil into the inner shrine. But such figurative language obscures the heart-touching reality—it is the way of His flesh, the mystery of His union with us in the affections of suffering 21 manhood. And He who is the way is also the priest, the great priest prophetically descried, who mediates as elder brother over the family 22 of God. Let us then draw near with genuine affection in the full assurance which faith gives of spiritual truth. Our ritual is complete; and it is a ritual in which the eternal pervades and overflows the visible. We are sprinkled, and at the touch of the blood of life each heart has been purged of the consciousness of its own evil. The body too has been bathed for its sojourn here with water of sacra- 23 mental purity. Let us hold fast the confession of our hope, so that what we professed at baptism may not swerve in trial; nor shall it, for faithful is the Master to whose promise our confession answered. 24 And let us study one another for the provocation of mutual love and 25 emulation in noble deeds; not neglecting the closer fellowship which comes from common worship—nay, sirs, such manners are not good —but rather contributing encouragement, and so much the more as ye behold the Day drawing nearer, that Day of the Lord, on which the hope of our confession was concentrated.

19. ἀδελφοί. As in iii. 1 exhortation is deepened by the sense of intimacy (cf. xiii. 22) and fellowship. So ἐν αἵματι instead of διὰ (ix. 12), and the encouragement of united worship in *v.* 25.

20. τοῦτ᾽ ἔστιν τῆς σαρκὸς αὐτοῦ. The Greek liturgies and almost all readers of the ep. understand this to refer to "the veil":

> "Onely this veyle which thou hast broke
> And must be broken yet in me,
> This veyle I say is all the cloke
> And cloud which shadows me from thee."
>
> H. VAUGHAN, *Cockcrowing.*

But Westcott, after considering all the legitimate senses which such an expression might bear, says, "it remains surprising that 'the flesh' of Christ should be treated in any way as a veil, an obstacle, to the vision of God in a place where stress is laid on His humanity (ἐν τῷ αἵματι Ἰησοῦ)." He therefore prefers, with Tyndale, Coverdale, the Great Bible and the Geneva Bible, to take τῆς σαρκὸς αὐτοῦ as gen. after ὁδόν: "By the new and living way which he hath prepared for us through the veil, that is to say by his flesh." Such emphatic final genitives are not uncommon; see e.g. xii. 11, Acts iv. 33, James ii. 1, and Luke ii. 14, where Origen considered that εὐδοκίας might be construed with εἰρήνη. Moreover the repetition εἴσοδον... ὁδόν, and the epithet πρόσφατον (which may have been supposed by the author to mean properly "fresh-slain") in antithesis to ζῶσαν, combine to keep the idea of "way" prominent throughout the sentence. The "common-sense" of readers is against this, and it is possible that Westcott, with the more exact expressions of S. John in his mind, has been needlessly offended by a verbal inconsistency in this author, who strikes out a first sketch of the sacramental language elaborated by S. John. That is possible but improbable; the subtle nicety of the author's phraseology and the sanity of Westcott's judgement grow upon the patient reader: Intr. III. 15.

21. ἱερέα...τοῦ θεοῦ. A reference, as in iii. 1, to Num. xii., but combined by ἱερέα μέγαν with the deep theology of Zech. vi. 11 ff.

22. ἀπὸ συνειδήσεως π. The prep. is recognised as natural when it is remembered that συνείδησις has not yet taken the definite modern sense: it is still a state rather than a part of mind.

λελουσμένοι. Washing the body is a natural symbol of inner washing, as has probably been always felt; cf. Aesch. fr. 32, καλοῖσι λούτροις ἐκλελουμένος δέμας | εἰς ὑψίκρημνον Ἱμέραν ἀφικόμην. But no doubt there is an allusion here to baptism, which throughout Acts and Epistles fills so much of the background: cf. Joh. xiii. 10. In the whole sentence we have an example of what Bengel rather loosely calls "chiasmus," and says is the characteristic figure of the epistle. Προσερχώμεθα, ρεραντισμένοι, τὸ σῶμα, ὕδατι, are the more metaphorical or visual terms ; καρδίας, συνειδήσεως, λελουσμένοι, καθαρῷ touch the spirit more directly. The antithetical weaving of the sentence draws the attention inward and onward to the unseen : ''Let us draw near, but to the unseen shrine of faith ; let us use ritual, but the simplest, the most cleansing ; let us rejoice in our baptism, but remembering that baptism is the appeal of conscience to God,'' cf. 1 Pet. iii. 21, 1 John iii. 19 f. We might say that the washing is general symbolism, but the associated thought of baptism gives further point as in Shakespeare, *H. V,* i. 2, '' That what you speak is in your conscience wash'd As pure as sin with baptism.'' It is possible to imagine another connexion between these two clauses, viz. that while λελουσμένοι points to baptism, ρεραντισμένοι points to the chalice of the Blood of Christ. The reader must consider whether or no such interpretation fits the whole context of the epistle ; Intr. ii. 4, iii. 21. For the ritual and moral significance of ρεραντισμένοι see Hort's thorough and profound examination into the nse of ραντισμὸν αἵματος I. X., 1 Pet. i. 2. He shows that '' The sprinkling of blood on the altar is represented by the sacrifice of the Cross...the virtue of which proceeded from nothing cognisable by the outward senses, but from the inner yielding up of the very life for the sake of men at the Father's will '' ; that '' Obedience was the form of moral good which the preparatory dispensation of law could best teach. Under the higher dispensation of grace it lost none of its necessity : the sprinkled blood enlarged its scope, while it filled it with a new spirit and sustained it with a new power '' ; and that to S. Peter and the seer of the Apocalypse '' The blood of martyrdom was in some sense comprehended in 'the blood of the Lamb,' of Him who is called 'the faithful Witness,' or Martyr.''

The punctuation might be made after πονηρᾶς. But apart from the considerations touched upon above, the abrupt commencement κατέχωμεν, κ.τ.λ. is quite in the manner of our author: Intr. v. 8.

23.   ἐλπίδος. ''Faith '' of A.V. was not found in earlier versions and is without authority. The mistake has affected A.V. heading. The slip was easy : in cod. armach. of vg. *fidei* was written and afterwards corrected to *spei* in vi. 11.

24.   παροξυσμὸν ἀγάπης. Such paradoxes are not unfrequent in N.T. ; cf. Mark iii. 5, 1 Thess. iv. 11 ; also Clem. R. lviii and lxii, ἐκτενὴς ἐπιείκεια. So in 2 Cor. iii. 17 the Bishop of Ely would read, οὗ δὲ τὸ πνεῦμα κυριεύει, ἐλευθερία, *JTS*, Oct. 1915.

25.   ἐπισυναγωγήν. In 2 Thess. ii. 1 of joining Christ in the

day of coming. And here, as in *Didache* xvi, gathering for worship
is connected with that hope. The common worship is preparation
for, even a sacrament of, the gathering together of all in Christ.
And this the more evidently because here Christ's immediate coming
in the crisis of the time is especially in view.

X. 26—31. IN GOSPEL TRUTH NO SUBTERFUGE FOR SIN.

Away with fastidious hesitation; the coming trial is of tremendous 26
import. For there is no more question of sins of inadvertence as in
the old Law; nay the whole of that old Law with its technical sin-
offerings is gone by. If we now persist in wilful sin after receiving
the knowledge which discerns real instead of conventional truth,
nought remains but an expectation of judgement, the more fearful for 27
our incapacity of defining it in terms of human imagination—it is
what the prophet meant when he told how God had predestined
"a fierce jealousy of fire to eat up His adversaries." Do not be
adversaries of God. When a man has set Moses' Law at nought, he 28
is out of reach of all human pity; "on the evidence of two or three
witnesses," we read, "he dies." How much worse, think ye, shall 29
be the estimate of his penalty who shall have trampled on the Son
of God, and accounted as a vile thing the Blood of the Covenant in
which he received his consecration to our Lord's service, and shall
have insolently used the Spirit who breathes God's grace? Argument 30
is needless; we know without telling Him who said, "Judgement is
mine, I will repay": and again, "The LORD will vindicate his own
people." It is a fearful thing to fall into the hands of God, the 31
living One.

26. ἐπίγνωσιν = knowledge; not in the abstract, but directed
towards a particular object. See Robinson, *Ephesians*, pp. 248—254;
and cf. John i. 17.

οὐκέτι...θυσία. Like vi. 4 ff., xii. 17, this almost appears to
contradict the doctrine of the forgiveness of sins. Yet closer examination shews that "sacrifice for sins" is an O.T. term, and that
the latter half of the verse is but a repetition of *v.* 18. What
does "remain" is indeed fearful. Here, as elsewhere, the ruin
involved in a base choice at the crisis with which the readers are
confronted is emphatically stated. Yet such ruin is too mysterious
to be humanly defined: hence the τις. As in 2 Tim. iv. 14, O.T.
language is quoted (Isa. xxvi. 11, LXX) to adumbrate what the
author presumes not to explain. And in all such fears or threats
S. Paul's principle (1 Cor. v. 5) is presupposed: Intr. III. 20.

28. ἐπὶ δυσὶν...ἀποθνήσκει. From Deut. xvii. 6. The curious addition in D𝕃 (vt.ⁿᵒⁿ ʳ) 𝔖 (hl.*) καὶ δακρύων after οἰκτιρμῶν, may be a modified reminiscence of a phrase in the same section of Deut., xiii. 8.

29. τὸ αἷμα τ. διαθήκης. From Ex. xxiv, as in ix. 20, but here raised to a higher power by the preceding " Son of God."

τὸ πνεῦμα τῆς χάριτος. The following reff. will shew how difficult it is for us, accustomed to the developed language of Trinitarian doctrine, to appreciate the delicate shades of meaning that attach to combinations of πν. with other words in N.T., Rom. viii. 15 cf. 1 John iv. 6, 1 Cor. ii. 12, 2 Cor. iv. 13, Eph. i. 13, 2 Thess. ii. 8. But it must be remembered that a heritage of Jewish thought made the personal conception of Spirit more natural than any vague idea of influence : Intr. III. 29.

" The grace " is the gift of new life which Christians received, not merely in general, but with special intensity for meeting their several trials. The Spirit of this grace is, from one point of view, the " breath " of God who brings the grace (cf. John xx. 22 f.) : from another, the breath of new life within springing from this grace.

30. ἐμοὶ ἐκδίκησις...κρινεῖ Κύριος. Quoted from Deut. xxxii. 35 f. The second sentence agrees with LXX, the former does not. But it corresponds exactly with a quotation of the same four words in Rom. xii. 19, and it represents the Hebrew fairly. Since it agrees with the Targum of Onkelos still more closely, we cannot certainly infer that the author remembered S. Paul's words when he wrote this verse, as is likely however, since the Pauline faith-text follows almost immediately in *v.* 37 ; cf. xi. 33, where there seems to be a reminiscence, not of the LXX of Daniel, but of some version which re-appears in Theodotion. More interesting is S. Paul's purpose in quoting. He gives the words the meaning they bear in the original context : God's people may be secure, for He will judge between them and their enemies. Our author seems to give them a precisely opposite meaning. Yet if the choice before his readers was between a false patriotism and "in quietness and confidence shall be your strength," the original intention of the sentence would presently recur to them.

X. 32—39. First Love an Education for the Supreme
Venture of Faith.

And call to mind the early days when, freshly enlightened by the 32
Dayspring of the Gospel, you faced like stout athletes much trial
of sufferings. On the one hand you were then a spectacle to the 33
populace by the insults and afflictions you endured; on the other
hand this gave you the assurance that you had really been made
comrades of the men whose chosen lot was a life like that. Your 34
comradeship you shewed by compassion towards our brothers in
prison; your own hardship you transformed by accepting the seizure
of your property with joy, recognising in your new knowledge that
so long as you were masters of yourselves you had a better possession
than material wealth, and a possession that abides. Do not then 35
cast off that daring mood which so became you then and is now
designed to reap a plenteous harvest. For brave endurance is what 36
the times now call for, in order that you may do the duty which
God wills and then carry home what the prophets have proclaimed.
For there is yet but "a very little while." He (thus we may render 37
the dim early oracle precise to day), He who "cometh shall come
and shall not delay. And to my righteous servant life shall spring 38
from faith." Yet there is another verse on another note: "If he
shrink back my soul hath no pleasure in him." Well, as for us, we 39
have nothing to do with shrinking back to ruin; our calling is the
faith that ventures all for a life in harmony with God's over-ruling of
the adverse world.

32. φωτισθέντες, cf. vi. 4. The reading of ℵ*, ἁμαρτίας ὑμῶν for
ἡμέρας, looks like a " western " audacity prompted by the idea of
baptism; cf. Rom. v. 8.

33. ἄθλησιν...θεατριζόμενοι. These metaphors are so like what
Clement (vi) says of the martyrdoms under Nero at Rome that they
seem to point to Roman Christians as the recipients of the letter.
But they are bookish metaphors (cf. xii. 1 f.), and the author may
possibly have S. Paul's phrase, 1 Cor. iv. 9, in mind. In D* ὀνει-
διζόμενοι stands instead of θ., which shews that the Neronian allusion
was not obvious in early days.

34. τοῖς δεσμίοις. Here the v. ll. ³⁴ δεσμίοις 𝔭¹³ AD*H 33
424** 442 1908 al. 𝔏 (vg.) 𝔖 (vg. hl.) 𝕮 (boh.) 𝕬 Chr. al.:
τοῖς δεσμοῖς μου ℵDᶜω𝔏 (vt.) 𝕮th Clem., Orig.ᶜᵒᵈ.: τοῖς δεσμοῖς
Orig.ᶜᵒᵈ.*: uinculorum tormenta 𝔏 (vt.ʳ) suggest that τοῖς δεσμοῖς
μου arose from an earlier mistake δεσμοῖς for δεσμίοις. Once ad-

mitted, τοῖς δεσμοῖς μου became an argument for Pauline authorship; cf. Phil. i. 7, 13 f., 17, Col. iv. 18, Philem. 10, 2 Tim. ii. 9; Intr. II. 2. The parallel to the true reading is xiii. 3 *infra*.

ἑαυτούς. ἑαυτοὺς 𝔭¹³ ℵAH *al. pauc.* 𝕷 ℭ (boh.) Clem. (Orig.) Cosm. ⅔ Euthal.*cod. al.* : ἑαυτοῖς D *al.* Chr. *al.* : ἐν ἑαυτοῖς *minusc. pauc.* ὕπαρξιν *sine additam.* 𝔭¹³ ℵ*AD*H* 33 𝕷 ℭ (boh.) ℭ𝔥 Clem. Orig. : *add.* ἐν οὐρανοῖς ℵᶜDᶜH**ω💲 (vg. hl.) 𝕬 Chr. Euthal.*cod.* Cosm. ⅔ *al.* Here again early corruption has marred the freshness of the thought, with which cf. Luke xxi. 19. Once the private will has been lost and found in God's will (x. 10), the self or soul is infinite riches. The addition of ἐν οὐρανοῖς imports an idea of future recompense which is quite alien to the context.

For a theological comment on the value of "self" see 2 Cor. xiii. 5, ἦ οὐκ ἐπιγινώσκετε ἑαυτοὺς ὅτι Ἰησοῦς Χριστὸς ἐν ὑμῖν; and Maurice's pathetic explanation of this to his troubled mother (*Life*, I. ch. xi) "...The truth is that every man is in Christ; the condemnation of every man is that he will not own the truth; he will not *act* as if this were *true*, he will not believe that which is the truth, that, except he were joined to Christ, he could not think, breathe, live a single hour....Separate from Christ, I can bear no fruit to God. Separate from Christ, I am separate from every one of my brethren...."

And cf. the language of Themistocles after Salamis : εὕρημα γὰρ εὑρήκαμεν ἡμέας τε αὐτοὺς καὶ τὴν Ἑλλάδα, νέφος τοσοῦτον ἀνθρώπων ἀνωσάμενοι...τάδε γὰρ οὐκ ἡμεῖς κατεργασάμεθα, ἀλλὰ θεοί τε καὶ ἥρωες, Hdt. viii. 109.

35. μὴ ἀποβάλητε. Field writes: "A.V. 'Cast not away....' The rendering of the Vulgate is *Nolite amittere*, which is the more common meaning of the word, 'Lose not, let not go,' the opposite of which is κατασχεῖν τὴν π. (ch. iii. 6)." He gives quotations which are highly illustrative of this ep.: δέδοικα μὴ τέλεως ἀποβάλητε τὴν παρρησίαν, Dio Chrys. *Or.* xxxiv. p. 425 ; νῦν δὲ τοῦ πλείονος ὀρεγόμενοι, καὶ τὴν τῆς προτέρας νίκης δόξαν ἀπέβαλον, Dion. Hal. *Ant.* viii. 86.

37. ἔτι γάρ. 𝔭¹³ omits γάρ, thus producing a vigorous abruptness as in *v.* 23.

The quotation is from Hab. ii. 3 f., introduced by a phrase from Is. xxvi. 20, another "advent" passage. The clause, ἐὰν ὑποστεί-ληται κ.τ.λ., precedes ὁ δὲ δίκαιος κ.τ.λ. in Hab. Here it is postponed to *v.* 38, and further emphasised by the prefixed καί. As here, so in LXX, there is some uncertainty about the insertion and position of μου. But what is important is the author's bold addition of ὁ to ἐρχόμενος, by which he adapts O.T. language to the Church's expectation of the coming of Christ. In LXX ἐρχ. ἥξει represents the emphatic Hebrew "shall indeed come"; who shall come, is left mysteriously vague. In the Hebrew it is "the vision" that comes. Thus Hebrew, LXX, and ep. represent three stages in Messianic thought, corresponding to the three periods to which they belong.

39. περιποίησιν. Cf. 1 Thess. v. 9, 2 Thess. ii. 14, both "advent" contexts. The noun seems a late formation from περιποιέω, cf. 1 Pet. ii. 9 with LXX of Isa. xliii. 21, Mal. iii. 17; also Plat. *Def.* 415, σωτηρία π. ἀβλαβής, and Haggai ii. 9, εἰρήνην ψυχῆς εἰς περιποίησιν. It is difficult to avoid recognising a reference to the saying of our Lord which in Luke xvii. 33 takes the form, ὃς ἐὰν ζητήσῃ τὴν ψυχὴν αὐτοῦ περιποιήσασθαι ἀπολέσει αὐτήν, ὃς δ᾽ ἂν ἀπολέσει ζωογονήσει αὐτήν. (Cf. Acts xx. 28, the only other place in N.T. except 1 Tim. iii. 13 where this verb is used.) In Luke too the context is an "advent" prophecy; but the verb seems to have been difficult to coarser understandings and in the later text became σῶσαι. Nor does the noun occur in N.T. except in the passages already referred to, and Eph. i. 14, εἰς ἀπολύτρωσιν τῆς περιποιήσεως, a difficult phrase which the Dean of Wells explains (as in 1 Pet. ii. 9) from the concrete idea of LXX; "that ultimate emancipation by which God shall claim us finally as His 'peculiar treasure.'" Westcott[1] however sees a larger promise in τῆς π.—"all that which God has made His own in earth and heaven, not men only who had fallen from Him, and earth which had shared the consequences of man's fall, but all created things, gathered together in the last crisis of their history...God in His infinite patience and love wins His creatures to Himself...The thought is of the complete fulfilment of God's purpose." This appears to suit the general character of Ephesians and the absolute use of π. in that verse. In our passage there is a difference; π. has changed position, and gaining the grammatical government of the phrase has lost its principality in the idea. Here the emphasis is on ψυχῆς, and the interest is in that process or crisis of life by which the "soul" reaches freedom. "A living being has a body; the soul takes possession of it and without intermediary has objectified itself in it. The human soul has much to do, before it makes its corporeal nature into a means. Man must, as it were, take possession of his body, so that it may be an instrument of his soul[2]." The author desires that his friends may so truly get possession of their souls that they may become masters of the circumstances which endanger them. They are to "come to themselves"; to realise the true harmony between the ideal of the Christian calling, and the difficulties pre-

---

[1] *St Paul's Epistle to the Ephesians*, Macmillan, 1906.
[2] *The Logic of Hegel*, transl. W. Wallace, § 208, cf. § 216.

sented by the seeming, external necessity of taking a lower choice. When this friction shall be serenely accepted as the divinely fit means of destined advance (cf. $\phi\epsilon\rho\omega\mu\epsilon\theta\alpha$, vi. 1) they will have entered upon "possession of soul," which is the happy state of faith, consequent upon the venture of faith.

CHAPTER XI

XI. 1—3. Faith and the Eternal Order.

And, let men say what they will, there is such a power as faith. 1
It is the heart of hope; it sifts fancy from reality when we reach into
the unseen. Faith is; for in the impulse and strength of faith alone 2
did the men of old time win their place in the roll of scripture heroes.
It is by faith that we get intelligence to comprehend how the ages 3
have been adjusted and re-adjusted by God's decree, so that we may
not think that the course of history has come about from the surface
play of passions and accidents.

For this description of faith see Intr. III. 33, v. 11. Add these
quotations from Windisch:

ἡ πίστις τοίνυν ἐστὶν ὄψις τῶν ἀδήλων, φησί, καὶ εἰς τὴν αὐτὴν τοῖς
ὁρωμένοις φέρει πληροφορίαν τὰ μὴ ὁρώμενα...ἐπειδὴ γὰρ τὰ ἐν ἐλπίδι
ἀνυπόστατα εἶναι δοκεῖ, ἡ πίστις ὑπόστασιν αὐτοῖς χαρίζεται· μᾶλλον
δὲ οὐ χαρίζεται, ἀλλ᾽ αὐτό ἐστιν οὐσία αὐτῶν, Chrysostom, t. xiii.
p. 197ᵃ·ᵇ.

διὸ καὶ πιστεῦσαι λέγεται τῷ θεῷ πρῶτος (sc. Ἀβραάμ), ἐπειδὴ καὶ
πρῶτος ἀκλινῆ καὶ βεβαίαν ἔσχεν ὑπόληψιν, ὡς ἔστιν ἐν αἴτιον τὸ ἀνω-
τάτω καὶ προνοεῖ τοῦ τε κόσμου καὶ τῶν ἐν αὐτῷ, Philo, de virt. 216,
p. 442.

μόνον οὖν ἀψευδὲς καὶ βέβαιον ἀγαθὸν ἡ πρὸς θεὸν πίστις...πλήρωμα
χρηστῶν ἐλπίδων...ψυχῆς ἐν ἅπασι βελτίωσις ἐπερηρεισμένης καὶ ἐφιδρυ-
μένης τῷ πάντων αἰτίῳ καὶ δυναμένῳ μὲν πάντα, βουλομένῳ δὲ τὰ
ἄριστα, Philo, de Abr. 268, p. 39.

Add also Coleridge, Aids, Moral and Relig. Aph. xii., "in all finite
quantity there is an infinite, in all measure of time an eternal; and
the latter are the basis, the substance, the true and abiding reality of
the former."

And Pindar, Ol. i. 28 ff., glancing half cynically, yet with an
artist's reservation, at the uncertainty of faith, has coincidences
with the language of the epistle:

ἦ θαυματὰ πολλά, καί πού τι καὶ βροτῶν φάτιν ὑπὲρ τὸν ἀλαθῆ
λόγον

δεδαιδαλμένοι ψεύδεσι ποικίλοις ἐξαπατῶντι μῦθοι.
χάρις δ', ἅπερ ἅπαντα τεύχει τὰ μείλιχα θνατοῖς,
ἐπιφέροισα τιμὰν καὶ ἅπιστον ἐμήσατο πιστὸν
ἔμμεναι τὸ πολλάκις·
ἁμέραι δ' ἐπίλοιποι
μάρτυρες σοφώτατοι.

1. ἔστιν, emphatic; the reality of faith rather than its definition
is insisted upon. Hence the following γάρ.

πραγμάτων, the order in ɰ¹³, πραγμάτων ἀπόστασις (sic) shews that
this word was read sometimes in the first clause. The rythm of the
true text seems better. So does the sense, for unless πρ. be taken in
the vaguest sense, it scarcely fits ἐλπιζομένων. Faith gives subsistence
to any hope, existence to invisible fact.

For ὑπόστασις see notes on i. 3, iii. 14. Ἔλεγχος is the "test"
or "trial" which shews a thing as it really is. Windisch quotes
from Epictetus, *Dissert.* iii. 10, 11, ἐνθάδ' ὁ ἔλεγχος τοῦ πράγματος, ἡ
δοκιμασία τοῦ φιλοσοφοῦντος. There it means the "account" which is
given in answer to this trial: so Socrates in his *Apologia* (39 c) said
that the Athenians would find, when he was gone, others to try or
expose their true characters with less sympathy than he had shewn
(οἱ ἐλέγχοντες), and that they vainly expected to escape "giving
account" (τοῦ διδόναι ἔλεγχον τοῦ βίου). A.V. "evidence" is almost
a confusion of the two senses. "Test" seems to suit the context
here.

2. ταύτῃ. αὐτῇ ɰ¹³ and two cursives; the same variation is found
at xii. 15 where ɰ¹³ seems again to be in group that gives αὐτῆς. Is
this the quietude of an Alexandrian corrector (Intr. ɪᴠ. 2)? Or did the
author himself throw the stress on the verb, ἐμαρτυρήθησαν, rather
than the pronoun? This verb is a striking one, and with its cognate
noun gathers deeper meaning as the argument proceeds; cf. xi. 39,
note.

3. αἰῶνας: cf. i. 2. The ref. is primarily to the creation, Gen. i.
But with this word the author takes a wider sweep. The idea of time
in αἰῶνας—"ages" not "worlds"—is extended into faith in the
growing process of God's already perfect will, cf. x. 10. Thus moral
purpose enters creation. To the first readers of the ep. their own
troubled days appeared disorderly. Their friend's faith, seeing life
steadily and whole, perceived the divine continuity of history.

φαινομένων: our borrowed word *phenomena* just expresses the
meaning. Blass, 75. 7, says μὴ ἐκ here = ἐκ μή, according to a
usage of good Greek, early and late. But it is more forcible to
construe μή with γεγονέναι, a perf. inf. which attracts the weight of

the sentence to itself; Goodwin, § 109. The result of intelligent faith is the conviction that "nullity and transitoriness constitute only the superficial features and not the essence of the world[1]." Blass quotes the parallel in 2 Macc. vii. 28, ὅτι οὐκ ἐξ ὄντων ἐποίησεν αὐτὰ ὁ θεός. Readers of Philo will notice how often this chapter seems to be connected with his writings. But the coincidences with the Maccabean books are quite as remarkable. With Philo a general community of thought and language is all that can be asserted. Intr. III. 32, 33.

XI. 4—16. FAITH AND THE PATRIARCHS.

"Still far beyond the range of actual touch, historical sympathy sets the individual amid a kindred of great names." Wallace.

By faith Abel offered to God a more abundant sacrifice than Cain, 4 and through that sacrifice he received witness of his righteousness, God himself witnessing to the rightness of his gifts; and through the sequel of the sacrifice he died and yet still speaketh.

By faith Enoch was taken away so as not to see death; he was 5 not found, says the Scripture, for God took him. God took him because He had pleasure in him, for before he was taken the witness is recorded that "he hath pleased God." Apart from faith it is im- 6 possible to please; for he who cometh to God's presence must by an act of faith decide that God is, and that to those who diligently seek Him He proves a good paymaster in affection.

By faith Noah received oracular warning of events not yet in 7 sight; he reverently heeded it, and prepared an ark for salvation, his family's salvation. Thus he openly condemned the opinion of the vulgar world, and became heir of the righteousness which developes along the line of faith.

By faith Abraham obeyed the call, while it was yet in his ears, to 8 go forth to a place which he was destined to receive as an inheritance; and he went not knowing whither. By faith he entered like a 9 sojourner into a foreign land; but it was indeed the home-land where the divine promise would realise itself. He came as a sojourner vowed to the life of tents, with Isaac and Jacob who were associated with him in the succession of the same promise; a sojourner in tents, for he looked away from earth to the city that hath firm foundations, 10 whose designer and creator is God.

By faith too Sarah herself (doubter though she seemed) was 11 invigorated for the seed-sowing even when past the seasonable age,

---

[1] Hegel, *Logic*, Wallace, p. 234, cf. *supr.* i. 10 ff.

12 since she did account Him faithful that promised. And so, from
one man, from a man as good as dead, were born children like
the stars of the sky in multitude and as the sand on the sea-shore
which is innumerable.

13   On the journey of faith these patriarchs all died; they did not
come home with the promises, but they saw them on the far horizon
and greeted them, and confessed they were strangers and pilgrims on
14 earth. "On earth"; for those who use that form of creed make
15 manifest their search after a native land beyond. And if they had
been merely re-awakening the memory of that land from which
they came forth, they would have had opportunity to retrace their
16 steps.   But now, you see, they are yearning for the better land,
that is the high heavenly one. And therefore infinite God is not
ashamed to answer to the homely title of "their God"; for He
prepared, for them, a city.

4. πλείονα. A picturesque epithet which lent itself to the author's
weakness for alliteration.

Hort's judgment on the readings of the clause μαρτυροῦντος ..τοῦ
θεοῦ—αὐτοῦ τοῦ θεοῦ ℵ° Dᶜ ω 𝕷 (vt.ʳ vg.) 𝕾 (vg. hl.) ℭ (boh.) 𝕬 Orig.
Chr. *al.*: αὐτῷ τοῦ θεοῦ 𝔭¹³ Clem.: αὐτοῦ τῷ θεῷ ℵ* AD* 33?
ℭ𝔱𝔥 Euthal.ᶜᵒᵈ· *—was that "the reading of the best MSS. (αὐτοῦ
τοῦ θεοῦ) is apparently a primitive error, due to mechanical permu-
tation, the true reading being that which Clem. alone has preserved." That reading is now supported by 𝔭¹³. Yet Gen. iv. 4 might
perhaps have justified the emphasis laid by αὐτοῦ on God's "own"
witness.

λαλεῖ: so 𝔭¹³ ℵA etc.; λαλεῖται Dω𝕷 (vt.ᵈ) ℭ𝔱𝔥 is the textus
receptus. Perhaps the influence of the Vulgate saved our A.V. from
such a jejune sentiment. "Immortality! Not here in human remembrance"; cf. Phil. *Quod det pot.*, p. 200, ὁ Ἅβελ, τὸ παρα-
δοξότατον, ἀνῄρηταί τε καὶ ζῇ. The pass. is rare; in this sense of a
person being spoken about, perhaps unparalleled; of the mid. there
seems to be no example.

5. μετετέθη. L. *translatus est.* Gen. v. 24 has καὶ εὐηρέστησεν
Ἐνὼχ τῷ θεῷ· καὶ οὐχ εὑρίσκετο ὅτι μετέθηκεν αὐτὸν ὁ θεός, which might
describe a calm and holy death. Wisd. iv. 10 is as reticent, unless
the part. be restricted in connexion to the verb, καὶ ζῶν μεταξὺ ἁμαρτωλῶν μ. Nor is Sirach xliv. 16 different, but in xlix. 14 something
miraculous is implied, οὐδὲ εἷς ἐκτίσθη οἷος Ἐνὼχ τοιοῦτος ἐπὶ τῆς γῆς,
καὶ γὰρ αὐτὸς ἀνελήμφθη ἀπὸ τῆς γῆς. Our author, full of the one
great wonder of the Person of Christ, prefers mystery to miracle, and
restrains himself from speculation.

6. μισθαποδότης. This does not imply mercenary religion, but trust which is really personal. *respondet curis aequatque amorem.* Notice the full-sounding compounds; but 𝔭¹³ has ζητοῦσιν.

7. εὐλαβηθείς. Cf. v. 7, xii. 28; L. *metuens* is inadequate.

κατέκρινεν. Cf. Luke xi. 31 f. This verb is rare compared with κρίνω in N.T., where only in Mark xvi. 16 and perhaps 2 Pet. ii. 6 is God's "condemnation" of man asserted.

τῆς κατὰ πίστιν δικαιοσύνης. S. Paul thinks rather of righteousness springing "out of" faith; Rom. ix. 30, x. 6; cf. Rom. iii. 22, iv. 11, 13, Phil. iii. 9.

8. For Abraham's "call" see Gen. xii. 1; from the human point of view, Gen. xi. 30 f. For his "sojourning," Gen. xxiii. 4. That thought is taken up again in *v.* 13. The stages of its spiritual development are to be observed in 1 Chr. xxix. 15 and Ps. xxxix. (xxxviii.) 12. It is the core of that "other-worldly" idealism which has always been characteristic of the Jew, appeared in utmost purity in the Galilean Gospel, and is interpreted for a rising generation in the rest of N.T. In this ep. the doctrine of faith is mainly an appeal for the revival of that enthusiasm.

9. γῆν τῆς ἐπαγγελίας. For this gen. of essential character cf. ix. 5. In ℵ* τῆς is omitted before the final αὐτῆς of this verse. A slip, no doubt; yet the promise which the land owned (cf. xii. 4) would be a pleasant thought.

11. καταβολήν is the proper word for "generation" rather than "conception," cf. Rom. ix. 10. Hence W.H. propose αὐτῇ Σάρρᾳ as alternative spelling; the early addition, [ἡ] στεῖρα οὖσα, would of course be incompatible with that. Perhaps the active verbal noun is not alien to the Greek language in which "we cannot say χαλεπὸν εὑρίσκεσθαι, but only χαλεπὸν εὑρίσκειν," Rutherford, § 339.

ἐπεὶ πιστὸν ἡγήσατο, as in *v.* 27, the author goes against the letter of O.T. (Gen. xviii. 12 ff.) to reach the general and profounder truth. For S. Paul's application of the incident cf. Rom. iv. 18 ff.

12. καθὼς τὰ ἄστρα, κ.τ.λ., from Gen. xxii. 17.

13. κατὰ πίστιν ἀπέθανον. Cf. *v.* 7 = "in the way of faith." In accordance with the metaphor that follows the author pictures faith in terms of space, whereas S. Paul hardly varies from terms of energy.

πόρρωθεν...ἀσπασάμενοι. Like pilgrims who see the minarets of the city on the horizon, and still must camp for one more night in the desert. T.R. inserts καὶ πεισθέντες after ἰδόντες with a curious paucity of authority or sense.

16. **νῦν...ὀρέγονται**, pres., because the author, as usual, realises written history as a vivid picture. Perhaps also because these pilgrim fathers were still living and still waiting, cf. *v.* 40. But **νῦν** must be a particle of logic; else **καὶ νῦν** would have been required.

ἐπαισχύνεται αὐτούς. The concordance seems to suggest that to the N.T. writers *ἐπαισχύνομαι* sounded more natural than *αἰσχύνομαι* when an acc. follows : yet cf. ii. 11 and the author's general tendency to use compounds. The meaning is rather "is not abashed before them"—a boldly imaginative figure--than "ashamed of their conduct." Cf. Plat. *Symp.* 216 B, πέπονθα πρὸς τοῦτον μόνον ἀνθρώπων, ὃ οὐκ ἄν τις οἴοιτο ἐν ἐμοὶ ἐνεῖναι, τὸ αἰσχύνεσθαι ὁντινοῦν· ἐγὼ δὲ τοῦτον μόνον αἰσχύνομαι. Note the emphasis, αὐτοὺς—αὐτῶν—αὐτοῖς.

ἐπικαλεῖσθαι, almost "to be surnamed," cf. Ex. iii. 15. The author dissents from Philo's philosophic reverence, and follows the early historians of Israel in dwelling on this homely, "human" condescension in God.

XI. 17—31. Faith: the consecration and redemption of Israel.

17 By faith hath Abraham fulfilled the sacrifice of Isaac, though the trial was hard: yea, the only begotten son was he in the act of
18 offering who had accepted the promises, unto whom it was said,
19 In Isaac shall a seed be called for thee. For he had made up his mind that God, even from the dead, can raise to life. And from the dead indeed, by a restoration that is a symbol for later faith, he did recover him.

20 By faith Isaac blessed Jacob and Esau, and his blessing reached into the purposes of God.

21 By faith Jacob, when he was dying, distinguished the two sons of Joseph as he blessed them; and with the reverent insight of infirm old age he worshipped leaning on the top of his staff.

22 By faith Joseph, as his end drew near, bade his brethren remember that the children of Israel should go forth from Egypt, and gave commandment concerning the removal of his own bones.

23 By faith Moses was hidden immediately after birth for three months by his parents, because they saw how goodly the child was, and they feared not the decree of the king.

24 By faith Moses, when he was grown a man, refused to be called
25 the son of Pharaoh's daughter, having made his choice rather to suffer abiding affliction with the people of God than to have enjoy-

ment of sin for a season. Greater riches in his reckoning than the 26
treasures of Egypt was the scorned estate of the Christ-bearing
nation; for he looked to the eternal service in which God pays the
wages.

By faith he left Egypt, but not because he feared the wrath 27
of the king; for he strengthened his resolution, as seeing Him who
is invisible.

By faith he celebrated the Passover (as Israel still does) and the 28
ritual of blood, that the destroyer of the first-born should not touch
them.

By faith they crossed the Red Sea as by dry land. But the 29
Egyptians had enough of sea and were swallowed up.

By faith the walls of Jericho fell after the procession had gone 30
round them seven times in seven days.

By faith Rahab the harlot perished not with the infidels, because 31
she had received the spies with the hospitality of peace.

17. προσενήνοχεν, κ.τ.λ., from Gen. xxii., but the perf. is in marked
contrast to the aorists of that narrative. "Sacrifice" is a metaphor
from ancient worship; the reality such language points to lies in the
union of man's will with God, cf. **x.** 10. Thus Abraham is ever to
be regarded as having in fact sacrificed Isaac, though the slaying of
the boy was stayed. To our author the main argument of Gen. xxii.
is the eternal consecration of the nation, through Isaac, to the LORD.
Cf. the somewhat narrower application of the same thought in Ep.
Barn. vii. 3, ἐπεὶ καὶ αὐτὸς ὑπὲρ τῶν ἡμετέρων ἁμαρτιῶν ἔμελλεν τὸ
σκεῦος τοῦ πνεύματος προσφέρειν θυσίαν, ἵνα καὶ ὁ τύπος ὁ γενόμενος
ἐπὶ Ἰσαὰκ τοῦ προσενεχθέντος ἐπὶ τὸ θυσιαστήριον τελεσθῇ. In Clem.
xxxi. Isaac himself is spoken of as a willing sacrifice, Ἰσαὰκ μετὰ
πεποιθήσεως γινώσκων τὸ μέλλον ἡδέως προσήγετο θυσία.

19. καὶ ἐν παραβολῇ. Cf. ix. 9; but Camerarius, in the sixteenth
century, proposed to take ἐν π.=παραβόλως, as though "in the very
crisis of the hazard"; another of the bold paradoxes of the ep.,
but hardly possible though a scholium on Thuc. **I.** 131 lends vague
support to it.

20 f. See Gen. xxvii., xlviii. The last words of *v.* 21 are quoted
from Gen. xlvii. 31, where LXX ῥάβδου represents a different pointing
of the consonants which signify "bed" in the traditional Hebrew
text. Latt. render *adoravit fastigium virgae eius.* But cod. D of the
vulgate inserts *super,* and our English paraphrase, "leaning upon," is
legitimate. Our author certainly, and the LXX probably, had no
idea of Jacob's worshipping an image carved on his staff; cf. however
Gen. xxxi. 19, 1 Sam. **xv.** 23, xix. 13, Hos. iv. 12.

23 ff. See Ex. ii., of which these verses are verbally reminiscent, as *v.* 28 is of Ex. xii. 21 ff. γεννηθείς might possibly be construed with πίστει as referring to Ex. ii. 1; his parents were careful of his pure Levitical descent.

26. τὸν ὀνειδισμὸν τοῦ χριστοῦ. A reminiscence of Ps. lxxxix. (lxxxviii.) 50 f., where "thine anointed," or "thy Christ," means the people of Israel; Intr. III. 6, 28, and i. 5, v. 5, notes.

27. μὴ φοβηθείς. This might refer to the exodus, and the addition of a clause about killing the Egyptian, in D*𝕴 (vt. vg.^{codd}), to *v.* 23, was no doubt meant to commend that explanation. But "as seeing the invisible" seems to point forward to the burning bush, and here as in S. Stephen's speech the spiritual education of Moses in the wilderness is the proper sequel to his secular education in Pharaoh's court, and the preparation for his redemptive work. The author deliberately corrects the letter of Ex. ii. 14 by the deeper truth of Moses' real courage, which he gathers from the whole context.

28. πρόσχυσιν: cf. ix. 21 f. The verb προσχεῖν is frequent in the ritual chapters of the Pentateuch for the dashing of the sacrificial blood against the altar, etc.

29. τὴν Ἐρυθρὰν Θ. So LXX for Hebrew "sea of reeds."

πεῖραν λαβόντες: cf. *v.* 36. Field would translate, "had experience of," adducing many parallels. And in *v.* 37 he suggests that ἐπειράσθησαν (which from the variety of readings might seem to have come in as a gloss) was originally ἐπειράθησαν and was intended to explain π. ἔλαβον there.

XI. 32—38.   FAITH: FROM THE JUDGES TO THE MACCABEES.

32   And what more am I to say? For time shall fail me if I tell the tale of Gideon, Barak, Samson, Jephthah, of David too and Samuel
33 and the prophets:—who by faith overcame kingdoms, wrought
34 righteousness, won promises, stopped lions' mouths, quenched fire's power, escaped the sword's edge, were made powerful when they were weak, and strong in war; they turned back armies of invaders;
35 women received their dead by resurrection; others were broken on the wheel, having refused the deliverance that was offered them so
36 that they might attain the better resurrection; others again had bitter experience of mockings and scourgings, of bonds too and of
37 prison; they were stoned, tortured, sawn asunder, died the death of the sword, went about in sheepskins, in goatskins; need, affliction,
38 evil estate was theirs continually; men of whom the whole world

was unworthy wandered about deserts, were fugitives in mountains and caves and holes in the ground.

32. Σαμουὴλ καὶ τῶν προφητῶν. Samuel, whose "ear the LORD uncovered" (1 Sam. ix. 15), inaugurated or restored the line of "inspired" prophets; cf. 1 Sam. iii. 20 f., Amos iii. 7, Deut. xxxiv. 10, and contrast 1 Sam. x. 10—13, xix. 23 f., 1 Kings xxii. 6 ff.

34. μαχαίρης. So 𝔭¹³ ℵAD* rightly; μαχαίρας ω : see Hort, Intr. p. 156.

ἐδυναμώθησαν ἀπὸ ἀσθενείας. Rendel Harris[1] sees a reference to Judith in this verse. Cf. Clem. lv. with Lightfoot's note.

παρεμβολάς. In the quotation, xiii. 11, this word has the meaning "camp," frequent in late Greek. Here it means "army in line of battle," as often in Polybius and LXX. This is however especially frequent in 1 Macc. And at this point the author seems to turn his mind almost entirely to the Maccabean heroisms, especially to the famous narrative of the Maccabean martyrs in 2 Macc. vi. and vii.—πρὸ μαρτύρων μέγιστοι μάρτυρες, as the Prayer Book of the Greek Church styles them. Thus "stopped the mouths of the lions" looks like a verbal reminiscence of Dan. vi. 22. But that particular Greek phrase is not in LXX of Daniel, we only know it from Theodotion's version, and the general reference might be to 1 Macc. ii. 60. The women who received their dead may be those mentioned in 1 Kings xvii. 17 ff., 2 Kings iv. 17 ff. But the thought of "resurrection" is greatly deepened if the mother of the seven martyrs is particularly included. See her noble words in 2 Macc. vii. 29. The "better resurrection" will then be a climax not a contrast, and the reality of her receiving will be like the saving of our Lord "out of death" in v. 7 f.

35. γυναῖκες. So of course the mass of MSS. But the consensus of ℵ*AD*, especially if as is probable 𝔭¹³ must be added to the group, shows that γυναῖκας is the reading which the most ancient line of transmission has preserved. Is it a "primitive error," or a faithful record of the author's own slip of the pen?

ἐτυμπανίσθησαν, *distenti sunt* vg. ; a late word for a late form of torture, which however can too well be translated into English "broken upon the wheel." Cf. 2 Macc. vi. 28 ff.

37. ἐπειράσθησαν. See note on *v.* 29 *supra*.

ἐπρίσθησαν. Isaiah is said in an apocryphal book to have been sawn asunder, but it would be strange to hark back here to an

---

[1] *Side lights on N.T. research*, pp. 170 f.

early prophet. Yet see Clem. xvii., who says that by those who went about "in goatskins and sheepskins preaching the advent of Christ," he understands Elijah, Elisha and Ezekiel. Intr. II. 4.

38. The punctuation of W.H. gives better rythm and more vigorous sense than is got by putting ὥν...ὁ κόσμος in parenthesis. The position of πλανώμενοι makes its slightly improper conjunction with "caves and holes" quite tolerable.

XI. 39—40. Deferred fruition.

39 And yet all these, though canonised through faith in the witness
40 of scripture, lacked fruition of the promise; inasmuch as God, with us to day in view, had provided a better fulfilment than they could conceive, that the completion of their blessedness might not be achieved without our co-operation.

39. μαρτυρηθέντες. This passage takes up the ἐμαρτυρήθησαν of *v.* 2. In xii. 1 (μαρτύρων) "being witnessed to" passes into "witnessing": at each stage in the salutary sufferings of the Christ the partakers of those sufferings become in their turn witnesses, and the earthly scene is filled with invisible as well as visible spectators. Indeed in xii. 1 we are not far from the idea of "martyrdom," cf. note on xi. 2 *supra*, also cf. 1 Cor. iv. 9, 1 Pet. i. 11 f. (where notice the affinity with our author's doctrine of angels), v. 1, 9, 1 Tim. vi. 13, and the testimony of the nations in Isa. lii. 13—liii.

40. μὴ χωρὶς ἡμῶν. In spite of xii. 23, it seems as though the author presses this argument here upon the little group of friends whom he is urging to their imminent duty—the perfect satisfaction of these O.T. saints waits for their hastening or hindering it. Intr. III. 23.

CHAPTER XII

Now we in our turn are on trial. Those whose faithfulness was 1
attested in the past are now to attest ours. They are spread round
us like a cloud of spiritual spectators as we stand in the arena.
Therefore, though hesitation to do our appointed duty clings to us
like the wrap which the anxious athlete shrinks from casting off, let
not hesitation become the sin of refusal. Let us cast it off and run
with steady resolution the race that stretches before us, looking past 2
the fears of sense to Him who leads us into the mysteries of faith and
will lead us to their consummation ; even Jesus, who in the trial set
before His manhood balanced pain with heroic joy, and with a noble
scorn of shame resolutely faced the cross. So hath He been enthroned on God's right hand. Mark Him well, for our contest is all 3
one with His ; what Korah-like gainsaying hath He so resolutely
endured from men who sinned against themselves in opposing Him.
Still men gainsay, and still His firmness gives us power, so that your
faint-heartedness need not end in failure.

1. νέφος. A common metaphor ; here particularly appropriate to
the gathering of "spirits," xii. 23.

εὐπερίστατον: not elsewhere except in passages dependent on this.
Vg. *circumstans* makes it active in sense like the preceding περικείμενον.
The strange *fragilem* (*sic*) in d seems to point to the passive sense
which is preferred by some. Isocrates' περίστατος ὑπὸ πάντων suggests "admired," the "specious" sin (cf. iii. 13), in which, if they
yield, their honour will stand rooted in dishonour. No vague
besetting sin is meant, but failure in the particular duty which the
ep. is written to urge. The picture here presented (cf. vi. 19 f.) is of
a race-course ; the O.T. heroes are watching to bear witness how the
readers of the ep. will acquit themselves : they, having Jesus now in
sight, who has run the same course and now sits visible on His
throne at the goal—note perf. **κεκάθικεν**, which at last marks a new

stage in the argument of the ep.—they are preparing to run the race. This picture suggests an active sense for εὐπ. The sin which presses on all sides upon the readers is like the wrap which the athlete, in the anxious moments before the start, shrinks from laying aside—ἀπο-δυτέον ἄρα τοὺς πολλοὺς ἡμῶν χιτῶνας, Porphyry, *de abstinentia.* Cf. Clem. vii. ἐν γὰρ τῷ αὐτῷ ἐσμὲν σκάμματι, καὶ ὁ αὐτὸς ἡμῖν ἀγὼν ἐπί-κειται. διὸ ἀπολείπωμεν τὰς κενὰς καὶ ματαίας φροντίδας...ἀτενίσωμεν εἰς τὸ αἷμα τοῦ χριστοῦ.

τρέχωμεν might be used figuratively of any contest, but the foot-race makes the best picture here.

τὸν προκείμενον. The Sixtine and Clementine vg. have *ad pro-positum certamen.* Hence A.V. in its original text "unto the race." Notice in the Prayer-Book how this passage helped Cosin to bring the 1549 version of the collect for IV Advent into its fine present form.

2. ἀρχηγὸν καὶ τελειωτήν : cf. ii. 10. This has been well rendered, "He who trod the path before us and trod it perfectly to the end[1]." Yet the idea of a captain in arms is included. In τελειωτὴν the author, who never labours his imagery, is passing from the romantic picture to the realism of *vv.* 3 f.

ἀντὶ τῆς προκειμένης αὐτῷ χαρᾶς. προκειμένης corresponds to προκείμενον in last verse. Not the future reward but the immediate "joy of battle" is meant. Cf. Father R. M. Benson, *Letters,* p. 201, "The joy which comes after peace is a spurious joy, an earthly one, if it is a joy because there is peace in our davs": Intr. III. 7.

ὑπέμεινεν takes up ὑπομονῆς from preceding verse (cf. x. 32, 36), and is echoed in *vv.* 3 and 7. The thought is characteristic of this ep. of the divine manhood. "The message of the cross to sufferers is this, that the highest and greatest victory that has ever been won in human nature was won by the perseverance of faith, hope and charity—in a word, by patience,—under the pressure of sufferings that were neither removed nor mitigated, but endured; and that, provided we can, by the grace of God, meet trouble in a spirit which is essentially the same, however much weaker in degree, we may win the same kind of victory in our measure[2]." Cf. note on iv. 15, and Intr. II. 15, III. 15.

3. τῶν ἁμ. εἰς ἑαυτούς. ἑαυτοὺς א*D* (αὐτοὺς p¹³ אc 33 Orig.) 𝕃 𝕾 (vg.) ℭ (boh.): ἑαυτὸν AP𝕃 (vg.codd.) 𝕾 (hl.): αὐτὸν DcωOrig. (?) Chr. The v.ll. shew the progress of error to αὐτόν. Probably αὐτούς, in nearly the same sense as ἑαυτούς, was the original word;

---

[1] *Foundations,* p. 192.
[2] F. M. Downton, in *The Cowley Evangelist,* June, 1914.

see Blass, 48. 2, 7, and cf. xii. 16 where most mss. have αὐτοῦ for ἑαυτοῦ of אּ*ACDᵇ ᵉᵗ ᶜ. The phrase is a reminiscence of Num. xvi. 37 (xvii. 2). Its bitterness is turned by the complementary utterance of our Lord, Luke xxiii. 34.

XII. 4—13. CHASTISEMENT THE REVELATION OF THE
FATHER'S LOVE.

In your wrestle with the threatening sin of these critical days you 4
have not yet had to face death, and you have forgotten the consola- 5
tion which comes to you like a father's voice pleading with his sons :
"My son despise not the chastening of the LORD, nor yet faint when
thou art reproved by Him; for whom the LORD loveth He chasteneth, 6
and scourgeth every son whom He receiveth." Wait manfully for 7
His chastisement. As with sons He dealeth with you, He who is
God. For is there ever a son whom a true father does not chasten? 8
If you stay outside the discipline of the divine family into which the
whole suffering world of men have been initiated, you must be
bastards and not sons. And further: if we accepted the fathers who 9
begat us as disciplinarians and so learned to respect them, shall we
not much more readily submit to "the Father of spirits" and so
rise to life? To the life, I mean, which is life indeed; for if they, 10
according to their poor judgement which looked forward but for a few
days, used to exercise discipline, He knows what is really for His
children's good and means them to share the holiness of His own
life. All chastening indeed seems at the moment to be a matter of 11
pain, not of joy: yet afterwards it yields fruit of peace to those who
have been trained thereby—the peace of righteousness. Wherefore 12
"the slackened hands and the palsied knees do ye set firm and
straight," and "straight paths be ye making for your feet," that 13
the lame folk be not led astray but rather be healed.

4.   τὴν ἁμαρτίαν. The article is significant: cf. note on iii. 13
and Intr. v. 5. The sin of failing in the one hard duty set before the
readers of the ep. at that very time is meant.

5.   ἥτις...διαλέγεται. As though discipline were a person, cf.
xi. 9, xii. 24. To our author the discipline of love raises natural
relationship into spiritual. Cf. Leonian Sacramentary: *DS qui
diligendo castigas et castigando nos refoves.*

The quotation is from Prov. iii. 11 f. It follows LXX with
the addition of μου, which is omitted in D* and a few other

authorities. Philo cites the verse with καὶ μὴ for μηδέ, and so ℘¹³ here.

7. εἰs παιδείαν. As often in the ep. some trial seems indicated which is nigh but not yet come, cf. 1 Pet. iv. 12. But in textus receptus the characteristic prep. has become εἰ, the foreboding is dulled, and the cheerful faith in God's fatherhood is made dependent on His creatures' resignation.

9. τῷ π. τῶν πνευμάτων. Cf. Num. xvi. 22, Apoc. xxii. 6, and v. 23 *infr.* Some printed edd. of 𝔖 (vg.) give "fathers of spirits" (i.e. "spiritual fathers"?) here. That is a misprint or misreading of the MSS. But the Armenian translation of Ephraem's commentaries seems to shew that he actually had this reading in the older version which he knew.

11. πᾶσα μέν. Another of our author's abrupt beginnings. The v.l. δὲ shews that it offended early scholarship.

12. τὰς παρειμένας...ἀνορθώσατε, from Isa. xxxv. 3; a close rendering of Heb.; yet there seems to be a reminiscence of LXX also.

13. τὸ χωλὸν, prob. concrete "lame persons," cf. οἱ πολλοί, v. 15; Intr. v. 5. But, giving a later sense to the verb, we might translate, "that your lameness grow not worse"; cf. Thuc. τὸ ἀνειμένον τῆς γνώμης.

An adaptation of Prov. iv. 26, LXX. Most MSS. have ποιήσατε, (℘¹³) א*P 33 ποιεῖτε. Is ποιεῖτε an Alexandrine correction of the unsuitable hexameter rythm? Intr. IV. 2, v. 12.

XII. 14—17.   CHARITY WITH LOYALTY.

14   Peace: Yes, "pursue peace" with all men. But do not, for the dream of peace, desert the consecrated fellowship outside of which no
15 one shall see the Lord at His coming. Keep that unviolated, continually interesting yourselves in the brethren lest there should be any one in lack of the common treasure of God's grace; lest any root of bitterness spring up into a noxious plant, and thereby the simple multitude
16 be defiled; lest any one be corrupted with lewd heresy or worldly ambition, as Esau was, who for one dish of food sold his proper birth-
17 right. For you know that when he did afterwards wish to claim his inherited blessing he lost his plea—no "place for afterthought" was allowed in that court—though with tears he had sought diligently to recover it.

14. εἰρήνην διώκετε. Cf. Ps. xxxiv. (xxxiii.) 14, Rom. xii. 18.

τὸν ἁγιασμόν. A Pauline word, but here used in the more special sense of LXX, the consecration which marks the people of God. So 2 Macc. ii. 17: ὁ δὲ θεὸς ὁ σώσας τὸν πάντα λαὸν αὐτοῦ, καὶ ἀποδοὺς τὴν κληρονομίαν αὐτοῦ πᾶσιν καὶ τὸ βασίλειον καὶ τὸ ἱεράτευμα καὶ τὸν ἁγιασμόν. It introduces a warning like those in vi. 4 ff., x. 26 f.; such a warning as was hardened later into *extra ecclesiam nulla salus.* This warning is in iambic metre and has almost a proverbial ring; but it is followed by a second iambic line which is too plainly due to the author's carelessness.

15 f. μή τις: for ellipse of verb see Blass, 81. 2. The clause μή τις...ἐνοχλῇ is from Deut. xxix. 18, where the corrected text of B (adopted by Swete) has μή τίς ἐστιν ἐν ὑμῖν ῥίζα ἄνω φύουσα ἐν χολῇ καὶ πικρίᾳ. B* has ΕΝΟΧΛΗ which makes no sense preceded by ἐστιν, and (like the addition of πικρίας after ῥίζα in AF) shews how N.T. affected the text of LXX. Ἐνοχλῇ is probably due to our author's adapting memory. Blass, 35. 5 *note*, thinks it was in his text of LXX. For the sequence of thought cf. this coincidence or reminiscence in Leighton quoted by Coleridge[1]: "The boasted peaceableness about questions of faith too often proceeds from a superficial temper, and not seldom from a supercilious disdain of whatever has no marketable use or value, and from indifference to religion itself. Toleration is a herb of spontaneous growth in the soil of indifference; but the weed has none of the virtues of the medicinal plant, reared by humility in the garden of zeal."

17. ἐκζητήσας αὐτήν. For Esau's profaneness and tears see Gen. xxv. 33 f., xxvii. 30—40. The αὐτήν might refer to "the blessing," and Gen. xxvii. 34 supports that explanation, which is adopted by W.H. in their punctuation. The sense is much the same, whether "blessing" or "repentance" be referred to. Esau's hopeless loss (which however is not represented in Gen. as eternal rejection from God) is a warning to the readers of the ep. whose hesitation involves a fearful risk of ruin. We find the phrase "place of repentance" in the Syriac Apocalypse of Baruch lxxxv., and the Latin 2 Esdr. ix. 12. In these books, which were consolations to the Jews after the fall of Jerusalem in A.D. 70, the doctrine is that in the day of judgement repentance will be no longer possible. In Wisd. xii. 10, 20, the same phrase occurs in praise of "the God of the fathers and Lord of his own mercy" who gives so many opportunities of repentance. Westcott quotes from Pliny's letter (x. 97) to Trajan on the Christians: *ex quo facile est opinari quae turba hominum emendari possit, si sit locus poenitentiae;* and from Ulpian, as though it were a term of

[1] *Aids,* Moral and Rel. Aph. xxvi.

Roman law, in the third century at least. The phrase had wide
applications and need not have conveyed to the first readers the
theological hopelessness it suggests here to us; Intr. III. 20.

XII. 18—27. THE TREMENDOUS HAZARD IN ETERNAL THINGS.

18   This is a stern warning, for in eternal things the issue of our
19 choice is tremendous.   In this crisis you have come near to no
material fire of kindled stuff, to darkness and gloom and storm and
trumpet-clang and sound of words, of the which sound those who
20 heard it begged that they might have no further explanation.   For
they had been moved beyond endurance by that awfully distinct
command, "If so much as a beast touch the mountain it shall be
21 stoned." And so fearful was the apparition, Moses said, "I am
22 beside myself with fear and all a-tremble." No, you stand on the
frontier of eternity, near to Sion the mount and city of the living
God, Jerusalem in heaven above; and myriads of angels in festal
23 assembly; and to the church of the firstborn, the patriarchal saints
whose names are enrolled in heaven; and to God the judge of all;
and to the spirits of those later saints whose righteousness has been
divinely perfected; and to the mediator of the covenant which now
24 renews its youth, even to Jesus; and to the Blood of that unearthly
ritual, tragic, personal, brotherly, which speaks, as Abel speaks,
unceasingly but with a meaning all divine.
25   See that you refuse Him not who is thus speaking. For if the
Israelites escaped not from God's purpose when in the limited and
earthly revelation at Sinai they had refused their human interpreter,
how much less we who are all but turning our back on our Lord who
26 speaks from heaven. That other voice at Sinai, the voice which
shook the earth, was His. And now too it is He whom we hear
proclaiming in the words of the ancient prophecy, "Yet once more
27 will I myself shake" not only "earth" but also "heaven." That
"once more" signifies the removal of the things that are shaken,
I mean the whole fabric of institutions human and divine, in order
that the realities which are never shaken may come and abide.

18—21. These verses are full of reminiscences of Ex. xix. 11—13,
Deut. iv. 11 f., cf. also Deut. v. 22, ix. 19. But ψηλαφωμένῳ is the
author's own.   Dω𝔖 (hl.) 𝔄 Ath. *al.* add ὄρει, but the authority for
omission אAC 33 1908 𝔏 𝔖 (vg.) ℭ ℭth Orig.ˡᵃᵗ· Chr. *al.* is decisive.
To "understand" ὄρει from *v.* 22 seems weak.   It is possible to take

the partt. as neuters, expressing vague horror: "Something tangible and seared with fire." But vg. has *ad tractabilem et accensibilem ignem.* Dr E. C. Selwyn¹ emends conjecturally πεφεψαλωμένῳ to be construed with ὄρει, and says that κ. πυρί could only mean "a fire burnt out." If so, "a tangible fire and presently burnt out" would stand in good antithesis with ὁ θεὸς ἡμῶν πῦρ καταναλίσκον, at the conclusion of this passage. But it is easier to explain the perfect from the primary meaning of καίω as "having been kindled." The author's addition ψηλαφωμένῳ governs the clause. Exodus and Deuteronomy express the terribleness of Sinai; he thinks of the material quality of its terror in contrast with the invisible, personal, spiritual richness of the mount and city of the living God, *vv.* 22 ff. It is that inherent quality which he tries to suggest by this perf. part.

19. παρῃτήσαντο, in all MSS. except ℵ*P and two cursives μὴ is added. This is probably a correction of scrupulous grammarians; for though παραιτοῦμαι with acc., as in *v.* 25 and Acts xxv. 11 (οὐ π. ἀποθανεῖν), or with direct inf., as Joseph. *de vita sua* 29 (θανεῖν οὐ π.), means "beg to be excused from," with acc. and inf. it would as a rule mean simply "beg."

21. τὸ φανταζόμενον. A nicely selected word; it gives to the whole description what Victor Hugo in his funeral oration on Balzac expressed as "je ne sais quoi d'effaré et de terrible mêlé au réel."

ἔντρομος. The agreement of ℵ*D has persuaded W.H. to preserve in mg. the otherwise unknown word ἔκτρομος.

22 f. For the heavenly Jerusalem cf. Apoc. iii. 12, xxi. 2, Gal. iv. 26 f. with Lightfoot's note on S. Paul's use of "an expression familiar to rabbinical teachers." In O.T. too Sion and Jerusalem have sacramental significance, see esp. Ps. lxxxvii. Whether Ἰερ. ἐπ. be joined with πόλει θ. ζ. or taken in apposition to the whole preceding clause, may be left to the reader's taste. Whether πανηγύρει be separated or not from ἀγγέλων is a more interesting question. Tradition, including versions and punctuated MSS., is on the whole for taking these words together; so vg. *multorum milium angelorum frequentiae.* The author's penchant for iambic cadences makes for this. For the liturgical tone of this passage see Intr. II. 4.

23. ἐκκλησίᾳ. In the first division of Acts which tells of the apostolic community in Jerusalem, ἐκκλ. is reserved, in technical sense—v. 11 is different—for the ancient Jewish Church. So probably in this ep. Hence the "first-born" are O.T. saints, who are enrolled in heaven, even though xi. 40 should imply that the realisation of their birth-right is delayed. The daughter Church, the disciples of Jesus, will then come in at καὶ πνεύμασιν. The universal κριτῇ θεῷ πάντων—looking back as judge and forward to His "all in all"—(1 Cor. xv. 28)—connects the two.

πρωτ. ἀπογεγραμμένων. Cf. Ex. xxxii. 32, Ps. lxxxvii. 6, Is. iv. 3, Dan. vii. 10, xii. 1: R. M. Benson, *Letters*, p. 220, "As the circle of affectionate memories becomes enlarged in the heavenly record, we learn increasingly the blessedness of the eternal bond which unites us in the company of all saints."

πνεύμασι δικαίων τετελειωμένων. See Intr. III. 23, 24, 25. D* has πνεύματι δ. τεθεμελιωμένων ͞spm *iustorum funditorum*: and Hilary explains, *spirituum in domino fundatorum*.

24. διαθήκης νέας. καινός, "new," has here become νέος, "young." Cf. Arist. *Eth.* i. 3, διαφέρει δ' οὐθὲν νέος τὴν ἡλικίαν ἢ τὸ ἦθος νεαρός. Since νέος can of course be used more generally, the quasi-personification (cf. xii. 5) is not bizarre; indeed it seems natural in this picture of exultant life. In Gilbert's reredos at S. Alban's Abbey the crown of thorns on the head of the Lord rising from the tomb is just breaking into leaf. When the High Priest entered the true sanctuary there was a renascence of the world. So in 1 Pet. i. 3, "Who according to his great mercy begat us again (ἀναγεννήσας) unto a living hope by the resurrection of Jesus Christ from the dead." Cf. Philo, *sacr. Abel et Cain*, p. 178, παρὰ τοῦ ἀγήρω καὶ νέου θεοῦ τὰ νέα καὶ καινὰ ἀγαθὰ μετὰ πάσης ἀφθονίας λαμβάνοντες ἐκδιδάσκωνται μηδὲν ἡγεῖσθαι παρ' αὐτῷ παλαιὸν ἢ συνόλως παρεληλυθός, ἀλλὰ γινόμενόν τε ἀχρόνως καὶ ὑφεστηκός.

μεσίτῃ, here with imaginative propriety; the mediator is not merely the *internuntius* of God and man, He links the ancient church with the new heirs.

25. τὸν ἀπ' οὐρανῶν. ℵ with limited but considerable support has οὐρανοῦ: cf. note on iv. 14.

26. The shaking of heaven and earth is quoted with added emphasis from Haggai (ii. 6), who prophesied when an older ritual had passed away and a new worship was beginning with little outward promise.

XII. 28—29. The Kingdom of God.

28   Those realities are what our fathers called The Kingdom of God; and that Kingdom which shall not pass away we are receiving in this final issue of the ages. Wherefore let us shew gratitude, and in the kingdom do loyal service well pleasing to God with reverence and

awe, for our God is, as He was of old, "Fire"—not material but **29** "consuming."

28. βασιλείαν. The "kingdom" or "reign" of God was the symbol by which salvation was preached and wrought in the Galilean gospel. After the synoptists and Acts it falls into the background of N.T. till the Apocalypse. But the primitive language now and then reasserts itself as here: Intr. II. 11, III. 32. For ἀσάλευτον cf. Dan. vii. 14.

ἔχωμεν χάριν. "ἔχειν χάριν, *habere gratiam*, pro eo quod est gratias agere, non est styli Apostolici : utuntur enim Apostoli passim verbo εὐχαριστεῖν," Estius. But this is one of our author's classical niceties. He does not mean "give thanks," but "shew gratitude."

א here joins an inferior group in reading ἔχομεν. That spoils the construction of the sentence, for λατρεύωμεν is a parallel independent subj., not as in the latinism of viii. 3, dependent on the relative.

εὐλαβείας καὶ δέους. δέους only here in N.T., and even here it has disappeared in the late text, αἰδοῦς καὶ εὐλαβείας. The true reading in Clem. ii., μετὰ δέους καὶ συνειδήσεως, is an almost contemporary witness to the originality of δέους in this passage.

29. πῦρ καταναλίσκον, from Deut. iv. 24; cf. *vv.* 18 ff. *supr.*

CHAPTER XIII

Сн. XIII. 1—6. Precepts of good churchmanship.

1 Let the brotherly love which has always bound together the family
2 of Christ continue to do so. Love is also due to those without, do not
forget it; for through that wider love some have entertained angels
3 unawares. Be mindful of people in prison—in these perilous times
you are as good as prisoners yourselves; and of those in misery or
want—the weakness of our mortal nature is the blessed source of
4 sympathy. Marriage? Everywhere honourable, and the marriage
bed always pure. I speak not of fornicators and adulterers; God
5 will judge them. A fine carelessness of money: everyone content
with daily bread. For it is the very *Ipse dixit* of God: "Be sure
6 I will not overlook thee; most certainly I will not forsake thee." So
we Christians must be of good courage and repeat: "The Lord is
my help, I will not fear. What shall man do to me?"

2. Cf. Rom. xii. 13, Gen. xviii. 3, xix. 2; for ξεν. in another
sense 1 Pet. iv. 4.

3. ὡς...ἐν σώματι. Cf. 2 Cor. v. 6 rather than Rom. xii. 5:
𝕃 rightly paraphrases, *tamquam et ipsi in corpore morantes*, and
Virgil would have understood—*mentem mortalia tangunt*.

5. ἀρκούμενοι. For this loose apposition see Blass 79. 10, but
cf. note on *v.* 8. The quot. is adapted from Deut. xxxi. 6, 8, Jos. i. 5:
that in the next verse is from Ps. cxviii. (cxvii.) 6.

αὐτός, emphatic: cf. Clem. xvi. of "Christ Himself, in whose
person the Psalmist is speaking."

6. ὥστε θαρροῦντας, with this martyr-courage cf. the *amorem
intellectualem Dei* of Plato: οὐκοῦν εἰ ἀεὶ ἡ ἀλήθεια ἡμῖν τῶν ὄντων
ἐστὶν ἐν τῇ ψυχῇ ἀθάνατος ἂν ἡ ψυχὴ εἴη, ὥστε θαρροῦντα χρὴ ὃ μὴ
τυγχάνεις ἐπιστάμενος νῦν, τοῦτο δ' ἐστὶν ὃ μὴ μεμνημένος, ἐπιχειρεῖν
ζητεῖν καὶ ἀναμιμνήσκεσθαι. *Meno* 86 B.

τί ποιήσει. This might be made dependent on φοβηθήσομαι,
according to the "Alexandrian and dialectical use of the interrogative

τίς instead of the relative ὅστις," cf. Mark xiv. 36, οὐ τί ἐγὼ θέλω,
ἀλλὰ τί σύ, Blass 50. 5. But, apart from the original context in LXX,
the more spirited interrogative form which W.H. prefer is far more
in keeping with the aphoristic style of this passage.

XIII. 7. MEMORIAL OF DEPARTED LEADERS.

Cherish the memory of your leaders, men who spoke to you the 7
word God gave them. And contemplating with ever fresh wonder the
supreme event of their career, be imitators of their faith.

7. τῶν ἡγουμένων. Clement uses this word and also προηγού-
μενοι (i., xxi.) of the officers of the Church in a general sense: cf.
Luke xxii. 26. But Clement also uses it of civil or military rulers
(xxxvii.), and it is often applied to the leaders of the Jews in 1 and
2 Macc. This passage seems to imply teaching as a function of the
leadership, and to hint at martyrdom—for it has a militant ring.
But it is impossible to guess whether they were bishops, elders,
presidents at the eucharistic service, or founders of the community
to which the readers belonged.

XIII. 8—16. THE SACRAMENT OF CALVARY.

Jesus Christ, yesterday and to day the same; yea, and while the 8
ages run. Elaborate precepts are rife which are as novel to Judaism 9
as to us. Do not swerve because of them from the onward course.
For it is a noble thing to have the heart founded deeper and deeper
by simple grace. But rules of food are mean—a trivial, disappointing
round. We are beyond such cares; the ministers of the tabernacle 10
partake of the sacrificial food; our altar is of a different order.
Indeed it is in outward appearance more analogous to the place out- 11
side the camp where the refuse of the high priest's sacrifice was (as
we read) burned. It was on Calvary, outside Jerusalem, that Jesus, 12
in order to sanctify the people of God, suffered as a criminal. There- 13
fore let us go forth to Him outside the camp, bearing the burden
which associates us with His shame. With His shame; but also
with the inward spiritual reality of His sacrifice, for the city which 14
we must now leave was never our abiding home; but, beyond the
shows of sense, we seek the city God has destined for us. By the 15
priestly mediation of our Lord Jesus let us offer up a sacrifice which
prophets and psalmists loved, a sacrifice of praise which ascends to
God unhindered by all the changes and chances of ritual; I mean
the "fruit of lips," the sweet mystery of language by which we

6 interpret our heartfelt devotion to His essential perfection. And do
not forget to be kind to one another and to share your earthly
goods; for such acts are also sacrifices with which God is well
pleased.

8. No verb is required. As in the original Hebrew of the
Shema' (Deut. vi. 4) this is a battle cry rather than a creed. Cf.
Maran atha="Lord come!" in 1 Cor. xvi. 22, and *vv.* 4 f. above.

9. παραφέρεσθε. T.R. has perpetuated the περιφέρεσθε of a few
ancient authorities; with that cf. Eph. iv. 14. But in this ep. the
danger is not of vague misbelief but of taking the wrong turn at
a particular choice; cf. ii. 1, xii. 13. This might seem to recommend
the reading of most mss., οἱ περιπατήσαντες, "those who have taken
to that walk," i.e. who have already made the wrong choice. But
the consensus of ℵ*AD*𝕷 is almost decisive for οἱ περιπατοῦντες,
and such a rendering of the aorist would not really suit the ep., in
which the trial is always envisaged as being imminent yet still future;
cf. vi. 4—9, xii. 5—7.

χάριτι: cf. note on iv. 16. Here, as in ii. 9, the main idea seems
to be of the absolute bounty of God which can neither be disputed
nor measured. Yet something further makes itself felt. How far
does χάρις in N.T. imply beauty of form or character—"the grace of
our Lord Jesus Christ"? There is certainly much feeling in N.T.
for that kind of χάρις; our Lord and the lilies; S. Paul in Phil. iv. 8;
the frequent καλὸς in this epistle; the ἀγγέλων πανηγύρει; the love of
language, often so delicate in pathos; the *desiderium* for the golden
splendour of the tabernacle, and (more exquisitely) for the tragic
simplicity of "the days of His flesh."

βρώμασιν. Cf. Rom. xiv., 1 Tim. iv. 3, Col. ii. 21 ff. The
reference is not to the rules of Leviticus, but to novel "unfitness
and irrelevance of teaching...barren and mischievous trivialities
usurping the office of religion[1]."

10 ff. Another picture, completing vi. 19 f., xii. 1 f. Here
Jesus, who in vi. is out of sight, in xii. in sight but distant, is to
be joined (13). And this imminent reality compels the author to
dissolve his picture almost while he draws it. The imagery is
thoroughly sacramental. When the Lord died on the cross, that
scene of "shame" (xii. 2), what could be seen was like the off-
scouring of a sacrifice (11; cf. Lev. xvi. 27). But what really took
place in the eternal sphere was the entrance of the divine High
Priest with His own sacrificial Blood into the presence of the Father.

[1] Hort, *Judaistic Christianity*, p. 134.

And the sacrament is complete, for we, says the author, are to appropriate its efficacy by doing as He did in visible shame and spiritual glory (13 f. ; cf. ii. 9, vi. 20, xii. 4, xiii. 7, 20). The imagery is borrowed from Levitical ritual, but no care is taken to make all the details correspond ; that ritual is not obeyed as a type, it is merely suggestive. Intr. III. 5 and 7.

15. Cf. Ps. l. (xlix.) 14, Lev. vii. 12 (2), 2 Chr. xxix. 31, Isa. lvii. 19 (Heb.), Hos. xiv. 2.

The "sacrifices" of these verses are not the same as that which informs the whole theology of the ep. Christ's one sacrifice could not be declined into the plural number. Here the idea is rather that even in the ritual of Christian worship there is a more than adequate substitute for the many sacrifices of Judaism. Nor was this doctrine altogether strange to Jews. Philo and other, especially Hellenistic, teachers had already recognised that it was enshrined in the Old Testament for the deepening of religion. Intr. II. 4, III. 13.

16. *talibus enim hostiis promeretur Deus,* vg. ; "promeretur passive dixit interpres, etsi parum latine," Estius: it is a survival from the Old Latin.

XIII. 17. LOYALTY TO THOSE ON WHOM THE BURDENS OF RESPONSIBILITY LIE HEAVILY.

Be pliant to your leaders' advice and commands. They bear the 17 weight of responsibility, and are watching through dark hours over you, the living souls entrusted to them; they know the account that must be rendered of such a charge. See to it that they may do their duty with happy cheer and no occasion for groaning—that would scarcely be to your profit.

17. ἀγρυπνοῦσιν. Can this be a reminiscence of the type of leadership, S. Paul? See 2 Cor. vi. 5, xi. 27. Or is it rather a grim touch of reality in this document of the warfare that occupied the corner of the apostolic Church to which this letter was written? There at any rate the command of the Lord was already approving itself as necessary ; ἵνα γρηγορῇ...γρηγορεῖτε οὖν...ὃ δὲ ὑμῖν λέγω, πᾶσιν λέγω, γρηγορεῖτε, Mark xiii. 35 f.

XIII. 18—21. COMMUNION IN PRAYER.

Think of us in your prayers; for we would fain believe that our 18 inmost mind is known to God, and we desire nothing else than to be true to His honour in all our dealings. And more than ever do 19

I 2

I beseech you to do this, in order that I may be the sooner restored to you.

20   And may God who makes peace in troubled times, who brought up from the dead the Shepherd of the sheep in the Blood of the Eternal Covenant, that great shepherd of prophecy, the transmuter of the ancient symbol of Life through Death into reality by His
21 obedience to God's will, even our Lord Jesus—may God confirm your shrinking resolution with all or any driving force of goodness for the doing of that duty which His will demands; while He continues to do with us (whose peace is already in His will) just that which is well-pleasing in His sight; may God do all this for you and us through Jesus, now exalted as Christ, to whom be glory for ever and ever: Amen, even so may God's will be done.

18. ἡμῶν. The author says little about himself, and we cannot tell precisely what he means by this plural. In *v.* 21, as well as here, it implies community in conscience at least as much as in circumstances (cf. iv. 3). It might even be a modest way of saying "me"; notice the modesty of assertion in πειθόμεθα, and contrast Phil. i. 25, πεποιθὼς οἶδα, with Lightfoot's note. It is perhaps worth remarking that a similar request for remembrance in prayer is introduced in Eph. vi. 18 f. by ἀγρυπνοῦντες (cf. *v.* 17 *supra*, ἀγρυπνοῦσιν).

20. This blessing sums up the doctrine and purpose of the epistle. It may be compared with the liturgical conclusion of Clement's epistle, but the form is different. Clement's prayer resembles the Greek liturgies; this is like a western collect, terse with close-knit movement, asking for a particular gift of grace: Intr. II. 4.

In *v.* 20 there is the solemn invocation: in *v.* 21 the main petition for the author's friends that they may be enabled to do their particular pressing duty (note the aor. ποιῆσαι), continued into the secondary petition for the author, and perhaps his fellow prisoners or fellow sojourners, that God's will may still be theirs. And all ends with the mediation of Jesus Christ, and a doxology which in the context seems to be addressed to Him in glory.

The passage from "our Lord Jesus" who did His duty in the days of His flesh, to "Jesus Christ" who has thus been perfected in His glorious office, is parallel to the passage from the author's petition for his friends to his petition for himself—their will is not yet lost and found in God's will, his own is. "Through Jesus Christ" is more than "through Him I offer prayer." It corresponds to the faith of the whole ep., that loyalty to Jesus the Lord is possible through His assumption of manhood into God. But all this antithesis and particularity is lost in the later text which gives παντὶ ἔργῳ ἀγαθῷ for the π. ἀγαθῷ of ℵD*ℑℭ (boh.) Greg.-Nyss. Euthal^{cod} Fulg., and ὑμῖν for the ἡμῖν of ℵDM 33 1908 ℥ (vg.) ℭ (boh.) 𝔄. Another addition, which did not get into textus receptus, is Χριστὸν after 'Ιησοῦν; so D* and some mss. of vg.; and so Andrewes has it in his *Preces Privatae*. All these are modifications which (like ἐπεσκέψατο for ἐπισκέψεται, Luke i. 78) fitted the special prayer of the author to the general conditions of church worship. So too, perhaps, the "Amen" at the end of the ep. which ℵ*33 ℑ (vg.^{cod.}) 𝔄 omit.

The αὐτῷ ποιῶν which W.H. place in mg. of *v.* 21 on account of its very strong attestation (ℵ*AC*33*ℭ (boh.?) Greg.-Nyss.) is thought by them to be a "primitive error" for αὐτὸς π. The correction actually appears in 1912 ℑ (vt.^d), and it would invigorate the "particularity" of the original prayer.

For the prophetic phraseology of *v.* 20 see Isa. lxiii. 11, Zech. ix. 11, Isa. lv. 3, Ez. xxxvii. 26.

"Amen" is explained by 2 Cor. i. 20, Apoc. xxii. 20.

'Εν π. ἀγαθῷ might be illustrated from the παντὶ τρόπῳ εἴτε προφάσει εἴτε ἀληθείᾳ of Phil. i. 18, or at any rate from 1 Cor. ix. 22, τοῖς πᾶσιν γέγονα πάντα ἵνα πάντως τινὰς σώσω. If "the living principle, the law within" them be not clear enough, then let any good motive be supplied that may drive them to the venture.

XIII. 22—25. Final words.

And, brothers, if this be too stern a treatise of exhortation, bear 22 with it. I exhort you now in quite another tone. For here you see I am sending you also a real letter.

You know—or let me tell you, that our brother Timothy is at 23 liberty. Accompanied by him, if he comes here reasonably soon, I will see you.

Greeting to all your leaders and to all the members of our holy 24 Church. The brothers of Italy send greeting to you.

And now, in the words of one we all know and shall ever love, 25 "Grace be with you all."

22. ἀνέχεσθε: more intimate and affectionate than the inf. of W.H. mg. The "exhortation" of the author has been long and sometimes stern. Like S. Paul at the end of Galatians, he "softens

the severity " by "Brothers." He adds a further courtesy; καὶ and
γὰρ may be taken separately, and the clause thus introduced will
refer to the kindly conclusion of a "letter" which had in its earlier
pages grown into a treatise: so apparently A.V. Nor would the
gentle play upon παρακαλῶ...παρακλήσεως be scorned. According to
this interpretation ἐπέστειλα is epistolary aor., " I write " or
"have just written." Clement, in his conclusion, uses ἐπεστει-
λάμην differently, of the main directions he has given in the body
of his epistle.

We do not know where Timothy, or where the author was. In
the next verse ἀσπάζονται ὑμᾶς οἱ ἀπὸ τῆς Ἰταλίας is a little more likely
to mean, "Your friends in Italy send you greetings from thence " than
"Your Italian friends send you greetings thither," because the former
is idiomatic Greek in which this writer would take pleasure. But
either rendering is perfectly justifiable. For the rest, the impression
left on unsophisticated minds by the whole conclusion, with its
reminiscences of Pauline phrases, and this mention of one Pauline
name, might be that a glimpse is given of a little company of apostolic
churchmen to whom S. Paul was a loved master, lately removed
by death. The writer has been near the apostle in his peril, and is
hastening to share a new peril which now threatens his friends.

INDEX

CPSIA information can be obtained at www.ICGtesting.com
Printed in the USA
LVOW08s0814160514

385979LV00001B/25/P